A very naive book $20—
full of inaccuracies —

HOMOSEXUAL BEHAVIOR AMONG MALES

HOMOSEXUAL BEHAVIOR AMONG MALES

A Cross-Cultural and Cross-Species Investigation

by Wainwright Churchill, M. D.

HAWTHORN BOOKS, INC. Publishers New York

HOMOSEXUAL BEHAVIOR AMONG MALES

First Edition: 1967

Acknowledgments

Grateful acknowledgement is made to the publishers, authors and organizations for permission to quote selected passages of the following books:

A History of Orgies, by B. Partridge; Anthony Blond, London.

The Homosexual and His Society, by D. W. Cory and J. P. LeRoy; The Citadel Press, New York.

Homosexuality, by D. J. West; Gerald Duckworth, London.

Homosexuality: A Psychoanalytic Study, by Irving Bieber, M.D., and Associates; © by Society of Medical Psychoanalysts; Basic Books, Inc., Publishers, New York.

The Origin and Development of Moral Ideas, by E. Westermarck; Macmillan & Co., Ltd., London.

Patterns of Sexual Behavior, by C. S. Ford and F. A. Beach; Harper & Row, Publishers, Incorporated, New York.

Sexual Behavior in the Human Female, by A. C. Kinsey, W. B. Pomeroy, C. E. Martin, and P. H. Gebhard; W. B. Saunders, Philadelphia.

Sexual Behavior in the Human Male, by A. C. Kinsey, W. B. Pomeroy, and C. E. Martin; W. B. Saunders, Philadelphia.

Sexual Life in Ancient Greece, by Hans Licht; Barnes and Noble, New York.

Towards a Quaker View of Sex, Friends Home Service Committee; Euston Road, London, N. W. 1 England.

To the memory of the
late Alfred C. Kinsey

Preface

Recent scientific investigations into the sexual behavior of human and subhuman animals have demonstrated beyond all reasonable doubt that homosexual responsiveness is a component of mammalian sexuality. It is as such, rather than as an abnormality, that it is viewed in this book. Although my own particular background is that of the clinician, I have specifically avoided writing a clinical book based upon the case histories of certain tormented individuals, all of whom have been nurtured in a very special environment. It has been too easy to treat homosexual phenomena simply as pathology and to ignore the part which this particular aspect has played throughout human history. Most of the clinical discourses on homosexuality and other sexual phenomena that fail to meet with approval in our culture seem to be only sophisticated substitutes for the more frankly moralistic tracts on sex which were fashionable several generations ago.

Thus, I have preferred to present the topic in its cross-species and cross-cultural dimensions. A word of caution, however. A nonclinical approach does not necessarily guarantee objectivity, and clinicians are not the only ones who have been ensnared by cultural bias on this subject. Although there are clinicians—too few, to be sure—who have escaped such bias, there are also sociologists, historians, and even anthropologists and students of animal behavior whose observations of homosexual phenomena have been obviously conditioned by conventional values. Unfortunately, one's own sexual predilections tend to color the way in which objective data are received and interpreted. Hence the exclusively heterosexual investigator will not always find the same meaning in the very same collection of data that the homosexually or bisexually inclined investigator may find. Indeed, so strong is the persuasion of sexual emotion, and the preferences and avoidances that always cling to it, that it is doubtful if there will ever be a fully objective account of any aspect of sexual life.

This book concerns homosexual behavior—not "homosexuality," at least not within the very narrow context with which some have invested this word. Still less is this a book about "homosexuals," whoever they may really be. No attempt has been made to emphasize, at the expense of other data, the peculiar forms of homosexual responsiveness within a particular culture or social minority, or to concentrate on any special personality type. Similarly, the discussion has not been confined to the behavior and

9

attitudes of males in whom a marked preference for like-sexed partners may be identified. I have not dwelt, for example, exclusively upon the homosexuality of males ratable on Kinsey's scale as 5 or 6—males in whom homosexual preferences are developed to a point where they more or less exclude heterosexual responsiveness. Most often homosexual responsiveness occurs among males who also respond vigorously to heterosexual stimuli, and it is entirely misleading to discuss it as if it were always, or even usually, a distinct phenomenon isolated from other aspects of mammalian sexuality. Most books on this subject are concerned only with the psychology of a special group of individuals within our own society who prefer homosexual to heterosexual contacts. Such sexual behavior as occurs between like-sexed partners among the infrahuman mammals, or between children or adolescents, or between persons who only occasionally participate in sexual contacts with like-sexed partners, is usually passed over lightly, or may even be entirely excluded from serious consideration with the comment that it is not "really" homosexual. But such assumptions are gratuitous, and no book on this subject may legitimately put aside the wealth of data which are available outside of conventional clinical sources. In this book the word "homosexual" is used in its historic and literal context to refer to any sexual phenomena that involve like-sexed partners, and all such phenomena are regarded as worthy of consideration.

In one way, however, this book treats the subject selectively: the investigation is confined to homosexual behavior among males. Because of the psychosexual differences between males and females, homosexual phenomena among females differ from such phenomena among males. Since, moreover, female homosexuality seems everywhere to have very different psychosociological repercussions, I have not wished to burden the text, or to confuse issues, by attempting to discuss both male and female homosexuality in a single volume. It is to be hoped that a book on female homosexuality which is outside the sin-crime-disease frame of reference will be forthcoming in the near future.

Throughout my book I have quoted often from the writings of other scientists and authors. The superscript numbers after the quotations refer to the numbered sources in the bibliography at the end of the volume. To each of the authors and publishers of the books from which I have quoted I wish to express my gratitude for the permission to reproduce their work.

No single source has provided as much reliable and informative material abount the nature of homosexuality as the monumental research of Alfred C. Kinsey, Wardell B. Pomeroy, Clyde E. Martin, and Paul H. Gebbhard, which was published by the W. B. Saunders Company in the two volumes *Sexual Behavior in the Human Male* (1948) and *Sexual Behavior in the Human Female* (1953). I have made extensive use of this research and have quoted often and liberally from the two volumes. To the authors and publishers of these volumes especially I extend my deepest gratitude for their generous cooperation. To Wardell B. Pomeroy, who has discussed with me at length many of his observations about homosexuality, I give special thanks. Above all, I wish to acknowledge my deepest respect and admiration for the late Alfred C. Kinsey, whose courage and genius opened new vistas in sexological research. It is to his memory that the present volume is dedicated with a keen awareness of the loss to science occasioned by his untimely death.

Wainwright Churchill
Rome, 1967

Contents

I

The Background and the Task

From earliest times man has been both mystified and alarmed by the urgency of his sexual drive. The manifold and usually intense passions associated with sex—love, hate, elation, disappointment, impatience, jealousy, joy, and remorse—along with the omnipresent character of the drive (for man's sexual proclivities, unlike those of the other animals, are not confined to a distinct period or season) have inclined him to regard this drive very differently than his other appetites. Under the persuasion of sexual arousal the sense of self-possession may diminish until the ego feels submerged in what the novelist Laurence Sterne called "an all consuming fire." This experience, no doubt, is what has prompted man so often to interpret erotic ecstasy in terms of possession by gods or demons. Witchcraft, sorcery, and magic are associated with libidinousness in every culture, and even in the more supposedly civilized and sophisticated areas of the globe, mystical and supernatural meanings are commonly ascribed to sexual phenomena of every kind. We know little, indeed, about man's psychological orientation to sex if we do not recognize the part that fear and consequent superstition play in it.

Since human beings have always been fearful of the range and intensity of their sexual desires and since human sexuality seems particularly apt to play some role in almost every kind of social and interpersonal relationship, men everywhere and at all times have attempted to regulate this drive. They have tried to direct its expression toward certain aims and away from others through the establishment of rigid attitudes, firm beliefs, and standardized moral directives that all too readily degenerate into dogma and taboo. Each society's aims, and the dogmas and taboos that are evolved in the interests of these aims, constitute what may be called a *sexual mystique*.

It must not be thought that the sexual mystiques of diverse cultures necessarily resemble one another. Although there may be considerable overlapping in certain particulars, especially between related cultures, and although a few predominant themes tend to recur, there is little agreement among diverse cultures as to what is acceptable and what is unacceptable sexual behavior. With the single exception of mother-son incest, virtually every possible type of sexual behavior has been condoned in one particular culture at the same time as it has been condemned in another. This is true even of such widely divergent practices as bestiality, pedophilia, and sadomasochism, and homosexuality. In some groups, for example, solitary masturbation meets with strong disapproval and the known offender may be severely penalized. In contrast, certain other groups regard this same behavior with indifference, or may actually encourage it.

Acceptance or rejection of a given type of sexual behavior is, however, seldom an all-or-nothing proposition. All kinds of provisos usually enter into sex codes of various groups. Such factors as age, sex, or social rank often determine the kind of erotic activities that are approved for the individual.

Thus solitary masturbation may be considered entirely innocent when practiced in childhood but it may be adjudged a form of depravity when engaged in by adults.

A male in our own culture must accept the stigma of inferiority, and in some quarters may even risk legal penalties, if it becomes known that he has participated in any kind of sexual contact with another male. Male homosexuality is harshly condemned in the sexual mystique of our culture on the grounds that sexual contacts between males are unprocreative and therefore grossly abnormal and "against the laws of nature." Yet sexual contacts between females in our culture, though certainly no more procreative, seldom arouse as much social anxiety. Female homosexuality has almost entirely escaped mention in the written statutes of Judaeo-Christian nations. Conversely, the sexual mystique of the ancient Greeks placed homosexual love among males on an exalted plane while female homosexuality, the odes of Sappho notwithstanding, was accorded an indifferent status.

The sexual mystique of both the ancient Egyptians and the Incas condoned brother-sister incest among members of the royal family, but incest among members of the lower classes was taboo.

Sadomasochistic practices may be highly esteemed when they occur in some mystical or religious context—for example, among certain North

American Indian groups, or among certain Christian sects of former times—but the same behavior may be adjudged entirely abhorrent in a secular context. Priestly castes in a great many cultures have often abided by a sexual mystique that is entirely at odds with that embraced by the laity.

Even the physiological status of the individual may play a part in determining the kind of sexual behavior that is acceptable to the group. Sexual activities of every possible kind may be forbidden the menstruating female in certain cultures, and she may be entirely isolated from the rest of the community and placed under a strict taboo that precludes the possibility even of social intercourse.

It must also be noted that there are some very important differences between cultures regarding the number and types of aims that they recognize in human sexual propensities. Virtually all cultures acknowledge the procreative aim of the drive, although, unlike our own Judaeo-Christian culture, not every other culture regards procreation as the only legitimate aim of sexuality. Some cultures, for example, stress the religious and mystical ecstasy that erotic arousal may produce in many individuals. One of the acknowledged aims of sex in such cultures is to inspire and to intensify religious experience. Often, too, the hedonistic aspects of sex have been highly valued; the pleasure afforded by the exploitation of human sexual capacities has been counted as a wholly legitimate aim in itself.

Most cultures have recognized the complexity and many-sidedness of human sexuality and have exploited it in the interests of the group. Cultures that encourage rather than set themselves in opposition to human libidinousness may, for the sake of convenience, be referred to as sex-positive. Other cultures have tended to view the sexual drive in more narrow terms and as a threat to the social organization. These sex-negative cultures—and our own must be considered an outstanding example—have attached value to only a single aspect of sexuality—usually procreation—while all others are deplored. Sex-negative cultures tend to regard sex as a kind of necessary evil, inherently dangerous, and to be hedged about on all sides by restraints and avoided except in very particular and very scrupulously defined circumstances.

Mention must certainly be made of the sexual mystique that prevails in our Judaeo-Christian culture, for this mystique has conditioned the thinking and attitudes of most of those who will read this book. It is not likely that anyone without some insight into the history of this mystique will be able to comprehend some of the paradoxes that surround the subject of homosexuality in our culture. This mystique, like most others, is based to a very great extent upon interpretations of sex that originate

in religious dogma and taboo. We must, therefore, first turn our attention
to the metaphysical and theological core of the Judaeo-Christian sexual
mystique.

We begin, of course, with the ancient Hebrews. This remarkable
people, different in so many ways from all the other peoples among
whom they dwelt, evolved one of the most prohibitionistic sex codes ever
known in history. Mosaic law included only thirty-six crimes punishable
by death—a relatively lenient code if compared with those of other
ancient peoples. But of these thirty-six capital crimes, one half—
eighteen—involved sexual relationships of one kind or another. We will
pass over a detailed discussion of this particular subject here since it
must be treated at greater length in the chapter on homosexuality and
the law. But the Hebraic effort to control sexual behavior by the use
of severe temporal sanctions, almost peculiar to the Jews among the
ancients, is a tendency with which we shall meet from the earliest phase
of our present culture.

With pious solemnity the ancient Hebrews bore the burden of the
moral superiority they felt, ever mindful that to themselves alone had
been revealed the nature of true morality. The "unnatural lusts" and im-
modest behavior of their "heathenish" neighbors scandalized the followers of Jehovah and caused them more than once to denounce the
Egyptians, Canaanites, Greeks, and Romans.

Not a little of their indignation was due to the pagan habit of exposing the nude body to view in all its details; for it is to the ancient
Hebrews that we owe the idea that nakedness is shameful, and the
feeling that the sexual organs and their functions are obscene. How
lewd and prurient, then, they found the naked images of the fertility
goddesses, the phallic symbols of the nature cults, and the representations
of the nude body in the sculpture of the Greeks and other pagans. They
deplored this "uncovering of nakedness" as a goad to what they deemed
corrupt impulses and base emotions. In place of an innocent attitude
toward nudity, they developed a morbid preoccupation with modesty.

Prudery permeated the Jewish attitude toward many other aspects
of life as well, and even extended to include phenomena that have very
little connection, if any, with erotic life. Delight in the life of the senses
became suspect; moralism often degenerated into frank asceticism among
the more zealous. We repeatedly hear of Jewish prophets and holy men
retreating to the arid desert to live a life of celibacy and complete
sexual renunciation made still more stark and painful by fasting and
other acts designed to mortify the flesh. Asceticism, which becomes so
prominent later in Christianity, was well established in Judaism long
before Christianity came into being. Nor should we overlook the significance of the rigorous dietary laws of the Hebrews, revealing a need

to surround the appetitive drives with prohibitions. We may even speak of a kind of alimentary prudery among the Hebrews.

All of the sexual prohibitions in Judaism and Christianity originate in a profoundly *erotophobic* psychology, a psychology in which sex is regarded not merely as somehow inherently evil, but also as somehow inherently dangerous. Although this erotophobia is rationalized in numerous and varied ways by those who have succumbed to it, none really understands its origin, any more than they understand the extent to which it is responsible for many of the beliefs and attitudes too often considered sober judgments of reality.

When it is felt that the erotic propensity itself is both evil and dangerous, it follows very logically that sexual phenomena will be surrounded with every possible type of restriction. Moreover, sexual pleasure will never be regarded as a legitimate goal in itself, and the acts that yield such pleasure will not be justified merely because of the pleasure, but only in terms of some other value that can be recognized in them or ascribed to them. Thus, the range of "legitimate" sexual phenomena is considerably narrowed in our culture; a whole array of sexual phenomena that are highly valued or at least considered harmless in other cultures, appear lewd, profane, and morbid to us. A single act, carried out under very special circumstances, is all that gains approval within the erotophobic atmosphere of Judaeo-Christendom. This single act, of course, is coitus, and the very special circumstances in which it is considered legitimate are those of the marital relationship.

The tendencies inherent in an erotophobic psychology would not allow for the approval of even monogamous marriage were society not forced to make some concessions to the imperious demands of the sexual drive and its procreative function. Chastity and celibacy are regarded with still greater favor than even marriage and parenthood, particularly in the Christian branch of this religious tradition, and so the more inspired religionists have tended to favor bachelorhood and sterility. Celibates existed among the ancient Hebrews, but since the advent of Christ, celibacy has become a requirement for the priesthood in some Christian sects, as well as an essential component of monasticism. The idea that chastity is a cardinal virtue has been reiterated as recently as during the pontificate of the late Pope Pius XII, and the Roman Catholic Church has never abandoned its position on the moral superiority of celibacy.

There is a good deal more evidence of erotophobia in the religion of the Hebrews. Consider, for example, the habit of circumcising males. Circumcision has been represented as a ritual symbolizing a covenant between the Hebrews and Jehovah. It may, of course, well be asked why this particular practice was believed by the ancient Hebrews to be praiseworthy in the eyes of God. Circumcision has been interpreted by psychoanalysts and others as a symbolic act of castration and however one may wish to interpret its unconscious or ritualistic meaning, it is nonetheless a form of genital mutilation. The psychosexual implications of routine circumcision are manifold and no doubt deeply rooted in an urge to maim the male sex organ.

Circumcision, along with the ancient Hebraic dietary laws, has been defended by latter-day apologists on hygienic grounds, and it has been argued that the early Hebrews, who were little more than ignorant barbarians at best, instituted these customs out of an appreciation of and respect for sanitation. These customs, however, were not defended by the Hebrews on medical but on religious grounds. The circumcision of males is not an unfamiliar custom among savages—for example, the aborigines of Australia, one of the most backward of all human groups—and it is the sheerest nonsense to imagine that this practice is prompted by hygienic considerations. The actual hygienic value of circumcision is in any case highly questionable.

There can be little doubt that circumcision and the dietary laws, along with all of the sexual prohibitions of the Hebrews, originated in irrational concepts of a metaphysical nature. What is most significant about them is the fear of and hostility toward the appetitive drives that they bespeak. That these practices are still adhered to by the pious in modern times (when plumbing, refrigeration, and other hygienic comforts are available to almost everyone) is due neither to a respect for sanitation nor even to a respect for tradition. The probability is that the same psychology that brought such practices into being in the first place is still at work.

One can hardly doubt that fear and hostility have always permeated the Judaeo-Christian attitude toward sex if one considers the concept of original sin, and the inferior sexual role dealt out to woman as a punishment for this sin. Ostensibly man's original sin consisted in his disobedience when he ate the fruit forbidden to him by Jehovah. But it is an insult to the dignity of religion to imagine that man should be eternally repentant for merely eating an apple. Nor has anybody ever really believed that the consumption of fruit had very much to do with original sin. The "forbidden fruit" has always been interpreted by human beings as a representation of *sexual pleasure* and, moreover, this interpretation is clearly supported by the nature of the punishment visited by Jehovah upon Eve. In wrath he curses her through Eternity for tempting Adam. It is clear that the punishment visited upon Eve is sexual in nature:

> I will greatly multiply thy sorrow and thy conception;
> In sorrow thou shalt bring forth children;
> And thy desire shall be to thy husband.
> And he shall rule over thee.

Thus, the feminine sex role is pictured in the Old Testament as a degradation in which the wife submits to the tyranny of her husband and sorrowfully brings forth children.

Because of Jehovah's punishment of Eve, religionists in the past opposed all medical efforts to facilitate painless childbirth, and because of it some religionists still argue against woman enjoying a dignified and equal status in society. But what is most important for us in this story is the light it throws upon the Judaeo-Christian orientation to sex.

The story of the fall of man and of original sin has been interpreted by the more esoteric during modern times in such a way as to emphasize the element of disobedience rather than the element of sex. But no matter how one may argue, and no matter how one may choose to interpret for oneself the meaning of original sin, the fact remains that the common people have always viewed it in a sexual context. It is this interpretation, whether accurate or erroneous, that has permeated the sexual mystique of our culture. The Adam and Eve story says simply to the average man that his sexual desires and the temptation that woman represents for him have put him (and her) on very bad terms with the Almighty; that he is, because of these desires, a "sinner" and as such has been punished and should be repentant.

It is easy to blame the common man for what one may regard as a naïve or oversimplified interpretation of the myth from Genesis; but a closer look reveals that the story is told in terms that encourage this interpretation. Consider, for example, the almost transparent phallic symbolism of the serpent, the suggestive meaning of "forbidden fruit," the couple's covering of their nakedness with fig leaves as their first act of repentance, and the nature of Eve's punishment. All of these elements and more encourage a sexual interpretation of original sin; and when such a myth arises in an erotophobic atmosphere it is foolish to imagine that men and women *en masse* will ascribe any other meaning to it.

But, it will be argued, the Old Testament does not condemn all sexuality; it lays, indeed, a great deal of stress upon the virtue of procreation. Did not Jehovah command man to "be fruitful and multiply"? Most certainly. But these words proved to be something less than an unmixed blessing— for woman especially. It is difficult to deny that the odor of original sin clings to *all* sexuality and, moreover, there is before us, always, the example of the holy men turning from sex to celibacy, from passion to chastity, with the unavoidable implication that sex is somehow evil. Nor should it be forgotten that, in spite of his commandment, Jehovah himself was a bachelor. Unlike many other religions, there are no celestial wives in the godhead of Judaeo-Christendom. Christ remains celibate, and so sinful is procreation that Jesus, the Man-God, is denied a natural birth. The idea of a "virgin birth" is the ultimate in erotophobia.

The sex-prohibitionistic attitudes and ascetic tendencies of the Hebrews passed directly into Christianity, where they became still more exaggerated. Although certain religious zealots among the Jews imposed ascetic disciplines upon themselves, the priesthood did not, and certainly it was not expected that the laity would do so. Indeed the Hebrews, a small group with big ambitions, encouraged childbearing and family life and looked upon virginity in the common man as something of a sin in itself. But the early Christians, believing that they faced the Final Judgment rather than a brilliant future on earth, had quite a different view of sex and marriage in the beginning. Unlike the Jews, the early Christians had no political ambitions and, indeed, very little interest at all in this world. This had much to do with their original attitudes toward sex, just as later, when they became a political force, their attitudes toward celibacy underwent revision.

It is important to remember that the moral code of the original Christians, as taught by Jesus, was predicated on the idea that the end of the world was directly at hand. Hence the remarkable indifference to economy, government, property, and all other worldly concerns. It was no longer a calamity to be a spinster or a childless husband or wife. Indeed, the abandonment of *all* family ties was urged. Jesus praised those who "leave house, or parents, or brethren, or wife, or children," and he followed his own precepts when he addressed his mother with the words, "Woman, what have I to do with thee?" No part of Christ's message was a source of greater consternation and misunderstanding among the people to whom he preached than that part of it which urged the abandoning of family ties in the interests of a higher life of the spirit in which all men and women were to be brothers and sisters.

The modern man, who is brought up on a reinterpreted and revised version of earlier Christian belief—a version designed to suit conditions in which the Church had come to dominate the State and the Final Judgment seemed far away in a different life, a version that speaks of the virtues of family life and of industry, love of country, and ordinary propriety—may find it difficult to comprehend some of the concepts preached by the first Christians. He may, if he reads the literal words of Jesus and even some of his disciples, find it necessary, with the aid of his priest or minister, to interpret these words in a highly allegorical sense so as to get from them a meaning more suitable to present conditions. Yet the statements in the New Testament, especially of Jesus, are admirably direct and clear in meaning and are seldom elusive or mysterious. When Jesus urged his followers to "leave house, or parents, or brethren, or wife, or children," he meant that the individual in search of his soul should dissolve all ties with this world and all ties that set him apart from other men, including those of family life.

There are yet other statements of Jesus which indicate that he had anything but the kind of view on family life that we find proper today. In Matthew XIX, 12, in answer to a question from his disciples concerning marriage, he spoke the following words:

> . . . For there are some eunuchs which were so born from their mother's womb: and there are some eunuchs which were made eunuchs of men: and there be eunuchs, which have made themselves eunuchs for the kingdom of heaven's sake. He that is able to receive it, let him receive it.

In the past various Christian sects have read a very sex-negative meaning into these words and some, therefore, have condoned self-emasculation for those who were "able to receive it." A number of outstanding Christian leaders castrated themselves in order to avoid what they regarded as sinful feelings of lust, among them the learned Origen, who, in a frenzy of religious ardor, mutilated his own genitals. Others too felt "able to receive it" and this sort of thing continued sporadically among Christians until the Church, alarmed by the possible consequences of such doings on any large scale, interdicted literal castration. It left intact, however, the symbolic castration of lifelong celibacy, which it has always placed on an exalted level of morality.

The sex-negativism so prominent today in Christianity stems more directly, however, from the teachings of Paul than from those of Jesus. There is really little in the attitude of Jesus toward sex that can be regarded as prudish or prohibitionistic. He associated with prostitutes and people who today would be considered low-life characters without, apparently, feeling any great need to emphasize to them their sexual sins. He was always more concerned with a broader, more constructive morality than that which has obsessed his followers up to the present time. One can never forget the words he spoke in defense of the woman taken in adultery:

"Let him who is without sin cast the first stone."

More than once Jesus is pictured in the New Testament as aloof from the petty prudery of the orthodox religionists of the communities in which he preached. He was more often disturbed by hypocrisy and what we today would call narrow-mindedness than by sexual irregularity. The attitude toward sex that we find so prominent in religion today has practically nothing in it that Jesus would have regarded as particularly uplifting, and much that he might very well have condemned. We look in vain for words from Jesus that lend any precedent for the harsh condemnation of sexuality uttered by Paul. Although, Jesus, no less than Paul, lived in a world in which prostitution, homosexuality, and premarital sex relationships were everywhere in evidence, it was Paul, not Jesus, who raged against "sexual vice."

Most of the founders of the great religions have taught a morality emphasizing ethical precepts that are only very tangentially connected with sexual relationships. It is their followers who stress sexual prohibition. When their doctrines are received by their disciples, they are invariably distorted and revamped to suit the needs of the mass mind, and what may originally have been an affirmation of life becomes merely cant designed to ward off the fear of death.

Jesus was not long dead before it seemed to his followers that his teachings would have to be interpreted in a different light and softened to meet the everyday needs of a continuing world. By Paul's time it was becoming clear that the end of the world might not be so close at hand, and Paul's comments on marriage are somewhat conciliatory, though, from a modern viewpoint, they are still shockingly condescending. He clearly expresses the opinion that marriage is but an inferior substitute for total renunciation of sexuality and that those, like himself, who are inspired by a higher devotion to virtue will choose a life of celibacy. Only the weaker sort may find it necessary to resort to marriage as a kind of refuge from a more serious form of immorality.

> I say therefore to the unmarried and widows, it is good for them if they abide even as I. But if they cannot contain, let them marry: for it is better to marry than to burn.

This sort of reasoning prompted Remy de Gourmont, in *La Cité du Soleil,* to observe, "For the Fathers of the Church there is no middle course between virginity and debauchery; marriage is nothing but a *remedium amoris* which God in his goodness has granted as a concession to human weakness."

The interpretation of sexual life that developed among Christians after the death of Jesus reinforced and greatly exaggerated the sex-prohibitionism of the earlier Jews. It is an attitude so guilt-ridden and so phobic that no expression of the sexual drive, even in marriage, can be accorded unambivalent approval. Under these conditions, it will always be felt necessary to justify sex by reference to "higher purposes" that, it is hoped, may expiate the sinfulness thought to be inherent in the drive itself.

Men who view the sexual drive as inherently evil and dangerous are likely to look upon the objects of their desire with both contempt and fear. The inferior status of women in our society comes, in part, from the feeling that they, like their prototype, Eve, are provocateurs of sin. They were constantly berated and condemned during the early history of the Church, as well as during the height of the Puritan epoch in England and America. The hideous practice of witch burning was, in no little part, due to the belief that women are "servants of Satan." The ancient Church Father Tertullian addressed woman in the crudest terms as "the gate by which the demon enters" and even went so far as to tell her that "it is on your account that Jesus Christ died." He urged all Christians to veil their daughters and bitterly castigated those who would not do so. In Puritan times girls were dressed in the most unbecoming way possible, under the guise of "modesty," so that they would not incite sinful feelings in men. Not a few of these girls who, in spite of their ugly garb, quite unknowingly aroused libidinous feelings in men were accused by them of witchcraft and black magic, and many of these victims of religious mania were actually put to the flames. In order to prevent the temptations that might divert one's mind from religious contemplation, women were separated from men in the various Puritan congregations of early America in much the same way that they still are in the congregations of the Orthodox Jews.

All such indignities put a breach in the amiable relationship of man and woman in sundry insidious and elusive ways.

Sex, then, in the Judaeo-Christian tradition, has become an object of guilt and fear, out of which strange and even fantastic notions have evolved. Mention may be made, however, of a somewhat more liberal interpretation of sexuality that has in very recent times enjoyed some favor among the more radical Protestant sects and among the less than orthodox Jewish sects. It is felt by some of the religious modernists that love alone—"real love"—is a transcendental force capable of expiating the evil which is supposed to be inherent in the drive. Sexual acts of any kind that take place between two loving partners in marriage are therefore regarded by those who embrace this philosophy as morally harmless even if these acts are nonprocreative in character. The loving partners are thought to be worshipping each other and God through the sexual union of their bodies. For some this view makes it possible to take a more friendly attitude toward contraception and family planning, and mitigates a certain amount of the odium traditionally associated with the so-called perversions, such as mouth-genital contacts or mutual masturbation. It is significant, however, that there is as yet in our culture no religious concept of sex as a legitimate force worthy of esteem on its own merits alone.

Since the procreative aspect of sex is emphasized, all nonprocreative sex acts are generally regarded not merely as *inferior* but also as sinful and unnatural. Many such acts are classed even by psychiatrists as psychological digressions from what they identify as "mature" or "healthy" erotic tendencies. Among the acts that are taboo in our culture are solitary masturbation, mutual masturbation, mouth-genital contacts, anal intercourse, sexual contacts between individuals of different species, sexual activities that are thought to exceed the bounds of modesty (exhibitionistic and voyeuristic acts), sadomasochistic acts, sexual contacts involving individuals below or above the age of fertility, and homosexual contacts of any kind. Almost every sexual act other than coitus in marriage is assigned, therefore, an inferior status in our culture. Many of these acts are specifically forbidden by law and evoke heavy penalties in the penal codes of certain Judaeo-Christian nations.

Moreover, since marriage is considered the only circumstance in which even coitus is legitimate, a number of other types of sexual behavior arouse condemnation. All casual sexual contacts—those involving "sex without love"—are deplored and are considered degrading. Sexual contacts in which more than two people participate are classed as debauchery and group perversion. Premarital and extramarital coitus are adjudged immoral and evoke censure under the terms "fornication" and "adultery." Any sexual favor bestowed upon another in return for monetary compensation is condemned. Thus prostitution is deemed a serious social and moral evil and a constant effort is made to suppress it through police methods.

Topics such as legalized abortion and contraception automatically become highly controversial in our culture. Abortion is almost always forbidden by law; in some areas even contraception is made an illegal practice. Still more often, laws forbidding public advocacy of birth control have been promulgated, making it extremely difficult for the average person to obtain information on family planning. The crushing reality of worldwide overpopulation and its many serious social consequences do not appear to the more fanatic defenders of the mystique to be sufficient argument in favor of contraception. Hence, a kind of promiscuous and irresponsible procreation thrives within certain elements of our population.

This is an imposing list of prohibitions, so vast that almost everything connected with sex is reckoned either socially taboo, illegal, pathological, or highly controversial. But there are still more elusive, though no less important, ramifications of this erotophobic mystique.

The failure of our mystique to recognize any function other than that of procreation in the sexual drive has brought about a very special attitude on our part toward the sexual needs of children and older people. Children in our culture are not expected to manifest any interest in sex or to engage in any frankly erotic behavior. Since they are too young to marry and raise a family, it is not believed that they could have any good reason to be interested in sex. Accordingly, children are stigmatized as precocious and even perverse if they manifest erotic interests, and a vigorous attempt is made to suppress such interests even, in many cases, through what amounts to intimidation and browbeating. They are also denied a realistic, frank, and meaningful sex education, with results that are extremely harmful both to the individual and to the group. Even the postpubertal child and the adolescent, in whom biological development is conspicuous and sexual desire at an apex never again to be equaled, are kept from giving full and natural expression to their sexual need.

No clinician, even though in many ways he may support and encourage acceptance of our sexual mystique, can fail to observe its harmful effects, especially upon children and, indeed, upon society at large. It is responsible for behavior and attitudes that often become frankly neurotic and sometimes even flagrantly psychotic. At the very least, the sex-negative atmosphere of our culture encourages feelings in the average man that can be considered neither healthy nor, in the most enlightened sense, ethical. This is a paradox, since it is as disease and immorality that almost all unapproved sexuality is condemned. But we are forced by neither reason, logic, nor objective observation of facts to assign the same definitions to these terms that enjoy current usage in our culture. Even at a superficial glance, it would appear that the vicariousness, hypocrisy, surreptitiousness, inhibition, and uneasy conscience engendered by our social attitudes toward sex are neither wholesome nor decent. But an unwholesome and indecent attitude toward sex is the very *least* that one can expect from this mystique. In many instances, it is a cause of far more serious consequences.

Clinicians for the last seventy years have pointed to the part sexual anxiety and guilt play in the etiology of neurosis, psychosis, and the more serious manifestations of emotional conflict. They have analyzed for us in considerable detail the origin of many psychiatric symptoms in distorted concepts of sex. This author has had ample opportunity in his psychotherapeutic practice to meet with some of the ill effects of the mystique. Too many times the most painful and debilitating symptoms have arisen in the implicit belief on the part of a patient that, for example, coitus is a form of assault and aggression, that mouth-genital contacts are a form of cannibalism, or that autoerotic practices are a form of self-abuse that drains the vital fluids of the nervous system and dries up the brain. These bizarre beliefs are not merely the result of ignorance or a lack of adequate sex education. They are due to maleducation in sex thrust upon the growing child as he absorbs our culture's fantasy-ridden mystique.

Not only is the young person denied any legitimate interest in sex, but the older person, too, is expected to be indifferent to this drive. If the erotic propensities of a man or woman outlast his or her procreative powers—which, especially in the case of women, they usually do—the older person is likely to meet with contempt and ridicule. Yet the sexual drive may continue to make demands upon men and women far beyond the point where procreation is desirable or even possible. The sociosexual problems of older people may be particularly aggravated when, as is not at all uncommon, they are without a spouse who shares their interests. Many older people are widowed or are married to a husband or wife who is sick, feeble, or sexually impotent. This problem is shunted off by society with the recommendation that continence and self-control be exercised as seemly virtues in the aging member of the community.

But older people continue to swell the ranks of our population as a result of scientific and medical advances. Many of these older people are, more-over, in good health and vigorous spirits. Many are far from sexually senile, even though they may be well beyond the age when parenthood is possible. Most have already raised families and are at a stage in life where the relaxation of familial responsibility provides them with the opportunity to enjoy pleasures that have been well earned. For a growing number of these people sexual contacts are among the pleasures that they wish to enjoy. The older person, especially the widow, in our society today no longer resigns himself or herself to the doubtful joys of a rocking-chair existence.

The age-old proprieties and taboos are even more ludicrous and harmful in this modern and changing world than they were in the past, because they tend to take into consideration fewer and fewer elements of an ever-expand-ing population. Not only do we have a greater number of older people who are still sexually vigorous but beyond the age of fertility, and not only is their number bound to increase, but we also have a growing number of young people not yet ready, economically or socially, for marriage. At present, for example, 50 per cent of the population in the United States is under twenty-five years of age. These young people are not, one may be quite certain, inclined to wait until marriage before they express their sexual needs. Nor are they likely, even after marriage, to confine their sexual activities to purely procreative acts. Neither the economy nor their own inclinations allow most young adults to raise families of ten or twelve children. The whole orientation of our moral concepts, and the laws that reflect it are out of step with reality and clearly oppressive to the individual. They always have been. But now the breach between reality and the mystique is greater than ever before. It is not surprising then, that we tend to find a growing number of people, especially among the young, who reject our traditional sexual conventions.

Because virtually all those who fail to conform to our sexual conventions are regarded as psychologically ill, the wayward husband, the promiscuous female, the prostitute and, above all, the "homosexual" and other so-called "deviates" have been characterized as psychopathic cases in recent clinical publications. Moreover, many would not hesitate, in the name of mental hygiene, to bring force to bear upon these supposed sufferers. In some jurisdictions, for example, psychotherapy has been made a condition of the probation given those who have been found guilty of having partici-pated in homosexual acts—for homosexual acts between males are still illegal according to the statutes of all but one (Illinois) of the fifty states in the United States. Psychiatric probation might appear generous and extremely progressive when compared to the prison sentences that were—and in many instances still are—meted out to the offenders against the sodomy laws. But a growing number of persons today feel that anything less than complete abolition of such antiquated and obnoxious statutes is not true progress.

The imputation of abnormality, if not outright illness, to all those who flout sexual convention is not new in our culture. Indeed, all deviations from the strict code of sexual behavior prescribed in the Jewish and Christian religions were viewed as monstrous and supernatural phenomena provoked by some diabolic force in opposition to the express will of God. In the mass mind there is but a meager distinction, if any at all, between sinfulness and disease. Originally the same devices were used to cleanse the body of illness that were used to purge the soul of sinfulness: exorcism, repentance, and penitence.

When true pathology is in fact involved and when, as in the case of venereal disease, it bears some tangible relationship to sexual vice, the mass mind finds it almost impossible to make any distinction. The existence of these ancient ailments has always been used by moralists to emphasize the dangers of sex. Indeed, it is not too much to say that the fear of venereal disease, along with the fear of unwanted pregnancy, have been the chief weapons with which moralists have attempted to intimidate the many. Especially during modern times, those who are at the forefront of moral crusades and clean-up campaigns claim that they are prompted mainly by a concern for public health when they officiously meddle in the private affairs of others. It might have been supposed that the discovery of a cure for syphilis and gonorrhea would have put an end to such rationalizations, but moralists have pointed to a recent increase in venereal diseases and have used this as a kind of scientific justification to "clamp down" on prostitution and all forms of sexual promiscuity. Moreover, much has recently been made of the fact that homosexual as well as heterosexual males are susceptible to these diseases. This discovery has served as an additional excuse to harass the homosexual minority, and to shut down taverns and other places where such people gather. There has been a concerted effort on the part of the police in America and to a lesser extent abroad, to eradicate male prostitution and to curb promiscuity among homosexual males. Some of these efforts have infringed upon the civil rights of individuals to such an extent that they have aroused criticism even among people who have no personal interest at all in homosexuality. Yet police raids, clean-ups, and arrests on morals charges have been defended by the police and by certain other groups on the grounds that public health and welfare are at stake.

It is not surprising to anyone who knows the history of venereal diseases that, after the steep decline in the incidence of syphilis and gonorrhea that occurred during the fourth and fifth decades of this century, there should now be an increase. Venereal diseases, like many other infectious diseases, have always followed a regular pattern in which they have reached almost epidemic proportions in one phase, only to be followed by a phase in which the diseases subside. This cycle has been repeated many times in the past. It is extremely doubtful that the recent increase in venereal disease has anything whatsoever to do with a hypothetical increase in sexual immorality. Efforts to restrict the sexual behavior of modern men are not likely to prove successful, but even if such efforts were to prove successful, there is little probability that they would have any substantial effect upon the incidence of venereal infection. Contrary to the claims of those who would seem to yearn for the worst, we are extremely fortunate that the present strains of disease-producing organisms are mild in comparison with the virulent strains of the past and, still more important, the present-day victim of venereal disease does have recourse to accurate diagnosis and effective cure.

But all will certainly agree that prevention is far better than cure. It is difficult to agree with the moralists and hypochondriacs, however, when they act upon the proposition that adequate prevention consists of efforts to enforce chastity or strict monogamy upon the masses. In more than 2,000 years, such efforts have not proved efficacious in the control of venereal disease. The only really effective way to control and perhaps eventually to eradicate these diseases is through the same method used against most other infectious diseases: immunization. If those who are now apparently so concerned about venereal diseases would abandon their ineffectual but obnoxious moral compaigns and instead direct their efforts, time, and financial resources toward the discovery of an effective vaccine, there is little doubt that far more would be accomplished. Why, if venereal disease is a serious threat to the health of the world, is there not a crash program to develop and to dispense adequate methods of immunization? One suspects that neither cure nor prevention is the real issue in the minds of a great many who raise a hue and cry over venereal disease and that moral rather than medical issues preoccupy these people. Certainly, as we have seen, venereal disease has provided moralists with a very noble excuse for officious acts that might not otherwise appear so noble.

R. S. Morton in his excellent book *Venereal Diseases* (Penguin Books, Ltd., 1966) concludes his discussion of prevention with the following observation:

> The venereal diseases show no tendency to yield to our best concerted legal, moral, psychological, sociological, political, or religious efforts. Nor do the contributions of medical science to their treatment give help to any notable degree. The addition of a prophylactic approach, with its commendable array of precedents, merits our earliest attention. Without it, hopes of solving the enigma look like being denied to us.

It is a disgrace that anyone today who is willing to avail himself of medical aid should have to be preoccupied with the risk of venereal infection. But no medical aid, in the form of an immuno-prophylactic agent, is yet available. Why not? Dr. John Knox gave it as his considered opinion in 1965 that if as much money were appropriated for syphilis research as went into research on poliomyelitis—which neither killed nor crippled as many people—a vaccine could be found within a matter of a few years. Billions are spent by national and international organizations on the development of destructive devices and sometimes, it appears, merely capriciously. Present programs to educate the public on the subject of venereal diseases and to offer inexpensive treatment are costly but are almost completely ineffective in the control of these diseases; and, as we have seen, often these programs involve moral crusades which, though ineffective, are a nuisance and even a threat to civil rights. The failure on the part of the proper authorities, both national and international, to support and finance an effective drive toward the discovery of an immuno-prophylactic agent against syphilis and gonorrhea suggests that the philosophy at work may be that the wages of sin—sexual sin—are disease and suffering.

Very briefly, in the preceding paragraphs an attempt has been made to convey some impression of the history and character of the mystique which surrounds sex in our Judaeo-Christian culture. It is obviously a mystique permeated by fear, superstition, negativism, and irrationality, and it is precisely these emotions, in an even more exaggerated form, with which we shall meet when we discuss homosexual phenomena between males in our culture.

So outrageous is this topic considered that until very recently there was practically no literature published on homosexuality. There existed only the traditional biblical admonitions, a few esoteric moral tracts and proclamations, and the few rather sleazy pornographic items that were sometimes offered through secret channels. But with the advent of modern psychiatry and psychoanalysis it became possible to publish books on this taboo subject—books that treated the subject exclusively in terms of psychopathology and disease—and, for the most part, it is still only clinical tomes that are published on homosexuality. But the research of Kinsey and his colleagues, first published in 1948, brought attention to the fact that homosexuality plays no small part in the histories of a great many Judaeo-Christian males. The shock occasioned by this realization, along with changing attitudes toward censorship, has led to an interest in homosexuality that goes beyond the traditional presentation of it as only sin, crime, and/or disease.

In very recent years the public has been exposed to a fair number of books that treat this subject frankly and unconventionally, although it must not be imagined that prejudice has been entirely overcome. Moralists still set their sights most especially against "the sins of Sodom and Gomorrah," and they are seldom appeased unless, at the very least, they may continue to regard all homosexuality as pathology. If any author presumes to write on the subject outside of this context, it is immediately assumed that he is himself accustomed to homosexuality and is an "apologist" who wishes to extend the sphere of homosexuality and make "converts." His book consequently—it is thought—could not possibly be objective or scientific. Books on homosexuality, according to this reasoning, are only objective if they condemn outright or at least leave sufficient scope for others to persist in the traditional condemnations of homosexuality.

All of this has given many capable authors who have a rich fund of knowledge on the subject pause to consider before writing a really frank book on homosexuality; after considering the risk to personal and professional reputation, most have decided against it. But facts are facts and no matter how an author may be condemned, any facts that he may bring forth will eventually be received. What may happen to him personally is not ever as important as the work he does.

When we direct our attention more exclusively to the subject of homosexuality we will find that it occurs in every possible type of circumstance and in every type of person. It occurs among people who make it an exclusive practice; it occurs among others who combine it with heterosexuality; it occurs among the young, the old, the middle-aged, and the adolescent; it occurs among blonds, brunettes, and redheads; it occurs among effeminate males and among masculine males; it occurs among neurotics and among those who are not so neurotic; it occurs among saints and it occurs among sinners; it occurs among aristocrats and it occurs among workmen, farmers, senators, artists, bankers, butchers, lawyers, morticians, policemen, thieves, hairdressers, iron-mongers, trapeze artists, poets, salesmen, doctors, log-rollers, priests, waiters, and psychiatrists; it occurs among Poles, Greeks, Americans, Russians, Germans, Mexicans, Irishmen, Frenchmen, Egyptians, Canadians, Persians, Moroccans, Italians, Puerto Ricans, Englishmen, Japanese, Hungarians, Eskimos, Turks, Hawaiians, and Jugoslavs; it occurs among Jews, Hindus, free-thinkers, Protestants, Mohammedans, Catholics, Buddhists, and atheists; it occurs among Negroes, Mongolians, caucasians, and pygmies; it occurs among savages, barbarians, and civilized men; it occurs among communists, monarchists, socialists, capitalists, anarchists, and fascists; it occurs among those who condemn it, those who condone it, and among those who are merely indifferent; it has always occurred in the past, it occurs in the present, and it will no doubt continue to occur in the future.

Therefore, one may well feel that this subject—so often passed over in silence or clamorously deplored—deserves some serious study in an atmosphere conducive to understanding and greater wisdom. Most men or women, of course, are more interested in heterosexuality than in homosexuality. But what is important for us to know also is that most men and women are nonetheless far more interested in homosexuality than has ever been generally acknowledged. We have spent so much time and effort pretending that homosexuality is rare, peculiar, and remote from everyday life that we have succeeded in believing our own propaganda.

In reality, however, homosexuality is neither particularly uncommon nor particularly remote from everyday life. It plays at least some part in the histories of a great many people, and it plays a very important part in the histories of a smaller but not insignificant number of people. If we consider all those who have ever had any direct experience with homosexuality themselves, and add to this the number all those who have had no such experience themselves but who in various ways have been affected by others close to them who have had such experience, we will find that we are dealing not merely in hundreds of thousands, but in many millions. Thus a vast number of people have every good reason to be intelligently concerned with this topic, and many more than ever before are willing to admit that they would like to know more about a type of human experience that is as old as the race itself.

It seems appropriate to bring the chapter to a close with an attempt to arrive at an adequate definition of homosexuality, for the word homosexuality has by no means been used by all people in precisely the same way.

Although for the last hundred years the word "homosexual" has been applied by scientists in a behavioristic context to all sexual phenomena that involve like-sexed partners, in recent years the term has been accorded a great many special meanings in different quarters. There has been no lack of argument among clinicians, and also among certain individuals who have a history of homosexual contacts, as to which type of sexual contacts between like-sexed partners are "really" homosexual and which are not. Often these arguments are reminiscent of the theological debates that were common during the Middle Ages, and the frequent concern with intention— or, as is said in more modern parlance, motivation—brings to mind the tortured moral discussions that may be found in scholastic philosophy.

Most clinicians have favored a definition of homosexuality that lays great emphasis upon psychodynamic factors and complex motivational constructs. Thus, contacts between like-sexed partners who manifest a clear preference for others of their own sex, or contacts between like-sexed partners in whom an aversion to heterosexuality may be identified are thought to be "really" homosexual. On the other hand, the more transitory, occasional, situational, or opportunistic contacts that may occur among prepubertal boys, adolescent youths, prisoners, sailors, male prostitutes, or others in whom a preference for heterosexual contacts may be claimed are thought by some to be "not really" homosexual.

Kinsey, Pomeroy, and Martin note that even clinicians have "come to believe that homosexual males and females are discretely different from persons who merely have homosexual experience, or who react sometimes to homosexual stimuli." [53] According to this view homosexuality is a function of that abstraction called the personality and is not limited or defined by actual behavior or by the reality of the concrete situation in which the person responds.

It might be argued that much of this sounds suspiciously like nonsense rather than scientific precision or perceptiveness, and it is perhaps not merely by chance that we find hair-splitting distinctions on this issue outside the clinical field as well. Certain of the more naïve elements of the general population have attempted to distinguish what is and what is not "really" homosexual behavior. Many males go through all of the sexual reflexes, including erection and orgasm, in sexual contacts with other males and insist to themselves and to others that they have done nothing homosexual because in such contacts they always played "the masculine role" or because they always fantasized their partners as women, or because the particular acts involved did not fit their definition of homosexuality. The homosexuality of mutual masturbation between males, for example, may not be recognized by some persons who insist that only anal intercourse between two males should be included in the definition of this word. Others insist that anal intercourse for the so-called active partner is not really homosexual because it is a "substitute" for heterosexual coitus. Interpretations like these seem to represent attempts to alibi what might otherwise be regarded as reprehensible behavior.

Further obscurantism may be noted when individuals with extensive homosexual experience claim that anyone with less experience, or anyone who is not aroused as exclusively by like-sex contacts as they, is "not really" homosexual. In definitions of this kind the word "homosexual" takes on an entirely relativistic and subjective meaning.

These efforts to distinguish between a supposedly genuine form of homosexuality and a supposedly spurious form seem to be related to the a priori notion that homosexuality is somehow unnatural and even clearly pathological. When, therefore, one points to instances of homosexual activity that cannot be readily identified with pathology—for example, the homosexual play of animals or children, the ritualized homosexuality found among various exotic peoples, or the so-called situational homosexuality of some typically "masculine" males in our own culture—it is argued that this is not really homosexuality at all. This is a very circular type of reasoning that is bound to confirm the premises or prejudices with which it begins. But we are in no way bound by reason to suppose that only obviously neurotic sexual relations between like-sexed partners are genuinely homosexual and that other relations not clearly linked with neurotic trends are not.

Throughout this book the word "homosexual" is used to refer to all sexual phenomena, overt or psychic, that involve like-sexed individuals. Individuals may respond sexually to stimuli originating in other individuals of the same sex in diverse ways and for virtually an infinite number of reasons. Some such responses may occur in a context that makes them appear fortuitous. In other instances such responses may occur in a context which makes them appear situational, experimental, transitory, opportunistic, compulsive, psychopathological, or in any one of a great number of other contexts. In either case the sexual nature of the response and the fact that it involves another individual of the same sex define the response as homosexual, rather than the context in which the response occurs. It is not too much to insist that contacts between two persons of the same sex that result in orgasm are homosexual, as are sexual contacts between like-sexed partners that do not result in orgasm. Similarly, the individual who does not make physical contact, but is erotically aroused by psychological or physical stimuli originating in another individual of the same sex has had a homosexual experience. Because the same individual may respond at other times, or even at the same time, to stimuli arising in individuals of the opposite sex does not mean that the former type of experience is not homosexual; homosexuality is not confined to a small and eccentric group of people who only respond to others of their own sex. We will continue our study of homosexuality with a more detailed consideration of this fact.

II

The Heterosexual-Homosexual Continuum

It would simplify matters considerably if all males learned a pattern of mutually exclusive sexual preferences so as to make it possible to divide them into distinct classifications, one heterosexual and the other homosexual. But, as Kinsey, Pomeroy, and Martin have noted:

> Males do not represent two discrete populations, heterosexual and homosexual. The world is not to be divided into sheep and goats. Not all things are black nor all things white. It is a fundamental of taxonomy that nature rarely deals with discrete categories. Only the human mind invents categories and tries to force facts into separated pigeon-holes. The living world is a continuum in each and every one of its aspects. The sooner we learn this concerning human sexual behavior the sooner we shall reach a sound understanding of the realities of sex.[53]

We must, accordingly, understand that the homosexuality of most males is not an all-or-nothing proposition. We do not mean to overlook the existence of individuals with a history of exclusive heterosexuality, nor the existence of other individuals with a history of exclusive homosexuality. The existence of exclusive heterosexuality and homosexuality has always been recognized and for the most part overemphasized. But what is important to understand also is that there is always a considerable portion of the male population in any culture whose members have learned to respond to both heterosexual and homosexual stimuli. There are some in whom heterosexuality predominates, some in whom homosexuality predominates, and others in whom the two types of responsiveness play a more or less equal part. We have traditionally referred to those individuals in whom heterosexual and homosexual responsiveness are more or less balanced as *bisexual;* on the other hand, we have referred to the remainder of this group as either heterosexual or homosexual. This method of classification, however, proves to be rather misleading, because it provides for only a three-point scale—heterosexual, bisexual, homosexual—whereas in nature there is a much more gradual transition between exclusive heterosexuality and exclusive homosexuality. This *continuum,* as we shall call it, is better described by a seven-point scale such as that devised by Kinsey, Pomeroy, and Martin.

In this scale (see the Appendix), 0 represents individuals with a history of exclusive heterosexuality, 6 represents individuals with a history of exclusive homosexuality, and 1 through 5 represent all those individuals with a history of varying combinations of heterosexual and homosexual experience. Those rated 1, for example, "have only incidental homosexual contacts which have involved physical or psychic response, or incidental psychic responses without physical contact." Those rated 3 "stand midway on the heterosexual-homosexual scale" and "they accept and equally enjoy both types of contacts, and have no strong preferences for one or the other." Those rated 5 "are almost entirely homosexual in their overt activities and/or reactions," but they "do have incidental experience with the opposite sex and sometimes react physically to individuals of the opposite sex." [53]

Since this is a seven-point scale, 3 is the midpoint in the classification; and, therefore, 0 is the opposite of 6, 1 is the opposite of 5, and 2 is the opposite of 4.

These ratings take into account not only the individual's overt experiences but also his psychosexual reactions. In those few instances in which actual behavior and psychosexual reactions are not in accord, the rating of an individual must be based upon an evaluation of the relative importance of the overt and the psychic in his history. The position of an individual on this scale is determined not by the absolute amount of overt experience or psychic reaction, but by the relation of the heterosexual to the homosexual in his history. In other words, all of the individuals in each classification show the same balance between the heterosexual and homosexual elements in their history.

Every person may be graded at some point in this scale in accordance with a reasonable representation of his sexual orientation. In this book we are interested in *all* those who rate from 1 through 6, rather than only those ratable as 5 and 6. Heretofore it has been those at the upper extreme of the continuum who have been the center of attention in most books on homosexuality. The serious neglect of those ratable from 1 through 4 has tended to obscure the full significance of homosexuality in the life of the adult human male. Thus in many cases statistical estimates of homosexuality in our culture have been misleading because they have tended to refer at most only to those with the highest rating.

It is presumably those ratable as 5 and 6 whom most people have in mind when they speak of the "homosexual." Yet it is impossible to be sure of what is meant by this elusive expression, since many people regard any person who has any homosexual experience whatsoever as a "homosexual." In the last war, for example, officials in the armed services categorized any serviceman known to have had homosexual experience as a "homosexual." Many such men were ignominiously expelled from service with a less-than-honorable discharge, a policy that often led to tragic circumstances for the former serviceman and his family. Similarly, under American law, an individual may receive the same penalty for a single homosexual experience that he would for a continuous record of homosexual experiences. Or, if he is employed by the federal government, an individual is likely to be excluded from his occupation, again often with tragic results, simply because he has had this elusive term applied to him. A husband who has worked out a very successful marital adjustment is likely to be rated a "homosexual" if his neighbors learn about a single contact he has had with another male. As Kinsey *et al.* observe, "All such misjudgments are the product of the tendency to categorize sexual activities under only two heads, and of a failure to recognize the endless gradations that actually exist." [53]

Definitions of the "homosexual" vary greatly and prove to be dependent upon criteria that are quite arbitrarily set up by people who wish to emphasize different aspects of homosexuality. Thus some people attach a great deal of significance to the frequency of homosexual experiences in the individual's history, while others stress the importance of the individual's attitudes toward his homosexual experiences rather than their number. Still others minimize these factors and instead stress the importance of certain personality traits or subconscious conflicts supposed to be in evidence in all "true homosexuals."

It does not seem that there is any worthwhile purpose served in the promiscuous use of the word "homosexual" as a substantive referring to persons. Whatever convenience there may be in the habitual use of this word as a substantive is offset by the confusion and abuse to which such a habit inevitably leads. Talk about the "homosexual" encourages generalizations that usually cannot be substantiated by reality, and one is never sure to whom this substantive really refers. Instead of being used as nouns the words "homosexual" and "heterosexual" are better used as adjectives to describe the particular nature of a sexual contact. Thus, a sexual contact between male and female is a heterosexual contact, though one cannot be absolutely certain that either partner is necessarily always a "heterosexual." Similarly, a sexual contact between two males or between two females is a homosexual contact, although once again one cannot be absolutely certain that either partner is necessarily a "homosexual."

The failure to recognize the heterosexual-homosexual continuum has also led to the erroneous belief that every individual is—even innately or inherently—either heterosexual or homosexual. From this tendency to over-generalize has arisen a stereotype of the "homosexual"—a stereotype, incidentally, that does not hold true even at the upper extreme of the continuum. Nevertheless, many people have come to believe that there is an intimate and regular relationship between an individual's sexual preferences and his personality, character, and even his physique and physical mannerisms.

> It is quite generally believed that one's preference for a sexual partner of one or the other sex is correlated with various physical and mental qualities, and with the total personality which makes a homosexual male or female physically, psychically, and perhaps spiritually distinct from a heterosexual individual. It is generally thought that these qualities make a homosexual person obvious and recognizable to anyone who has a sufficient understanding of such matters. Even psychiatrists discuss "the homosexual personality" and many of them believe that preferences for sexual partners of a particular sex are merely secondary manifestations of something that lies much deeper in the totality of that intangible which they call the personality.[53]

Many clinicians have elaborated detailed descriptions of "the homosexual personality," and in most cases they have identified various environmental influences and emotional conflicts supposed to be found regularly in his history. Descriptions of "the homosexual personality" and accounts of its origin differ widely among the various schools of clinical thought. We shall not discuss these theories in detail here since they are mentioned later in this book. We may note at this point, however, that a number of psychological inventories and "tests" are in current usage that purport to identify the "homosexual." These are used both in psychiatric clinics and in industry. (Many employers, for reasons not entirely clear, refuse to hire anyone whom they regard as a "homosexual," and some have relied upon these psychological techniques to identify him.) For the most part these diagnostic inventories are dependent upon preconceptions about homosexuality found within the various schools of clinical thought, and they are not infrequently also dependent upon an even cruder characterization of the so-called homosexual personality.

Many characteristics have been attributed to males with homosexual preferences. It is commonly believed, for instance, that such males tend to be physically weak and that their body structure resembles that of the female, especially around the hips and thighs. They are supposed to have delicate skins, fine complexions, and high-pitched voices, along with ob-

vious hand movements, peculiarities of gait, and other effeminate mannerisms. Artistic interests are ascribed to all these males and they are also
said to be temperamental, emotionally unbalanced, oversensitive, difficult
to get along with, and undependable. It is also believed that "homosexuals"
manifest the same interests as females and that they have "a female soul
in a masculine body." They are supposed to have a predilection for certain
occupations such as ballet, hairdressing, window display, interior decorating, acting, religious service, teaching, social work, and other trades, arts,
and professions that are thought somewhat effeminate by some males in
our culture.

This stereotype, unfortunately, has been encouraged in the psychiatric
literature until recent times. As but a single example, we may point to
Karpman's remarks in *The Sexual Offender and His Offenses:*

> The homosexual male shows a feminine carrying angle of arm; long
> legs, narrow hips, large muscles, deficient hair on face, chest, and
> back, feminine distribution of pubic hair, high-pitched voice, small
> genitals, scrotal fold. Often he has excess fat on shoulders, buttocks,
> abdomen. Occasionally the penis is very large, the hips unusually
> wide.[50]

So-called "constitutional factors" are attributed to homosexual males
throughout psychiatric literature even in many of the texts that are regarded as authoritative, and this fact no doubt is what prompted Kinsey
et al. to remark somewhat laconically, "The characterizations [of 'homosexuals'] are so distinct that they seem to leave little room for doubt that
homosexual and heterosexual represent two very distinct types of males." [53]

Clinicians in particular continue to ascribe various mental characteristics
to all "homosexuals." In a book entitled *Sexual Deviation,* first published
in 1964, Dr. Storr asserts that "an excessive fear of physical injury is more
commonly found in male homosexuals than in heterosexuals." [74]

It is impossible to know with certainty what scientific evidence, if any,
allows Dr. Storr to make this broad generalization, for the statement is
undocumented by any research in his text. We may suppose, however, that
this opinion is based upon the psychoanalytic research of Bieber *et al.*[8]
These authors reported that such fears were prevalent in a group of 106
homosexual psychiatric patients. But it is quite untenable to generalize
that the entire homosexual population, including those who are not psychiatric cases, commonly suffers from the same fears. Indeed, it is quite
impossible to make any broad generalization about this population, since
no valid cross-section of the homosexual population has ever been studied
scientifically. We can accordingly say very little that is reliable about the
physical, intellectual, spiritual, emotional, or psychiatric status of this
population. Nevertheless, sweeping generalizations are continually made

about the "homosexual" on the basis of a few psychiatric studies of small groups of emotionally disturbed individuals. These generalizations are passed on from one writer to another, often when the original source is entirely forgotten, until they tend to form a kind of tradition. This is mythology rather than science.

When one learns something about the incidence of homosexuality and becomes aware of the heterosexual-homosexual continuum, it appears quite obvious that these generalizations about the "homosexual" apply, at most, to very exceptional cases. Even if attention is narrowed to the upper extreme of the heterosexual-homosexual continuum, those who conform to the stereotyped picture of the "homosexual" are the exception rather than the rule. A majority of males ratable even as 5 or 6 fail to display the various emotional, characterological, and physical attributes ascribed to the "homosexual," and most of these males possess no peculiarities, apart from their sexual preferences, that set them apart from other males.

There are of course some effeminate males in the homosexual group who conform to the stereotype. Some of these men, generally referred to today in the vernacular as "faggots," "fairies," "pansies," or "queens," have identified with this stereotype, and some even go so far as to imitate openly the female. It is important to realize, however, that these represent a small minority of the homosexual group. Indeed, it must be pointed out that effeminacy per se does not necessarily indicate a preference for other males as sex partners. There are highly effeminate males, some of whom appear to be "pansies" and "faggots," who rate 0 on the seven-point scale. There are male transvestites who have no interest at all in other males as sex partners, and there are, on the other hand, males with a lifelong rating of 6 who in every respect except for their sexual preferences possess all the characteristics identified with the "heterosexual" in our culture. Effeminacy, therefore, may be associated with heterosexual preferences, or it may be associated with homosexual preferences; it is not a characteristic peculiar to either the heterosexual or the homosexual group.

When we take into consideration all those ratable from 1 through 6— some 50 per cent of the male population—the numbers alone make it quite clear that most of the attributes thought to be linked with homosexuality— effeminacy, emotional disease, moral degeneracy, etc.—cannot be found in the vast majority of those males in whom homosexual interests have become manifest. It would be somewhat preposterous to imagine that one out of every two males fits the stereotype of a "homosexual" and is a "faggot" and a moral degenerate. The overwhelming majority of these males fail to suggest this stereotype, even in minor details. Within the homosexual group at every level including the higher ratings, every type of male may be found. "Acceptance of the fact that homosexuality affects a substantial proportion of the population," as West observes, "means the

abandonment of some common notions about homosexual types. . . .
Among the homosexual multitude all types of physiques and character
may be found." [78]

It is quite impossible to identify an individual's sexual preferences in
terms of his character, personality, physical type, mannerisms, choice of
occupation, emotional adjustment, or any of the other criteria that have
been used to arrive at such a diagnosis. The vast majority of all males—
whether ratable as 0, as 1, as 2, as 3, as 4, as 5, or as 6—resemble one
another in more ways than they differ from one another. Almost all males
react in terms of their genetic sex and are masculine beings both psychologically and physically. When, in a later chapter, we discuss the psychosexual
characteristics of males, we shall see that homosexual males are very
typically masculine beings.

There is perhaps only one characteristic that is found commonly—
though not necessarily regularly—among individuals with a history of
homosexuality in our culture: a sense of guilt. We do not have to look
far afield for the source of this guilt. It is clear that the homoerotophobic
atmosphere of our culture encourages this feeling. But what is of more
interest for the moment is the fact that most males with a history of homosexuality resemble most others who lack such a history, so that within the
homosexual group there are as many "types" as may be found in the
heterosexual group. It is ironical that this fact has provided certain theorists
with material with which to characterize the "homosexual" along certain
narrow lines. West has discussed this circumstance very well in the following paragraph:

> Apart from their characteristic sense of guilt, homosexuals vary
> so much that it is virtually impossible to pick out any one feature
> common to all. Writers on the subject, even medical writers who
> should know better, carelessly throw out generalizations without an
> atom of validity. One reads that homosexuals are depraved, or ex-
> hibitionists, or (and this usually from the homosexuals themselves)
> that they are more "alive" and "sympathetic" than the humdrum mass
> of humanity. In reality some homosexuals suffer from neurotic fears
> and anxieties, and some are self-assured and hard as nails; some are
> vain and ostentatious and some are shy and quiet; some are cow-
> ardly and some are heroes; some are effeminate and some are
> brutes. Since all these types are represented, psychologists can all
> too easily pick out examples to suit their own pet theories. Those
> who choose to believe the condition is a sign of moral degeneracy,
> on a par with drug addiction, alcoholism, and criminal tendencies,
> can find plenty of examples among the prison and criminal population
> of men who readily satisfy any and every sexual whim without the
> slightest pang of conscience. On the other hand, those who believe
> that the over-attachment of the young boy to his mother causes homo-

sexuality can equally well pick out examples, especially among only children, of shy, pampered men who have never broken away from an adoring mother. Those who believe that homosexuality springs from narcissism—that is to say, love of self to a pathological degree coupled with inability to form a give-and-take relationship with other people—can readily point out vain, attention-seeking individuals who are prepared to put on a show of simpering mannerisms for the benefit of any male willing to dally with them.[78]

It is easy, then, to find whatever one is looking for in the homosexual population simply because this population is *not* homogeneous.

But certain of these facts are beyond the experience of the armchair theorist who has never bothered to make a quantitative study of sexual behavior. In the limited and very special atmosphere of the study, the library, or the clinic, many of the broader truths of life are dimmed and one's perspective may become narrow. It is particularly necessary for the sexologist, like any student of behavior, to approach his subject from a quantitative as well as a qualitative standpoint. If his generalizations are to have any basis in reality, he must always make it a point to have as broad a knowledge of his subject as is possible. He must have a firsthand acquaintance with the social and psychological atmosphere in which various types of sexual behavior arise, and he must possess the rare talent of being able to gain the confidence of other human beings to such an extent that it is possible for him to circulate among them in, as it were, their native habitat, not as a prying stranger but as a sympathetic confidant. If he is not able to do so he will never be able to accumulate enough experience to speak with true authority, and his understanding will be necessarily limited.

As far as homosexuality is concerned, the scientist who studies it must be able to enter with ease a number of different social environments, some of which may not be generally accessible to the average person. He must be able to look with emotional detachment, and also with moral detachment, upon the data that become available to him when he is successful in gaining entry into the private world of his subjects. He must have at his command a wealth of such data drawn not only from his own immediate culture and environment, but also from other environments, with which to compare the new data that became available to him. If he lacks the perspective that comes from a broad knowledge of his subject he will be apt to misinterpret the data, and he will find himself constructing interesting but fanciful theories rather than recording substantial realities. The second-rate scientist tries to hide his ignorance by making a theory when he should be accumulating facts. He is usually firm in his theoretical convictions to the same extent that he lacks sufficient data to support them.

The scientific student of homosexuality who is keenly aware of the heterosexual-homosexual continuum knows that it is necessary to have an adequate statistical impression of sexual behavior before one conjures up theories of meaning, etiology, and prognosis.

Consider the idea, common in clinical circles as well as in the population as a whole, that the "homosexual" is an anxiety-ridden, shy person who, because he has some deep fear of the opposite sex, uses his homosexuality as a "defense" against heterosexuality or as an "escape" from it.

Of course, it may be true in the case of certain individuals that the capacity to respond homosexually is used as a defense against some deep-seated fear of heterosexuality. But the question is, how often is this true? To what extent can we explain all homosexuality as an escape from heterosexuality? To what extent can we explain even most homosexuality in these terms?

If we hand-pick our cases and disregard a great number of data we will be able to establish a convincing argument for the above interpretation of homosexuality. But if we look at the total picture we will see immediately that this very often is an entirely inadequate account of the etiology of homosexuality. It does not fit all the facts that are at one's disposal, or even most of them. It might be argued that fear of heterosexuality supports a homosexual adjustment in the case of the 4 per cent of the male population that maintains a rating of 6 throughout life, or even in the case of the 8 per cent of the population that maintains this rating for an extended period of time. Such an interpretation might even fit the homosexuality of those ratable as 5. But how well does it fit the homosexuality of those ratable as 1, 2, 3, or 4—all of whom have a substantial history of heterosexuality that often exists simultaneously with homosexuality? Let us assess the value of this theory in the light of the facts presented in the following quotation.

> Some of the males who are involved in one type of relation at one period in their lives, may have only the other type of relation at some later period. There may be considerable fluctuation of patterns from time to time. Some males may be involved in both heterosexual and homosexual activities within the same period of time. For instance, there are some who engage in both heterosexual and homosexual activities in the same year, or in the same month or week, or even in the same day. There are not a few individuals who engage in group activities in which they may make simultaneous contact with partners of both sexes.[53]

We must assume, since we can be sure that sexual preferences are learned rather than inherited, that the individual's position in the heterosexual-homosexual continuum depends to a large extent upon the type of learning favored by his culture. In some cultures, for example, almost 100 per cent of the males cluster around a rating of 3. In these cultures homosexuality is expected and is encouraged along with heterosexuality. In other cultures close to 100 per cent of males may be rated less than 3. Homoerotophobic cultures tend, naturally, to favor a large per cent of lower ratings, and homoerotophilic cultures tend to favor a larger per cent of higher ratings. But it is very important to realize that no culture, whatever its orientation to heterosexuality and homosexuality, is ever successful in bringing about a uniform rating for all members of the group, simply because *influences other than cultural attitudes also play an important part in the acquirement of sexual preferences.*

Consider, for example, America, a subculture of the Judaeo-Christian tradition. In America homoerotophobia is at a height that is unprecedented even in the other subcultures of Judaeo-Christendom. In the United States male homosexuality occasions more social and personal anxiety than in any other civilized society known to science. Not only is homosexuality discouraged by the mores and condemned by public opinion on all sides; it is proclaimed a serious mental disease by American medicine and evokes heavy penalties in the numerous American statutory sex codes. Yet, the research of Kinsey *et al.* has revealed that homosexual responsiveness plays some part in the histories of one out of every two males in America.

Since these data are the most thorough and reliable we have on homosexuality from any culture, an examination of this research will provide us with a substantial insight into the nature of the heterosexual-homosexual continuum. It will reveal, as well, certain of the influences that play a part in the acquirement of various patterns of sexual behavior. We will not, of course, learn all that is important about homosexuality by studying its manifestations in only one culture, but we may begin here.

Identification with the verbalized ideals of our culture led many people in the past to believe that homosexuality is a rare and therefore also abnormal phenomenon confined to the activities of a very few eccentrics. Pre-Kinseyan estimates of the incidence of this behavior ranged from 2 to 4 or 5 per cent at most.

Because homosexual activities incur severe disapproval in most areas of Judaeo-Christian culture, and because, in America at least, such activities may actually involve serious legal consequences, few persons have ever been willing to disclose publicly any history of homosexuality. When, however, Kinsey and his colleagues, in the effort to determine what people *do* sexually, were so bold as to inquire directly into this area of sexual life, they were surprised to find that a substantial number of males and about half the same number of females freely admitted that homosexual contacts played some part in their sexual history as adults. It was found that in the privacy established through assured anonymity and in the atmosphere of rapport created by these skillful investigators, a far greater number of people than anyone had ever anticipated were willing to discuss their homosexual experiences. When the results of these thousands of interviews were tabulated, even the investigators themselves were surprised to find that homosexual experiences constituted a part of the sexual pattern of what then seemed to be an unbelievably large number of males.

Because these scientists were anxious to obtain a reliable account of the sexual behavior of American males, and because the findings in this area were so far beyond what any scientist had previously estimated, they were skeptical of their own findings. They proceeded to question the results they had obtained. Since the possibility existed that those who had volunteered their histories represented only a special segment of the community—a segment that, for example, might have an especially high incidence of homosexuality—Kinsey and his colleagues set about testing the validity of their findings. Their tests were designed to reveal among other things, whether or not the results of the study as a whole represented a valid cross-section of the entire country. One method used to ascertain this was to compare the results obtained from an entire community with those obtained from only part of a community. Since it must be presumed that data obtained from all the members of a given community cannot be involved in any problem centered around a valid cross-section, it was possible to use those data to check the data that were obtained from communities in which only certain individuals volunteered information. When these comparisons were made it was found that the same proportion of males reported homosexual activities in both cases. Other checks as well were applied, and the results always confirmed the validity of the data obtained. It is of interest to quote the authors on this point.

> These figures [on homosexuality] are, of course, considerably higher than any which have previously been estimated; but, as already shown . . . they must be understatements, if they are anything other than the fact.
>
> We ourselves were totally unprepared to find such incidence data when the research was originally undertaken. Over a period of several years we were repeatedly assailed with doubts as to whether we were getting a fair cross-section of the total population or whether a selection of cases was biasing the results. It has been our experience, however, that each new group into which we have gone has provided substantially the same data. Whether the histories were taken in one large city or another, whether they were taken in large cities, in small towns, or in rural areas, whether they came from one college or another, a church school or a state university or some private institution, whether they came from one part of the country or from another, the incidence data on the homosexual have been more or less the same.
>
> While the validity of the data on all of the sexual outlets has been tested and retested throughout the study . . . especial attention has been given to testing the material on the homosexual.

The authors then outline twelve specific tests that were applied to the data on homosexuality. The conclusion at which they arrived from the results obtained from these tests is summarized as follows:

> If we had arrived at the present incidence figures by a single cal-. culation based on a single population, one might well question their validity. But the determination of the extent of the homosexual in the population is too important a matter to be settled on anything but an elaborately devised system of samples. When twelve ways of obtaining data give results that are as consistent as those which are to be found in the tables and charts listed above, there can be no question that the actual incidence of the homosexual is at least 37% and 50% as given above. The tests show that the actual figures may be as much as 5% higher, or still higher.[53]

The results of this research have pleased few people, since few have been prepared to approach the subject objectively. Most people who are at all concerned with it have already arrived at a preconceived estimate of the incidence of homosexual behavior and are not particularly disposed to abandon their notions, since these may not be based so much on a desire to know the truth as on a desire to prove a foregone conclusion.

On the one hand, people who thought homosexual behavior less frequent were convinced that it is abnormal and therefore rare. They could not accept the idea that this type of behavior involves so large a portion of the population. On the other hand, those people who thought the incidence of homosexual behavior much higher than it proved to be were convinced that homosexual impulses play some part in the sexual history of virtually everyone. Most of this latter group were either "homosexuals" themselves, or psychoanalysts who, on the basis of certain theories, maintain that homosexual impulses, at least on an "unconscious level," are universal.

The reasoning of those who have disputed these statistics is interesting. All agree that homoerotophobia plays some part in what they believe to be the erroneous conclusions arrived at in the Kinsey investigation. But the two groups described above each offer a different interpretation of the effect produced by this homoerotophobia. Those who favor a lower incidence point out that since, so to speak, no respectable person would either feel homosexual urges or admit to them, those who did report such urges were psychopathic or exhibitionistic types who made use of an opportunity to expose themselves. It has also been argued by this group that "homosexuals" flocked to Kinsey to report their histories in order to create the impression that homosexuality is universal. All of these arguments, of course, are refuted by the various tests applied to the data, and especially those that were designed to test whether or not a representative cross-section was interviewed.

Those, on the other hand, who favor a higher incidence argue that many people who might have reported homosexual urges and experiences were prevented from doing so by guilt, shame, and anxiety. They believe, were it not for homoerotophobia, that a much greater number of subjects— even all of the subjects—would have reported some history of homosexuality. Kinsey and his colleagues have suggested themselves that any change in the incidence reported would probably be in the direction of greater magnitude. It is another thing, however, to imagine that it would be, for instance, doubled, or that it would approach 100 per cent.

On the basis of the tests applied to the data, and on the basis of the methods used in interviewing the subjects, we must assume that the figures which we are about to consider represent a very close approximation of the actual incidence of homosexuality in American society. It is also instructive to note that even when smaller statistical populations are studied the results clearly tend to confirm the Kinsey findings.

The statistics which follow do not refer to the number of so-called homosexuals in the population for, as we have already pointed out, it is quite impossible to know at what point, if at all, an individual should be characterized as a "homosexual." "It is only possible to record the number of those who belong to each of the positions on such a heterosexual-homosexual scale as is given." [53]

The absurdity of a rigid and categorical sexual classification is obvious when the two following examples are considered.

A so-called homosexual from a large city in the eastern United States who was notorious for his promiscuous activities with other males, adopted the name "Midnight Mae" and "cruised" the public parks in "drag" over a period of years, subsequently married, abandoned "the gay life" completely, became the father of seven children and so far as anyone knows, never again felt any pressing need to engage in homosexual activities. Such cases may be rare, but in absence of more precise scientific knowledge it is difficult to say just how rare they actually are.

Conversely, a prominent and respected physician who until the age of fifty-six had experienced heterosexual arousal exclusively and could remember no earlier tendency to become aroused by other males, consulted the author in a state of anxiety because a chance experience with a younger man who had seduced him a year earlier had so encouraged the establishment of a homosexual pattern that he had lost all interest in women and was no longer able to perform sexually with his wife. This father of four children who, until the age of fifty-six, imagined that homosexual behavior is confined to little boys, apes, and a few rare neurotics, became the impassioned lover of a man younger than his oldest son, and a frequent client of male prostitutes.

While it is fruitless to try to decide at what point an individual with a history of homosexuality becomes a "homosexual," and it is therefore impossible to say how many "homosexuals" there are in the world, it is nevertheless possible to speak with considerable authority on the number of individuals who become involved to varying extents in homosexual activities. On the basis of the data collected by Kinsey, Pomeroy, and Martin, we may gain some impression of the role homosexual responsiveness plays in the sex life of the human male within the American subdivision of Judaeo-Christian culture.

All of the figures which follow refer to males who have reached sexual maturity—or more precisely, to males between adolescence and old age (roughly between sixteen and fifty-five years of age). These figures, therefore, do *not* account for the homosexual activity of those under sixteen. If the homosexual activities of these younger males were counted the figures would be substantially higher.

It is also important to note that these figures refer to the white male population and do *not* account for the homosexual activity that occurs among American Negro males.

In the light of these considerations and others, these percentages may be accepted as *minimal* for the American male population as a whole. Moreover, since the American male population is undoubtedly harassed by more anxiety over homosexuality than males in any other culture or subculture, including even males in other subcultures of Judaeo-Christendom, we are forced to conclude that *the incidence and frequency data which follow must be absolutely minimal in terms of the world population of males.*

Of the total male population, 37 per cent—more than one out of every three males that one may meet—has *at least some overt homosexual experience to the point of orgasm* between adolescence and old age. Another 13 per cent of males have experienced manifest homosexual urges without ever having had overt homosexual contact to the point of orgasm. It may be seen, therefore, that *approximately 50 per cent of the male population become directly involved emotionally and/or physically with homosexuality to some extent after sexual maturity.* A more precise breakdown of these figures follows. For the moment, however, let us consider some of the implications of the above figures.

That 37 per cent of males with some overt homosexual experience represents a group that, according to current laws in the United States, is composed of "sex offenders." All of these males would be subject to arrest and imprisonment if the precise details of their homosexual activities were known to the police. If we include all other sexual behavior that is illegal in the United States, this figure rises to a point at which almost every American male (approximately 95 per cent) is a "sex offender" in terms of the laws of his country. No further comment is necessary regarding the need to revise sexio-legal codes of the fifty states. The total unreality of these codes is patent.

Of the 13 per cent of males with unfulfilled homosexual urges, there must be a considerable number of disturbed, frustrated individuals. It should be understood that a number of these individuals are oriented predominantly or even exclusively to homosexual stimuli but cannot bring themselves to seek the contacts they desire.

The cumulative incidence of homosexuality has been cited as approximately 50 per cent. Since only 4 per cent of the male population are exclusively homosexual throughout life, it may be seen that 46 per cent combine varying degrees of homosexual and heterosexual responsiveness. Of this 46 per cent some are more homosexual than heterosexual in orientation, some are more heterosexual than homosexual in orientation, and a smaller number are equally homosexual and heterosexual in orientation.

Since the cumulative incidence of the homosexual is 50 per cent, there is another 50 per cent who are exclusively heterosexual throughout life and have never become aware of any tendency to respond to homosexual stimuli. This latter group is the analogue of the 4 per cent of males who are exclusively homosexual throughout life.

These two groups taken together would seem to represent a refutation of, or at least a challenge to, the psychoanalytic proposition that the psychosexual orientation of all males is basically bisexual. The undisputed fact that from birth on we possess the capacity to respond sexually to any sufficient stimulus, and that therefore we are all potentially bisexual, should not be taken to indicate a manifest or even an implicit bisexual orientation on the part of all males. For this study reveals that 50 per cent of all males never exploit the capacity to respond to homosexual stimuli and that 4 per cent of all males never exploit the capacity to respond to heterosexual stimuli. Thus, 54 per cent of American males must be described as monosexual rather than bisexual in orientation.

Let us now clarify the part homosexual activities play in relation to heterosexual activities in the life of the American male. All of the following figures also refer to white, adult males, and they are valid in each instance for at least a three-year period. Some of these males, therefore, continue to respond homosexually over a much longer period of time.

One out of every three males (30 per cent of all adult males) has at least *incidental homosexual experience or reactions,* i.e., rates somewhere between 1 and 6 throughout a period of at least three years.

It is easy to confuse this group with the 37 per cent mentioned earlier. To be classed in the 37 per cent group it was necessary only that the individual have at least one homosexual experience to the point of orgasm as an adult. The present group includes all those who rate 1 through 6. In a certain respect this statistic is even more significant than the 37 per cent—

which is more often quoted—because it refers to a population in which homosexual responsiveness *continues over an extended period of time.*

One out of every four males (25 per cent of all adult males) has *more than incidental homosexual experience or reactions,* i.e., rates from 2 through 6 throughout a period of at least three years.

One out of every six males (18 per cent of all adult males) has *as much of the homosexual as the heterosexual* in his history, i.e., rates 3 to 6 throughout a period of at least three years.

At this level we begin to approach a highly significant proportion of homosexual behavior in terms of the mores. These individuals would be regarded at least as "bisexuals" according to psychiatric and other conventional criteria. Many journalists and others, among them Jess Stearn, the author of a recent book on homosexuality, regard all of the individuals within this group as "homosexuals." More importantly, however, one out of every six males—a group of males equal in number to the largest minority groups in the country—become involved at least as much with homosexuality as with heterosexuality during a period in their lives of not less than three years duration. On the basis of this statistic it is folly to imagine that the homosexual minority is a small or potentially insignificant one. If this group were coordinated and began to act in its own interests, it could bring enormous pressure to bear. This, however, is not an imminent possibility, since this is a rather fluid group and in most ways a highly heterogeneous group, burdened with a great deal of ambivalence and many misgivings concerning its own sexual behavior.

The fact remains that at any one time one out of every six males is deeply involved in homosexuality—a disturbed and a disturbing element within the atmosphere of Judaeo-Christian culture. It is shocking to imagine the number of unhappy and restless people represented by this figure, which alone is enough to call for a re-evaluation of our traditional attitudes toward homosexuality.

One out of every eight males (13 per cent of all adult males) has *more of the homosexual than the heterosexual* in his history, i.e., rates 4 to 6 throughout a period of at least three years.

This group constitutes what may be considered the "hard core" of the homosexual minority although, because of the anxiety homosexuality occasions in our society, any of those ratable from 1 through 6 may develop attitudes peculiar to members of a minority group. It is in the next group, however, that we must assume that the full social burden of homosexuality is most often and probably most deeply experienced.

One out of every ten males (10 per cent of all adult males) is *more or less exclusively homosexual,* i.e., rates 5 or 6 throughout a period of at least three years.

One out of every thirteen males (8 per cent of all adult males) is *exclusively homosexual,* i.e., rates 6 throughout a period of at least three years.

The magnitude of this figure is unprecedented when it is realized that most pre-Kinseyan estimates of homosexuality (which, presumably, would relate most directly to the sexual pattern of this group) were in the neighborhood of 2 per cent. The Army induction centers reported an estimate of 0.1 per cent, while Havelock Ellis estimated 2 per cent to 3 per cent. Even Hirshfeld's more liberal estimate of from 2 per cent to 5 per cent is dwarfed by the Kinsey finding, which almost doubles it at the upper extreme.

In conclusion we may note that 4 per cent of all adult males are *exclusively homosexual throughout their lives* after the onset of adolescence.

The members of this latter group would certainly be regarded as "true homosexuals" according to current thinking. It is perhaps this group that earlier scholars had in mind when they attempted to estimate the incidence of homosexuality, but it is hard to be certain of this since they did not define what they meant when they referred to those who are "really homosexual." Even this group represents a very large number of males, well exceeding the million mark in America alone.

So far as these ratings are concerned, Kinsey *et al.* note:

> The people who are identified as "homosexuals" in much of the legal and social practice have rated anything between 1 and 6 on the above scale. On the other hand, there are some persons who would not rate an individual as "really homosexual" if he were anything less than a 5 or 6. Nevertheless, it should be emphasized again that there are persons who rate 2s or 3s who, in terms of the number of contacts they have made, may have had more homosexual experience than many persons who rate 6, and the clinician, the social worker, court officials, and society in general are not infrequently concerned with persons who rate no more than 2s and 3s. Many who rate only 1 or 2 are much disturbed over their homosexual experience, and they are frequently among those who go to clinicians for help.
>
> Finally, it should be emphasized that the social significance of an individual's history may or may not have any relation to his rating on the above scale.[53]

What then is the extent of homosexuality in our culture? We have already pointed out that it is quite impossible to say how many "homosexuals" there are in our society, since this depends on the definition. But certainly homosexuality may become a personal problem for any of the 50 per cent of males who become involved in it. When we come to the group ratable from 3 to 6, a group in which homosexuality is at least as pervasive as heterosexuality, there can be little doubt that most of the people in this group have more than a casual interest in this topic. This group, as we have seen, represents 18 per cent of the male population, or

1 out of every 6 males. It is therefore clear that this type of sexual responsiveness can in no sense be considered rare or uncommon even in our own society.

An examination of the statistics of those who have had homosexual experience to the point of orgasm if they remain unmarried until the age of thirty-five reveals an interesting manifestation of the differential effect of formal education: 58 per cent of the males who belong to the group that goes into high school but not beyond, 50 per cent of the grade-school level, and 47 per cent of the college level. The single male at all educational levels, presumably because he has fewer opportunities to enjoy heterosexual coitus, will accept homosexual contacts more readily than the married male.

The *frequency* of the homosexual—as contrasted with the *incidence* of the homosexual—is very low:

> In any particular age group, in any segment of the population, it is never more than about 5.5% of the males who are having homosexual relations that average more than once every other day (3.5 per week). Calculating only for the males who actually have homosexual experience, there are never more than 5.2% that have frequencies averaging more than 6.0 per week during their most active years. Considering that it is 25% of the entire population which has total sexual outlets which average more than 3.5 per week, and considering that 24% of the married males have outlets that average more than 6.0 per week in their most active period, it is apparent that outlets from the homosexual are definitely low.[53]

This great discrepancy between the incidence of the homosexual and the frequency of homosexual outlets is remarkable and calls for comment.

It must not be imagined that these low frequencies are due to biological or any other extracultural factors. Homosexual males are no less motivated to seek sexual outlet than any other males. Indeed, it is thought by many that homosexual males are extraordinarily promiscuous and exceptionally hedonistic. These low frequencies are the result, as Kinsey *et al.* note, of social influences. It is clear that the American male who has a strong desire for homosexual relations enjoys far fewer opportunities to find satisfaction than the American male who desires heterosexual relations. He is faced with a great many more frustrating circumstances that require self-control and sexual renunciation than other people. In his everyday life he encounters many situations that for him are seductive and that arouse desire but do not allow for satisfaction. Males are prone to expose themselves to other males in locker rooms, gymnasia, public lavatories, and similar surroundings. These daily encounters may constitute temptations for the homosexually inclined male. But although the homosexual male may be frequently tempted he must also, because of the nature of his environment, be frequently frustrated. Nor is there any socially acceptable situation in which he may meet with those who share his sexual interests, as other males may. He is always forced to seek satisfaction surreptitiously, under the most dangerous and most anxiety-producing circumstances.

It is hardly surprising, then, if he seems more tense and nervous than others. Many people who experience homosexual urges react to them with virtual panic at the thought of their immorality. Others who have better accepted these urges in themselves, nevertheless live in constant fear and apprehension of the consequences that may result if their sexual desires become known to others. They are confronted with the possibility of the loss of employment, the loss of reputation, and the loss of personal dignity; there is also the very real possibility of an encounter with the police. In this nightmarish atmosphere the homosexual male may often renounce the possibility of sexual satisfaction altogether, or if he is incapable of doing so—and most people are—he may allow himself satisfaction only on rare occasions. Kinsey has remarked on this.

> There are some males who are primarily or even exclusively homosexual in their psychic responses, but who may completely abstain from overt relations for moral reasons or for fear of social difficulties. Left without any sociosexual contacts, some of these persons have essentially no outlet, and some of them are, therefore, very badly upset.[53]

To expect constant self-control from any person, or to require sexual abstinence of the average man amounts to little less than cruelty, however well this cruelty may be rationalized by appeals to moralism. We must challenge the wisdom of those who, because of their own religious beliefs, insist that no room whatsoever be allowed for any person to experience gratification of homosexual needs. The urge to punish may be considered by many to be no less immoral than the urge to sin. We feel very strongly that this unbending attitude is not only unwise and very unrealistic, but that it is also difficult to defend on ethical grounds in a free society.

Those responsible for the enforcement of law, along with certain others, may remark upon the promiscuity of the "homosexual." Only recently this author participated in a conference on homosexuality that included lawyers, psychologists, police officials, court psychiatrists, and members of the clergy. The idea was brought forth in this conference that the "homosexual" is a shortsighted hedonist who is interested in quick and frequent gratification at any cost. This impression was offered by individuals whose experience with so-called homosexuals is limited to the type of person who gets into difficulties with society, and who may well fit the description of a shortsighted hedonist. But it is highly questionable if generalizations about an entire group may be made on the basis of behavior that only certain individuals within this group display. This picture of the "homosexual" is certainly not confirmed by the frequency data that we have just encountered.

No doubt certain very experienced persons in the larger cities succeed in racking up for themselves a large number of "conquests," and still more persons may spend many hours each week searching for outlets. But apparently only a few ever have much success. This searching or "cruising," as it is called, may consume a great deal of the free time of some of these people; that does not mean that every adventure results in a successful contact. But many more people who have had a few homosexual experiences and who would like to have more never learn the technique of finding such experiences, never "cruise," and only very seldom, through chance, meet with another with whom they may find satisfaction. Many others may have learned full well the technique necessary to establish contact with a homosexual partner, but they may not elect to run the very serious risk that finding such a partner usually entails.

For every "homosexual" observed on the prowl by the police or some other person "in the know," there must be any number of others sitting alone in their rooms or searching for some means to sublimate their urges, for as we have seen, the frequency of outlet even for those at the upper extreme of the continuum is very low. Those who manage to cope with the limitations imposed upon their desires—and apparently they are in the vast majority—never come to the attention of the authorities or of other more promiscuous males.

Although no reliable frequencies among males with homosexual histories have been reported from Europe—to say nothing of the frequencies that may prevail outside of Judaeo-Christendom—it is safe to assume that frequencies among males with homosexual histories outside the United States are substantially higher. This would be consistent with the greater sexual freedom accorded the individual elsewhere in the world. The absence of laws prohibiting homosexual acts, although not necessarily contributing to an increase in the number of "homosexuals," provides greater opportunity for those who have learned homosexual preferences to find more frequent outlets.

If as many factors conspired to depress the average frequency of heterosexual outlets as do to depress the average frequency of homosexual outlets in the United States, it is very likely that a large number of predominantly heterosexual males would begin to manifest the neurotic attitudes associated with predominantly homosexual males in the United States. Many of them would find themselves constantly "on the prowl"—and do in any case. Many would resort more often to breaking the laws that restrained them. Many would feel extremely persecuted and would tend to congregate with others whose misery they shared; many others would simply fall into one of the clinical syndromes that may develop out of chronic frustration of the sexual drive. Those who had mastered the various techniques necessary to cope with such barriers against sexual satisfaction would no doubt, like many "homosexuals," tend to over-estimate the importance of their sexual "conquests." Nothing argues for the idea that frustration of heterosexual impulses would lead to results very different from those to which frustration of homosexual impulses seems to lead in so many cases.

Through the Kinsey research it was also found that homosexual activities occur in a much higher percentage of those males who become adolescent at an early age, and in a definitely smaller percentage of those males who become adolescent at a later age. The highest incidence and frequencies in masturbation and in heterosexual contacts are also to be found in this group. It is this same group that evinces the greatest sex drive both in early adolescence and in later life.

The fact that homosexual activities occur much more frequently in this group suggests that it is males with the strongest sex drive who respond most vigorously to a variety of sexual stimuli and who more often find it necessary to breach convention in order to satisfy the imperious demands this drive makes upon them. The fact that these same males also mature sexually at an earlier age increases the possibility that they may become more readily conditioned to respond to numerous stimuli. Males with weak drive are less readily conditioned to any type of response. Here we may see yet another line of evidence that reveals the importance of conditioning in the acquirement of sexual tastes.

Homosexual activities occur with greater frequency among those who live in towns or cities and less frequently among rural groups. However, in certain of the most remote rural areas there is a substantial amount of homosexual activity among those engaged in outdoor occupations such as hunting, mining, prospecting, cattle-raising, and lumbering. The homo-sexual activity of these men is said to interfere only rarely with heterosexual relations, and there is a minimum of social conflict or personal disturbance over this activity.

Kinsey suggests that this is the type of homosexual experience in the histories of the explorers and pioneers of earlier days in America.

Few people today recognize the part homosexuality played in the life of the early American male. In the early days there were more men than women, particularly on the frontiers. Frontier-life occupations isolated men from women for long periods of time. Under these conditions men turned to one another for the satisfaction of their sexual needs, and homo-sexuality was largely taken for granted. This continued throughout the period when the West was settled. Many of the famous cowboys and gun-fighters would be considered homosexuals by modern American standards.

Billy the Kid, for example, was homosexually oriented. His handsome appearance more than once stirred up rivalries among the men with whom he associated. It has been suggested that the revenge of a jealous lover may have played some part in his death. Homosexuality was also very common among the troops of both the North and the South during the Civil War, and there are accounts of male prostitutes who followed the armies.

The extent of homoerotophobia in the United States in contemporary times is extraordinary and gives one pause to wonder about the psychodynamic relationship that may exist between present-day fears and the homosexuality in the past history of the country. Usually human beings only fear evils that they feel strongly attracted to.

In keeping with the effects of cultural conditioning, it was found by the Indiana team that homosexual contacts occur less frequently among devout Catholics, Orthodox Jewish groups, and active Protestants, whereas such contacts occur most frequently among males who are not especially active in church connections. Religious indoctrination may do little to prevent the development of homosexual interests, but it may do much to prevent the satisfaction of such interests.

Mention must be made of the wide difference in the incidence of homosexuality among males as compared with females. When the Kinsey team studied sexual behavior in the human female, it was found that the accumulative incidence of homosexuality among females reached 28 per cent as compared with 50 per cent among the males. The accumulative incidences of overt contacts to the point of orgasm among the females had reached 13 per cent as compared with 37 per cent among the males. In other words, homosexual responses had occurred in about half as many females as males, while contacts that had proceeded to orgasm had occurred in about a third as many females as males. There were, moreover, only about a half to a third as many females who in any age period were primarily or exclusively homosexual.

It must also be pointed out that a much smaller proportion of the females had continued their homosexual activities for as many years as most of the males. Females also, it was found, tended to be far less promiscuous than males. Indeed, 71 per cent of the females had restricted their homosexual contacts to a single partner or two, whereas many of the males had had contacts with scores or even hundreds of sexual partners. Only 51 per cent of the males had restricted their contacts to a single partner or two. In this respect as in most others, the homosexually inclined male is typical of most other males, and the homosexually inclined female is typical of most other females. Promiscuity and aggressiveness in seeking sexual partners are typically masculine sexual characteristics that make for much misunderstanding between males and females. The social implications of this difference between the sexes are great. Because of his greater promiscuity and more pronounced aggressiveness the homosexually inclined male, like the heterosexually inclined male, is more often found in socially provocative circumstances than females. Homosexually inclined females do not come into conflict with social conventions nearly as often, not only because our society is much more tolerant of female homosexuality, but also because the homosexuality of females seldom involves as much socially provocative behavior.

These facts contradict the earlier opinions of clinicians and of the public at large. Earlier estimates of female homosexuality, based upon guesses, were almost always higher than the estimates made of male homosexuality.

From the statistical data gathered it must be concluded that the verbalized ideals of the community with regard to sexual behavior, and specifically with regard to homosexual behavior, bear little relationship to the actions of the people who espouse such ideals. Hypocrisy in these matters seems to be the rule for the vast majority of Americans, as doubtless it is among all other peoples. Surely we cannot continue to imagine that homosexual interests are rare among American males, or even that the tendency to act upon these interests is rare. Indeed, it is not too much to say that homosexual responsiveness constitutes a part of the sexual experience of a very great number of males even within most cultures that attempt to minimize or to suppress completely such responsiveness. Because they are drawn from a highly homoerotophobic environment, the Kinsey data perhaps more than any other tend to bring into focus the likelihood that homosexual behavior is rooted in tendencies that are characteristic of mammalian sexuality. This should not be overlooked by serious scientific and philosophic thinkers whose role it is to formulate and to reinforce by legal and social sanctions the sexual prohibitions and religious ideals of our culture.

The high incidence of homosexuality among American males reported by Kinsey may raise some doubts about what Americans *really* believe about sex. If you ask the average American male what he thinks about homosexuality he is apt to give a very negative reply indeed, for the religious and sexual creeds he accepts condemn homosexuality unequivocally. But what does the average American male really believe about homosexuality? We can form some impression of his true beliefs and feelings by being aware of his actions. The words of George Bernard Shaw are very apposite in this connection: "What a man believes may be ascertained, not from his creed, but from the assumptions on which he habitually acts."

From the data in this chapter it is apparent that heterosexuality and homosexuality are not antitheses in the sexual world and that, indeed, these two types of responsiveness may occur at different times, or even simultaneously, in the same individual. It is apparent, moreover, that in the population as a whole there is a continuum between exclusive hetero-sexuality and exclusive homosexuality in which virtually every combina-tion of heterosexuality and homosexuality may be found. The fact that both heterosexual and homosexual stimuli may elicit sexual response in the same individual has enormous theoretical significance, and we will in-vestigate its implications in a later chapter.

When we discuss later the cross-cultural data on homosexuality we will find many more examples of this same coexistence between the two types of responsiveness. In quite a few cultures the coexistence of heterosexuality and homosexuality is even more frequent than in our own culture and often more emphatic and pronounced. As a matter of fact, our own culture places heavy stress upon exclusiveness in the sexual area and favors circum-stances that give rise to 0s and 1s and 5s and 6s more than to 2s, 3s, and 4s. In spite of this emphasis upon exclusiveness, however, the heterosexual-homosexual continuum remains a substantial reality in our culture, and Judaeo-Christian males manifest, at least to some extent, a nonexclusive sexuality like that more commonly found among other males.

III

The Phylogenetic Basis of Homosexuality

Belief in the idea that the sexual drive is exclusively in the service of reproduction and that it is dominated by an "instinct" that directs an animal's behavior into certain preordained channels has caused scientists in former days to ignore homosexual behavior among the lower animals.

The impression that infra-human mammals more or less confine themselves to heterosexual activities is a distortion of the fact which appears to have originated in a man-made philosophy, rather than in specific observations of mammalian behavior. Biologists and psychologists who have accepted the doctrine that the only natural function of sex is reproduction, have simply ignored the existence of sexual activity which is not reproductive. They have assumed that heterosexual responses are a part of an animal's innate, "instinctive" equipment, and that all other types of sexual activity represent "perversions" of the "normal instincts." Such interpretations are, however, mystical. They do not originate in our knowledge of the physiology of sexual response, and can be maintained only if one assumes that sexual function is in some fashion divorced from the physiologic processes which control other functions of the animal body. It may be true that heterosexual contacts outnumber homosexual contacts in most species of mammals, but it would be hard to demonstrate that this depends upon the "normality" of heterosexual responses, and the "abnormality" of homosexual responses.[54]

Objective observation of the sexual behavior of lower animals has revealed that sexual contacts between individuals of the same sex occur in almost every species of mammal that has been extensively studied. Homosexual behavior, for example, has been observed by scientists among monkeys, dogs, bulls, rats, porcupines, guinea pigs, goats, horses, donkeys, elephants, hyenas, bats, mice, lions, rabbits, cats, raccoons, baboons, apes, and porpoises. Among these and other animals homosexual contacts between males are more conspicuous and occur more frequently than between females.

Moreover, homosexual contacts between infrahuman females never appear to result in orgasm. But it is not certain how often infrahuman females ever reach orgasm in any type of sexual relationship. Between males, however, homosexual contacts may proceed to orgasm for the male that mounts another male.

Homosexuality among animals below the level of the primates seems, more often than not, to be entirely fortuitous. It often results from a failure to identify the sex of the intended partner. The sexually aroused animal will attempt to mate with the nearest partner. This indicates the absence of any "heterosexual instinct" and suggests that all that is innate is an undifferentiated drive toward the release of sexual tension. This drive, of course, is subject to conditioning so that older experienced animals may come to associate sexual satisfaction with heterosexual coitus. When the drive is present and a heterosexual partner absent, however, the animal will seek contact with others of its own sex. Just as there is no inherent heterosexual instinct, there is, likewise, no inherent tendency to avoid homosexual contacts among the lower mammals. The learning of rigid heterosexual or homosexual patterns and the learning of patterns of avoidance are much more common among human animals. Even at the human level, however, "degree of need" or "strength of drive" may, under special conditions, overcome learned patterns and cause the individual to participate in sexual behavior that he has not previously learned to associate with satisfaction.

Although well-defined patterns of homosexuality are seldom in evidence among the lower mammals, they may become exclusively conditioned to homosexual stimuli if exposed to an environment that favors such learning. Male rats have been taught to be homosexually oriented and to reject females altogether. An excellent description of the experimental techniques used to bring about this kind of conditioning is provided by Broadhurst in his book *The Science of Animal Behavior* (1963).

But often the lower mammals may also become positively conditioned to homosexual stimuli outside the laboratory. Homosexual behavior, for example, is very common in domestic stock. R. H. Denniston in *Sexual Inversion* (Basic Books, Inc., 1965), calls attention to such behavior among bulls:

> Young bulls or steers are often used as "teasers" to arouse mature bulls in preparation for the collection of ejaculates for use in artificial insemination. As a matter of fact, if a heifer has been used several times as a "teaser" for a bull, the bull will then react more readily to a "teaser" of his own sex than to a female.

Ford and Beach, reporting the observations of McBride and Hebb (1948), point to an interesting case of spontaneous homosexuality between two male porpoises. These aquatic mammals have been found to have a psychologic status considerably above that of most terrestrial mammals such as dogs, cats, cows, and horses. McBride and Hebb noted that adult male porpoises repeatedly attempt to engage in sexual contacts with younger members of their own sex. Even in cases where male porpoises have been courted by a receptive female, they may avoid her and promptly attempt to copulate with another male. This is clear evidence that a definite if temporary preference for a like-sexed partner may occur spontaneously among subhuman mammals. An example follows.

Two male porpoises formed a close attachment to each other and after some time one of the pair was removed from the observation tank for three weeks. The following reaction took place upon the reunion of the two:

> No doubt could exist that the two recognized each other, and for several hours they swam side by side rushing frenziedly through the water. For several days, the two males were inseparable and neither paid any attention to the female. This was in courting season, and at other times the two males seemed bent only on preventing the other's copulation with the female.[62]

Behavior of this kind suggests a much more well-defined form of homosexuality than has heretofore been observed among the lower mammals, where homosexual behavior is usually less continuous and usually arises without much suggestion of preference.

It is only in very recent years that systematic studies of the homosexual behavior of lower mammals have been made. On the basis of what has been found thus far it is reasonable to assume that with continued investigation more detailed accounts of the nature and extent of this behavior will be available. It may already be seen that even the lower mammals demonstrate a distinct capacity for response to homosexual stimuli.

There can be little doubt that homosexual contacts as a more frequent means of sexual outlet increase as we ascend the scale of evolution. The more highly evolved mammals display more of this behavior and, more important, the type of homosexuality that they display tends more often to suggest an element of preference or choice. This may be explained in part by the fact that primates and other of the higher mammals are especially susceptible to the effects of experience. They may more readily learn, as a result of prepubertal homosexual play, that sexual satisfaction may be experienced with other males. Certain male primates, for example, are highly receptive to homosexual contacts, and some tend to invite sexual advances from other males.

In spite of the mammalian capacity to respond homosexually, however, heterosexual behavior is always more in evidence than homosexual behavior. The following points specified by Kinsey, Pomeroy, Martin, and Gebhard explain why.

> In actuality, sexual contacts between individuals of the same sex are known to occur in practically every species which has been extensively studied. In many species, homosexual contacts may occur with considerable frequency, although never as frequently as heterosexual contacts. Heterosexual contacts occur more frequently because they are facilitated, (1) by the greater submissiveness of the female and the greater aggressiveness of the male, and this seems to be a prime factor in determining the roles which the two sexes play in heterosexual relationships; (2) by the more or less similar levels of aggressiveness between individuals of the same sex, which may account for the fact that not all animals will submit to being mounted by individuals of their own sex; (3) by the greater ease of intromission into the female vagina and the greater difficulty of penetrating the male anus; (4) by the lack of intromission when contacts occur between two females, and the consequent lack of those satisfactions which intromission may bring in a heterosexual relationship; (5) by olfactory and other anatomic and physiologic characteristics which differentiate the sexes in certain mammalian species; (6) by the psychologic conditioning which is provided by the more frequently successful heterosexual contacts.[54]

The six factors described above combine to facilitate the learning of a heterosexual behavior pattern in animals and humans. These factors rather than any instinct account for the greater frequency of heterosexual contacts among most animals. Because heterosexual behavior is more common and often tends to form a pattern it is interpreted as "normal," while homosexual behavior, being less frequent and more fortuitous in character, is interpreted as "abnormal." But such interpretations are mystical; they are based on a priori notions and philosophic bias rather than upon scientific insight into the cause and meaning of sexual behavior.

When we ascend the phylogenetic scale to the level of the primates— monkeys, apes, and men—we find a type and incidence of homosexual behavior that is far less frequently encountered among the lower mammals. Homosexuality among the apes is highly significant since man is in the same order of animal life. It has long been recognized that study of the lower primates affords many clues to a deeper understanding of man.

Before proceeding to an account of directly homosexual behavior among the lower primates, however, it is necessary for us to consider a type of behavior that has been described by biologists and animal psychologists as "inversion."

Male animals of both higher and lower mammalian orders may sometimes display mating behavior like that of the receptive female. Among lower mammals this behavior is rare but has been observed in several instances. Some males will react to the sexual advances of other males with coital reactions typical of the female in estrous. These males temporarily reverse their sexual behavior, but this "feminization" is never permanent and those males who adopt such behavior inevitably prove to be vigorous copulators when placed with a receptive female. Other males become much more attentive to an inverted male and may attempt copulation with him but, when given a choice, male rats, for instance, will attempt to mate with a receptive female sooner than with an inverted male.

In view of the inverted animal's willingness to mate with the opposite sex, it is clear that inversion should not be confused with homosexuality. In referring to humans the term inversion has been used to signify homosexuality, and even in classical psychoanalytic terminology it refers to preference for homosexual contacts. This is unfortunate since it causes some confusion. An inverted male animal is by no means necessarily a homosexual male, and males who indulge in homosexual behavior may not manifest any of the signs of inversion.

The kinds of inverted behavior found among some males of the lower mammalian orders has an analogy in the behavior of certain human males who adopt characteristically feminine attitudes and social behavior. Such inverted behavior may or may not be associated with homosexual behavior. Some homosexual males are extremely effeminate and go to great lengths to imitate the behavior patterns of females. On the other hand, the majority of homosexual males do not behave in this inverted way. The problem is further complicated by the occurrence of this kind of inversion among fully heterosexual males, some of whom go so far as to dress in female attire. Yet many of these transvestite males manifest a vigorous sexual preference for females and have never been aware of any homosexual interests.

The physiological basis for inversion among the lower mammals is not understood. It does not, however, appear to be related to abnormal glandular function. Ford and Beach have described the effects of castration upon an inverted male rat. After castration the feminine behavior disappeared within a few days. When the animal was supplied with the male hormone (androgen), both male and female mating patterns were restored. Administration of estrogenic hormones may evoke some feminine behavior but less so than when androgenic hormones are administered.

Since there is nothing to suggest that inversion is dependent upon physiological or anatomical bisexuality, Kinsey *et al.* have suggested that *inversion of sexual behavior* would be a more accurate way of referring to this phenomenon. Inversion of sexual behavior may often be observed among the lower primates, where it may also serve to stimulate and to facilitate homosexual contacts.

Kempf, Hamilton, Carpenter, Bingham, Zuckerman, and Maslow have all offered descriptions of homosexual behavior among subhuman primates, and their most arresting findings have been reviewed by Ford and Beach in their important book *Patterns of Sexual Behavior*. Since they summarize the main issues, we may continue to follow their treatment of this topic.

Homosexual arousal is much less frequent among female subhuman primates. Male primates, on the other hand, respond readily to homosexual stimuli. Mutual grooming, genital examination, sexual mounting, inversion of sexual role, phallic-anal penetration, mutual masturbation, erotogenic play, homosexual orgasm and even oral-genital explorations have been described in the literature. There can be no doubt that subhuman primates, particularly *males,* provide ample evidence of a tendency toward a kind of homosexuality analogous to that found among humans. This is to be expected in view of the close evolutionary connection between man and the other primates, and it serves to demonstrate the phylogenetic basis of this behavior in human beings.

With a few exceptions, such as were discussed previously—though these few exceptions may be multiplied as research in this area is extended—it is among the primates that we first encounter homosexual relationships that appear to be more than fortuitous and intermittent. No animal other than man has ever provided evidence of a lifelong form of exclusive homosexuality, but among the subhuman primates we get a glimpse of semi-exclusive homosexuality. These animals, like their human relatives, are highly social in their behavior, and this is expressed in the way they manifest homosexual tendencies. To begin with, there is much "role playing" in the homosexual behavior of subhuman primates. Younger primates may assume a feminine posture in the effort to secure the attention and protection of an older male. These young males may offer themselves in homosexual intercourse with a dominant older male. The male that is playing the feminine role may reach backward and handle the penis of the partner and sometimes the "passive" male masturbates while the "active" male copulates with him. Identical behavior may be observed in human homosexual males during copulation. Homosexual friendships may arise in which frequent sodomy, mutual embracing, and social protection of the young animal by his full-grown partner take place.[35]

Not all homosexual behavior among subhuman primates is confined to relationships between older and younger males or to relationships in which the younger male always assumes the passive role. Prepubertal and adolescent males engage in homosexual relations together; on occasion they may also mount older males and attempt to carry out intercourse with them. Bachelor baboons who have no female mates sometimes form homosexual friendships and for a time a masculine pair may remain together constantly. Homosexual behavior seems to be especially common among baboons, and not infrequently whole groups of male baboons are involved in sexual alliances.[86]

In the subhuman primates it does not appear that masculine homosexuality is solely a substitute for heterosexual relationships. Two observations definitely preclude the possibility that these relationships are entirely in the nature of a substitute for heterosexual relationships: Hamilton has provided evidence that some adult male monkeys carry on homosexual alliances during the same time that they engage in heterosexual activities;[35] and Zuckerman reports that adult male baboons mount other males just before or just after sexual relations with a receptive female.[86] This behavior, then, is not entirely in the nature of a substitute for heterosexuality. Nor is it surprising that animals as highly evolved as the subhuman primates should provide evidence of the capacity to become positively conditioned to homosexual stimuli, especially when the opportunity for a good deal of homosexual experience arises throughout childhood, puberty, and adolescence.

Ford and Beach note, "In general, all mature male monkeys and apes show a distinct preference for heterosexual as opposed to homosexual partnerships, although in many cases this is not exclusive." [22]

Homosexual behavior is more common among young male primates. Hence, certain theoreticians, particularly of psychiatric persuasion, have concluded that the tendency to respond homosexually is indicative of emotional immaturity. Allen (1958) asserts that "with the monkeys and apes homosexuality is immaturity and the adult ape drops it because he finds copulation with the female more enjoyable." [6] This, obviously, is intended to have ominous portents for adult human homosexuality. The idea that homosexual behavior is "immaturity" fits the psychiatric view; but it does not wholly fit the facts. We have just seen how some adult primates may not only respond to homosexual stimuli but may do so just before or just after copulating with a receptive female, and that some adult monkeys carry on homosexual alliances concurrently with heterosexual activities. Moreover, immature apes and monkeys may, indeed, indulge in a good deal of homosexual behavior; but they generally do so with adult males of their species. Therefore we must accept the fact that adult apes and monkeys also participate in their share of homosexual activity. The difference is, of course, not that subhuman primates generally avoid homosexual relations upon attaining maturity, but that they commence an active heterosexual life upon attaining maturity.

The tendency, peculiar to our society, of thinking in terms of exclusiveness in sexuality causes many people to subscribe to theories that uphold or rationalize exclusive forms in the face of data indicating that such exclusiveness is far from generally the case with men or monkeys. Even within our own particular society, where every effort is made to assure exclusive heterosexuality, we find that only about half of the males adhere to this limitation throughout life, and that only a small minority of males maintain an exclusive form of homosexuality. Later, when we consider other societies that do not put such a premium upon exclusiveness, we will see that there is little to suggest that humans in these other cultures practice an exclusive form of sexuality throughout adult life.

A number of observers have discussed the factor of social dominance in connection with homosexual behavior among the subhuman primates. Some (Kempf, for example) have suggested that "comparative inferiority, physical weakness, and biological impotence are implicitly acknowledged by any male that allows himself to be used as a sexual object by another member of his sex." Ford and Beach, however, point to the advantages that accrue to a smaller, younger animal who submits to a more dominant partner. The older adult tends to protect the young homosexual favorite who, in addition, may receive other favors. Not to be overlooked is the fact that homosexual activity may constitute the only available form of sexual satisfaction for a younger male under circumstances in which the older males hoard the females for themselves.

Many of these efforts to explain homosexual behavior among the higher animals and man tend to become rather complicated and unnecessarily speculative. In many cases this seems to result from an anthropocentric and ethnocentric bias on the part of observers who find it difficult to imagine that homosexual stimuli could of themselves provide sufficient motivation for sexual behavior. Consequently, many theorists search for elaborate and sometimes extraneous explanations of homosexual behavior when it may be sufficient to realize that *any animal, in the absence of negative conditioning, is capable of responding to any adequate stimulus including, of course, homosexual stimuli.*

Concluding their discussion of these points, Ford and Beach make the following observations:

> Identifications of "first causes" would be difficult if not impossible until the evidence is more plentiful. For purposes of the present discussion it is appropriate to disregard questions as to the existence of a specifically homosexual developmental stage and of the social patterning of this form of behavior between adult males. The significant fact would seem to be that, regardless of its origins and of its functions as an indicator of social dominance, homosexual behavior does occur. Furthermore, in some cases at least, it is preceded and accompanied by signs of erotic arousal and, perhaps, even of satisfaction.[22]

The data on homosexual behavior among infrahuman mammals indicate that it occurs among the lowest as well as among the highest mammals, but that as we ascend the phylogenetic scale both the frequency and the complexity of this behavior increase; among the subhuman primates we get a clear inference of the type of homosexuality that exists at the level of human life. The complexity of any animal's behavior is a function of the complexity of the nervous system of the animal.

The mammalian record thus confirms our statement that any animal which is not too strongly conditioned by some special sort of experience is capable of responding to any adequate stimulus. This is what we find among young children who are not too rigorously restrained in their sex play. Exclusive preferences and patterns of behavior, heterosexual or homosexual, come only with experience, or as a result of social pressures which tend to force an individual into an exclusive pattern of one or the other sort. Psychologists and psychiatrists, reflecting the mores of the culture in which they have been raised, have spent a good deal of time trying to explain the origins of homosexual activity; but considering the physiology of sexual response and the mammalian backgrounds of our human behavior, it is not so difficult to explain why a human animal does a particular thing sexually. It is more difficult to explain why each and every individual is not involved in every type of sexual activity.[54]

The phylogenetic basis of homosexuality is often denied by certain clinicians and others who are dedicated to the belief that all human homosexuality is always pathological and that, in the words of Bieber *et al.,* "At any age, homosexuality is a symptom of fear and inhibition of heterosexual expression." [8] Those who insist upon this interpretation of homosexuality are forced to disparage the phylogenetic data, and they do so by emphasizing the sporadic and seemingly indiscriminate nature of homosexual behavior among infrahuman species. These authors do not believe that there is any connection between infrahuman homosexuality and the homosexuality of human beings, "where cognitive and highly complex patterns are involved and where, at least in our society, fear of heterosexuality is salient." [8] But this contention overlooks the fact that subhuman primate homosexual behavior is not, by any means, entirely "sporadic" nor altogether "indiscriminate," as we have seen in this chapter. The fact that human homosexuality involves "cognitive" and "highly complex patterns" of course is a function of the complex central nervous system of human beings and only demonstrates the obvious: namely, that human beings humanize every type of behavior in which they become involved.

Authors who are dedicated to the clinical interpretation of homosexuality are often likewise forced to disparage the significance of the homosexual behavior of human beings outside our own culture, because such behavior usually does not meet with the criteria emphasized in clinical theories. But we have no right to elaborate theories on the origin and meaning of homosexual behavior that ignore or disparage the homosexual behavior of infrahuman individuals or the behavior of other human beings simply because their attitudes do not conform to what we have come to regard as normal in our Judaeo-Christian culture.

On the basis of the phylogenetic data, and on the basis of the cross-cultural data that follow in the next chapter, it is not too rash to assume, as

West did, that "Homosexual behavior seems to arise from some deep-rooted natural urge which finds different expression in different cultures." [78]

This "deep-rooted natural urge" is related to the phylogenetic basis of homosexuality and cannot be entirely overlooked merely for the sake of convenience. How one may wish to regard it from a moral standpoint is an entirely separate question; but scientists have no right to overlook the phylogenetic factor. This entire issue resolves itself into the question of whether there is any "natural" basis for homosexuality. In answer to this we must agree with Dr. F. A. Beach, the famous expert on animal sexuality, who said of human homosexuality:

> In our society sexual contact between members of the same sex is considered extremely undesirable. Various social goals and ethical laws are violated by the homosexual individual, but to describe his behavior as "unnatural" is to depart from strict accuracy.[5]

Nothing, of course, is ever "unnatural," as Goethe pointed out in his great essay on Nature. The task of the scientist is not to separate the "natural" from the "unnatural" but rather to discover what function a given phenomenon fulfills in nature. In referring to sexual phenomena it is common for people to use, indeed to abuse, such expressions as "natural," "unnatural," "normal," "abnormal," and the seemingly endless list of synonyms that, in recent times especially, have been invented to replace the more obviously conventional jargon. But we should not attempt to skirt the important issues merely by inventing new clichés for old prejudices. It is necessary to be absolutely clear about this. However desirable or undesirable from some other standpoint a given type of sexual behavior may be, it may not, from a scientific standpoint, ever be described as "unnatural." This issue is succinctly expressed in a comment ascribed to Kinsey, who is reported to have said, "The only kind of abnormal sex acts are those which are impossible to perform."

No sexual behavior, whether heterosexual, homosexual, or autoerotic in character, is without a firm foundation in phylogeny and developmental history of the species. In this chapter some of the phylogenetic data on homosexual behavior have been presented. It is clear that such behavior is not an exclusively human phenomenon. Neither, as we will see in the next chapter, is such behavior peculiar to human males nurtured in our own culture. It is well to keep these considerations in mind when one seeks an objective rather than merely a conventional understanding of homosexuality and other sexual phenomena.

IV

The Cross-Cultural Data

In view of the data on subhuman primates and other infrahuman animals, one would expect to find homosexual behavior conspicuous among human males. A review of anthropologic and historical literature confirms this expectation. In fact, homosexual behavior may be noted in all groups that do not make a pronounced effort to suppress it and, more often than not, it may be noted even in groups which do condemn it—our own, for example. There are, however, significant cultural variations both in the incidence of homosexuality and in attitudes toward it. Research usually shows that sexual phenomena between like-sexed partners are relatively common or, where this does not seem to be the case, well-defined social sanctions suppress such behavior. This generalization has been expressed clearly by Ford and Beach who observed that "Among societies in which adult homosexual activities are said to be very rare, definite and specific social pressure is directed against such behavior." [22]

It is not necessary to belabor the implications of the observation made by Ford and Beach. The fact that homosexual behavior regularly occurs even among adults wherever specific social sanctions do not interfere, and even often despite social prohibition, accords with the data on subhuman animals and reveals the continuity of this behavior throughout the mammalian class. Such behavior reflects capacities that are a part of the phylogenetic heritage of the human animal.

Although homosexual behavior of one kind or another is probably never totally absent in any group, it is not always easy to identify. Margaret Mead (1961) has pointed out that statements on absence of homosexual behavior are not reliable; she emphasizes the difficulties that arise when anthropologists attempt to assay the part homosexuality plays in a given culture. She believes that the incidence of such behavior may go unnoticed by some investigators who are ill equipped to ascertain the actual situation. Such factors as "language barriers, unbreakable cultural taboos, needs for personal privacy, distrust of Caucasian investigators, retrospective falsification, and even, in some non-literate societies, conventions of courtesy that demand telling a questioner what he presumably wants to hear" often prevent the student of sexual behavior from getting an accurate picture of the facts (see J. Marmor, *Sexual Inversion,* Basic Books, Inc., 1965).

These problems are further aggravated because different investigators view and define homosexuality in very different terms. Some fail to report sexual relations that occur between like-sexed partners because, in their opinion, such relations may appear only "incidental," "situational," or "fortuitous," and therefore "not really homosexual." Not a few anthropologists have been unduly influenced by current psychiatric opinion on this subject and often fail to identify homosexual phenomena that do not resemble those more commonly found in our own culture. Some, for example, ignore homosexual behavior that does not involve changes in the gender-role pattern defined by the group. Others are concerned only with homosexual behavior that is acknowledged, condoned, and even formalized by the group; hence illicit or secretive homosexual alliances may go unnoticed and unreported. Nonetheless, cross-cultural studies have revealed what to some may appear an alarming incidence of homosexual behavior within diverse groups. In this chapter, however, we shall be concerned with the attitudes toward homosexual behavior rather than with the incidence of this behavior per se.

Although homosexuality, among males especially, has aroused anxiety and disapproval within a number of cultures, a majority of cultures have provided some approved means of outlet for the homosexual needs of males and have attempted to *regulate* rather than to *suppress* homosexual behavior. The distinction between regulation and suppression is important and deserves the careful consideration of scholars, philosophers, legislators, and others who may be responsible for formulating and enforcing those social sanctions that are directed toward the sexual behavior of individuals within our own group.

We have seen that sexual behavior, whatever form it may assume, is always a focal point of social anxiety; this is particularly the case, though not exclusively, with societies like our own in which the religious code is inordinately erotophobic. Few societies, even those which may be described as sex-positive, are content to leave any type of sexual behavior entirely within the province of individual decision. Virtually all societies attempt to regulate sexual behavior and to direct it along certain lines predetermined by the prevailing religious, moral, and ethical convictions of the group.

For example, heterosexual behavior everywhere evokes social concern and is subject to certain rules that affect premarital, marital, and extra-marital sexual relationships. Certain patterns of behavior are favored and approved by the community, and certain other patterns may be subject to severe restrictions. Thus, the age at which a given type of heterosexual relationship is thought appropriate, the specific types of behavior that may be enjoyed by heterosexual partners, the acceptability of one type of partner as compared with another, as well as many other aspects of heterosexual life may be determined by the mores that prevail within a given culture. To be sure, these may differ widely between unrelated cultures, and it may be quite impossible to demonstrate upon any objective basis that the mores of one group are superior to those of another. But it is certain that sexual mores of one kind or another will be in evidence.

Similarly, homosexual behavior will be subject to social regulation through the mores where it is approved. Although only about one-third of the cultures of which we have any specific knowledge attempt to suppress homosexual behavior completely, almost all cultures attempt to determine the forms this behavior may assume. Thus, only certain types of homosexual contacts may be considered acceptable; anal intercourse may be favored and oral-genital contacts or mutual masturbation may be disfavored. The age of the partners or their social rank may become a moral issue in certain groups. Only those relationships between an older and a younger male may be approved, or only those relationships taking place between partners within the same age group may be sanctioned. Certain mutual responsibili-ties may fall upon homosexual partners as a result of their alliance. The older partner, for example, may become responsible for the religious edu-cation or the social behavior of the younger partner and he in turn may be required to follow the instructions of the older partner and to regard him as an authority.

In most cultures homosexual relationships precede and facilitate the de-velopment of adequate heterosexual relationships. Indeed, it is almost axi-omatic that within societies that approve certain types of homosexual relationships, these do not displace or supplant heterosexual relationships for the vast majority of men involved. Often homosexual relationships are approved for young unmarried males; these relationships may be abandoned later in life. Not infrequently, however, homosexual alliances coexist with marriage and parenthood, and it is regarded as one of the duties of an older male to maintain a homosexual alliance with a younger male. In this latter case homosexuality may constitute a part of the sexual behavior of males throughout their lives. But nowhere is *exclusive* homosexuality required of any large or substantial portion of a population. Wherever homosexuality is required or expected of all males in a community it coexists with hetero-sexuality.

In contrast, there is some evidence to suggest that exclusive forms of homosexuality occur more often and on a larger scale within societies such as our own that provide no socially acceptable outlet for these impulses. This is, of course, a paradox. But it is not too difficult to understand this paradox if one considers the emphasis societies like our own place upon the factor of exclusiveness in matters touching upon sex.

Thus, the individual who turns to homosexuality in spite of social disapproval is likely to make of it an exclusive way of life, just as he would have made heterosexuality an exclusive way of life had he not been homosexually inclined. Many such individuals actually feel confronted by a choice between homosexuality and heterosexuality and cannot, on moral grounds, reconcile the coexistence of both heterosexual and homosexual trends. Others in whom both tendencies are well developed may abandon one or the other in favor of an exclusive form of sexuality because our society provides even less acceptance of the "bisexual" than the "homosexual." Such an individual, if he does not attempt to maintain an exclusively heterosexual pattern, may develop a pattern of exclusive homosexuality simply because he feels he must become a part either of "the gay world" or "the straight world." Thus in attempting to suppress homosexuality completely, our society actually gives rise to a greater number of exclusively homosexual individuals than other societies that make some provision in the mores for homosexual tendencies.

Because homosexual behavior, like heterosexual behavior, is usually subject to social regulation, some scholars who are indoctrinated with the attitudes of our own particular culture imagine that this form of sexual outlet is wholly unacceptable to the society that attempts merely to regulate it. Any attempt on the part of another society to *regulate* rather than to *suppress* homosexual relationships is interpreted by these scholars as a complete rejection of all forms of homosexuality. For example, the effort on the part of the ancient Greeks to suppress prostitution among free-born boys has been seized upon by a number of scholars as proof that the Greeks disapproved of all types of sexual contact between like-sexed partners. Abundant evidence makes it clear, however, that the Greeks had no intention of eliminating sexual contacts between males. The tendency to project the attitudes and value judgments of our own culture onto other cultures is common even among scholars, and the conscientious reader of sexologic literature must be forewarned of this.

Far from suggesting a fundamental rejection of homosexuality, attempts to regulate homosexual activities clearly indicate that the society in question recognizes a legitimate sphere in which these activities may flourish. Our own society, of course, like certain others, recognizes no such legitimate sphere for the realization of homosexual needs; but this affords no basis for the assumption that efforts on the part of other societies to regulate homosexual behavior represent total rejection of all forms of homosexuality.

In reviewing the sanctions of various cultures with regard to homosexuality, no discrete pattern related to geography, historical circumstances, or the evolutionary stage of the culture is conspicuous. Homosexual relationships have been approved or even encouraged by various peoples at the highest levels of civilization as well as at the lowest levels of savagery in every age and within diverse geographical environments. They have been deplored or even severely punished by various peoples at similar levels of civilization or savagery in analogous ages, and within equally diverse geographical environments. We cannot, therefore, generalize that either the acceptance or rejection of homosexual behavior is regularly correlated with any known circumstance related to geography or the complexity of a given society.

In spite of this, some scholars have found various conditions responsible for the cultural acceptance or rejection of homosexual behavior. Thus, warlike or militaristic cultures have been supposed to favor the acceptance of male homosexuality, but cultures whose populations were low have been supposed to look upon male homosexuality with disfavor. These theories were advanced in the past on the basis of only a few samples before the accumulation of any large number of historical and anthropological data. None has been verified by an adequate number of data, and the data we now possess tend to contradict all the classical opinions on this subject.

Other explanations have been offered for these differences in cultural attitudes toward homosexuality. It has been suggested, for example, that male homosexuality is more prevalent within groups in which the social status of females is inferior, but although this may sometimes be the case, other instances exist in which male homosexuality thrives in the midst of equality between the sexes. It has been claimed that puritanism and an exaggerated regard for the "chastity of women" encourage the acceptance of homosexuality, but far more often it is precisely in environments where puritanism prevails that homosexuality is regarded as one of the most monstrous of sins. Homosexuality has often been explained in terms of economic factors; it may, for example, be difficult for many young men in highly competitive societies to accumulate enough wealth to acquire a wife. These men may therefore turn to other males for satisfactions that otherwise would be realized in marriage with a woman. But such economic barriers against marriage might be more likely to increase premarital heterosexual relations rather than homosexual relations, especially if one accepts the idea that homosexuality is morbid. In our own culture the rise of "momism" and the feminine revolution has been made responsible for an alleged increase in male homosexuality, supposedly as a result of the failure of many males to develop "healthy masculine identifications."

All of these opinions may have relevance in a particular case but certainly none has relevance in all cases. It is in reality not possible, at least at this time, to offer any generalizations as to why certain cultures approve homosexual behavior while others do not. We must surmise that the reasons for approval or disapproval are peculiar to the particular culture and are more often related to belief in the supernatural than to past or present realities.

It is quite unscientific to argue, as some have, that homosexuality is a form of decadence and that social approval of homosexuality spells the doom of a culture. As a matter of fact, history and anthropology show that homosexuality has thrived within some cultures during their most vital phases, and that, in other instances, it has thrived during periods of decadence and devolution. The opposite is also true: Homosexuality has been severely restricted within some cultures during periods of great vitality as well as during other cultures' devolutions.

The decision as to whether we within the Judaeo-Christian culture should modify our attitude toward homosexuality should not be based upon unscientific hypotheses relating to the social desirability or undesirability of homosexual behavior, but rather upon a recognition of the incidence and frequency of this behavior and the extent to which we are prepared to accord some autonomy to the individual in formulating his own moral standards. This is an ethical rather than a scientific question. The answer must depend upon our concept of freedom. Science may offer some clues that are helpful in arriving at an enlightened answer—mainly by indirection—and it may relieve certain fears that are based upon misunderstanding and ignorance. It is foolish to suppose that science could do more, and fatuous to suppose that it should do less. But ethics, not science, must provide the final answer to this question.

It remains for us to see what the attitudes of various groups toward homosexuality are. In gathering our sample we may draw from the past as well as from the present, for it is important to note that cultural attitudes toward homosexuality change in time, sometimes entirely reversing themselves. More often than not, the specific reason for the change is incomprehensible.

For example, the ancient Hebrews before the Babylonian Exile (circa 700 B.C.), like their neighbors, accepted homosexual practices and even accorded status to male temple prostitutes. At this earlier period in Jewish history both mouth-genital contacts and homosexual activities were associated with religious practice, as they continued to be among other peoples of the Near East. Subsequently, the attitude of the Hebrews toward homosexuality became absolutely phobic and prohibitionistic.

On the other hand, the Persians of early antiquity originally frowned upon homosexual practices, whereas at a later date we find them embracing such practices with little less than enthusiasm.

Within ancient times the practice of homosexuality was recognized by such divergent peoples as the Celts, Greeks, Scandinavians, Egyptians, Etruscans, Cretans, Carthaginians, and Sumerians, to offer but a few examples from Europe and the Near East. In fact, certain forms of homosexuality seem to have received approval among the earliest peoples of civilization. It is precisely in the so-called cradle of civilization—the Tigris-Euphrates Valley, the Nile Valley, and the Mediterranean Basin—that homosexuality received the greatest approval during very ancient times and largely still enjoys such approval today in spite of the rise of Judaism, Christianity, and Mohammedanism.

We learn from the Old Testament that homosexuality was rampant among the Canaanites, Chaldeans, and Egyptians. The British psychiatrist Clifford Allen (1958), multiplies a number of other scholarly errors in his chapter on "Nature, Causation, and Treatment" (of homosexuality) when he writes, "It is definite that the Egyptians (like other ancient peoples) regarded sodomy as the ultimate humiliation." [6] We have been unable to locate any reliable source for this assertion. The classical scholar Licht (1932), however, points to documentary evidence that the Egyptians, like most of their neighbors, did practice homosexual relationships guiltlessly from an early point in their history:

> The oldest literary testimony hitherto known dates back more than 4,500 years, and is to be found in an Egyptian papyrus which proves not only that paederasty was at that time widespread in Egypt but also that it was presumed to exist amongst the gods as a matter of course.[59]

With the exception of the Hebrews and possibly though not certainly the Assyrians, we can find no evidence that the ancient peoples of the Mediterranean and the Near East ever attempted to suppress the practice of homosexual love. Statutory law among certain of these peoples did attempt to regulate homosexual behavior. Thus, for example, Hittite law forbade homosexual contacts between father and son. But this is an injunction against incest, not homosexuality. Likewise, among most of these peoples, various statutes were designed to protect the very young against rape, violence, or other forms of exploitation. Nowhere, however, except in the Old Testament and in the teachings of the Zoroastrians, do we find an all-encompassing denunciation of homosexual relations among any of the peoples of antiquity.

Prichard (1950) has suggested that a homosexual theme is present in the Gilgamesh Epic, an important Middle Eastern literary text dating from the second millennium B.C. or earlier. According to this scholar the epic contains passages that indicate that the heroes, Gilgamesh and Enkidu, were homosexual lovers.

It is significant that homosexual relationships are not prohibited in the codes of either Lipit-Ishtar or Hammurabi. It was once thought that an exception to this was found in the Middle Assyrian Laws (twelfth century B.C. or earlier) that appeared to prescribe castration as a punishment for homosexual relationships; but a more recent translation suggests that this punishment was preceded by homosexual contact between the convicted man and his punishers.[54]

The ancient Greek attitude toward homosexual love is well known and the Greeks have left us with a great deal of information on this subject, much of which provides food for thought. Likewise, homosexuality enjoyed approval among the Romans until the adoption of Christianity as the religion of the Empire, and homosexuality was practiced among the various peoples of Italy without incurring any serious obstacles from the very earliest times until the Christian Era. We hear of it among the Etruscans, who inhabited Italy before the peoples who later merged with them to become the Romans. The following descriptions of the earliest Italian attitude toward erotic life is informative. It was made by the Greek historian Timaeus.

> It is not considered objectionable among the Tyrrhenians to have to do with boys openly, whether actively or passively, for paederasty is a custom of the country . . .
> When they are with friends or relatives their custom is the following. When they have stopped drinking and are going to bed, servants bring into them courtesans, beautiful boys, or women, while the lamps are still burning. When they have enjoyed themselves sufficiently with these, they fetch young men in their prime, and let them enjoy themselves with these courtesans, boys, or women. They pay homage to love . . . They are very fond of women, but find more pleasure with boys and young men. These are very beautiful, since they take the greatest care of their persons and remove all troublesome hairs from their body.[59]

Among the ancient peoples of the Mediterranean, homosexual love was so common as to be a constant component of the social life of the times. The practice was cultivated not only throughout Greece, but all the way around the coast of southern Europe and as far north as Marseilles (Massalia). "The city of Massalia, according to the testimony of several witnesses, was one of the chief seats of homosexuality, whence the (ancient Greek) proverb, 'Ship to Marseilles!' "[59]

Nor were socially accepted homosexual practices limited to the Mediterranean and the Near East in ancient times. We hear of such practices throughout Gaul among the Celts, and also among Germanic and Scandinavian peoples.[79]

Homosexuality has enjoyed acceptance in China and Japan from ancient through modern times. In the case of Japan, the acceptance—indeed, the celebration—of homosexual love seems to have reached a pinnacle during

the feudal period of that country. At that time homosexual love was considered more manly for the knight than heterosexual love. Erotic lore
favored such relationships above all others. That homosexual love was
never abandoned by the Japanese in modern times may be seen in the
fact that teahouses with male *geishas* still existed in Japan until the end of
the Second World War, when they were suppressed by the American
occupation forces. Since the Americanization of Japan homosexuality is
less flagrant there although the Oriental attitude toward this subject remains permissive in spite of Western pressure.

The Chinese, too, have allowed wide scope for homosexual interests
throughout the centuries. Homosexual practices seem to have constituted
a part of the sexual repertory of all classes in China during ancient and
modern times. Male brothels were common in that country as recently as
the beginning of this century. The Communist attitude toward homosexuality in China today is unknown to this author, but if we may judge from
Russia—which we may not with certainty do—the official attitude in China
today is negative. In a most unhistoric way, Communists have denounced
homosexuality as a form of "bourgeois decadence." The ridiculousness of
such an interpretation is patent in the light of history and anthropology,
since homosexuality is in no way peculiar to capitalist cultures and if anything has more often been suppressed within "bourgeois" communities
than within any others except modern Communist communities.

The attitude toward homosexuality in India is more equivocal than in
China or Japan. On the one hand we know that homosexual activities are
common among Buddhists and Moslems, in the former instance among
the priests and monks themselves. We hear of "peg boys," boy prostitutes
trained to cater to the paederastic urges of older male clients. On the other
hand, the Hindus of India seem to have a more puritanical attitude toward
sexual practices in general, and homosexual activities are one among a
number of other sexual activities that are considered improper. We who
in our culture abhor homosexuality, and in the past have punished it with
death by fire and in recent times by imprisonment, may find it instructive
to note how the Hindus deal with this behavior:

"According to the 'Laws of Manu,' a twice-born man who commits an
unnatural offense with a male, or has intercourse with a female in a cart
drawn by oxen, in water, or in the daytime shall bathe, dressed in his
clothes, and all these are reckoned as minor offenses." [79]

There is a subtle but important point connected with this article in the
"Laws of Manu": it is possible to disapprove of homosexuality, and even
to exact penance for it, without standing in such horror of it that the
penalties become barbaric. To equate homosexual acts with heterosexual
intercourse "in a cart drawn by oxen, in water, or in the daytime" and to
prescribe as a penalty the simple act of voluntary self-ablution is a far cry

from death by fire or state-imposed imprisonment. This suggests that among the Hindus, erotic relationships between males are of an order of importance quite below that ascribed to them by more homoerotophobic peoples.

Within most Mohammedan cultures homosexual practices are common. "The Mohammedans of India and other Asiatic countries regard paederasty, at most, as a mere peccadillo." [79] In North Africa and the Near East this behavior is so commonplace that it does not even occasion comment.

Mohammedanism is related to Judaism and, like Christianity, has borrowed a good deal from Old Testament teachings. In this way the Mohammedan religion has taken over the ancient Hebraic taboo on homosexuality, but in a greatly modified form. This particular taboo, however, is practically nonoperative today, and it is doubtful whether it was ever very effective in suppressing homosexual behavior. According to religious law, sodomy, like fornication with which it is equated, is supposed to be punished severely—unless the offenders make a public act of penitence. "In order to convict, however, the law requires that four reliable persons shall swear to have been eye-witnesses, and this alone would make the law a dead letter, even if it had the support of popular feelings; but such support is certainly wanting." [79]

Judaeo-Christian travelers to the Near East and Far East, when confronted by the widespread practice of male homosexuality in those areas, have usually been scandalized and have ascribed these practices to "oriental decadence" as they have ascribed similar practices among primitive peoples to "barbarism" or "savagery." On this subject Westerners tend to be excessively provincial. Since few people ever enjoy being looked down upon, non-Judaeo-Christians throughout the world have tended to hide and in some cases even to deny the existence of homosexuality in their midst in more recent times. As a result of colonialism, Judaeo-Christian attitudes toward homosexuality have left their mark upon exotic cultures. The emulation of the Western world has brought about a more furtive attitude toward all sexuality and a corresponding growth in puritanism in other parts of the world.

One of the earliest anthropologic accounts of homosexuality was published in 1906 by Edward Westermarck. By calling upon the reports of scholars, travelers, missionaries, and others, Westermarck was able to compile a great many data on the homosexual practices of diverse peoples in many parts of the world. His research revealed that this behavior is common among aboriginal peoples within such widely separated areas of the world as North America, Europe, South America, Asia, Oceania, Africa, and Australia. In the course of his investigations he came across evidence that homosexuality is accepted as natural in the lives of a great many different peoples. Less surprising was his discovery that certain other cultures, like our own, have attempted to suppress any manifestation of homosexual responsiveness. His findings concur with those of later investigators that homoerotophobic cultures are definitely in the minority. Westermarck's research, unlike that of Ford and Beach which we will presently consider, includes data on a great many highly civilized and literate peoples. For this reason it complements the work of the later investigators and commends itself to our attention.

It is from Westermarck that we learn of the phobic attitude toward homosexuality that was characteristic of Zoroastrianism and that, along with that of Judaism and Christianity, represents the most extreme stand against homosexuality known in history. The religion of Mazda was practiced among the ancient Persians, who, if we are to believe Herodotus and certain other ancient authorities, nevertheless practiced homosexuality with particular zest throughout ancient times. This is interesting in view of the religious attitude toward homosexuality that we are about to encounter.

> In the Zoroastrian books "unnatural sin" is treated with a severity to which there is a parallel only in Hebrewism and Christianity. According to the Vendidad, there is no atonement for it. It is punished with torments in the other world, and is capital here below. Even he who committed it involuntarily, by force, is subject to corporal punishment. Indeed, it is a more heinous sin than the slaying of a righteous man. There is no worse sin than this in the good religion, and it is proper to call those who commit it worthy of death in reality. If anyone comes forth to them, and shall see them in the act, and is working with an ax, it is requisite for him to cut off the heads or to rip up the bellies of both, and it is no sin for him. But it is not proper to kill any person without the authority of the high-priests and kings, except on account of committing or permitting unnatural intercourse.[79]

Few religions, except among the most homoerotophobic peoples, have specified death as a penalty for homosexual acts. This penalty represents a fanatic effort to suppress such behavior. We may, incidentally, detect remnants of this fanaticism in certain practices within Judaeo-Christian quarters today. An interesting example of this is the not uncommon practice of acquitting young murderers of their offense where it can be proved that "unnatural vice" figured in the crime. Not infrequently, so-called homosexuals have been murdered with impunity in some European countries and in the United States most particularly, as recently as the last few years. We refer to those cases in which judges and juries have been persuaded to bring in a verdict of "not guilty" when the murderer had been a supposed "victim" of homosexual seduction, even though the law does not provide for such a defense. The implication of such a verdict is that sexual virtue and propriety, within this context at least, are above life itself.

In reviewing the anthropologic and historic data on homosexuality we cannot fail to be impressed by the frequent association of this mode of sexual expression with magic and religion. The most primitive connection between homosexuality and religious practice seems to be *shamanism*. The shaman is a religious specialist believed to possess supernatural power, a kind of priest or medicine man.

Among many so-called primitive peoples it is not uncommon for certain males to dress like women. These transvestite males (called *berdaches*) perform women's tasks and adopt some aspects of the feminine role in sexual activities with male partners. Often the berdache becomes the "wife" of another man and lives with him. In addition to his berdache "wife" the husband may have another wife with whom he carries on a heterosexual marriage. The berdache, too, may carry on heterosexual relations with a mistress: children are often born of such unions. Among the Koniag of Alaska some males are raised from early childhood as females. When mature, such a male becomes the wife of one of the important men in the community. We find this same institution among peoples as widely separated from the Koniag of Alaska as the Lango of East Africa and the Tanala of Madagascar.

The berdache may and usually does enjoy considerable social prestige, and he often becomes a powerful shaman believed to possess supernatural powers. Sexual contact with a shaman is thought to confer religious and magical benefits. In this way homosexual practices may become associated with belief in supernatural events.

Among more literate peoples, homosexuality has often played a unique role in religious and mystic rituals, especially in the religious cults of the earliest civilizations in the Near East, from whence they spread to Europe during antiquity. The Romans were acquainted with these cults, and during the later days of the Empire the Praetorians elected an emperor, Heliogabalus, who was raised from boyhood as a homosexual priest in such a cult. It has already been mentioned that among the ancient Hebrews, in addition to *kedeshoth,* or female prostitutes, *kedeshim,* or male prostitutes, were attached to the temples. The word *kadesh* properly denotes a man dedicated to a deity, although it is often translated "sodomite." These kedeshim were consecrated to Dea Syria, the mother of the gods. Homosexual acts committed with these male temple prostitutes, like sexual relations with priestesses, probably were believed to confer blessings on the worshippers.

In addition to its role in shamanism and priestcraft, homosexuality often plays a substantial part in the puberty rites of less civilized peoples. Anal intercourse between mature men and adolescent boys, with the youth playing the passive role, is thought to endow the young man with strength and courage. Keraki bachelors of New Guinea universally practice sodomy with younger males in connection with puberty rites. After a year of playing the passive role, the Keraki youth spends the remainder of his bachelorhood playing the active role with the newly initiated. Passive anal intercourse is thought to be necessary for the health and character of the growing boy. Similar rituals are common within other groups as well.

It is interesting that homosexual rather than heterosexual relations are so often chosen as a means of initiating the pubertal youth into manhood; but this undoubtedly results from the idea that homosexual union confers magical benefits. When the boy has proved his prowess as a homosexual lover and has "absorbed" some of the strength of the older male, he is then thought ready for heterosexual relationships, although these may not necessarily terminate his homosexual activities. More often than not homosexual activities continue beyond the period of initiation, at least through bachelorhood and sometimes beyond, and the initiated brave must then perform what is regarded as his duty toward younger males. These same peoples often believe that heterosexual intercourse drains the strength of the male partner which, they believe, may be renewed through homosexual contact.

Often these rituals and practices, though fully sanctioned by the men, are supposedly kept secret from the women; not, as we might think, because of embarrassment or guilt, but because these practices are regarded as exclusively and peculiarly masculine behavior. It is not uncommon to encounter segregation of the sexes in the religious and mystical practices of primitive and ancient peoples.

One of the most recent and comprehensive studies of the sexual behavior of human beings and animals was published in 1951 by C. S. Ford and F. A. Beach. In this book, *Patterns of Sexual Behavior,* the authors have used the cross-species and cross-cultural approaches; that is, they have compared the sexual behavior of different species of animals and of different human groups. The results are highly informative. We shall, of course, only be concerned in this chapter with the findings that pertain to human male homosexual relationships.

For the sake of convenience, we may divide human groups into two categories: the first, which we will call *homoerotophobic,* represents those groups, like our own, in which homosexual behavior is considered unacceptable for all members of the community under any circumstance; the second, which we will call *homoerotophilic,* represents those groups in which homosexuality is considered acceptable under certain circumstances for at least some members of the community. It must be recognized that this classification is highly schematic, since few societies ever completely reject or completely accept any form of sexual behavior. Even the most permissive societies impose some limitations, and even the most restrictive societies tend to wink at certain exceptions, so that in speaking of these categories we refer more to the professed ideals of the society than to the actual behavior of every member of the group.

In twenty-eight of the seventy-six societies for which data are available, homosexual activities on the part of adults are either totally absent, rare, or carried on only in secrecy. Thus 36 per cent of the sample studied, or approximately one-third, may be considered homoerotophobic. The authors remark, "It is to be expected, however, that the estimate would run considerably below actual incidence, since this form of sexual expression is condemned in these societies." [22]

Thus, the Mbundu of central Angola in Africa discourage homosexual behavior by holding it up to ridicule, although it is said to occur in secret among both men and women. Among the Alorese of Indonesia this behavior is frowned upon in both children and adults, although it may not be punished. The social sanctions against homosexuality among the Goajiros, a suspicious and warlike people of the Goajiro Peninsula, Colombia, are so effective as to suppress this behavior entirely. Investigators found no evidence of overt homosexuality among these people. In Haiti homosexual behavior occurs, especially in urban areas, but such behavior is nonetheless condemned. This behavior is said to occur only rarely among the Manus of the Admiralty Islands north of New Guinea. Homosexuality in Bali seems to be confined to prostitution according to these authors. The Kwoma head-hunters of New Guinea regard sodomy as unnatural, and the Rwala Bedouins stand in such abhorrence of homosexuality that they sentence female as well as male offenders to death. A unique exception is found in the Siriono of eastern Bolivia. Homosexual behavior is said to be very rare among these people although no known social sanctions that would prevent such practices exist among them. This is curious since, as we have seen, homosexuality is rare only when specific sanctions exist against it. Ford and Beach observe that the major anxieties in this culture center about food rather than sexual behavior.

Virtually all the groups that seem to be more or less successful in suppressing homosexual behavior are very sparsely populated. The Alorese live in small villages in the mountainous interior of Timor in Indonesia. The Manus are limited to a population of two thousand distributed in eleven villages; the Goajiros comprise a population of only eighteen thousand. Under conditions like these it may be expected that there is little privacy for the individual and little opportunity for the individual to indulge in behavior that is disapproved by the group. The likelihood of social sanctions being carried out is very great. It is important to remember this when we expect that the social sanctions of our own immensely populated and complex culture will have the same effect. In a society such as ours natural behavior which meets with social disapproval is likely to occur in spite of all efforts to suppress it. In any highly populated and complex society, homosexual behavior, especially among males, may never accurately be described as rare, whether or not it meets with social approval. One might, therefore, argue that it is wiser to attempt to regulate homosexual behavior than to attempt to suppress it completely. Most groups have recognized this and have attempted to make some provision for the satisfaction of homosexual needs.

In forty-nine of the seventy-six societies studied—64 per cent of the sample, a distinct majority—"homosexual activities of one sort or another are considered normal and socially acceptable for certain members of the community." [22]

The berdache, the homosexual shaman, and the puberty rites represent the most common forms of institutionalized homosexuality. Approved homosexual practices, however, also occur on a more informal basis involving a larger segment of the male population:

> Among the Siwans of Africa, for example, all men and boys engage in anal intercourse. They adopt the feminine role only in strictly sexual situations and males are singled out as peculiar if they do not engage in these homosexual activities. Prominent Siwan men lend their sons to each other, and they talk about their masculine love affairs as openly as they discuss their love of women. Both married and unmarried males are expected to have both homosexual and heterosexual affairs.[22]

Male homosexual behavior most often seems to involve anal intercourse. Mutual masturbation and oral-genital contacts between males are much less frequently reported. In societies that favor anal intercourse between males, oral-genital contacts may be frowned upon or may even be considered unnatural, and homosexual contacts involving mutual masturbation may be considered childish and unsatisfying. Such behavior, however, has been reported in the anthropological literature:

> Manual stimulation of the genitals of one young boy by another is described only among the Hopi; childhood sex play apparently consists far more frequently of attempts to copulate with another member of the same sex. For the Wogeo, however, homosexual relations between adult males seem confined to mutual manual manipulation of the sexual organs. In Africa, Dahomean and Nama men practice mutual masturbation as the only form of homosexual behavior. Tikopia men manipulate their own genitals in the presence of other members of the same sex, although mutual masturbation apparently never occurs.
>
> Sodomy apparently is absent among the Crow Indians, although oral-genital contacts are fairly frequent.[22]

Anal intercourse, or attempts at anal intercourse, seem to be the most common mode of homosexual behavior among subhuman males also, although a diversity of homosexual techniques have been observed among monkeys and apes. Anal intercourse, often preceded by a number of other techniques, seems also to be the most common type of homosexual contact among civilized peoples both in modern and ancient times. Some states in America, it may be noted, outlaw only anal intercourse between males— "sodomy" or "buggery"—and ignore other types of sexual contact between males. In such cases it is usually supposed necessary to prove penetration in order to convict, although in practice this law has been extended to cover all types of homosexual contacts. There is some evidence that mouth-genital contacts are more common among males during more recent times than in the past and that such contacts are also more common today than in the past between heterosexual partners. Whatever significance these distinctions may have remains to be elucidated, but they are worthy of mention.

The cross-species and cross-cultural data on homosexuality accord well in a number of important particulars which must be emphasized by way of summary.

These data suggest, if not demonstrate, an inherent capacity on the part of all mammals, both human and subhuman, to become sexually aroused by stimuli that originate in other individuals of the same sex. In referring to this fact Ford and Beach go so far as to use the word *tendency* rather than the word *capacity*. "The cross-cultural and cross-species comparisons . . . combine to suggest that a biological tendency for inversion of sexual behavior is inherent in most if not all mammals including the human species." [22]

Homosexual responsiveness is far more frequent among males than females. Whether one speaks of the lower mammals, ancient societies, "primitive" societies in the present, or our own society, the picture is always the same: far more males than females manifest homosexual interests and become involved in homosexual contacts.

The cross-species and cross-cultural data also reveal that homosexual contacts occur most frequently and most characteristically between a younger and an older male rather than between mature males of the same age. Often there is considerable disparity between the ages of the partners. An encounter between two infrahuman adult males most often leads to a display of aggressiveness that may terminate in open conflict. Fully developed males usually regard each other as sexual rivals rather than as sexual partners. On the other hand, an encounter between a younger and an older male, especially if the younger male is not fully mature, may lead instead to sexual responsiveness on the part of both. Younger, less physically developed males of course are not as differentiated from females in either appearance or temperament, and they are usually more passive and less aggressive than older males, making sexual union easier and more successful between the two. At the human level these biological factors may be no less important, but in addition psychologic factors seem to play a big part. The youth's admiration for an older, stronger, and socially more effective male, and the man's desire to play the role of mentor and guide may set the scene for emotions that are easily eroticized. Men ordinarily do not compete with boys, as they do with other men and, for their part, boys do not ordinarily compete with men; they tend rather to emulate them. Also, a grown male with fully developed heterosexual capacities may more easily respond sexually to a younger male than to another male of his own age; the psychological transition from erotic responsiveness to a woman to erotic responsiveness to a boy or youth is less abrupt and more facile than the psychological transition from erotic responsiveness to a woman to erotic responsiveness to another mature male. Though for obvious social and legal reasons, it is denied by most males within our own society, most fully developed males who respond sexually to other males prefer partners who are younger than themselves. This may be reflected by the overwhelming percentage of male prostitutes, and certainly the most sought after of them, who are adolescent youths and young men usually not much beyond the very early twenties. No doubt biologic and psychologic factors combine to raise the incidence of homosexual relations between partners of divergent ages among animals as well as humans.

In our Judaeo-Christian culture, especially in Anglo-Saxon and American subcultures and to a lesser extent in Northern Europe, perhaps no other sexual event is considered more sinful—or more criminal—than the homosexual seduction of a younger male by an adult male. The anxiety that such seductions arouse in the community is often rationalized by the claim that the younger partner may be morally corrupted and seriously injured psychologically. Seduction has even been claimed as the cause of exclusive, lifelong homosexuality, and many continue to make this claim although there hardly remains a single scientific investigator, either in the clinical or experimental disciplines, who gives credence to it. So strong is the taboo against homosexual acts involving men with boys that even in the more "liberal" countries where homosexual acts are not penalized these acts are usually permitted only between adults, although the age of consent in some of the continental countries of Europe may occasionally be as low as sixteen or seventeen.

It is clear from the cross-species and cross-cultural data that our moral judgments and our anxieties in this matter are at considerable variance with both the facts of nature and the moral judgments of most other non-Judaeo-Christian peoples.

Homosexual behavior, like most other sexual behavior, is more frequent among the young, and fewer adult males than youths may at any one time be involved in such behavior. This has been accepted by some as proof that homosexuality is "immaturity." But this argument may not be easily reconciled with the persistence of homosexual responsiveness among a lesser but nonetheless significant number of adult males—most of whom are completely adequate heterosexually. Similarly, although homosexual activity is common among animals and humans, it is never more common than heterosexual activity, at least among adults. In the vast majority of cases, the presence of homosexual responsiveness does not exclude heterosexual responsiveness. Both moral preceptors and clinicians have made much of these facts and have put forth the argument that the predominance of heterosexual over homosexual behavior is proof that homosexuality is "abnormal." But the circumstances that favor the learning, reinforcement, and retention of heterosexual behavior patterns have been discussed within the previous chapter.

In turning our attention exclusively to humans we may note that a distinct majority of societies expect some homosexual behavior and make some provision for it in the sex mores. In 64 per cent of the societies for which data on homosexuality are available, homosexual activities of one sort or another are considered normal and socially acceptable for certain members of the community. In some societies virtually all males engage in homosexual relations and individuals are singled out as peculiar if they do not indulge in homosexual relations. Although homosexual relationships may receive generous approval within certain cultures, they are not considered more acceptable than heterosexual relationships, except in the rare cultures in which homosexual love is surrounded by an aura of religious or philosophic piety and is extolled as superior. Even in these cases, it is always expected that the individual will participate in heterosexual as well as homosexual relationships.

There is a distinct tendency for homosexuality to become associated with belief in the supernatural within both homoerotophilic and homoerotophobic cultures. This association often has a prominent bearing upon popular attitudes toward the subject. More often than not either approval or disapproval of homosexual phenomena may result from superstitious attitudes and belief in the supernatural. Our own society is no exception to this generalization.

On the basis of their study of the cross-cultural data, Ford and Beach make the following observation with which we may conclude this chapter:

> The basic mammalian capacity for sexual inversion tends to be obscured in societies like our own which forbid such behavior and classify it as unnatural. Among these peoples social forces that impinge upon the developing personality from earliest childhood tend to inhibit and discourage homosexual arousal and behavior, and to condition the individual exclusively to heterosexual stimuli. Even in societies which severely restrict homosexual tendencies, however,

some individuals do exhibit homosexual behavior. In our own society, for example, homosexual behavior is more common than the
cultural ideals and rules seem to indicate. Within the societies which,
unlike our own, provide socially acceptable homosexual roles, a
number of individuals, predominantly men, choose to exhibit some
measure of homosexual behavior.[22]

V

Theories on the Origin of Homosexuality

Since homosexuality has always been considered grossly abnormal during Christian times in the West, explanations of it have been sought far and wide. It has been felt that the origin of this behavior must be as eccentric as the behavior itself appears in our society. Hence, almost every type of extraordinary circumstance has at one time or another been made responsible for the development of homosexual preferences. The theories of causation that have enjoyed favor at different times, however, have always reflected contemporary attitudes toward the subject.

Thus, in the Dark Ages and during medieval times, when homosexuality was thought to be a supernatural state of mind, it was attributed to possession by devils, and the cure was exorcism by bell, book, and candle. A hundred years ago, when it was regarded as a vice, it was attributed to depravity, excessive "self-abuse," satiation, and the search for new sensations. The cure was public censure and private penance. Seventy years ago, when homosexuality was regarded as a form of moral and neurological degeneracy, the cause was attributed to the "bad seed" of one's ancestors, and there was no cure because it is impossible to reverse heredity. Twenty-five years ago, when endocrinology was all the rage, homosexuality was thought to be a glandular disease, and the cure consisted of hormonal injections. Today psychiatric explanations of almost every sort of health problem, short of those that require immediate surgery, enjoy wide currency. Accordingly, homosexuality is regarded as an emotional ailment, and is attributed to complicated psychodynamic conflicts that arise during childhood. Clinicians differ among themselves as to

89

the precise conflicts that are supposed to be responsible for homosexuality, but all agree that the cure involves long-term psychotherapy.

There is in reality no need, however, to cast about in mysterious realms for the origin of most homosexual behavior. It is only because we have learned to regard homosexuality as extraordinary that we have insisted upon an extraordinary explanation of it. From the data already presented in these first chapters it should be evident that homosexuality is not paricularly uncommon, either in our own society or in most others. If homosexuality arose in the very special and very exotic circumstances that are generally made responsible for it, it would be much rarer than it actually proves to be. We must look for an explanation of this behavior that is sufficiently comprehensive to account for the incidence found among the lower mammals, among men of diverse cultural background, and among average men in our own culture.

We believe that such an explanation can be found only in the accepted and familiar principles of learning and conditioning and that it is not only unnecessary to look elsewhere for an explanation but also misleading to do so. Sexual tastes and sexual preferences are acquired in exactly the same way as any other tastes and preferences. The principles which are involved in the learning of homosexual preferences are exactly the same as those which are involved in the learning of heterosexual preferences. Certain factors, which were discussed in Chapter III, favor the learning of heterosexual responses and bring about a higher incidence of heterosexuality than homosexuality. But homosexual responsiveness is never a rare phenomenon in any large group of human beings, and circumstances that favor the learning of homosexual responsiveness, though less pronounced than those which favor the learning of heterosexual responsiveness, are never rare in any complex social organization. The sooner we learn these facts about homosexuality the sooner we will be able to deal with the disturbing problem that it presents both to the individual and to the group in our society.

But before discussing the principles that are involved in the learning of homosexual tastes some mention must be made of certain other factors that have been made responsible for the incidence of homosexuality. Among these are: willful depravity and perversity, heredity and constitution, glandular imbalance, and deep-seated emotional conflicts.

These causative factors must be judged in terms of all the available data on homosexuality and not simply in terms of those data which one may choose to accept because they harmonize with an a priori interpretation of homosexuality. They must account for the homosexuality of all those ratable from 1 through 6. They must also account for the cross-cultural and phylogenetic data on homosexuality. Clinicians in particular have refused to acknowledge any significance in the statistical data on homosexuality from our own society just as they have generally refused to acknowledge any significance in the cross-cultural and phylogenetic data. But it is easy to manufacture any theory if one selects only those facts that seem to support it and rejects any other facts that seem to contradict it. In this book we must insist upon judging the validity of various theories on the origin of homosexuality in the light of the facts summarized in the first four chapters. Among the most important of these are:

(1) Homosexual responsiveness may occur in any mammal and is not limited to human primates. (Chapter III)

(2) Homosexual responsiveness does not preclude the possibility of heterosexual responsiveness but rather, in a vast majority of individuals who are homosexually responsive, coexists with heterosexual responsiveness. (Chapters II, III, IV, V)

(3) In any human population of males there is a gradual continuum between exclusive heterosexuality and exclusive homosexuality. (Chapters II, IV)

(4) Cultural attitudes toward sex seem to affect the incidence of the various ratings on the seven-point scale, so that homoerotophobic environments tend to favor the incidence of lower ratings, while homoerotophilic environments tend to favor the incidence of higher ratings. (Chapters II, IV, V)

(5) Exclusive homosexuality, throughout the course of an entire lifetime, may be found only among human beings, and the number of individuals who are exclusively homosexual throughout an entire lifetime constitutes only a small percentage of any population. (Chapters II, III, IV)

(6) Homosexual responsiveness is much more common among males than among females in all mammalian species including human primates. (Chapters II, III, IV)

With this background in mind, we may now discuss some of the factors that have been offered in explanation of homosexuality.

One of the oldest and most persistent explanations for homosexuality is that it results from willful depravity and perversity. Thus it has been claimed that certain individuals take up a life of homosexuality as a result of distorted conscience. These individuals are thought to have become bereft of all knowledge of right and wrong. It was quite generally believed in the past, for example, that certain roués and rakes who had run the gamut of heterosexual experience turned from women to boys in a desperate search for new thrills that might whet their sated appetites. It was seriously believed also that excessive masturbation—"self abuse," itself regarded as a monstrous perversion—weakens the moral fiber and even the brain, and leads from bad to worse until eventually one sinks to the level of every known "perversion." Overcome by the ill effects of onanism, self-pollution in dreams, and fornication, broken in spirit and soul by the evil burden of vicious habits, the "moral degenerate" turns to ever greater wrongs until, at last, he is reduced to sodomy and "unnatural vice." If saved in time by a moral reawakening and by an appropriate feeling of repentance, he might be able to renounce his evil ways and turn once again to the joys of a virtuous life.

Of course, such an explanation is no longer acceptable for even the person of average sophistication and intelligence, at least when phrased in the language above. Few today would offer willful depravity or moral degeneracy as explanations of the homosexuality of the Greeks, Siwans, Chinese, or even the homosexuality of some of our own citizens. We have learned to look for more substantial causes, and we are apt to rephrase the moralistic jargon of the past. Yet the *spirit* of this interpretation may be recognized in a great deal of what is said today about homosexuality, and even the *substance* of this type of interpretation has not altogether vanished from the contemporary scene.

Consider, for example, a recent book entitled, *Morality and the Homosexual,* by Rev. Michael J. Buckley, D.D., a Roman Catholic priest from England. This book presents homosexuality entirely as a moral problem which, as such, can only be properly dealt with by the Church. Father Buckley clearly rejects the idea that homosexuality is a disease, and he also rejects the idea that it has any connection with the individual's heredity or physiology. It is, according to him, however, "an unnatural condition." But Father Buckley does not think that a priest should be "deterred by the false claim that homosexuality is essentially a medical or psychiatric problem." Instead, he argues, "Modern scientific theories are but mists which some moralists use in their attempts to obscure the teaching of the True Church." This book, which received the imprimatur in 1959, specifies reorientation to heterosexuality through pastoral guidance as the task in all these cases. But where this may not be possible, the individual must instead make "an adjustment to his condition in the only way acceptable to Catholic moral theology—a life of chastity." [9]

We may see, therefore, that the theory of willful depravity has never really been abandoned. If in addition to the more forthright expressions of this idea we recognize as well all the more subtle versions, it remains the most common explanation of homosexuality in our culture. Certainly our laws treat homosexuality as a form of willful depravity that should be punished, and much of the moral disapproval such behavior incurs seems to be founded on the conviction that homosexuality is merely a vice voluntarily embraced by those who lack the moral stamina to abjure it.

Other than to point out that this theory is extremely maladroit from a psychological point of view, we will not attempt to offer any detailed criticism of it. It is not our task here to speculate on philosophical issues.

The idea that homosexuality has an hereditary or constitutional basis has been encouraged in the psychiatric literature on the subject up until recent times. Indeed, we are still apt to meet with this theory in various guises. Certain inherent physical and emotional characteristics are believed, especially by those of the constitutional school of psychiatry, to be linked with homosexual preferences. Even Freud was not entirely beyond this belief and Fenichel, one of Freud's most learned disciples, specifies constitutionality as a factor in the development of homosexuality.[21]

It is difficult to define precisely what psychiatrists mean by constitution; probably no two people ever use this word with exactly the same meaning in mind. The following extracts taken from the *Psychiatric Dictionary* of Hinsie and Campbell, however, may help the reader to gain some impression of what is meant by constitution.

> Few expressions in contemporary medical literature are applied with so little unanimity and exactness as is the term *constitution*. Its identification with the phenotype, body build or genotype of an individual is almost as common as its usage—with or without the epithet "hereditary"—for denoting the general biological make-up or the particular genetic structure of an organism . . .
> The classification of constitutional disease groups as clinical entities was bound to remain useless, because there is no disease which is purely constitutional, and there is no constitutional system which is alone the pathogenetic basis for a specific pathology.
> According to the principles of modern physiological genetics the furthest one can go is to distinguish between predominantly hereditary and predominantly peristatic disease . . . Consequently, the concepts of heredity and constitution have become practically inseparable, although it is clear that the constitution is not to be identified with either the genotypical structure or the phenotypical make-up of a person . . . It is therefore best understood as an auxiliary concept of medical classification and general pathology . . .[41]

We hear less and less about heredity and constitution as more and more data which show that sexual preferences of any kind are acquired rather than inherited become available. Nevertheless these theories are still favored by some clinicians, as well as by a great many preponderantly homosexual males who feel that they were "born that way."

West, in his book *Homosexuality* (1960), has made an important observation about heredity in these cases.

> Although no physical abnormality has yet been discovered, the assumption that there must be some underlying constitutional defect would receive some support if it could be shown that homosexuality is hereditary. Many difficulties stand in the way of an answer to this question. In the case of some rare and clear-cut defect, like a missing finger, the mere observation of several instances in the same family affords good evidence of a hereditary factor. But homosexuality is so common that the discovery of a number of cases in the same family

would have no significance. Even if investigation revealed some families with an unusually high proportion of homosexuals in several successive generations, this still would not amount to proof of hereditary causation. Like infectious disorders, homosexual tendencies might be transmitted by association.[78]

Similarly, it was supposed for some while that homosexuality is due to a disequilibrium in the body chemistry, particularly with regard to glandular secretions. Some endocrinologists believed that male homosexuality results from a lack of male hormones (androgens) and an overabundance of female hormones (estrogens). Accordingly, homosexual males were treated with injections of male hormones in the expectation that they would become disinterested in homosexual contacts. Such treatments proved disastrous in many cases because androgenic hormones increase the sexual drive of the male without altering habitual patterns of sexual response. Many males treated with these injections therefore merely became more avid for homosexual contacts, with the consequence that the endocrinological treatment of homosexuality has been abandoned in contemporary medicine. It is not likely that such treatment would have been used in the first place if certain data on homosexuality had been known and properly interpreted.

The widespread incidence of homosexuality within certain cultures makes the proposition that this behavior regularly arises in some pathological context extremely untenable. There are, as we have seen, some groups in which virtually all males engage in homosexual behavior. It is difficult to suppose that all such males suffer the ill effects of hereditary, glandular, or psychiatric pathology. This is emphasized by Ford and Beach in connection with the idea that homosexuality has some basis in glandular imbalance.

> The fact that a majority of males in some societies engage in homosexual relations has a direct bearing upon certain interpretations of such behavior that are current in our own society. Some clinicians assert that the homosexual individual is characterized by an abnormal glandular imbalance. This or any other exclusively physiological explanation for homosexuality seems to be contradicted by the cross-cultural evidence.[22]

In their critique of the hormonal explanation of male homosexuality, Kinsey, Pomeroy, Martin, and Gebhard made the following adroit observation: "It is curious that psychologists and psychiatrists, who are the ones that most often emphasize the importance of psychologic conditioning, so often look for hormonal explanations of any type of sexual behavior which departs from the Hittite and Talmudic codes." [54]

It has been generally recognized in scientific circles for the last ten or more years that sexual preferences have little or nothing to do with heredity, constitution, hormones, or the like, and that, instead, sexual preferences are a topic for *psychological* investigation.[53, 54, 22, 78, 8, 6]

But, unfortunately, many of the psychological explanations of homosexuality that have been offered in the clinical literature are open to the same objections that may be raised in connection with the other explanations. Complicated psychodynamic accounts of the origin of this behavior may find some limited applicability in certain isolated instances, but such accounts can hardly explain homosexuality in the majority of instances in which it occurs. The assumption that homosexuality is but a symptom of some pervasive disturbance within the total personality and that homosexual interests can only develop in a pathogenic context is based, no doubt, upon the fact that homosexuality is studied by clinicians in people who are, in fact, neurotic and emotionally upset. It is not surprising to find all kinds of emotional conflicts in the history of psychiatric patients, whether or not these patients are homosexual. But clinicians insist that in the history of homosexual patients there are particular types of conflict that do not appear as often, or do not appear at all, in the histories of exclusively heterosexual patients.

This contention is maintained, for example, in a psychoanalytic report by Bieber and others on the therapy of 106 homosexual patients.[8] Generalizing from their findings with their patients, these authors lay great emphasis upon childhood conflict in the nuclear family as an important factor in the psychogenesis of homosexuality along with other factors that seem to favor "hidden but incapacitating fears of the opposite sex" in adulthood. They found that their homosexual patients, more often than their heterosexual patients, had a history in which a "detached-hostile father" and "a close-binding-intimate mother" could be identified. When the homosexual patients were compared with their siblings it was found that, "The homosexual son emerged as the interactional focal point upon whom the most profound parental psychopathology was concentrated." Thus, the homosexual patients were regarded as victims of the psychopathology of their mothers and fathers.

Bieber *et al.* make no attempt at all to relate these findings to the statistics on homosexuality in our own culture, nor to the cross-cultural and phylogenetic data. Indeed, these data were referred to somewhat contemptuously. Apparently it is felt by these authors that the homosexuality of the patients in their study is the only "real homosexuality" and that in all cases of "real homosexuality" the same factors are always present. But there is nothing in this study to prove or even to suggest strongly that this must be the case. From a study of only 106 individuals, all of whom are seriously neurotic and most of whom represent a highly select population in a number of other important respects, we can hardly feel certain that these generalizations may be applied to every individual who is homosexually oriented, even in our own society. When, in addition, these generalizations seem to have little or no applicability to a number of important data on homosexuality—consider, for example, their lack of relevance to the homosexual behavior of subhuman primates and other of the lower mammals—we are forced to be skeptical of them. It may well be that there are many—even a great many—males in our culture who become involved in homosexuality because of the reasons suggested in this study; we cannot know just how many until much more research has been carried out on a larger and more representative population of homosexual males. But that every male, even at the upper extreme of the continuum, who becomes involved in homosexuality has a similar history, or is motivated to homosexual behavior out of incapacitating fears of heterosexuality, seems, to say the least, unlikely. It does not seem tenable, for example, that males who are ratable as 3s or 4s, and who therefore have a substantial history of heterosexuality, or that males who combine in the same moment homosexual and heterosexual interests can be properly described as incapacitated by a fear of heterosexuality. Most males who manifest homosexual interests, as we have already seen elsewhere, continue to function well heterosexually. Nor can we see any general applicability of the factors stressed in the Bieber study to the homosexuality of most non-Judaeo-Christian peoples. To imagine, for example, that all Siwian males participate in homosexual relations and enjoy them because of the damaging effects of a relationship with a detached-hostile father and close-binding-intimate mother is a bit strained.

We are forced to conclude, therefore, that these findings, insofar as they have any general applicability, must be relevant to some subgroup at the upper extreme of the heterosexual-homosexual continuum in our own culture. But we cannot feel at all certain that even all 5s or all 6s have a history like that described in the Bieber study, or that all of these more predominantly homosexual males suffer from the same anxieties that were identified in the population of patients studied by Bieber and his colleagues. It does, however, seem likely that some highly disturbed males in our culture are victims of the emotional circumstances described in the Bieber book, and that many of these males enter into an exclusively homosexual way of life because they have been conditioned by early childhood conflicts to avoid heterosexual contacts.

Recognition of the fact that the homosexuality of most males must be nonpathogenical and unrelated to pervasive emotional conflicts does not mean that there is never any homosexuality that originates in a psychopathological context. It is extremely probable that a pervasive pattern of homosexuality in our culture may not only *cause* serious conflict in some people, but also that a pervasive pattern of homosexuality may *originate* in serious emotional conflicts during childhood. The total failure to develop heterosexual interests may be related not only to the factors stressed by Bieber and his psychoanalytic colleagues, but also to certain other dynamics emphasized by other clinicians. Freud's contention that narcissistic self-love may encourage homosexual preferences, Wulff's suggestion that so-called father fixation may play a part in the development of such preferences, or even the "masochistic pseudo-aggression" which Bergler makes responsible for homosexuality, all may be meaningful interpretations of the homosexuality of certain individuals.

The fundamental objection that must be raised against most clinical interpretations of homosexuality is that they are offered as explanations for all homosexuality when, in fact, they fail to explain most of the data which we have on this subject. Moreover, most clinical interpretations are based on an a priori conclusion that all homosexuality in adults is pathological, another assumption that does not seem to fit a great many facts.

Exclusive homosexuality throughout an entire lifetime is rare almost everywhere except within our own culture, and exclusive homosexuality over any prolonged period of time is virtually nonexistent in infrahuman mammals. Exclusive sexuality of any kind is uncommon among most mammalian males, particularly the younger males; but where exclusiveness exists it is usually exclusive heterosexuality rather than exclusive homosexuality. It is not too presumptuous, therefore, to imagine that where homosexual tastes among humans completely exclude heterosexual tastes over a very extended period of time, complicated psychodynamic factors related to anxiety over heterosexuality may be often involved.

Similarly, one can hardly doubt that a strong element of homoerotophobia is responsible for the exclusive heterosexuality of a great many people in our culture. Fixation at either extreme of the heterosexual-homosexual continuum may be related to neurotic attitudes toward sex, and sexual neuroticism is the rule rather than the exception throughout our culture. We are not in the habit of regarding 0s as pathological types, and most of them are not. It may nevertheless be recognized that much exclusive heterosexuality in our culture is related to phobic attitudes toward homosexuality as much as to complete satisfaction with heterosexuality. Many persons never allow themselves even to contemplate the possibility of a homosexual experience, not necessarily because they are perfectly adjusted to heterosexuality but sometimes only because they fear homosexuality. The aggressively "masculine" pose of some males; the vainglorious pride they take in the sociosexual role assigned to them; the contempt they often have for females and for any other males whom they do not regard as "regular fellows"; the fervor with which they espouse the superiority of their own attitudes, their own preferences, and their own opinions, and the bitterness with which they condemn every type of sexual heresy suggest something less than a wholly comfortable or secure adjustment to sexual life.

Certain people may become as neurotic about heterosexuality as others do about their homosexuality. Although it may be easy for most of us to recognize that exclusive homosexuality may originate in and be maintained by neurotic fears, we are less often able to recognize that neurotic fears may play some part in the origin and maintenance of certain cases of exclusive heterosexuality, because it is regarded as unreservedly "normal" in our culture.

Belief in the idea that homosexuality is always "abnormal" and that heterosexuality is always "normal" is based on an interpretation of the sexual drive as *instinctual* in nature. According to this interpretation, the sexual drive is *innately* directed toward certain heterosexual aims and objects, and unless diverted—or, as one says, "perverted"—during the course of its development this drive will compel one toward the type of sexual behavior that receives approval in our culture. Those who do not manifest such behavior are thought to be involved in what amounts to a transgression of instinctual life. This, in substance, is the psychoanalytic approach to the sexual drive, for all of the stages in psychosexual development of which psychoanalysts speak are thought, under "normal" conditions, to terminate in exclusive heterosexuality of a kind, moreover, that is compatible with monogamy. This, however, is not so much a scientific as it is a moralistic interpretation of sex.

In reality there are no innate aims in the sexual drive other than discharge of tension, and no innate objects in this drive. Any aims and any objects that become attached to this drive do so only as a result of experience. Young male mammals who have not been previously conditioned will react to any sufficient sexual stimuli, whether these are autoerotic, heteroerotic, or homoerotic in character; and they may, moreover, become *conditioned* to any of these stimuli. Heterosexuality, therefore, no less than homosexuality, is *learned* in the context of one's experience, and neither has anything to do with "instinct." Ford and Beach emphasize this in the following passage.

> Men and women who are totally lacking in any conscious homosexual leanings are as much a product of cultural conditioning as are the exclusive homosexuals who find heterosexual relations distasteful and unsatisfying. Both extremes represent movement away from the original, intermediate condition which includes the capacity for both forms of sexual expression. In a restrictive society such as our own a large proportion of the population learns not to respond to or even to recognize homosexual stimuli and may eventually become in fact unable to do so.[22]

In speaking of sexual phenomena of any sort, the words "natural" or "unnatural" serve no worthwhile purpose; but if the word "natural" is ever to be applied at all, it is neither to exclusive heterosexuality nor to exclusive homosexuality that it has the most relevance. Strictly speaking, the most "natural" expression of the sexual drive is one in which neither heterosexuality nor homosexuality exclude the possibility of the other—that is, the "intermediate condition which includes the capacity for both forms of sexual expression," of which Ford and Beach speak. Many societies, especially those which tend to be sex-positive rather than sex-negative, expect and encourage this "intermediate condition." But this observation should not be used to encourage sexual chauvinism among so-called bisexuals.

Any sexual preference (heterosexual, homosexual, bisexual, or auto-erotic) may be learned in a nonpsychopathological context in which anxiety and guilt play no part. Any of these preferences also may be learned in a distinctly psychopathological context in which anxiety and guilt favor the development and fixation of one type of preference over another. Although certain psychodynamics that have been identified by psychiatrists and clinical psychologists may play some part in the exclusive homosexuality of some people, and although certain other dynamics less often identified may play some part in the exclusive heterosexuality of some people, it is to the ordinary principles of learning and conditioning that we must turn for an explanation of most homosexuality as well, of course, as most heterosexuality. The principles of learning and conditioning may be fully reconciled with an explanation of homosexuality in terms of the six points outlined at the beginning of this chapter. It may be seen that no other type of explanation is fully reconcilable with all of the six points. Let us, therefore, consider in greater detail the factors that are involved in the learning of sexual preferences.

VI

The Acquirement of Sexual Preferences

Modifiability is one of the intrinsic qualities of living protoplasm. All living creatures, from the most simple to the most complex, are modified by the experiences through which they pass. Learning is but one among a number of other instances of the modifiability which is characteristic of living things.

All living organisms show some capacity for learning, and zoologists have revealed that even so lowly and modest a creature as the one-celled paramecium is capable of a kind of learning. When, for example, this tiny blob of protoplasm is presented with a number of food choices it will experiment and, as a result of experience, will tend to repeat in the future the "right choice" more often than the "wrong choice." Maier and Schneirla speak of primitive learning among the lowest forms of life and describe a number of changes in the behavior of protozoan animals that arise in connection with experience.[61]

As one ascends the phylogenetic scale the capacity to modify behavior in connection with experience—that is, the capacity to learn or to become conditioned—increases with each step as life becomes more complex, and conditioned responses replace purely mechanical or unconditioned responses until, at the level of the higher mammals, learning has become the most important determinant of the individual's behavior. The primates are almost entirely dominated by their capacity to become conditioned by the stimuli present within the environment, and human survival is dependent upon man's extraordinary capacity for learning.

It is not surprising to biologists and psychologists that conditioning should play such a formidable role in determining the attitudes, feelings, and behavior of human beings, for the capacity to learn is directly dependent upon the evolution of the cerebral cortex. Man's greater capacity to become conditioned by experience has reduced the role of innate, unlearned responses to the barest minimum. A few simple reflexes, such as the sucking reflex, are present at birth, but even these are subject to modification through experience. Man, therefore, is an animal almost completely devoid of anything resembling the instinctive (unlearned) patterns of behavior that may be observed among some of the simpler forms of life. He must learn almost every type of response which he will make to a given stimulus, and in the interest of survival this learning begins immediately at birth and continues throughout life.

There are no sexual instincts in man. Human sexual behavior, as we have seen, varies widely from individual to individual and from culture to culture, and human sexual behavior is entirely dependent upon learning and conditioning. The tastes, preferences, goals, and motives that determine the individual's pattern of sexual behavior are *acquired* in the context of his unique experiences and are in no sense innate or inherited. Only if this fact is thoroughly integrated and absorbed is it possible to discuss human sexual phenomena from a scientific standpoint.

Before the development of experimental and statistical psychology it was generally assumed that all mammalian sexual behavior, including human sexual behavior, depends upon certain innate, unlearned tendencies called *instincts* that are quite independent of the experiences with which an individual meets in his environment. These instinctual influences were thought to lead the individual through a preordained pattern of sexual behavior in which learning plays little or no part. There were few, if any, scientific data on the sexual behavior of animals to contradict such a view, and the data on human sexual behavior, such as they were, were subjected to this interpretation, whether or not they confirmed it.

The sexual "instinct," of course, was interpreted in terms of procreation, and procreation was thought to be an *inherent* aim of sexual drive. It is not difficult to see that this view of sex reflected and rationalized moral and religious concepts of sex. It was not known that experience and learning are essential elements even in the procreative behavior of infrahuman animals; and in the case of human sexual behavior, both ignorance and hypocrisy tended to mask and to minimize the extent of nonprocreative sexuality. Nevertheless it was impossible to ignore completely the existence of such phenomena as homosexuality, masturbation, and some of the other nonprocreative manifestations of sexual drive. These, however, in the light of the instinct theory, had to be regarded as highly exceptional and rare events representing "perversion." It was only in the case of these so-called perversions that experience was accorded any significance. Thus it was assumed that in what was interpreted to be a normal course of events instinct would lead the individual to conventional norms of sexual behavior; but in the case of unconventional sexual behavior certain extraordinary influences of a necessarily pathological character were thought to have "perverted" supposedly instinctive tendencies. At first, as we have seen in the previous chapter, these pathological influences were regarded as hereditary, constitutional, glandular, or otherwise physical in nature, and the "pervert" was considered a victim of neurological degeneration. Later, however, under the influence of psychoanalytic thinking, experience rather than physiological pathology was accorded some role in the etiology of these so-called perversions. Thus, certain traumatic events and conflictual experiences were made responsible for "perversion." Psychoanalysts for the last seventy years have been discussing the particular traumas and conflicts that are supposed to be responsible for unconventional sexual behavior. Since this view continues to influence the thinking of many clinicians and is met often in popular literature, we must take some note of it in this chapter.

Psychoanalysts believe that the sexual drive is instinctual in nature and that, as such, it has certain inherent and preordained aims and objects which, in the course of "normal" development, lead the adult individual to an exclusive interest in heterosexual coitus in a monogamous relationship. Analysts have predicated a regular sequence of sexual events which, since it is thought to be instinctual, is pictured as more or less independent of the individual's unique experience. Psychosexual development is pictured along lines in which autoerotic and masturbatory phenomena predominate at first, followed by homosexual phenomena during late puberty and early adolescence, and, in late adolescence and early adulthood, by exclusive heterosexuality. According to this hierarchy, therefore, certain sexual phenomena are interpreted as more mature while certain others are interpreted as less mature. Masturbatory and homosexual interests on the part of an adult are interpreted as evidence of "fixation" to a supposedly earlier stage of psychosexual development, or as a subsequent "regression" to such a stage, and both are also interpreted as instances of emotional immaturity.

But no such regular sequence of events has ever been substantiated by any objective study of a sufficiently large and representative sample of males and females in our culture or in any other culture. At best such a hierarchy must be regarded merely as a hypothetical proposition. Since it involved the largest and most representative sample ever studied, the research of Kinsey, Pomeroy, Martin, and Gebhard offers some clues concerning early sexual growth and activity.

These observers found that a certain number of individuals did in fact have a history in which autoerotic phenomena were followed by homosexual and subsequently heterosexual phenomena. But a majority did not. A number of different developmental patterns were identified, and no one of them could be established as a norm. In the history of some individuals heterosexual responsiveness preceded homosexual and autoerotic responsiveness. In others the sequence was homosexual, autoerotic, and heterosexual. In others still the sequence was heterosexual, autoerotic, homosexual. What is even more significant, perhaps, was the fact that more often than not there were no discrete "stages" at all; autoerotic, homosexual, and heterosexual phenomena coexisted from early childhood throughout life, and the existence of one type of responsiveness did not preclude the simultaneous existence of another type. There are males, for example, who have worked out an excellent adjustment in marriage in which both they and their wives are satisfied sexually, and yet not a few of these males continue to participate in homosexual contacts from time to time, and some also continue to engage in solitary masturbation. All of the three basic types of sexual responsiveness were found in a large number of males during both childhood and adulthood. Homosexual contacts during childhood were reported by 48 per cent of the older males and 60 per cent of the boys who were preadolescent at the time they contributed their histories. The mean age of the first homosexual contact was about nine years, two and a half months. The fact that, on the whole, homosexual play was found in more histories, occurred more frequently, and became more specific than preadolescent heterosexual play certainly does not tend to lend any credence to the view that homosexual responsiveness is unnatural or anti-instinctual. Neither does it suggest that homosexuality is more natural than heterosexuality during childhood and therefore more immature; for heterosexual play was found to begin even earlier. The average age for the beginning of preadolescent heterosexual play was about eight years and ten months—approximately five months earlier than the average age at which homosexual play began. Heterosexual play was found in 40 per cent of the preadolescent histories.[53]

Kinsey's data clarify the important part that both heterosexuality and homosexuality play in the histories of Judaeo-Christian males, not to mention the part that autoerotic activities play, and once again we are faced with the responsiveness of the human male to all three classes of sexual stimuli both during childhood and later in life. The fact that homosexual and autoerotic stimuli become less prominent later in life is no reason to assume that either homosexual or autoerotic interests are unnatural or immature. The older male in our culture is simply more conditioned by the sexual values of the culture than the younger male. But in spite of such cultural influences both homosexual and autoerotic stimuli continue to elicit response from a highly significant number of older males.

Because autoerotic, homosexual, and heterosexual interests and activities were all found in a very large number of children and adults, it would appear to be arbitrary and even somewhat misleading to promulgate a hierarchy according to which one particular sexual modality is more or less "mature" than another. There are no specific sexual modalities peculiar to a given age group, nor, so far as any one knows objectively or with certainty, to any group that may be identified on the basis of "emotional maturity." It is assumed, of course, that adult individuals who engage in autoerotic and/or homosexual activities are involved in behavior that is in some way peculiar to children, and that these individuals manifest numerous symptoms of emotional immaturity apart from their sexual activities. Neither assumption has ever been verified and both, accordingly, must be considered sophisticated prejudices.

The interpretation of sexual phenomena in terms of instinct continues to influence the thinking of many people, including not a few clinicians, and the sexual drive is still generally referred to by most people as an instinct. But nowadays scientific students of behavior no longer speak of instinctual or unlearned sexual responses. Science today recognizes that all human sexual patterns, and most infrahuman sexual patterns are a product of learning and conditioning. All mammals possess the basic physiological capacity to respond sexually to any sufficient stimulus. Unless an animal is deformed or otherwise physically incapacitated, he will, providing he has not been conditioned by previous experience, respond identically to identical stimuli, whether these stimuli emanate from some part of his own body, from an individual of the opposite sex, or from another individual of the same sex. Thus, it is misleading and actually incorrect to imply that any human or infrahuman mammal at birth or before learning has taken place, is possessed of any instinct or predisposition toward a particular class of sexual stimuli. Experience determines the pattern of sexual responsiveness that becomes characteristic of any individual.

Few, if any, serious students of sexual behavior, including even clinicians, deny nowadays the capacity of all mammals at birth to respond to varied sexual stimuli. To deny the capacity for diverse sexual response would be to deny virtually a whole list of undeniable behavioristic data. But some theorists have obscured the issue and have opened the way for instinct theory by making a distinction between *capacity* and *tendency*. The fact that every mammal is born with the capacity to respond to autoerotic, heteroerotic, or homoerotic stimuli must not be taken to mean that the individual is born with a tendency to respond to any one of these three classes of stimuli more than to another. It is incorrect to speak of an original tendency or predisposition toward either autoeroticism, heterosexuality, or homosexuality. Some scholars have attempted to minimize the factor of learning by substituting the word tendency for the word instinct. Bieber and his colleagues, for example, speak of a tendency toward heterosexuality:

Capacity is a neutral term connoting *potentiality* whereas *tendency* implies the probability of action in a specific direction. In our view, the human has a capacity for homosexuality but a tendency toward heterosexuality.[8]

It is more correct to say that humans—and other mammals—have a capacity for heterosexual response and a capacity for homosexual response at birth, but that they do not have an inborn tendency toward either heterosexuality or homosexuality. After the drive has been conditioned one way or the other or both ways—in other words, after the *capacity* for response has been exploited and learning has begun—we may speak of a *tendency* toward heterosexuality and/or a tendency toward homosexuality. But this tendency is *acquired* and is a product of learning rather than a part of the individual's biological inheritance. To speak of a tendency toward heterosexuality or homosexuality that is independent of learning is simply to invent a new vocabulary for the old concept of instinct.

We believe that Bieber and his colleagues, like most other psychoanalysts, do indeed work on the supposition that sexual drive is guided by instinct and that these authors have merely confused rather than clarified these issues for themselves and their readers by introducing a new terminology for an old concept. It would have been much more to the point if they had simply said that heterosexuality is instinctual, and homosexuality is anti-instinctual, for that is what their statement amounts to.

The word "learning" may be somewhat confusing. In the mind of the average person it suggests a very special situation involving the cooperation of the learner and is usually associated with the acquirement of abstract knowledge or specific skills. In reality, learning may take place with little or no cooperation on the part of the learner, and the range of responses it covers far exceeds the intellectual or symbolic spheres of mental life. Emotional responses and even attitudinal postures are also learned, more often than not without the knowledge or cooperation of the learner.

One specific complex of events is almost always associated with the learning process: A living organism tends to repeat those experiences which are pleasurable and tends to avoid those experiences which are painful.

Gratification of the felt needs of an individual constitutes what is probably the greatest single motivational factor for the establishment of learning. When a given response leads to the gratification of a felt need and at the same time is not accompanied by any element of pain, the likelihood is very great that the same stimulus will evoke the same response in the future.

The optimal conditions for the establishment of a learned response are present when the response gratifies a felt need, when it evokes no pain, and when alternative responses do occasion pain. When, on the other hand, a particular response affords no gratification of felt needs and also leads to pain, the optimal conditions for future avoidance of the response are present.

Throughout this chapter we have used the word "experience." We have in mind the same definition of this word that is offered by Maier and Schneirla:

> The term *experience* as used here . . . refers to the effect of stimulation of the organism. Consciousness may or may not accompany such stimulation, but this cannot really be known [in the case of infra-human animals] and really makes no difference. We have therefore used the term in its broad sense and have not used it as a reference to consciousness. To limit the meaning of the term *experience* to a conscious state is likely to imply that consciousness is an important determiner of behavior and therefore worthy of a terminology which refers to it. The point of view of this treatment opposes any such assumption.[61]

With this definition in mind we may proceed to three important generalizations: Precedence of experience, intensity of experience, and recency of experience all affect the future behavior of the individual. This has been summarized very well as follows: "Other things being equal, the first experiences, the most intense experiences, and the latest experiences may have the maximum effect on the individual's subsequent behavior." [53]

One never knows what new experiences or combination of experiences may change or widen the erotic orientation of an individual even after the formative period of childhood. Childhood experiences are important because of the weight precedence carries in the establishment of learning. But the importance of childhood experiences can be overemphasized:

> Freud and the psychiatrists, and psychologists in general, have correctly emphasized the importance of one's early experience, but it should not be forgotten that one may continue to learn and continue to be conditioned by new types of situations at any time during one's life. It is incorrect to minimize the importance of all except childhood experiences in the development of adult patterns of behavior.[54]

No matter how strongly conditioned an older person may have become to a given class of sexual stimuli, and no matter how strongly conditioned to the avoidance of some other class of sexual stimuli, the acquisition of new tastes remains a possibility. There are instances in which persons who have been exclusively heterosexual for many years have developed homosexual interests, and other instances in which persons who have been exclusively homosexual for many years have developed heterosexual interests. Although dramatic and extreme changes in the sexual pattern are not common in later life, such changes do sometimes occur. Most often persons tend to repeat the same pattern of sexual preferences that has become established by early adulthood. Complete reversals from exclusive heterosexuality to exclusive homosexuality or vice versa are far less common later in life than a movement toward a bisexual pattern of preferences. But most sexual preferences, whatever their nature, tend to be fairly stable after adolescence.

The idea that seduction during childhood may cause the individual to prefer homosexual contacts in later life is an oversimplification of the facts and often a dangerous conclusion. But if one knows how to evaluate the true importance of early sexual experience during childhood one is in possession of valuable knowledge. It has been observed repeatedly, "The type of person who first introduces an individual to particular types of sociosexual activities may have a great deal to do with his or her dissatisfactions with other types of activity." [54]

Generally speaking, if a young person is introduced to any type of erotic situation in the absence of strong learned avoidance by a kindly and sympathetic person of his—or her—own age, or older, the chances are great that the young person will respond positively and will tend to repeat the same behavior in the future. The reverse may be equally true; early experiences with an unsympathetic or obnoxious person may bring about avoidance of such experiences in the future. Some early seductions, for example, condition the child negatively rather than positively. This may be the case whether the seduction involves homosexual or heterosexual contacts.

Let us recall some of the factors mentioned above that contribute to learning, and let us hypothesize a rather complicated example of the interplay of these factors.

Suppose that the first erotic contact a young person experienced involved another person of his own sex. Precedence for homosexual responsiveness would be established. But suppose (perhaps as a result of learned avoidance, physiologic incapacity, or unpleasant environmental conditions) that this youth did not experience sufficient pleasure in connection with this contact, or that he experienced displeasure. Suppose that he subsequently did experience intense pleasure in connection with a heterosexual contact. It would be safe to assume that in such a case the factor of intensity would displace the factor of precedence. If reinforcement through repetition occured, and if the most recent contact he had experienced pleasurably were also heterosexual, it would be likely that the next time he sought erotic outlet he would seek it with an individual of the opposite sex. The reverse of all this could also take place and lead to homosexual tendencies.

Thus neither precedence, intensity, nor recency *alone* usually determine the future behavior of an individual. Each may have different significance under varied circumstances or within a particular permutation.

Certain other factors that are important in the acquirement of erotic preferences and tendencies must be considered. These include vicarious sharing of experience, reactions to associated objects, sympathetic responses, and the significance of gender in the tendency to become conditioned to psychologic stimuli.

Because of the human being's extraordinary capacity for symbolic thought and communication he may share *vicariously* in the erotic experience of other human beings. As a result of the development of speech and the invention of writing, plastic and pictorial representation, and other devices for the communication of ideas and feelings, we are able through fantasy to participate in the experience of others. This vicarious sharing of experience may act as a conditioning factor and may contribute to the learning of certain sexual preferences.

Vicarious sharing of experience may greatly modify the significance of one's first *overt* erotic contacts, particularly in those cases in which the first experience occurs relatively late in the individual's history. For example, the boy who has his first sexual contact with another male but who all his life, and especially since the onset of puberty, has been stimulated by and has developed a pattern of responsiveness to literary or pictorial representations of feminine erotic stimuli will not readily be influenced in the direction of a homosexual pattern of responsiveness.

To an appreciable extent almost all of us have been conditioned to respond to or to avoid various sexual stimuli long before we have ever experienced direct erotic contact with another human being. Indeed, it is this earlier, vicarious form of conditioning which usually determines the nature of the first overt contacts. The effect of earlier conditioning tends to push us toward the sort of erotic contact with which we have already learned to associate gratification. For this reason the numerous stories of adolescent youths who became "homosexuals" as the result of "seduction" are usually unfounded or are a gross oversimplification of the facts. Adolescent boys who accept a primary homosexual contact with someone of their own age or with an older man usually do so because they have *already* fantasized such a contact; under such conditions, they often either facilitate the contact or directly seek it out. In other words, such youths have already acquired a tendency toward homosexuality. Other youths, not so predisposed by earlier conditioning, tend to avoid homosexual contacts because they have no interest in them and because they have learned that homosexual relations are taboo. If homosexual contacts occur solely on the basis of some ulterior or extra-erotic motive as, for example, monetary gain, they are usually of little weight in establishing a well defined pattern of homosexual responsiveness. It is not often that young men are sexually victimized by the schemes of some diabolic pervert or that they are led astray into the paths of fixed homosexuality unless they have already acquired homosexual tendencies through a number of convening circumstances. It would appear that the myth of "corruption" is circulated by those who do not wish to face the fact that many young males are predisposed to respond positively to homosexual contacts, and even to seek them out.

Any animal may be conditioned to respond to stimuli which are associated with the primary stimulus. If, for example, satisfaction was obtained with an individual of the opposite sex one is more likely to respond to other individuals of the opposite sex. If the previous experience was with an individual of one's own sex, one may, because of association with the previous experience, respond again to other individuals of one's own sex. Even a very simple experience may evoke a number of associated stimuli. Thus, for example, an intense love affair with a redheaded girl may predispose a young man to favor other redheads. In the future redheaded women may seem more "sexy" than blondes or brunettes. Sexual stimulation by things one sees, hears, smells, or tastes often depends upon the association which they evoke rather than upon the direct physical stimulation they provide in themselves. While this is true of all the higher mammals, it is particularly true of humans. There seems to be no end to the list of things which may become part of and contribute to erotic responsiveness. Through association many objects and many circumstances which in themselves have no erotic significance may come to act as sexual stimuli.

As an example, let us consider the stimulating erotic effect that furtiveness and even anxiety may come to have for some males. We will choose an instance in which homosexual stimuli are involved, although the same reaction could easily arise in a heterosexual context. Some homosexual males have learned to experience erotic arousal in such tense and furtive circumstances that tension and furtiveness may become essential components of the erotic situation for them. Some may reach a point at which it is no longer possible for them to respond sexually to another male in a relaxed and secure atmosphere of privacy. Thus, they may come to prefer furtive sexual contacts in a public lavatory or bath house, where danger of exposure and arrest are ever present.

Some of these males may have become so conditioned to anxiety in connection with sexual arousal that they deliberately seek partners whom they cannot trust or who they feel may cause them some sort of trouble. They can only enjoy sexual contacts when they feel they are "playing with fire." Some such males have even reported to this author that they are grateful for the laws prohibiting homosexuality in the United States, because these laws foster the kind of furtive and anxiety-ridden sexual contacts that they have come to prefer. This of course is only one among many paradoxes that such legislation and the psychology upon which it is based has brought into being.

Many people, both homosexual and heterosexual, can only enjoy sexual contacts that they can interpret as "forbidden fruit" because sinfulness has become through association an essential component of the erotic situation. Some males, for example, can only reach a high pitch of sexual excitement if they feel that they have seduced a girl against her will or in a context in which her cooperation appears to be a "conquest" on their part.

All of these seemingly strange attitudes and reactions are quite comprehensible, though not necessarily any more socially desirable, when it is recognized that associated stimuli may come to assume erotic significance on their own. Sadomasochistic preferences may often be traced to this source.

Not infrequently associated phenomena may come to act as even stronger stimuli than the direct physical stimulation provided by a sexual contact. This is always the case where so-called fetishism is involved. Most people are acquainted with the fact that some males are more aroused by a pair of pink silk panties, or some other article of clothing associated with women, than they are by direct physical contacts with women. But even in cases where associated stimuli do not take on an autonomous character they may be very important in bringing about full sexual arousal, and associated stimuli play an important role in almost all sexual relations.

Males in particular respond to the erotic excitement of another individual. Sexual partners often respond to the responses made by each other. These sympathetic responses are akin to reactions to associated stimuli and to vicarious sharing of experience. An observer may become aroused by the sexual excitement of some third party. In this way it is possible that what arouses the party being observed may also come to arouse the onlooker. If this happens, an individual may become conditioned to a particular type of response simply because that response was meaningful to another individual. This response may subsequently become an independent part of the individual's own erotic repertory. Many aspects of erotic responsiveness are learned in this way.

Not a few of the sexual responses that are conspicuous in our culture are acquired by the young in succeeding generations simply because they are stimulating to the older generation. There can be little doubt, for example, that many younger males learn to respond to heterosexual stimuli because they see that these stimuli arouse other males, and the heterosexual arousal of other males calls forth a sympathetic response in them. Similarly, the homosexual arousal of older males in ancient Greek society no doubt encouraged homosexual arousal in younger males. The

sex stimuli that are emphasized in any particular culture are easily acquired and tend to be perpetuated in successive generations not simply
because, as is believed in the culture, they are "natural," but also because
of sympathetic response and the other influences emphasized in this
chapter.

The factors which we have been discussing do not have equal significance for males and females. Sexual learning and conditioning play a
more prominent and important role in the histories of males. Females do
not seem to be as often influenced by psychological stimuli as males. It
is important for us to note this difference between males and females and
to discuss it at some length. The psychosexual differences between most
males and females are considerable, and if we are to arrive at an understanding of the problems sex presents, we must be aware of them. Kinsey,
Pomeroy, Martin, and Gebhard draw attention to some of these differences:

> In general, males are more often conditioned by their sexual ex-
> perience, and by a greater variety of associated factors, than females.
> While there is a great individual variation in this respect among both
> females and males, there is considerable evidence that the sexual re-
> sponses and behavior of the average male are, on the whole, more
> often determined by the male's previous experience, by his associa-
> tion with objects that were connected with his previous sexual ex-
> perience, by his vicarious sharing of another individual's sexual ex-
> perience, and by his sympathetic reactions to the sexual responses of
> other individuals. The average female is less often affected by such
> psychologic factors. It is highly significant to find that there are evi-
> dences of such differences between the females and the males of infra-
> human mammalian species, as well as between human females and
> males.[54]

Ford and Beach also refer to this difference between males and females
in their studies of the sexual behavior of infrahuman animals, and they too
consider the difference impressive.

> We are strongly impressed with the evidence for sexual learning
> and conditioning in the male and relative absence of such processes in
> the female. In as much as learning is known to depend heavily upon
> the cerebral cortex, the implication is plain that the sex difference
> derives directly from the unequal role which this part of the nervous
> system plays in masculine and feminine mating behavior.[22]

This psychosexual difference between males and females may also be
observed in the case of homosexuality. Homosexuality, we have already
seen, is much more common among males than among females, and homosexual contacts appear to have a very different meaning for the two sexes.
It is important to be aware of these distinctions when attempting to eval-

uate the homosexual behavior of males and females. Ford and Beach comment upon these differences:

> Like self-masturbation, homosexual activities are more common among males than among females. This holds true for the vast majority of human societies and for all the other primates as well. Here again the relative ease with which the genitals of the two sexes can be stimulated may be important, particularly in the case of sub-human animals. This cannot, however, be the complete explanation. In human beings the relative infrequency of feminine homosexuality probably reflects the fact that for most women sexual satisfaction demands more than simple genital stimulation. It usually rests upon a complex type of interrelationship with the masculine partner. Paradoxically enough, this point of view receives confirmation from the accounts of exclusively homosexual women who affirm that they prefer feminine lovers because the latter are more sentimental, more considerate than men. This simply emphasizes the fact that for the human female, physical climax in and of itself is less sufficient than it is for most men.[22]

The propensity of the male to find sexual stimulation in a great number of things, situations, and relationships is what makes him so much more "perverse," as the psychiatrist would term it; and all of these so-called deviations result from the masculine capacity to become aroused by and to respond to diverse psychological stimuli. As a result of their greater capacity to become conditioned by psychological stimuli, many males learn to respond sexually to stimuli that seem to have little or no connection at all with conventionally acceptable sexual stimuli. A not inconsiderable number of males respond energetically to articles of clothing, to various parts of the anatomy of the female, or to other associated stimuli. These males are labeled "fetishists" in the older sexologic literature, and their behavior is considered psychopathological by many. Other males are intensely aroused by visual stimuli, or they may be aroused by the act of exhibiting their genitalia. This so-called deviant behavior, taken as a whole, is very common among males although it is seldom encountered in females. Hardly any of the clinically defined "perversions"—with the possible exceptions of sadism and masochism—are found among women. Fetishism, exhibitionism, voyeurism, and transvestism are almost exclusively masculine phenomena and all of this so-called sexual pathology results from the masculine capacity to become aroused by and to respond to diverse stimuli of a psychological order.

Even in the case of homosexuality there is a startling difference between males and females. The male with a homosexual history as in all things erotic, showed himself to be far more promiscuous than the female. The female with a history of exclusive homosexuality, maintained monogamous relations much more often than did the exclusively homosexual male.

Many would immediately assume that sociological factors account for this difference. Kinsey does not agree:

"Apparently, basic psychologic factors account for these differences in the extent of the promiscuity of the female and the male." [54]

The psychosexual difference between male and female is not obscured or even minimized in the case of homosexual-oriented individuals. Certain schools of psychiatry have encouraged belief in the idea that homosexual males have "identified" themselves with their mothers, or some other significant female in the early environment, and from thence proceeded to "play a feminine role." But homosexual males do not present a picture of feminine psychosexuality. Their sexual pattern, except for the choice of partner, is typical of all other males. Similarly, homosexual females display a typically feminine pattern of erotic responsiveness in all respects other than choice of partner. The notion of "psychological inversion" as a result of identification with the parent of the opposite sex is not borne out by a study of the sexual and erotic behavior of males and females who respond erotically to others of their own sex.

> The idea that homosexuality is a sexual inversion is dispelled when one hears homosexual females criticising homosexual males for exactly the same reasons which lead many wives to criticize their husbands, and when one hears homosexual males criticize homosexual females for exactly the things which husbands criticize in their wives. In fact, homosexual males, in their intensified interest in male genitalia and genital activity, often exhibit the most extreme examples of a typically male type of conditioning.[54]

The homosexual male must be understood as a masculine being, indeed, as a typically masculine being. Males, whatever the vicissitudes of their individual experiences, react to these experiences as males. The same is true of females. To this extent gender may be considered of the utmost importance in the determination of what the individual will learn in the context of his environment.

Most of the social problems with which the homosexual male meets and most of the problems that he creates within the context of Judaeo-Christian culture, are the result of his psychosexual masculinity rather than the result of any hypothetical "inversion" of this masculinity into psychosexual femininity. The homosexual female, on the other hand, meets with fewer problems and inspires less controversy within our culture, as within most cultures, because of her fundamental femininity; she is less aggressive and less promiscuous.

These differences could only have been recognized clearly after a thorough study of male and female patterns of sexual behavior such as that done by Kinsey and his colleagues. Until we were able to recognize the psychosexual differences between males and females, it was not possible to understand a number of problems associated with male homosexuality. These enigmas were further obscured by the belief, still prevalent within many quarters, that the homosexual male more closely resembles the female than the heterosexual male, and that the homosexual female more closely resembles the male than her heterosexual sister. These errors may have resulted from an overestimation of the superficial appearance of certain effeminate males and certain "mannish" females.

Before leaving the topic of masculine and feminine psychosexuality, further mention must be made of the greater need on the part of the male for regular sexual outlet. We may once again call upon Kinsey and his colleagues for an account of this difference.

> After the initial experience in ejaculation, practically all males become regular in their sexual activity. This involves monthly, weekly, or even daily ejaculation, which occurs regularly from the time of the first experience. Among approximately 4,600 adolescent males, less than 1% (about 35 cases) record a lapse of a year or more between their first experience and the adoption of a regular routine of sexual activity. This means that more than 99% of the boys begin regular sexual lives immediately after the first ejaculation. In this respect, the male is again very different from the female, for there are many women who go for periods of time ranging from a year to ten or twenty years between their earlier experiences and the subsequent adoption of regularity in activity. The male, in the course of his life, may change the sources of his sexual outlet, and his frequencies may vary through the weeks and months, and over a span of years, but almost never is there a complete cessation of his activity until such time as old age finally stops all response.[53]

The sociosexual implications of this, especially for the single male, are enormous. Consider, for example, our social attitudes and legal statutes in so far as these concern premarital sexual activities. English and American law, and the attitudes upon which these laws are based, by making illegal all premarital sexual activities except nocturnal emissions and solitary masturbation, force most boys and a great many older men into illicit activity. Males who for various reasons will not or cannot marry— and this includes a large number of predominantly homosexual males— are forced by prevailing laws and social attitudes into illicit sexual activities throughout life. Many unmarried males who may not wish to enter illicit activities are confronted by a regular need for sexual outlet, and may be bewildered as to how to handle their sexual problems. Homosexual males who rate high on the scale may, in particular, be confronted by both a moral and a legal problem, and they cannot, as other males may, look forward to an end to this problem in marriage.

Marriage is the only solution our Anglo-Saxon society provides for regular sexual outlet, and if one considers the promiscuous tendencies of most males and the extent and frequency with which they may become aroused, especially during their prime, one is forced to admit that marriage is not a wholly realistic solution to this problem. It is a very unrealistic solution—in fact, no solution at all—when it is realized that the demands made upon a man by his sexual drive are at a height which he will never experience again, precisely at a time in his life when marriage is out of the question—from sixteen years old through the early twenties.

But the predominantly homosexual male can find no solution at all to his sexual problems in marriage; for even if he married he would not find adequate satisfaction. Hence the life he leads appears highly immoral to others and often even to himself, not merely because his activities are interpreted to be aberrant and immoral, but because his failure to find stability in marriage also propels him toward a great many promiscuous and casual sexual contacts. If, as occasionally he does, he turns toward a steady relationship with another male, and if this relationship is anything more than sexual and includes some of the nonsexual social components of heterosexual marriage—living together in companionship, sharing of economic burdens, etc.—the likelihood of exposure as a "homosexual" is very great. Most males do not feel that they can risk such exposure and may therefore remain with their families or live separately in loneliness. But loneliness itself may favor escape into sexual promiscuity. A vicious circle of illicit sexual indulgence and loneliness is often brought into being by these circumstances. Since we refuse to offer the "homosexual" any legitimate solution whatsoever to this dilemma, we should not be surprised if we find him somewhat miserable. Under these conditions there is no particular reason to suppose, as is often done, that something intrinsic in the very nature of his sexual preferences brings about this misery. If there is anything intrinsically pathological about homosexuality, we can feel quite certain that it is emphasized and supplemented by the frustrating social position in which these individuals find themselves.

Chief among the stimuli impinging upon human animals are those which arise out of the particular character and quality of the culture in which they are reared. Man is a social animal and the society in which he has been nurtured and in which he lives determines many of his attitudes and a great deal of his behavior. This generalization is particularly applicable to erotic attitudes and behavior. These are constantly affected, positively and negatively, by social stimuli.

The role of culture in the conditioning of sexual behavior has been stressed by many investigators. Indeed, some have put forth the proposition that sexual behavior is entirely a function of cultural conditioning. Frumkin (1961) and others have suggested that feral man—that is, an individual outside of culture—does not display sexual behavior upon attaining physiological maturity. In another paper Frumkin stresses the social origin of sexual behavior.[30, 31]

> There is no sexual instinct in man. And man's sexual behavior is symbolic, since it is social, learned, it is always shaped in a particular culture milieu and oriented by the values of the society maintaining that milieu. The nature of sexual behavior in man, like *all* his truly human behavior, *varies* with his culture, with reference to the society in which he is socialized and in which he becomes a human, social being.[30]

In spite of the truth in all this, to overlook entirely the physiological basis of the sexual drive is imprudent. Recognizing the physiological basis of the sexual drive does not imply accepting the notion that the sexual drive is governed by "instinctual" forces that emanate entirely from within and which are disassociated from the learning process. But, on the other hand, recognizing the physiological component in sexual behavior in no way precludes comprehending that specific patterns of sexual behavior originate in the experience of the individual.

The experience of the individual *in toto,* rather than only that part originating in the broader social scene, determines sexual preferences as well as other aspects of individual psychology. Those who have overemphasized the role of cultural conditioning have sometimes failed to accord sufficient weight to the fact that complex cultures such as our own are always subdivided into a great many diverse social units, some of which may differ considerably from one another. Simply because all men in Western civilization share in a common culture does not mean that all men are exposed to an identical and homogeneous social milieu. Sociological differentiation begins, as a matter of fact, in the nuclear family, and sociological stimuli, which ultimately mean the stimuli provided by interpersonal relationships, are different for every individual. This is complicated further because every individual reacts differently to the same constellation of sociological stimuli. Some rebel; others conform; still others work out some kind of compromise or adjustment.

Curiously enough, one of the strongest objections to the behavioristic explanation of the etiology of the homosexual pattern is based upon what amounts to an exaggerated emphasis of the role played by cultural stimuli in the determination of sexual preferences. This is curious because the objection originates in psychoanalytic circles, which usually are not noteworthy for the importance they ascribe to cultural stimuli. This objection, which requires attention, has been stated very clearly by Marmor in his Introduction to *Sexual Inversion* (Basic Books, Inc., 1965):

Within the matrix of contemporary Western civilization, with its abhorrence of and hostility to homosexual behavior and its powerful pressures toward heterosexual conformity, it does not seem likely that a homosexual object-choice, even if it were initially determined by positive conditioning, could maintain itself in a hostile and punitive environment, *unless there were concomitant anxieties of equal or greater strength blocking the path to heterosexual adaptation.* For our time and culture, therefore, the psychoanalytic assumption that preferential homosexual behavior is always associated with unconscious fears of heterosexual relationships appears valid.

This opinion opens the way for the consideration of several important issues that constantly arise in most discussions of human homosexuality. Of course, insofar as Marmor's remarks have relevance, it is only to the preferential homosexuality of certain males who have entirely avoided heterosexual relationships. Explanations of homosexuality that posit the fear of heterosexuality have little if any applicability at all to the homosexuality of males in whom heterosexual trends are also well developed and functional, and this means probably 90 per cent or more of the males who have a history of homosexual responsiveness. One cannot expect to explain homosexuality in terms of the fear of avoidance of heterosexual relationships if heterosexual relationships are neither feared nor avoided.

But even in the case of distinctly preferential homosexuality, fear of heterosexuality need not always nor perhaps not even usually be conspicuous. It is not necessary to assume, for example, that because a man prefers the color red to the color green, and usually or even always acts upon his preference, that he is afraid of green. It would be as illogical to suppose that preferential heterosexuality is based upon a fear of homosexual relationships as to suppose the opposite, and indeed, there may be a significant number of instances in which either assumption proves true. But Marmor and the psychoanalysts insist that all preferential homosexuality provides evidence of the fear of heterosexual relationships.

The above formulation, moreover, presupposes the existence of unconscious fear. But there is still no ineluctable proof that unconscious feelings of any kind actually exist; it remains but a theory that there is an "unconscious mind." In the absence of more certain knowledge of these things it may be rash and even quite prejudicial to insist that every case of preferential homosexuality involves a repressed fear of heterosexuality.

But far more important than any of this is Marmor's assumption that simply because our culture is hostile to homosexuality all men will become heterosexual unless forced by fear into a homosexual "adaptation"; here, it would appear, cultural and social factors are being overstressed or at least misinterpreted.

The fact that some males become positively conditioned to homosexual stimuli although the culture in which they live is antihomosexual affords no sufficient reason to insist that concomitant anxieties of equal strength are blocking the path to heterosexual adaptation. The example of preferential homosexuality in our culture does not cast doubt upon the determinative effects of positive conditioning in the acquirement of sexual preferences; rather, it demonstrates the weak effects that negative social conditioning sometimes produce in certain people. Most of us, but not all of us, acquire a great many of our tastes and opinions from the social environment. The predominantly homosexual individual may be one type of person who does not; there are others as well.

Acceptance of the principles of learning and conditioning does not imply acceptance of the idea that all people are equally affected by the social environment in which they live, nor does it imply acceptance of the idea that the social environment of every individual within the same culture is identical. We cannot speak of society in global terms when we discuss the psychology of the individual; there are many "societies" within a single culture. Western civilization, viewed in its totality, is certainly antihomosexual; but not every social unit, even in Judaeo-Christian culture, is antihomosexual. Indeed, some homosexual males have created a "gay society" of their own which in no small measure may reinforce early positive conditioning to homosexual stimuli. Social dynamics are involved in "the homosexual way of life" that cannot possibly be discussed at length here; but it is perhaps sufficient to point out that the global society in which the homosexual male lives seems to insist upon some exclusive form of sexuality, even if it is homosexuality! The fully homosexual male in our culture may actually have fewer pressing social conflicts than a male ratable as 2, 3, or 4. He at least may find a subgroup into which to retire. Consideration of the precise nature of homoerotophobia in our culture should not be overlooked in this discussion. It is not entirely correct to say that homosexuality is hated in our culture so much as that it is *feared*. Moreover, there are some less conspicuous aspects of social life in Judaeo-Christian culture that inadvertently encourage homosexuality at the same time as they encourage enormous guilt over homosexual feelings. Indeed, the outstanding feature in the psychology of prepotently homosexual males is not so much their fear of heterosexuality as their sometimes unreasonable guilt feelings about being homosexual.

Quite apart from these more subtle and intricate psychosociological considerations, preferential homosexuality, in order to exist at all, must originate in an early and pervasive positive conditioning to homosexual stimuli. If such conditioning does not take place, no amount of fear of heterosexual relationships can bring about a pattern of homosexual object-choice. It is not enough to view preferential homosexuality merely or only as a flight from heterosexuality, for it is possible to escape binding heterosexual relationships in other ways that do not involve homosexual alternatives. Homosexual preferences must be accounted for not only in negative but also in positive terms; after all, such preferences do yield pleasure and this fact also needs to be accounted for.

Many males may become positively conditioned to homosexual stimuli early in life at a time when broader social attitudes are neither perceived nor valued. Later, when the individual recognizes the social dangers such preferences must invoke, he may simply rebel or cling stubbornly to pleasures that seem to afford sufficient recompense for the hostility he has to face in the broader environment. These reactions are not necessarily fears; men throughout history have sacrificed much for the satisfaction of their libidinous appetites and tastes.

Learning and conditioning account for every type of behavior pattern and every type of sexual preference that may be found in mammalian species. But the discrete experiences that in the case of a particular individual favor the acquirement of a particular sexual pattern vary so widely that it is impossible to establish any single type of experience as a regular cause. In the case of homosexuality, for example, childhood seduction, segregation from the opposite sex, traumatic experiences with the opposite sex, and various "complexes" elaborated in the psychiatric literature have been urged as regular causes. But in the absence of any carefully controlled, wide-scale research, all of the specific causes for homosexuality, even those which are most widely accepted at the moment, must be recognized as merely provisional.

If we had at our disposal the means of determining every experience that contributed to the learning of a homosexual pattern of responsiveness in the case of a specific individual we would find, no doubt, that scores of different experiences had played their part, and it would probably be equally evident that hundreds of other experiences continue to contribute to the reinforcement and maintenance of the pattern.

It may be that certain types of experience are especially powerful agents in conditioning the individual to respond selectively to homosexual stimuli. One must be extremely cautious, however, about accepting a single cause (or a small number of interrelated causes) for the acquirement of homosexual preferences in the case of each and every individual. Because it is very likely that these differ widely in different people, the best that we may do is to specify the process that brings about a pattern of homosexual preferences. The same, of course, must be said of all other patterns of sexual preference, for they all originate in the same psychological process.

It is appropriate to conclude this chapter with a summary from Kinsey *et al.*:

> The inherent physiological capacity of an animal to respond to any sufficient stimulus seems, then, the basic explanation of the fact that some individuals respond to stimuli originating in other individuals

of their own sex—and it appears to indicate that every individual could so respond if the opportunity offered and one were not conditioned against making such responses. There is no need of hypothesizing peculiar hormonal factors that make certain individuals especially liable to engage in homosexual activity, and we know of no data which prove the existence of such hormonal factors. There are no sufficient data to show that specific hereditary factors are involved. Theories of childhood attachments to one or the other parent, theories of fixation at some infantile level of sexual development, interpretations of homosexuality as neurotic or psychopathic behavior or moral degeneracy, and other philosophic interpretations are not supported by scientific research, and are contrary to the specific data on our series of female and male histories. The data indicate that the factors leading to homosexual behavior are: (1) the basic physiologic capacity of every mammal to respond to any sufficient stimulus; (2) the accident which leads an individual into his or her first sexual experience with a person of the same sex; (3) the conditioning effects of such experience; and (4) the indirect but powerful conditioning which the opinions of other persons and the social codes may have on an individual's decision to accept or reject this type of sexual contact.[54]

VII

Homosexuality in a Sex-Positive Environment

Since the balance of this book will be concerned with the many problems that homosexuality occasions both for the individual and the group within our homoerotophobic culture, and since many of the circumstances associated with homosexuality in our culture present a rather sordid and even brutal picture, it was felt necessary that the reader should have the opportunity of learning something about homosexuality within a more homoerotophilic environment as well. Either Chinese or Japanese culture would have provided an example, or we could have dwelt in more detail upon one of the more homoerotophilic primitive groups. But, for several reasons, we have chosen the ancient Greeks and Romans for such an example instead. First of all, there is a greater wealth of material more readily available concerning homosexuality among these peoples. Second, it was felt that, being direct ancestors, they are less remote to the modern Westerner than perhaps even the contemporary Easterner. Third, by studying the ancient Greeks and Romans we may round out the background of our own attitudes toward homosexuality in the West today. If, in rehearsing the subject of Greek and Roman homosexuality, we offend such scholars as Clifford Allen (who thinks that this subject has been discussed "ad nauseam") we may only apologize and hope that they will find something new and useful in this account. If not they may skip this chapter and go on to the next.

The Greeks bequeathed to us the fundamentals of rational thought and hence the fundamentals of ethical living. Nowhere did they apply their penchant for rational thought and ethical living more clearly than in the area of homosexual love. Nowhere are such values more to be sought today.

It has been suggested that the Greek attitude toward homosexuality was rooted in their concept of *Hedone*. Hedone is translated and defined by Licht as "the cheerful enjoyment of life, especially of the joys of love." [59]

It is a great tragedy that no people in the Western world other than the Greeks themselves have ever succeeded in grasping the full significance of philosophical hedonism. The Romans, for example, misinterpreted this concept and degraded it into a mere rationalization for debauchery. It has been interpreted similarly in modern times, and teachers of the Judaeo-Christian ethos condemn hedonism as a philosophy which justifies unbridled lust and vice. It would appear that the human intellect can only very imperfectly and only very briefly make the distinction between ethical hedonism and amoral self-indulgence. In our own culture we have come to believe that morality consists almost exclusively of sexual renunciation, and even of inhibition of the appetitive drives. But the pre-Christian attitude, and particularly the Greek attitude, was almost completely at variance with this.

The extent to which the Greek approach to life and love differed from ours may be realized when it is remembered that according to Judaeo-Christian belief life is a "vale of tears," a mere interval in an infinite existence during which the individual is to determine by his will and actions whether his post-mortem fate will be that of eternal bliss or eternal damnation. Earthly existence, pictured in these terms, is a period of trial terminating in a colossal and superhuman Judgment. In such an atmosphere the sensuous aspects of life take on a satanic lure and are charged with dangerous implications. One's chief moral task becomes that of spurning all things sensual and repenting when one has "fallen into the ways of the flesh." The joys that accompany the satisfaction of the appetitive drives are disparaged as human frailties or even condemned outright as vices or sins.

This orientation to the life of the senses often deteriorates into frank puritanism. One journalist, writing in a satirical vein, defined a Puritan in the following terms: A Puritan is a person who lives in mortal fear that someone, somewhere, somehow may experience a moment's pleasure.

In contrast to us, the ancient Greeks placed an enormous stress upon the value of pleasure and the righteousness of joy. To live the good life meant to dwell within the bounds of rational pleasure. Such concepts as moderation and the golden mean were valued only because excess leads to pain. The ancients saw no virtue in renunciation for its own sake. Were it possible to sustain the most heightened pleasures indefinitely, they would have found nothing immoral in doing so. For them there was no antagonism between that which is good and that which is sensual, any more than between that which is sensual and that which is rational. Indeed, the aim of most Greek ethical philosophy was to rationalize the life of the senses with the express purpose of achieving and maintaining pleasure in this world. Beauty was an object of desire; pleasure an inspired goal of life. They knew little of any other world and had only the most shadowy notion of any other life. They were concerned with the improvement of the only world they knew and with the enjoyment of a life that was the only one which had substance for them. To heighten the intensity of this life in a world they loved implied, they thought, the cultivation of three branches of philosophy: ethics, logic, and aesthetics. They were always concerned with the good, the true, and the beautiful; this concern was evident in their attitudes toward the life of the senses.

This orientation helps to explain many features of Greek life, including, of course, the Greek attitude toward sex. Since all things capable of affording pleasure or associated with pleasure were admired and sought after by the Greeks, youth was ever a source of delight, and the decay of human beauty through old age or death was horrible to them. They almost always blamed the aged and only seldom the young. Youthful beauty and zest were a cause of forgiveness for almost anything. Yet their passion for youth did not rob them of the capacity to admire and to be guided by wisdom when it appeared in the old.

Wine and other liquors were indulged in to the point of intoxication because under the influence of wine the joy of living is intensified. They would have regarded the prohibition of alcohol as ignorant and barbaric. No people were more given to Dionysiac festivals and revelries, but we never hear of habitual drunkenness or neurotic alcoholism among the Greeks as we do among the Romans and later Judaeo-Christians.

They enjoyed wealth and luxury with an unhypocritical candor which is refreshing to remember after witnessing the overweening materialistic greed of modern men who espouse a philosophy that extols the virtues of poverty and the evils of luxury. If they were gifted with personal beauty the Greeks took joy in the fact without feeling any pressing need to affect false modesty; they did everything they could to enhance whatever elements of personal beauty they possessed. Cultivation of the body and development of athletic grace were essential components of a Greek education along with the cultivation of mental agility, artistic taste, and the use of logic. They took pride in their beautiful language. No educational measure was spared to ensure that the growing youth learn to speak his native language with eloquence and clarity. Poetry, drama, sculpture, music, architecture, and the other arts, as well as philosophy, were admired and cultivated with results that have placed the Greeks foremost among the aesthetic and intellectual innovators of world history.

A song is left us by the Greeks that conveys very well the flavor of their ethos of Hedone. "Best for mortal man is health; second best, charming personal beauty; third, wealth obtained without fraud; fourth, to be young amongst one's friends."

This little song expresses an affirmative approach to life that is simple, honest, and eloquent. It is interesting to note how this view contradicts fundamental tenets of our own moral tradition that, characteristically, are stated in negatives.

Not least among the pleasures of life to which the Greeks paid homage were those of a directly erotic order. They celebrated the joys of physical and spiritual love in both word and deed. These were a source of inspiration to philosophers no less than to writers, poets, and artists. In an atmosphere in which the legitimacy of the sexual drive was recognized, its varied manifestations were valued, and love was not limited by consideration of gender. The greatest and most renowned Greeks, along with the most modest, spoke openly of their love of women and of men without the shame and guilt that we have come to learn. It would not have occurred to them to suppress joy in an object of erotic desire. Indeed, as Sigmund Freud noted in the extraordinary observation quoted below, the erotic factor in a relationship, according to the ancients, would have only served to enhance rather than to degrade the nature of that relationship. To the ancients and especially to the Greeks, sexual passion was regarded as an ennobling experience.

> The most pronounced difference between the love life of antiquity and ours lies in the fact that the ancients placed the emphasis on the instinct itself, while we put it on its object. The ancients extolled the instinct and were ready to ennoble through it even an inferior object, while we disparage the activity of the instinct as such and only countenance it on account of the merits of the object.[28]

With this view of sex it would have been impossible to disparage homosexual passion or to put any manifestation of sexual passion on an inferior plane. The number of celebrated homosexual love affairs among the Greeks is legion. Socrates, for example, attracted to himself the flower of Athenian youth. Plato was the lover—and not merely a "Platonic" one—of Alexis. For three generations, the position of head of the Platonic Academy passed from lover to beloved; Xenocrates loved Polemon, Polemon loved Crates, and Crates loved Arcesilaus. But these loves were not, as some have imagined, limited to followers of the Platonic school of philosophy. Aristotle was the lover of his pupil, Hermias, whose virtues the great philosopher celebrated in a famous hymn. Everywhere among the elite of Greek culture we find these loves. Euripides the tragic dramatist was the lover of Agathon; Phidias the sculptor, was the lover of Agorocritus of Paros; Themedon the physician, was the lover of the astronomer Eudoxus of Cnidus.

So much a part of Greek culture were these loves that they were attributed to the gods themselves. Zeus is supposed to have loved the boy Ganymede whose beauty is said to have moved the celestial patriarch to rape. The love of the god Heracles for Iolanus was celebrated in Thebes in a yearly festival, the Iolaeia, consisting of gymnastic and equestrian games. At Sparta a festival was celebrated yearly in honor of Hyacinthus, the beautiful youth loved by Apollo. All of the most important male deities are paired off with youths of exceptional quality of whom they were supposed to be the lovers.

It was argued by many of the more idealistic scholars of the last century that these masculine love affairs of which we hear in antiquity seldom or never involved overt sexual contact. Some scholars have defended the chastity of Greek and Roman homosexual love affairs by pointing to the philosophy of Plato in which spiritual, nonphysical love is accorded a higher status than sensual love. This, in all events, is the meaning that has become attached to "Platonic love."

It is doubtful, however, if "Greek love" was ever very often "platonic" or if the ancients themselves ever expected that it should be. While homosexual affairs were highly idealized, and while these affairs were regarded with an air of seriousness rather than with an air of levity and were utilized in the interests of the common good of the community, it would not have occurred to most ancient Greeks that physical love and sexual union could in any way render a relationship base or inferior. The hedonistic orientation to life was too well developed among the Greeks for such an idea to flourish. The notion that sexual feeling may debase a relationship is more peculiarly Judaeo-Christian. The Greeks, it appears, recognized that for a relationship to be superior it is necessary that other values, in addition to erotic values, be present, but not that the absence of sexual feeling makes for a superior relationship.

Few scholars today imagine that homosexual friendships among the ancients, even in the case of the loftiest intellectuals, were devoid of libidinous content, or that these friendships did not involve overt sexual relations in a vast majority of instances. The sexual nature of "Greek love" may be easily detected in the poetry to which it gave rise. Moreover, we are in possession of a great deal of other information which clearly reveals a physical component in this love. Xenophon, for example, frankly states that love between a man and youth was considered entirely as a conjugal union. Other contemporary accounts confirm Xenophon.

The Greeks, and it seems most of the other ancient peoples of the Mediterranean Basin and the Near East, were susceptible to youthful masculine sexual attractiveness even on a more casual basis than that involved in extended affairs. We know, for example, that houses of male prostitution flourished and were recognized by the state to an extent in which they were taxed. Everywhere in antiquity, and especially in the Hellenized areas, homosexual arousal was accepted as an ordinary part of life. No major culture of antiquity, unless it be the culture of the Hebrews, had completely succeeded in resisting the open acceptance of "paederastia." It should be remembered by those who adhere to the theory that homosexuality was a cause for the decline and fall of the Roman Empire that paederastia flourished during the apex rather than during the nadir of ancient civilizations. On the other hand, this fact does not afford irrefutable proof that the acceptance of homosexuality is always associated with the "golden age" of a culture.

The history of Greek homosexuality must certainly go back as far as the Cretan period, which is to say that the history of Greek homosexual love is as old as the Greeks themselves. Like the Egyptians, they attributed homosexual propensities to the gods in their myths. Such an attribution usually indicates one or both of two things: Either the practice assigned to the gods is very ancient among the people themselves, and/or the practice is regarded in high esteem. It is, therefore, rather gratuitous to imagine, as some scholars have, that homosexual love was unknown or repudiated by the Greeks of the Homeric era. Westermarck (1906) wrote, "No reference is made to paederasty either in the Homeric poems or by Hesiod, but later on we meet with it almost as a national institution in Greece." [79]

Hans Licht does not agree, and provides sufficient evidence for his view:

> The first beginnings of the Greek love of boys are lost in prehistoric times, even in the darkness of Greek mythology, which is completely saturated with stories of paedophilia. The Greeks themselves transfer the beginnings to the oldest times of their legendary history. The assertion, often naïvely made, that in the Homeric poems there is as yet no trace of the love of boys to be met with, and that it was a phenomenon which first appeared during the so-called decadence is, in my opinion, false, for I have already shown . . . that the bond of friendship between Achilles and Patroclus . . . however ideal it was, yet contains a high percentage of homoerotic sentiment and action; that the Homeric epos also abounds in undoubted traces of ephebophilia [erotic attraction to strong young men], and that no one in the ancient times of Greece ever supposed otherwise.[59]

The wrath of Achilles upon the people who slew the beloved Patroclus was bitterly cruel. Twelve noble youths of Troy were offered in sacrifice before the funeral pyre of Patroclus. Hector, who killed Patroclus, was slain by the half-crazed Achilles. It is a highly significant touch on Homer's part that when Priam, the aged father of Hector, comes to claim the body of his son, he is represented in the *Iliad* as pausing to gaze upon and admire the beauty of the youth who has killed his son. This detail prompted one scholar to observe:

We must accordingly form a higher idea of the beauty of Achilles than the charms of Helen; for Priam, on whom the most unspeakable sorrow has been inflicted by the former, admires it and is able to be surprised at it, at the very moment when he is begging for the dead body of his son. (Gerlach; quoted by Licht.)

Nor is the Odyssey without its allusions to homosexual relationships:

It is clear from the Odyssey . . . that, after the death of Patroclus, Antilochus took his place with Achilles, meaning, of course, that Homer is unable to imagine the chief hero of his poem without a favorite. From this passage we further learn that Achilles, Patroclus, and Antilochus were buried in a common grave, as the three were often named together in life.[59]

Proof that Homer was acquainted with homosexuality may be seen also in his reference to the rape of Ganymede by Zeus. The boy is expressly described as having been of beautiful figure. Homer also knew of an extensive trade in boys, some of whom were bought by Phoenician sailors or were carried off to fill the harems of pashas. At the reconciliation of Agamemnon and Achilles, Agamemnon offers Achilles several noble youths as gifts of honor.

Thus homosexual love affairs are prominent even during the earliest period of Greek history, and we know a good deal about the physical side of Greek homosexuality as well. According to Licht, "How the exercise of its sensual functions was handed down to posterity by formal documents is sufficiently shown in the rock inscriptions of the island of Thera—the modern Santorin—in the Cyclades." [59]

Licht points to the fact that in the Greek language the words "paederasty" and "paederast" did not convey the defamatory meanings attached to them today in modern European languages. There were, however, words in ancient Greek which did convey a defamatory meaning, such as those words that may be translated to mean "one who stares at or spies after boys," or "one who has a frenzied, uncontrolled passion for boys." On the other hand, an expression that may be translated "one who especially loves beautiful boys" had a laudatory meaning and was bestowed upon Sophocles in Athens as a title of honor. There were also terms which referred to the beloved youth (or "listener," as he was called) and to the lover (or "inspirer"). These were more serious terms. But common parlance also included terms such as "lamb" or "kid" for the beloved, and "wolf" for the lover. In an epigram, the poet Straton wrote:

Going out in revel after supper, I, the wolf, found a lamb standing at the door, the son of my neighbor, Aristodicus, and throwing my arms around him I kissed him to my heart's content, promising on my oaths many gifts.[59]

As in our own society, very young children were shielded from the sexual advances of adults by legal restrictions that certain naïve scholars have interpreted as evidence that the Greeks condemned all types of overt homosexual contact. This protection, however, did not extend beyond the arrival of puberty, except in the case of violence or outright rape. Marrou suggests that the Greeks considered the ideal age for the "listener" was between fifteen and nineteen. Regarding the question of age, a contemporary, Straton, makes the following observations:

> The youthful bloom of the twelve year old boy gives me joy, but much more desirable is the boy of thirteen. [He who has arrived at puberty.] He whose years are fourteen is a still sweeter flower of the Loves, and even more charming is he who is beginning his fifteenth year. The sixteenth year is that of the gods, and to desire the seventeenth does not fall to my lot, but only to Zeus. But if one longs for one still older, he no longer plays, but already demands the Homeric "but to him replied." [59]

The Homeric "but to him replied" refers to the demand for the return of love. This is a particularly informative item since it tends to suggest that amorous relationships with boys from twelve to seventeen years old were regarded as playful and less serious, while those with young men from eighteen years on implied a more serious attachment in which reciprocity was expected. Admiration of beauty in a very young boy, however, was a common response. We hear a great deal in Greek literature about "beardless boys" with only the first down of the beard upon the chin. Aristophanes, the great comic dramatist, also praises Greek boys in the same manner, but the down he speaks of in his humorous obscenity is not the down of the cheeks and lips.

Homosexual love, or "paederastia" as the ancients called it, was not merely a form of erotic outlet to be enjoyed without responsibility. It played an important role in several aspects of Greek life and culture. Its effects may be seen in the educational system of the Greeks; in the development of Greek patriotism, military valor, and "esprit de corps"; in Greek aesthetic and ethical philosophy; and in certain aspects of the Greek religion. It may be observed that, although homosexuality was practiced among all of the ancients with a freedom unknown in modern times anywhere in the West, it was mainly among the Greeks that this type of erotic relationship became spiritualized and was put in the service of civilized objectives. "Greek love" became a model for homosexual love throughout the rest of the ancient world. When this model perished under the impact of Christianity, homosexuality was stripped of all cultural significance and became a perversion quite beyond the pale of acceptable social living. As such it has failed, except in the most indirect way, to make any substantial contribution to civilization in modern times. Those who become involved in it do so at their own risk and often at their own loss, rather than discovering a means for the enrichment of life. It is pitiable that so substantial a part of the human erotic tendency should be shunted into social oblivion where it becomes devoid of all cultural significance and social value.

It is from a passage in Strato that we learn of the early form which paederastia assumed. In Crete the young man, "eromenos," was virtually abducted by his older lover with the connivance of those around them. The eromenos was introduced into the "men's club" by his abductor. Then the two, along with their friends, left for a two months' holiday in the country, where they celebrated their "honeymoon," as it were, with banquets and hunting. On return from this sojourn they were feted with solemn ritual. The eromenos received from his lover, among other gifts, a suit of armor and henceforth became the older man's shield-bearer. By these solemnities the youth was accepted in the "Order of Illustrious Men." He could then participate in the life of an adult nobleman and was given a place of honor in the choirs and gymnasia.

All of this suggests that homosexual love became a means of recruitment to an aristocratic military brotherhood early in Greek history. But this should not be taken to mean that homosexual relationships did not exist apart from this context, nor that these relationships did not survive the period of Greek military aspirations. Marrou points out that, apart from its origins, the practice of paederastia persisted as an integral part of Hellenic civilization even after the Greeks had abandoned their military way of life. It is in the context of a militaristic brotherhood, however, that the formal elements of paederastia seemed to originate.

Living at a period in history not unlike our own, when personal combat was necessary both for defense and for national expansion, attributes of physical bravery and valor were highly prized by the Greeks, and they repeatedly asserted that the outstanding development of these traits among them was due to homosexual attachments. Paederastia, they insisted, was essential to character development and was always associated not with weakness, effeminacy, and cowardice, as in our culture, but with patriotism, bravery, and manly virtue. According to Athenaeus, the Greeks "were convinced that in the comradeship of a pair of friends fighting side by side lay safety and victory." Plato points to the military advantage derived from such attachments. It was held in the Socratic circle that the most formidable army would be one composed of pairs of lovers, each inspiring the others to deeds of heroism and self-sacrifice. This ideal was realized in the elite corps formed by Gorgidas which Pelopidas made into a "sacred band." Aelian said that one who loves in battle is inspired by two gods, Ares and Eros, but he who does not love in battle is inspired only by Ares. Plutarch mentioned that when a young soldier uttered a painful cry in battle the lover of the boy was punished by the State, presumably because the older man had failed in his educative duty toward the boy. "Even of the ideal of Greek heroic might, of Hercules, it is related that his mighty deeds became easier when he carried them out before the eyes of his beloved, Iolanus . . ."

Licht quotes a later commentator, Theodor Däubler (1923), who affirmed the importance of homosexual love among the Greeks for us, as their cultural progeny:

> Anyone who is unable to regard the love of the Hellene for boys, or Sappho's inclination for her own sex, as something elevated and sacred, denies it in the face of Greece. We are more indebted to their heroic lovers than to mankind's most glorious art for Europe's freedom and the complete destruction of the Persian despotism in face of the diversity of the natural impulses in man . . . Any attack on the love of boys in Sparta's prime would have acted with destructive effect, would have been considered unwholesome, and as a betrayal of the people.[59]

Apparently, until the time of the great lawgiver Solon—himself much given to homosexual inclinations—there were no major statutes which dealt with this issue. Solon promulgated a legal code that, among other things, included several items dealing with the regulation of homosexual relationships. A slave was not allowed to enter into a homosexual relationship with a free-born boy. Free-born youths were not available for erotic contact during the prepubertal period although, interestingly, this statute does not protect the prepubertal slave boy. Still another law deprived those of their civic rights who incited free-born boys—once again not slave boys—to the practice of prostitution.

These laws are typical of the laws dealing with homosexuality that we find throughout antiquity, and virtually never are other types of homosexual contact forbidden. But modest as they were, these laws were seldom enforced, and could hardly have been so. It must be noted, in the first place, that they affected only free-born boys, and only Athenians possessing full citizenship. The great mass of "Xenoi," that is, non-Athenian immigrants, had complete freedom in these matters. The adult Athenian citizen had complete freedom in these matters with all but free-born Athenian boys.

These laws, such as they were, soon became a dead letter. Even the free-born boys could, if they wished—and many apparently did—sell their erotic favors. By claiming that erotic acts were carried out with affection, and that their gains were merely gifts from the supposed lover, these youths could escape the charge of prostitution.

Outright male prostitution, like female prostitution, abounded in Greece and in most other parts of the ancient world. In Athens and other harbor towns, there were brothels in which boys and young men were available either alone or with girls. Hire of boys also existed by contract for longer periods of time. Sometimes boys were hired out in this fashion to entertain at social gatherings, and sometimes they were hired out to be at the disposal of the client alone. Often the inmates of male brothels were young boys who had been taken as prisoners of war and sold into slavery. But often enough they were free youths who entered the profession voluntarily. These boys— especially those hired out on contract to entertain at parties and festivals —were required to meet with high standards of proficiency not only as sexual partners but also as musicians and entertainers.

The Greek attitude toward male prostitution was somewhat ambivalent. On the one hand, these houses were surely well patronized, and the patron never felt that *he* was particularly an object for scorn, as in the case of modern males who consort with female prostitutes. The Greeks did not, however, have unreserved admiration for the boy prostitutes, because they regarded homosexuality not merely in terms of physical passion, but also in terms of love. The type of homosexual relationship which they most admired included elements of sentiment and idealism. It was a relationship to be entered into freely and one that involved mutual responsibilities of an uncommercial kind. There are many complaints within Greek literature on the part of lovers who found that their favorites expected money and handsome presents. One such follows from the poet Straton:

> Woe is me! Why in tears again and so woe-begone, my lad? Tell me plainly; I want to know; what is the matter? You hold out the hollow of your hand again to me. I am done for! You are begging perhaps for payment; and where did you learn that? You no longer love slices of seed-cake and sweet sesame and nuts to play at shot with, but already your mind is set on gain. May he who taught you perish! What a boy of mine he has spoilt! [59]

Some writers, in the face of the most substantial evidence to the contrary, have insisted that homosexuality among the ancients was an entirely aristocratic phenomenon confined to the upper-class intellectuals, and that even within this group it was wholly "platonic" in character. Such conclusions can be based only upon ignorance of the available data on the one hand or, on the other hand, upon the belief that homosexuality is so "abnormal" that it could never have become a part of the behavior of any large segment of the population (the same sort of reasoning that has made some people doubt Kinsey's statistics on male homosexuality within our own culture). But we have no reason at all to doubt the overt homosexuality of the Greeks because, unlike us, they never made the slightest effort to hide it. And moreover, we know that homosexual interests were manifest at all social levels in ancient civilization. A few examples of this follow.

The renowned Greek sculptor Phidias inscribed "beautiful Pantarkes" (the name of his favorite) on his mighty statue of Zeus at Olympia. This may not be particularly surprising to a modern Westerner in the case of an artist and intellectual who, we suppose, might be different from other men.

We are apt to make some allowance for what we regard as the eccentricities of artists. But a brick is preserved from ancient Greece upon which, in like fashion, a workman inscribed, "Hippus is beautiful! So it seems to Aristomedes." That a common workman would confess his response to the beauty of a boy is much more difficult for the modern mind to grasp or accept.

The inscription "beautiful boy" occurs on a great number of articles from antiquity. Licht says, "The word beautiful is sometimes found alone, more frequently in the form 'the boy is beautiful' or combined with a name as an inscription on Greek vessels; also on columns, shields, basins, footstools, pillars, altars, chests, bags, discus rims, and a large number of other objects." [59]

The habit of writing or etching the name of a loved one is characteristically masculine. Wall inscriptions and other *graffiti* are common in our own culture. But it is not common for females to make such inscriptions.[54] We must therefore, assume, even if we had no other evidence for doing so, that the inscriptions made on various objects were addressed by one male to anotner. In most cases there is no reason to doubt this as the names of both parties are mentioned.

Nor, as we have been told, was homosexuality peculiar to the aristocracy and the intelligentsia in Rome. The greatest of Roman poets, Virgil, did not think it would strain the credulity of his readers when, in his second Eclogue (which is a homosexual love poem), he pictured a common shepherd, Corydon, as passionately enamored of a boy. Corydon is probably Virgil himself, and the boy in the poem, Alexis, is probably Virgil's favorite. The poet did not hesitate in portraying himself as a shepherd in love with a youth. He had no fear that this would appear ridiculous to his contemporaries. In the end the young shepherd consoles himself over the rejection he receives from Alexis.

> Corydon, Corydon, what is this madness that has got you down? You have left your vines half pruned, and the elms they grow on thick with leaves. Rather than this, why not get busy on a useful piece of work and plait a basket with some osier-twigs or pliant reeds? If this Alexis treats you with contempt, you'll find another.

It is, apparently, quite feasible to the shepherd boy that he will experience this passion again with another young man.

There is other evidence that homosexual relationships occurred among lower-class Romans as, undoubtedly, they did among lower-class Greeks. Kiefer (1934) suggests, for example, that the murder of the prefect Pedonius Secundus by his slave was a "crime passionnel" in which the slave killed his master "because he was in love with a youth and could not bear to be supplanted by his master." [52]

The part played by homosexual love in the Greek educational system during classical times is of the utmost importance not only for an understanding of Greek culture, but also because of the indirect effects which it had upon Roman education and upon education in later Christian times. The role of paederastia is stressed by H. I. Marrou.

> For the Greeks, education . . . meant, essentially, a profound and intimate relationship, a personal union between a young man and an elder who was at once his model, his guide and his initiator—a relationship on to which the fire of passion threw warm and turbid reflections.
> Public opinion—and, in Sparta, the law—held the lover morally responsible for the development of his beloved. Paederasty was considered the most beautiful, the perfect form of education . . . Throughout Greek history the relation between master and pupil was to remain that between a lover and his beloved: education remained in principle not so much a form of teaching, an instruction in techniques, as an expenditure of loving effort by an elder concerned to promote the growth of a younger man who was burning with the desire to respond to this love and show himself worthy of it.

This love provided classical education with its material conditions as well as its methods. These relationships were always between an older and a younger male with at least as much difference in age as that between an elder and a younger brother. The lover (erastes) admired the beloved (eromenos) for his beauty; if not the beauty of his body then at least the beauty of his soul. He wished to gain the affection of the boy and shine before him as a hero and mentor. (How often these relationships continue to exist in our own times between younger males of slightly different ages, although the directly sexual component tends to be minimized in our culture.) The younger boy, for his part, regarded his hero as a model to whose exalted level he aspired.

Other peoples besides the Greeks have recognized the importance of the erotic factor in education, and among them are some of the most highly civilized and cultivated peoples of history. The Chinese, for example, fostered a system of cultural initiation in which homosexual relations were encouraged between master and disciple, as well as between disciples of the same master. Our technologically obsessed civilization, however, in which so many particular skills must be imparted, and in which our democratic fervor inclines us to believe that everyone is educable rather than merely trainable, hardly enables us to provide cultural initiation on a one-to-one basis.

Roman education, like our own, was carried out in classes conducted by an instructor who had very little emotional contact with his several pupils. But the aim of Roman education and its results were different from the aim and results of Greek education. The Romans were little concerned with philosophy, which they regarded as a rather dangerous activity from the point of view of conformity to the State. Their object was to train students in what they regarded as the "practical" areas of learning. A few wealthy Romans enjoyed a Greek education, but they were not necessarily considered the most valuable citizens by the State. Periodically the teaching of Greek philosophy was forbidden in Rome.

The course pursued in history by the Romans was altogether different from that pursued by the Greeks, and the differences between the Roman and Greek attitudes toward sex, which will be discussed briefly later, are related to fundamental differences in the Roman and Greek character and mentality. It is the Roman rather than the Greek educational system that we must blame for some of the calamities of our own educational system.

The type of relationship among the Greeks which we have been describing was fostered by a combination of forces that are hardly duplicated in our own society. The center of Greek life for the male was the community, not the home. The adult Greek male was first and foremost a citizen and only secondarily a husband or father. In a democratic community like that of the ancient Greeks every free man was expected to participate in the political life of his nation. The Greek male contributed to the political decisions of the State. He also contributed a substantial portion of his life to defending that State as a soldier. Most of his life was spent outdoors: in the agora, in the palaestra, in the military camp. And most of his associations were with other men. He was apt to meet with women only at home.

The family could not be the educational center. The wife was devoted to the home and to the rearing of the smaller children. She took care of the babies, but when the male child was seven he was taken out of her hands. The Greek father, unlike the Roman father, was no great patriarch; most family decisions were made by the mother.

This removal of the child from the home and from the father and mother at so early an age encouraged the Greek to regard his nation as his family, and perhaps it also freed the Greek from the narrower interests of a family-oriented psychology. It was always public rather than private life that interested the Greek male. As a very young boy he lived with other boys at the palaestra. Thus, paederastia not only provided a basis for the education of the boy, it also gave the boy the close personal tie with an older person that he otherwise lacked.

All of this might appear quite horrible to the Jewish and Christian reader whose ethos is rooted in the sanctity of the family. But it must be remembered that under this system the Greeks were able to develop a culture that in many respects has hardly ever been paralleled for profundity, variety, and originality. They were able to recognize and define ethical and aesthetic values that are still cherished by us today. Under this system they developed the concept of democracy, they made the first substantial contributions to science and to philosophy, and they excelled in the major arts. They were, moreover, an admirably healthy, happy, and constructive people. There is relatively little that requires an apology in Greek culture, and while it was far short of perfection and lacked completeness, particularly in its attitude toward women, Greek culture can compare very favorably with the best that we have to offer.

Particularly was it a culture in which robust physical and mental health seemed to thrive. Sanity seemed to characterize the Greek mentality. At home in the intellectual, the sensual, and the spiritual aspects of life, the Greek was able to draw upon the deepest resources of his mind. He was little inhibited by many of the less admirable psychological traits that we find among the ancient Hebrews and Romans—traits such as rigidity, compulsivity, authoritarianism, excessive shame, doubt, guilt, and the like. The Greeks were surprisingly free of many of the neurotic traits and psychological ills that are to be found among the Romans and among modern Judaeo-Christians. There was, for example, little evidence of alcoholism among the Greeks. Brutality, cruelty, and debauchery seemed to play little part in their character. Juvenile delinquency and adult criminality were rare among the Greeks. Their attitude toward sex was explorative, permissive, and fundamentally naturalistic in contrast to that of the Romans whose original rigidity and moralism soon gave way, under the impact of imperial grandeur, to a morbid exhibition of sexual eccentricity and sadism.

The relative lack of serious psychopathology among the Greeks is all the more remarkable when it is realized that, according to our beliefs, "perversion," in the form of homosexuality, played so large a part in the life of both the Greek male and the Greek female.

The passionate nature of "Greek love" may be detected, along with its spiritual intensity, in much of the poetry to which it gave rise. Virtually every Greek poet of any fame has left us with examples of homoerotic poetry. The few examples that follow are drawn from an extended period in ancient history. They are chosen more for the insight they give into the nature of Greek homosexuality than for their value as poetry, although some of them are admired as among the best lyrical poetry in world literature. In each case, the following poetical quotations are from Hans Licht.[59]

We begin with what seems to be a letter written by Philostratus, accompanied by a gift of flowers. This note is of interest because it sheds some light on what a courtship between man and boy was like. In this instance there is a note of tenderness that would be appropriate if the writer were addressing a girl. This poem and others that follow resemble the romantic poetry inspired by heterosexual love; many of the same themes, images, and sentiments are expressed in both.

> These roses desire with longing to come to you and their leaves as wings carry them to you. Receive them kindly as a memorial to

Adonis, or as the purple blood of Aphrodite, or as the choicest of fruits of the earth. The crown of olives adorns the athlete, the towering tiara the great king, the helmet a warrior; but the rose is the ornament of a beautiful boy, since it resembles him in fragrance and in color. It is not you who will adorn yourself with roses, but the roses themselves with you.

On another occasion the poet sent flowers, presumably to the same youth, with the following brief note:

I have sent you a crown of roses, not (or at least not exclusively) to give you pleasure, but out of affection for the roses themselves, that they may not fade.

Aside from the well-known discourse on love in his *Symposium,* the great philosopher Plato left several epigrams addressed to boys. One, written to his favorite, Dion, declared that he "filled the heart with the madness of love." Another was written to a boy of unusual beauty whose name was Aster, which in Greek means star. The poet plays upon the name of the beloved and declares that he envies the sky, which looks down upon Aster with many eyes when he, himself a star, looks up at the stars. In another epigram to a different youth, he wrote:

When I kissed you, Agathon, I felt your soul on my lips: as if it would penetrate into my heart with quivering longing.

The poet Ibycus was described by his contemporaries as "the most frenzied lover of boys." In the Palatine Anthology he is referred to as one who did "cull the sweet bloom of Persuasion and of the love of lads." This passion continued to work in him even in the latter part of his long life. Plato commented upon the homosexual propensities of Ibycus. Of himself and his great capacity for love, he wrote:

In spring the quinces, watered by the river streams, bloom in the unspoiled gardens of the maidens; and the first shoots of the vine, guarded beneath shady leaves, grow and blossom; but for me love— that, like the Thracian north wind, blasting beneath the lightning and rushing, dark and fearless, from Cyprus with scorching madness—is never at rest, and holds possession of my mind throughout my life.

Of his favorite boy he wrote:

Euryalus, offshoot of charming graces, object of the fair-haired maiden's care, Cyprus and mild-eyed Persuasion have reared you in the midst of rosy flowers.

The poet Anacreon, described by his friends as "cheerful and amiable," lived to the age of eighty-five. Like Ibycus, he was devoted to love throughout his long life and pursued it in relations with both males and females. His favorite was a Thracian youth named Smerdis, to whom he dedicated many poems. Upon the death of Anacreon, his friend Simonides wrote the following epitaph in which he recalled the poet's attachment to Smerdis:

> Alone in Acheron he grieves not that he has left the sun and dwelleth there in the House of Lethe, but that he has left Migistheus, graceful above all youth, and his passion for Thracian Smerdis.

This prolific poet and versatile lover, Anacreon, penned the following verse, which has had many imitators:

> Oh boy, with a maiden's look, I seek thee, but thou dost not hear, not knowing that thou ridest thy chariot over my heart.

The writer Pindar has been described as the greatest and most powerful of all Greek lyric poets. The story is told that he prayed to the gods to give him the most beautiful thing there was in the world. His favorite, Theoxenus, was the gift. When he became ill during a gymnastic contest in Argos, he sought the comfort of Theoxenus and died in his arms. Among the poetry of Pindar are the following lines expressing his strong feeling for Theoxenus and its sensuous basis:

> Right it were, fond heart, to cull the flower of love in due season, in life's prime; but whoever, when once he hath seen the rays flashing from the eyes of Theoxenus, does not swell with desire, his black heart with its frozen flame is forged of adamant or iron.

In one poem the famous Theocritus chastises his youthful love, accusing him of inconsistency, and reminds the boy of the old age that threatens. This idea suggests a parallel with Shakespeare's sonnets to the unknown young man, "Mr. W. H."

In another passage, Theocritus contrasts his own happiness in love with the unhappiness of a friend, Aratus, a famous physician who had the misfortune of loving and being rejected by a coy youth, Philinus. Theocritus attempts to console Aratus in the following lines that give us a brief picture of the life of the times:

> Yet you, winged hoast of the Loves, with cheeks red as peaches, now hit Philinus with curly hair, awake in him desire for my friend. After all, he is not so young now, already the girls chaff the fool— "Ay, Ay, Philinus, you see your beauty is already gone!" So now take my heartfelt advice. Let the foolish boy run and let some other pretty ones, my dear friend Aratus, feel this deep sorrow.

To console his friend still further Theocritus wrote a longer epic poem describing the intense love of the god Heracles for Hylas. It is not known what eventually transpired between Aratus and Philinus, but it seems that the physician had a difficult lad on his hands.

Meleager wrote often of his love, Myiscus. In typical Greek fashion, he was also known for his many erotic episodes with women. In contrasting the love of women with the love of men he wrote:

> It is Cypris, a woman, who casts at us the fire of passion for women, but Love himself rules over the desire for males. Whither shall I incline, to the boy or to his mother? I tell you for sure that even Cypris herself will say, "The bold brat wins."

In more amorous vein, Meleager wrote the following lines, so clearly expressive of physical passion that it is extremely difficult to know how certain scholars have managed to convince themselves that "Greek love" did not have any libidinous content:

> Love brought to me under my mantle at night the sweet dream of a laughing boy of eighteen, still wearing the chlamys; and I, pressing the tender flesh to my heart, culled empty hopes. Still does the memory of the desire heat me, and in my eyes still abideth sleep that caught for me in the chase that winged phantom. O soul, ill-starred in love, cease at last even in dreams to be warmed all in vain by beauty's images.

Meleager, in still another verse, vents his enthusiasm for the youthful Andragathus who is away at sea.

> The South Wind, blowing fair for sailors, O ye who are sick for love, has carried off Andragathus, my soul's half. Thrice happy the ships, thrice fortunate the waves of the sea, and four times blessed the wind that bears the boy. Would I were a dolphin that, carried on my shoulders, he could cross the seas to look on Rhodes, the home of sweet lads.

A rather charming picture is painted by Asclepiades, a poet of Samos who was the teacher of Theocritus and left eleven epigrams addressed to young men:

> Wine is the proof of love. Nicagoras denied to us that he was in love, but those many toasts convicted him.
> Yes! he shed tears and bent his head, and had a certain downcast look, and the wreath bound tight round his head kept not its place.

Callimachus was one of the greatest epigrammatists of the Alexandrian period. He was a North African who lived about 310–240 B.C. In the following poem he gives frank expression to the inconstancy of his passion:

> It is but the half of my soul that still breathes, and for the other half I know not if it be Love or Death that hath seized on it, only it is gone. Is it off again to one of the lads? And yet I told them often, "Receive not, ye young man, the runaway." Seek for it at . . . for I know that it is somewhere there that the gallows bird, the love-lorn, is loitering.

The quotations above do not by any means exhaust the record of homosexual sentiment in the poetry of the ancients. Even from this scanty sample, the reader may begin to form some impression of the feelings that were involved in paederastia. One can hardly escape the implication that the Greeks were moved in a deeply sensual way by young males of comely appearance. At the same time, they were able to idealize and to poetize their response without compromising its physical basis. They dwelt upon the somatic characteristics of the beloved and proved one of their firmest beliefs: *Love arises out of the longing for beauty.* This hedonistic precept is of great importance for an understanding of the Greek attitude toward love. Love was fundamentally an aesthetic experience, though in no way divorced from libidinous interests. Once homosexual love had arisen it was used in the interests of education and other social goals. But one should never forget that it began as a somatic reaction fully reconciled with a hedonistic point of reference.

The celebration of homosexual love was represented in the plastic arts of the Greeks as well as in their prose and poetry. The ancient ideal of beauty was personified in the male body. "Fair hair, black flashing eyes, ruddy complexion, tight sinews, and broad shoulders" are catalogued as marks of manly beauty by one contemporary. This insistence upon the superiority of masculine beauty represents one of the most fundamental differences between ancient and modern European culture. In modern European culture the aesthetic ideal is feminine.

The poet Straton gave frank expression to the ancient preference for beauty in the male when he confessed, "I am not charmed by long hair or by needless ringlets taught rather in the school of Art than of Nature, but by the dusty grime of a boy fresh from the playground, and by the color given to his limbs by the gloss of oil. My love is sweetest when unadorned, but an artificial beauty has in it the work of a female Cypris."

In addition to education, literature, and the plastic arts, paederastia played a part in Greek religion and public festivals.

Hermes was the patron god of boys. In every palaestra and gymnasium there was an image of the youthful god which boys kept crowned with evergreen, hyacinths, and wreaths of violets. Feasts involving homosexual acts were dedicated to Hermes and celebrated by the youths in the gymnasia. A law, apparently never very successfully enforced, stated that "the owners of gymnasia shall not allow anyone beyond the age of boys to sneak in with them at the feasts of Hermes; otherwise he is to be punished according to the law concerning the violation of the body." The presence of an older man in this environment, which was supposed to be dedicated to the god, was taken to indicate an impious intrusion engaged in for immoral motives. In later times Aeschines, the scholiast, wrote, "In the inner part of the house at schools and palaestrae there were columns and chapels, with altars to the Muses, Hermes, and Heracles. There was also drinking

water there, but many boys under the pretence of drinking came in and
practiced immorality."

Although most ancient Greek festivals accorded prominence to the beauty
of male youth through song, dance, and athletic display, certain festivals
featured this and were, in fact, celebrations in honor of the homosexual
ventures of the gods. Each city seems to have had its own way of celebrat-
ing these occasions. At Megara, the celebration of the Diocleia included
contests between boys and youths in kissing. Prize songs on the love of boys
were sung at Thespiae during the festival of Eros, the god of love. At Sparta
the Gymnopaedia (festival of naked boys) was celebrated, and also the
festival in honor of Hyacinthus, the beautiful youth loved by Apollo, for
whom the flower is named. One of the great festivals, the Iolaeia, was celebrated in Thebes in honor of the love between Heracles and Iolanus. Arms
and brass vessels were awarded as prizes to the victors who took part in
the gymnastic and equestrian games that were part of this festival. A gymnasium and shrine in honor of Iolanus existed in Thebes until compara-
tively late times.

Because Greece is favored by strong sunlight and mild weather during
most of the year, the Greeks were able to practice nudism in these festivals
—for which they were condemned by the Hebrews and Romans. But the
Greeks did not consider display of the nude figure to be reprehensible. In
the palaestrae and gymnasia clothes were never worn by the young athletes,
but only by old men who wished to hide the ugliness that age imposes upon
the human form. After the Romans had transformed their earlier priggish-
ness into voluptuousness and immorality, they became more tolerant of
nudism in their public baths. But they were never altogether certain about
the innocence of the nude body and from time to time imperial decrees
were issued in an attempt to suppress this "Greek habit."

Our account of homosexual love among the Greeks may cause some
readers to form the impression that the Greeks had no interest in heterosexual relationships. This is of course far from true. The Greeks had a
healthy interest in heterosexual love and celebrated this love in some of
their greatest artistic and intellectual achievements. It is incorrect to characterize the Hellenes as a homosexual people, as so many have done. Homosexuality obviously played a much greater part in the life of the average
Greek male and female than it does in the life of the average Judaeo-
Christian male or female. But Greek culture is more appropriately described as bisexual than homosexual. No entire culture is ever really
homosexual, although some cultures are far more bisexual than others. In
spite of the high regard in which paederastia was held in Hellenic culture,
every grown man was expected to marry and beget children. Bachelors
were less well tolerated among the Hellenes than they are among us today.
They were heavily taxed, and the unmarried male adult beyond a certain

age was subject to various other penalties at times. Many traits associated with homosexuality in our culture were no less frowned upon by the Greeks. They ridiculed effeminacy, transvestism, and the like much as we do, with the exception that their ridicule seems to have been far more good-natured than ours and seldom if ever led to the physical violence with which the "sissy" and "faggot" often meet in our culture.

Highly effeminate males—especially those who refused marriage and adopted the passive role as adults in a homosexual relationship—were called "kinaidos." These half-men are an object of comedy in the dramas of Aristophanes and Menander in which they are often given feminine nicknames. There was also a great deal of humorous reference to the amplitude of the posterior of the kinaidos. A favorite reference to them was a word which can only be translated as "broad bummed."

Refinement of taste, interest in the arts and in intellectual matters, and receptivity to homosexual stimuli were not attributes associated with effeminacy among the Greeks. Indeed, these were qualities to which all Greek males aspired. A kinaidos was a male who practiced exclusive homosexuality as an adult and affected feminine behavior, gestures, mannerisms, and sometimes even feminine dress, like the "faggot" of our own culture. The kinaidos painted his face and used other cosmetic devices to imitate the female. Today this type of male is considered a psychological curiosity to the educated few, and an object of coarse ridicule and even physical hostility among the many, especially in Anglo-Saxon and American cultures. In ancient times opprobrium for the kinaidos seems to have been expressed entirely through humorous ridicule.

Homosexuality among the Hellenes very seldom assumed a form that could convincingly be described as perverse. It undoubtedly originated in and was maintained by the material and social conditions described earlier in this chapter and was further encouraged by the hedonistic ethos of the Hellenes. Neither these material and social conditions nor this ethos can be found among the ancient Hebrews, nor among the Europeans after the adoption of Christianity into the Roman Empire. Hans Licht has summarized the ethos that surrounded homosexuality among the Hellenes very well:

> If we are to draw conclusions from what has been said as to the ethics of Greek love of boys, the following emerges as an undeniable fact: The Greek love of boys is a peculiarity of character, based upon an aesthetic and religious foundation. Its object is, with the assistance of the State, to arrive at the power to maintain the same and at the fountain-head of civic and personal virtue. It is not hostile to marriage, but supplements it as an important factor in education. We can also speak of a decided bisexuality among the Greeks.[59]

VIII

The Dissipation of a Sex-Positive Culture

When we turn to the Romans we find a somewhat different picture of homosexuality. Homosexual practices were known and tolerated—indeed, accepted not only among the early Romans but among virtually all of the peoples who inhabited Italy before them, and simultaneously with them. But the Romans, like us, developed no original ethical concept of homosexual love. In the later days of the Republic and throughout the period of the Empire, they did, however, import and adopt the Greek attitude toward this phenomenon, just as they imported and adopted many other elements of Greek philosophy and culture. We know that Greek slaves tutored the offspring of noble Roman houses and that the Greek language, philosophy, and literature were studied by cultivated Romans. A number of outstanding Roman leaders from the earlier days of the Empire to the very end, were passionate grecophiles and did a great deal to emphasize Greek ideas among their subjects.

The Roman adaptation of Greek paederastia, like most of its other adaptations from Greek culture, did not represent the original very faithfully. The Romans had too strong an ethos of their own, and it was almost in complete contradiction to the Greek ideal of Hedone. Consequently, we find homosexual relationships among the Romans, as among their neighbors, but usually of a rather inferior ethical status. More often than not they involved sheer voluptuousness, particularly during the imperial period. Then, especially, sadomasochism also became involved in both heterosexual and homosexual activities. Time and again we hear of sexual activities among the Romans that involved either the exploitation of slaves and other defenseless elements of the population, incomprehensible relationships between equals, or bizarre behavior of one kind or another.

Nero, for example, thought himself so much a Greek in sympathy and culture that he exempted Greece from Roman taxation. His adaptation of Greek paederastia, however, like most Roman adaptations of Hedone, lapsed into psychotic distortion and cruelty. He caused a youth, Sporus, to be castrated, then "married" him in public and declared the boy to be his "Empress." This shows how wide of the mark Nero was from anything resembling the Greek love of boys. While the Greeks were charmed by the masculinity of their favorites and looked upon their passion as an opportunity to better the condition of the beloved, it was necessary for Nero to remove the clearest evidence of masculinity in Sporus, to feminize him and to degrade rather than to elevate him. Such cruel and eccentric acts were not at all uncommon among the Romans, but had virtually no precedent in the history of the Greeks.

The Romans were never hedonists. Only certain Christians who have a distorted notion of what is meant by hedonism imagine otherwise. Roman debauchery was held up to scorn by the Church as a typical example of hedonism. Hedonism is often still misrepresented as the kind of lecherous self-indulgence common among the Romans during their decline. From this the impression has developed that all "pagans" were hedonists, and that all hedonists are sadistic brutes fallen into a state of depravity. But whoever associates Roman decadence with Greek hedonism does so at the expense of reason and fact.

At their philosophical best, the Romans were stoics. No doubt it was their stoicism—certainly not hedonism—that enabled them to conquer and to rule the world. From their earliest days elements of prudery, rigidity, and authoritarianism were apparent in the Roman personality. And it is precisely these qualities in the Roman personality that, under the catalyst of world dominion, gave rise to the lasciviousness, moral corruption, and sadism that thrived among the Romans in later days and was confused by them and by their later critics with hedonism. The Etruscans who antedated the Romans in Italy, represented, in the words of Burgo Partridge, "a half-way house between Greek and Roman civilizations." They approached the Greek ideal of Hedone much more closely than the Romans.

When men who follow a restrictive ethos denying the legitimacy of the life of the senses revolt against this ethos—as, sooner or later, they are bound to do in large numbers—they are apt to adopt, as an alternative to their ascetic tendencies, an attitude toward the life of the senses which is more properly described as voluptuous or licentious than hedonistic. This is really the greatest psychological danger inherent in any fundamentally anti-hedonistic philosophy. This is also the essential difference between the ancient Greek approach to sexual life and the approach to sexual life that we find among the ancient Romans, Hebrews, and Christians. When a man revolts against an anti-hedonistic philosophy, he does not ordinarily become a hedonist. He is much more apt to veer from excessive moralism toward excessive immorality.

It has always been of special interest to this author as a psychologist to observe how some of the most wanton criminals reveal themselves, upon examination, to be deeply entrenched, thinly-disguised moralists of the most benighted order. They are in a desperate revolt against the restrictions that their negative attitude toward the life of the senses places upon them. Many alcoholics, rapists, sadists, drug addicts, compulsive gamblers, "moral degenerates" of every conceivable type, and even murderers are in the most fundamental sense Puritans who despise and fear their own and other people's appetitive drives. Indeed, this author is thoroughly convinced that there is a direct and perhaps even causal relationship between certain types of psychopathology, particularly of the antisocial variety, and morbid moralism. More often than not, the criminal and the so-called moral degenerate, far from being a man without a conscience or a man without moral values, is a man with an exaggerated and unrealistic sense of right and wrong. We most often become aware of his presence when he is in revolt against the superhuman concept of right he harbors within himself. As one example, mention may be made of Jack the Ripper who, like a great many other sadistic murderers and rapists, felt that his atrocious crimes were committed in the interests of the highest moral principles. Violent sex criminals in particular seem to suffer from antihedonistic, puritanical attitudes toward sex.

If, on the other hand, one admits and accepts the complete legitimacy of all the appetitive drives, including the sexual drive, and recognizes that the avoidance of pain and the quest for pleasure are entirely virtuous tendencies, it then becomes possible to consider how the appetitive drives may be satisfied in the most *ethical* context and for the greatest good to oneself and the community.

Partridge (1958) has pointed to the fundamental psychological and sexio-social differences between the Greeks and the Romans. His observations are well worth quoting in some detail:

> In his everyday life the Greek . . . displayed an unmistakable zest for life which was accompanied by grace, style, and understanding in and for the art of living. . . . One of the first impressions that one receives in reading about this aspect of the lives of the two peoples is that the Greeks controlled their sexuality, but that the sexuality of the Romans became their master, that they abandoned themselves to this master, and that he destroyed them as they had foreseen and partially intended.
> Greek sexual life was extraordinarily free from perversions. (I ex-

clude homosexuality from this category, since it does not arise from a mistaken concept of sexuality.)

The literature of the Greeks contains many references to homosexual love but . . . this love is always idealized, admired and mystified: the whole Greek attitude indicated an appreciation of and admiration for the possibilities of purely sensual delights, undefiled by the heresy that it is impossible to mix intellectual and physical pleasures, which leads inevitably and undesirably to the sacrifice of one to the other.

When we look at the Romans we see something different . . . an obsession with cruelty, more important, an *attitude towards cruelty*, which is to be seen nowhere in the literature of the Hellenes.

Partridge later continues his analysis of the Roman personality with a highly pertinent observation.

Behind the sado-masochistic idea lies an equation of violence and copulation. This implies various preliminary ideas. First that in sex there exists something foul and criminal, second . . . that the active participants are committing an offense on the passive. Following this will come the impulse-desire toward retribution.

The possessor of either of these perversions [sadism or masochism] has, at some level of his consciousness, gone astray. Either he has, by a tortuous and mistaken process of subconscious thinking, decided that he must sacrifice his sexuality to save his conscience and the people with whom he comes in contact. Or, in the case of the sadist, he will be tortured by a well-founded guilt.[65]

Nothing could be more applicable to the classic Judaeo-Christian concept of sexual relationships than the comments in the last two paragraphs. In its overesteem of sexual chastity, expressed in both the obsession with monogamy and the obsession with celibacy; in its traditional view of women as poor and defenseless creatures who must be protected against the onslaught that the sexual act is interpreted to be; in its attempt to apply rigid controls to sex and even to suppress it as a dangerous force by the use of almost every conceivable technique (including legal statute), Judaeo-Christian culture expresses, even more emphatically than ancient Roman culture, the sadomasochistic misconception of sex as an innately violent, foul, and criminal drive.

Because sex is regarded in this way, the active partner is thought to be committing an implicit offense against the passive partner. Thus the erotic impulse must be surrounded by sanctions designed to render it harmless. It must be alibied at all times by every possible rationalization —usually love, marriage, procreation. And it must provoke anxiety and guilt rather than a sense of well-being and fulfillment. When—as in the case of homosexuality or the "perversions"—no sufficient alibi can be found for it, the expression of the erotic impulse is, as we have seen, regarded as a moral and sometimes even a criminal offense.

Partridge's description of the Romans is borne out by the very extensive historical record we have of them. Their history begins with a story of rape—the rape of the Sabine women—and rape, cruelty, and debauchery permeate the balance of the record. There were, of course, exceptions. One should not be unmindful of these. But exceptions they always were, and they stand out in contrast to the main tendency of Roman life.

During Republican times, before the establishment of the Principate, the sadism of Roman life, when not directly expressed against others by aggression and conquest, was directed largely against the self in pious attitudes of stoicism, duty, and obedience to authority. The image of a tyrannical father imposed itself upon the Roman mentality, much as in the case of the ancient Hebrews who personified this in Jehovah. Roman women and children lived in an atmosphere of subservience. A Roman matron who was unfaithful was often punished by her husband with death. Even as late as the first century, Caesar's wife was supposed to be "beyond suspicion." (These ladies were to have their vengeance in succeeding centuries of the Roman Era.)

Narrow-mindedness was an outstanding component of the Roman personality, and it expressed itself in the Roman attitude toward philosophy. The Romans never quite trusted the Greek habit of inquiring into the meaning of virtue, for to them as to us today, the meaning of virtue was clear. It could be summarized in four words: duty, courage, obedience, and justice. Unfortunately these high-flown and somewhat stilted values were usually placed in rather negative connotations. Too often duty meant the abandonment of self-realization, courage meant brutality, obedience meant masochistic surrender to both personal and impersonal authority, and justice meant punishment and revenge. They had an innate distrust of the subtleties of the intellect, the refinement of taste, and the cultivation of manners, and were concerned with practicality, mastery of the physical world around them, and the acquisition of wealth and power. Their mentality and philosophy were ideally suited to the military goals that they set themselves and that they were to realize with amazing success.

It is not surprising that when they had the world and its resources in their grasp, their stoical approach to life became almost unbearably burdensome. In the face of the temptations produced by enormous power and wealth, and in the absence of any deep knowledge of the real pleasures in life, they surrendered almost every component of morality and ethics. Brutality, cruelty, avarice, greed, cowardice, egoism, licentiousness, preversity, idleness, and vanity became outstanding features not only of their leaders but of the common people themselves. This is the danger that success brings to all Puritans, and the increasing luxury of our own civilization in the absence of an enlightened attitude toward pleasure begins more and more to resemble certain features of the ancient Roman scene.

Having never thought much about pleasure, and being rather inept in handling ideas, the Romans imagined that in pursuing a life of voluptuous luxury, unencumbered by either thought or taste, they had realized .the Greek ideal of Hedone. They borrowed this concept and made it a rationalization for debauchery. But all of this, of course, was only the other side of the coin. For an unflinching moralism they had substituted immorality, thinking that in this manner they could escape from the inner restrictions that moralism imposed. But it is clear that, in their frantic excess of vulgarity, the Romans never learned the meaning of pleasure. One may wonder if pleasure was what they truly sought. To the end, they remained intellectual and spiritual parvenus; having failed in their experiment with hedonism because they never understood the meaning of it, they turned readily to a philosophy of self-abnegation. The stage was set for Christianity. Mortification of the flesh and an unhealthy mysticism ending in asceticism were substituted for unbridled lust in a world which had been too much with them and in which they never learned to find substantial joy. They were ready for the philosophy of the Dark Ages.

The brutality that is the outstanding feature of Roman life cannot be explained merely by the militaristic ambitions and habits of the people. If anything, these were encouraged by a tendency toward brutality. We will not attempt any further analysis of this trait here, but it is of interest to note that much of the cruelty of Roman men was not only tolerated by Roman women but wholeheartedly encouraged and embraced by them. We hear of the Roman woman's cruelty to slaves, the delight she shared with men in witnessing the gory spectacle of the arena, and the active part she played in sadistic orgies of a religious nature. A number of these orgies are described by Partridge and others. As for their place in the religion of Rome, Juvenal complained of the breakdown of Roman religion as a result of the "drunken emancipation of women."

It is an unfortunate fact in the history of the Greeks that women never enjoyed the full benefits of social freedom. Their place however was probably not as inferior as it is often pictured by many Christian scholars who have learned to worship rather than to love women. Greek women were confined almost completely to the home, although we do hear of a number of outstanding intellects among them such as Sappho and Aspasia.

The spread of homosexuality among Greek males has been offered as an explanation of the inferior status of Greek women. But it is difficult to know where if at all, causal relationship begins. It is equally possible that the sequestered status of Greek women encouraged homosexuality among males. We shall see, however, that emancipation of women does not in any respect guarantee a decrease in male homosexuality, any more than suppression of male homosexuality guarantees a superior status for women. For homosexuality among males undoubtedly increased in Rome along with the emancipation of women, and such may also be the case in our own culture.

Roman women enjoyed a much greater degree of freedom throughout a great part of their history than any other women of antiquity, and more than most other civilized women until modern times. They gained the right to inherit and own property, and contributed a great deal to decisions within the family. In addition, they occupied important positions within the religion of the State. Time and again we see the part they played in the politics of the Empire; their influence in this sphere was formidable. Many of the emperors and other public men owed their positions to the initiative of women whose resourcefulness and cunning has never been surpassed. Though in numerous ways despicable, the Roman woman was always interesting, often attractive, and sometimes laudable. The personalities of a great many women are imprinted on the history of Rome. Among the beneficiaries of their resourcefulness and unscrupulousness were not only such lunatics as Nero and Heliogabalus, but such savants as Hadrian. Often they could bring about the success or ruin of a man. That happened in the case of Emperor Heliogabalus, and Nero ordered the murder of his mother in order to escape a similar fate.

The traditional farewell of the Roman mother to her war-bound son— "Return with your shield, or on it"—gives a clue to the part women played in the development of Roman military courage—and fierceness.

By the latter part of the second century, Roman women participated fully in the cultural and social life of the Empire. They organized and took part in intellectual circles, debated in public on an equal footing with men, and learned the classics and argued their meaning in public gatherings with men. They were completely free to choose whom they wished to marry, and equally free to instigate proceedings for divorce. They accumulated vast fortunes in their own right, advised generals as to what tactics to use in warfare (often in the presence of the troops), hunted, wrestled, joined in the sports and amusements of men, and dressed, if they chose, in masculine attire, as many women do today. Their vices could be matched with those of any man; they ate and drank with the heartiest of libertines, engaged paramours, caroused from dawn to dusk—often even in public gathering places—and did precisely as they pleased.

This new-found freedom of women caused a great deal of scandal and much serious comment from time to time. The work of Roman writers and journalists is filled with commentary on this subject, most of it negative. But none of this had any effect. Women continued to demand and to gain additional freedom until their status reached the point at which it was scarcely, if at all, inferior to that of men. Some of these emancipated women displayed the finest traits of character. Not a few accepted the tragic circumstances that befell their husbands in a society dominated by despots. For all of the unseemly a pects they were capable of displaying, Roman women remain among the most interesting and complex females in history.[10]

These conditions undoubtedly influenced the attitude of men toward homosexuality. It would appear that the Roman male tended to associate the passive role in a homosexual relationship with femininity and thus with effeminacy. Homosexual preoccupations became associated with effeteness during the latter part of the Roman epoch. There was a great deal of resemblance between the homosexual milieu of Rome and that of modern-day Judaeo-Christendom. Homosexuality among the Romans earlier in their history seems to have followed the pattern of homosexual relationships among other Mediterranean peoples. For a time, the Greek model was followed, and many educated Romans imitated Greek paederastia. Hellenized affairs of this sort continued among certain educated elements until the adoption of Christianity. But it was always difficult for the Romans to maintain a philosophical approach toward any aspect of life. More often than not, homosexual relationships were crude affairs that could hardly be imagined to satisfy any requirements other than those dictated by lust. As was the case with other aspects of sexual life, these relationships tended to deteriorate into pathology of a strongly sadomasochistic variety. Sometimes, as in the case of the young Emperor Heliogabalus, the sadomasochism was psychological rather than directly physical in nature, involving prostrating oneself before another male or dressing in feminine attire. This unfortunate and insane youth, raised by iron-willed women who used him to realize their own ambitions, included in his numerous fantasies the idea of castrating himself. He settled for circumcision. His eccentric activities were tolerated by the blasé Romans who had long since grown accustomed to bizarre behavior on the part of high officials.

> At night he would go to a brothel, drive out the prostitutes, and wearing a wig, stand in the door himself, soliciting trade . . .
> He tried to induce the physicians to make him into a woman, promising them large sums of money should they succeed. That there was a masochistic element in his character need not surprise us. According to Dio Cassius he liked to fantasize himself as a particularly lewd woman, taking pains to be caught *in flagrante delicto* by his "husband" so that he should be severely beaten.[65]

Sadomasochistic homosexuality of an even more extreme sort was known among the Romans. Youths of defeated nations and even impoverished Roman youths were sold into slavery and were bought by some psychopaths to be used as victims in sadomasochistic orgies. Some of these boys were maltreated and subjected to mutilation in order to excite lustful feelings in their owners. Sometimes slave boys who were purchased for their sexual charms were treated kindly; some were even loved. But we know from a later edict that forbade the mutilation of slaves for erotic pleasure—not for punishment!—that in a great many instances these boys were mishandled and were submitted to brutal acts of a kind virtually unrecorded among the Greeks. The same fate befell many slave girls at the hands of men and women alike.

It would be altogether too pat and too inhuman if this sordid picture were unrelieved by any element of contradiction. There were periods in Roman history—brief when compared with the full history of that long-lived State—when sanity, though never pervasive hedonism, prevailed. The early period of the Republic was flinty and unbending, but at least not lecherously cruel in spirit. One cannot love these earlier Romans, but one can feel some measure of respect for them.

Later there were a few brief intervals of truly civilized refinement. The period of the Antonine Emperors was one such interval. But it soon gave way again to the brutality and vulgarity exemplified and encouraged by leaders like Commodus and Caracalla.

The poetry which the Romans have left us is not without examples of homosexual ardor and, like most pagan peoples, the Romans were success-ful in combining this with a sanguine appreciation of the charms of women. Catullus addressed a poem to his young friend Juventius in which the innocence of the ancients regarding any contradiction between homosexual and heterosexual sentiments is vividly portrayed. This poet, famous for his highly erotic poetry addressed to the lustful Clodia-Lesbia, felt no hesitancy in writing to the well-made youth:

> O if you would let me, fair Juventius,
> I would be kissing your honeyed eyes forever.
> Three hundred thousand times I would kiss you
> with new rapture,
> nor could find enough of this blissful pastime
> promised in my dreams. Even if your kisses
> grew to such profusion
> they outnumbered sheaves
> ripening in the wheat field.
>
> (trans. Horace Gregory) [1]

The frank sensuality of this poem is not marred by any suggestion of debauched lust. It is possible to imagine the poet taken with a genuine, if rapturous, affection for the youth.

During the reign of Hadrian (a Spanish Roman by birth and early education), Greek enlightenment shone upon the Empire with renewed vigor. This rare Roman was a passionate grecophile as well as an energetic traveler. He admired scholarship, philosophy, and the arts. Although a somewhat restrained and thoughtful man rather than a man of sanguine appetites, there was room in his view of life for genuine pleasure. The Greek youth, Antinous, became the object of his love and favor. He managed to exalt this boy without at the same time, in traditional imperial fashion, feeling a need to castrate either Antinous or himself. A great deal of their time together was apparently spent in study, discourse, travel, and sport. The boy's enthusiasm for athletics was to play some part in his death.

While on a journey in Egypt, when he was nineteen years old, the young Greek was drowned in the Nile. It is unknown whether he was killed as a result of a plot or an accident. Some historians have suggested that Antinous received word that the Emperor's extraordinary devotion to him had provoked great jealousy and plotting, and that the boy, not wishing to endanger his beloved friend's life, immolated himself. At the death of his idol the grief of the Emperor was great. He fell into a depression, which finally he brought under control, but Hadrian never became reconciled to Antinous's death. He defied the dead boy and had statues of him erected throughout the Empire with the result that we have many representations of his face and form.

Marguerite Yourcenar's account of the relationship between the Emperor and Antinous is at once touching and informative. In her book, *Memoirs of Hadrian,* she puts the following thoughts, which seem very probable, into the mind of the Emperor:

> I fought against my grief, battling as if it were gangrene: I recalled his occasional stubbornness and lies; I told myself that he would have changed, growing older and heavy. Such efforts proved futile; instead, like some painstaking workman who toils to copy a masterpiece, I exhausted myself in tasking my memory for fanatic exactitude, evoking that smooth chest, high and rounded as a shield. Sometimes the image leaped to mind of itself, and a flood of tenderness swept over me: once again I caught sight of an orchard in Tibur, and the youth gathering autumn fruits in his tunic, for lack of a basket. I had lost everything at once, the companion of the night's delights, and the young friend squatting to his heels to help Euphorion with the folds of my toga. If one were to believe the priests, the shade was also in torment, regretting the warm shelter of its body and haunting the familiar habitations with many a moan, so far and yet so near, but for the time too weak to signify his presence to me. If that were true my deafness was worse than death itself. But after all had I so well understood, on that morning, the living boy who sobbed at my side?

Hadrian was one of the few emperors who died a natural death. Only a few years after his removal from the hurly-burly of Rome to the sedate villa he had built in the section outside of the city which today is called Tivoli, the Emperor was laid to rest. One of the most beautiful parts of this royal dwelling that has been excavated is the reconstruction of Canopus and the temple of Serapis in Egypt which the Emperor had built as a reminder of his travels, and also, perhaps, as a reminder of his deified beloved. In the center of this temple, facing outward toward a beautiful artificial lake, stood a huge statue of Antinous in the form of the Egyptian god.

The Antonine enlightenment could not last. Ranged against the philosophical and humanistic tendencies of emperors like Hadrian, Antoninus Pius, and Marcus Aurelius were the brutal forces in the Roman character that again became manifest in men like Commodus and Caracalla. Two hundred years later the structure of Roman statecraft in the West had collapsed, leaving Europe a prey to the unopposed vandalism of barbarians. Before this debacle, however, the Emperor Constantine had issued the Edict of Milan; Christianity had risen to a place of honor in the Empire and paganism was on the wane.

The adoption of Christianity was not the transformation that it has been pictured. The elements of the death wish so clear in later Roman life had come into the ascendant and were to dominate European civilization for the next thousand years, leaving an imprint that has never worn away.

> The Romans, although the most spectacular, must also be considered the most contemptible people who have ever attempted the orgy-experiment . . . With the exception of a few true Hedonists, such as Petronius, they had none of them any true understanding of the nature of pleasure. Lacking grace and elegance, contemptuously disposed toward the actions which they pretended to admire, it cannot be wondered if their behavior has about it a suspicious odour of the death-wish. Present or no, this wish was presently consummated with the arrival of the Christian era.[65]

That the Christian sexual ethos should have followed the mad excesses of Roman decadence—that, indeed, the adoption of Christianity itself was but a new expression of this very decadence—seems to have been inevitable. But for all there is to criticize in the ancient Roman attitude toward erotic life, it should not be imagined that the Romans ever reached the spiritual and intellectual depths that lay ahead in the Dark Ages. Voluptuousness, though in every way inferior to ethical hedonism, stands a notch above asceticism, practiced off in the desert of North Africa or in the musty atmosphere of a somber monastic cell. The Romans may have embraced vulgarity, intemperance, and sadism; but they did so, for the most part, at least honestly. The vulgarity, intemperance, and sadism of the Dark Ages and of Medieval Christendom are even of more sickly caste, hidden as they were in the disguise of piety and religious ardor. Sadism was never abandoned; it was turned inward to become a form of religious masochism and self-abnegation. Self-flagellation, self-emasculation, the wearing of hair shirts, and all the other items in the ascetic repertory of the saints represent no genuine improvement over the worst features of Roman decadence in the erotic sphere. Such practices are, in the words of Oscar Wilde, "remnants of savage mutilation."

When the excesses of Roman heteroerotic life began to spread to the homosexual sphere, Roman authority dealt with it as it dealt with almost everything else—through fiat. The first indication among the ancient Mediterraneans that we get of an official condemnation of homosexuality *in toto* occurred during the reign of the Christianized though still officially pagan Emperor Alexander Severus (A.D. 208–235). He was a cousin of the lunatic Heliogabalus and followed him in the imperial succession. The depraved behavior of his kinsman, homosexual and otherwise, must have left a deep impression on the more pious youth who through his Christian mother was acquainted with the sexual ideals of the new religion. He was raised in an atmosphere of asceticism and sexual renunciation. His love of Greek and Latin literature was curbed by his mother, who impressed upon him the need to yield these interests to others that would better equip him to organize and to rule a world Empire. Moral reform became an outstanding passion with him, and early in his reign he imposed a severe censorship upon public morals that included the arrest of prostitutes and the deportation of many actively homosexual men in public life.

The reforms of Alexander Severus established a precedent, but one not rigorously pursued by succeeding emperors because the ancient mentality had not yet become fully permeated by erotophobia. It required three hundred more years of living with the new theology before the ancient mind could absorb the idea that there is anything seriously sinful in erotic passion. Throughout this period sporadic efforts were made to suppress "Greek love," especially after the formal adoption by Constantine of Christianity into the Empire. But homosexual contacts were never irrevocably outlawed until the reign of the Byzantine Emperor Justinian (A.D. 483–565).

Terrified that "sodomistic practices" might incur anew the wrath of Jehovah and bring upon his realm a fate similar to that of Sodom and Gomorrah, Justinian initiated a methodical effort to suppress paederastia throughout the Empire. No cruelty was thought too excessive if it was effective in putting down what by then had come to be thought of as "unnatural lust." In an atmosphere of fear, intolerance, superstition, and religious bigotry, paederastia was ruthlessly attacked as idolatry, heresy, and witchcraft.

The classical attitude of the ancients toward sex, as we have seen, was entirely tolerant, and it would never have occurred to the ancient mind to condemn sexual passion in any form as unnatural. Now, however, it was no longer possible for the individual to veer in any way from the rigidly defined sexual dogmas of the Church Fathers. The sexual heretic was treated like any other heretic: he was hunted down, condemned, implored to renounce his devious ways, and if he failed to do so was excommunicated and delivered to the secular authority to be burnt as a criminal.

The Greeks had civilized homosexual love and had found in it another source for the creation of civilization. And this had not made them in any way insensible to the suasive and propelling force of love between the sexes. They had the happy faculty of being ignorant of sexual prejudices and were, therefore, innocent of their deathly grip. Unused to the habit of repression, they set up in its place expression, and from that fount came the origins of the finest elements within our civilization. But after the adoption of Christianity and the suppression of "pagan life" things were quite different, and some of the changes that were wrought particularly affected the character of homosexual relationships.

Now stripped of all social approval, devoid of any constructive purpose in the new order of things, and regarded as monstrously sinful, homosexual tendencies became an affliction to the individual and a lingering disease in the community. Those so afflicted retreated into a half-world of secrecy and uneasy conscience, and the sordid picture of sexual heresy that we still see in our midst had entered the scene of Western civilization. As the Dark Ages descended upon Europe, erotophobia—and homoerotophobia in particular—became abiding components of the Judaeo-Christion mentality. Western man had invented a new sin, a new crime, and a new disease.

IX

Homosexuality Within a Sex-Negative Environment

We have explored the manifestation of homosexuality within a sex-positive culture; now we must focus our attention upon homosexuality within a culture in which not only homosexuality but almost all sexual phenomena have become an object of fear and suppression.

The different subcultures of Judaeo-Christian civilization do not all regard homosexuality in precisely the same light by any means, although all Judaeo-Christian subcultures are affected to varying extents by anxiety and superstition on this subject. Some mention will be made of other nations; but it is the American attitude toward homosexuality and the peculiar sociological consequences of this attitude that will receive the most detailed consideration in this chapter.

The inordinately erotophobic character of American society and its long and almost exclusive history of puritanism, along with certain other forces that are more difficult to particularize, have brought homoerotophobia in particular to an apex that has no parallel in civilized society of modern times. The mere imputation of homosexuality in America may be enough to ruin a man's reputation, his livelihood, his relationship with his government, and any hopes he has for future happiness. Beyond these calamities, moreover, the American male who becomes involved in homosexual contacts must actually fear for his freedom; for to the more ordinary social perils of this behavior have been added the threat of outright persecution under the law. In the United States various "sodomy" laws, long since dropped by almost all other civilized nations, still fill the statute books, and one hears periodically of certain perfectly peaceable citizens who have been arrested on a "morals charge" for behavior that might not even occasion comment elsewhere in the world. Even more incredible is the elaboration and strenghtening of this type of moral legislation in recent years and the conscientious enforcement insofar as it is physically possible. But the topic of homosexuality and the law is sufficiently important and complicated to be the subject of a separate chapter.

The American attitude toward homosexuality has drawn comment from scholars within the country as well as from observers abroad. No one who is informed in the sexological area can fail to be impressed by the extent of the problem that homosexuality presents in the United States. About the intensity of American homoerotophobia Kinsey and his colleagues remarked:

> In our American culture there are no types of sexual activity which are as frequently condemned because they depart from the mores and the publicly pretended custom as mouth-genital contacts and homosexual activities. There are practically no other European groups, unless it be in England, and few if any other cultures elsewhere in the world which have become as disturbed over male homosexuality as we have here in the United States.[53]

The American attitude toward male homosexuality has reached such heights of phobia that any behavior that might even tend to suggest homosexual interests is frowned upon and avoided. Thus an affectionate embrace between males in public or in private is looked upon askance and usually avoided, even between fathers and sons. When President Johnson, in a moment of exuberance, embraced a prominent official in public, it was deemed sufficiently noteworthy to draw comment in the newspapers and for a brief time became an occasion for ribald jests.

Any type of gesture or behavior which might remotely suggest the possibility of homosexual interests may occasion notice and even outright ridicule. The number of items connected with taste that are associated with effeminacy in our culture are legion; until very recent times, the avoidance of some of these items has made the average American male somewhat stilted and something of a caricature. American males have been raised in an atmosphere that encourages behavior that conceivably might have served a useful purpose on the farm or on the frontier, but that seems to have no meaning in an atmosphere of leisure and refinement such as is found in most urban communities today.

Within very recent times, no doubt under the civilizing influence of American women, a notable number of males have to some extent abandoned the taste, manners, and speech of the frontiersman. Increasingly American males have acquired characteristics that their grandfathers would have undoubtedly regarded as effeminate. Some, for example, have even taken to highly scented after-shave lotions that are almost as pungent as the perfumes worn by many continental Casanovas. Speech among males has become a bit more relaxed, and it is now possible to convey some measure of manly affection without a cloak of obscenity or horseplay.

Younger American males in particular seem less anxiety-ridden about adhering to the traditional stereotype of the "he-man" than their fathers, although this change must be described as a trend rather than a substantial or pervasive reality in the present. No doubt this trend is related to the fact that American society is far less insular than in the past. Higher education reaches a much greater number of people today, travel abroad is far more common, and the media of public communication tend to bring the habits, manners, and attitudes of other peoples to the attention of the average man. More often confronted by a varied picture of life and not so strongly or so exclusively conditioned as the older American to traditional stereotypes, the younger American is in a transitional phase the end of which no one at present may predict. It seems quite probable that a very real change is in process in American society, a change that eventually may have a substantial effect upon many of the factors we shall be discussing in this chapter. American youth is a dynamic force that must be reckoned with, and although burdened by tremendous problems heaped upon them by the errors and prejudices of the old, young Americans of today are not likely to perpetuate some of the abuses that their parents held forth as virtues. But we must discuss the present here and not the future.

The changes to which we have referred, as timid and as modest as they are, along with an hysterical misreading and misrepresentation of the Kinsey statistics have caused some older people to propagate with alarm the idea that homosexuality and "perversion" are now on the increase in America, when in fact there is little reliable evidence to back up such an assertion. It is of course true that there is today, as in the past, more homosexuality than the mores would ever lead one to believe. And it is also true that our more candid times have brought homosexuality into greater prominence. We do not pretend as often that homosexuality does not exist. But the incidence and frequency of homosexual behavior and the amount of homosexual interest among American males cannot be shown to be measurably greater—or, for that matter, less—than in the recent or remote past. It would appear that the greater freedom of our times to discuss and even to confess an interest in homosexual and other erotic activities, has been misconstrued as evidence of an increase in the incidence of homosexual behavior.

In spite of the relaxation of censorship and a more composed attitude on the part of younger people toward this entire subject, however, the contemporary American male continues to suffer from what is undoubtedly more than his share of homoerotophobia, and it has greatly impaired the interpersonal relationships of many of these males by creating a breech between them that often seems to preclude the possibility of warmth, emotional spontaneity, and affection. One need only spend a few hours in a typically male environment to discover how shallow, overconventionalized, and brittle the relationships between many men are. The coarse banter that passes for humor, the monotony of the conversation constantly on the lips of some of these men (cant, clichés, and overworked slang expressions that are in essence impersonal and give no clue to the true character of the individual), the rigid formula of taste, mannerism, and interest that make one fellow appear exactly the same as the next, the endless wisecracking and horseplay, the stereotyped enthusiasms and the equally stereotyped aversions, all reveal a failure on the part of the person not only to develop his innate and unique resources as an individual, but also to really communicate with others. No doubt myriad factors play some part in bringing about this type of personality restriction; but there can be little doubt that chief among these factors is the inhibition resulting from an element of homoerotophobia. So many men so desperately seek to be "regular guys" and so fearfully avoid being "odd balls" that they have neither time nor energy left to be themselves. Having failed to be themselves they have little to offer in a relationship with another person.

A great deal of this urgency is merely a function of the compulsion found among so many Americans, male and female, to *conform* at all costs. But in the case of males in particular, this urgency to conform with a stereotype of one's sex is based upon a deep-seated fear of being (as the double-entendre itself so clearly reveals) "queer." In no other language, to this author's knowledge, except in the American language, has the word "queer" been used to denote homosexuality. Even in British English this word has never had any homosexual connotation—except in recent times when it has been borrowed from American usage.

Thus masculine interpersonal relationships have often been distorted by an element of homoerotophobia; but in a great many cases the individual's relationship to himself has also been damaged, perhaps with even more tragic consequences.

The need for warmth, cooperation, affection, and even a degree of intimacy in social relationships between persons of the same sex is as great as in social relationships between persons of the opposite sex. Perhaps one of the most depressing aspects of the social scene today is the lack of strong and meaningful friendships like some of those prominent during other periods of our history. The entire atmosphere of our times seems to be pervaded by a sense of loneliness and alienation. This is so striking as to have become a major theme in contemporary literature and drama. It is difficult to escape the impression that a great many social relationships today, especially between persons of the same sex, are somewhat shallow and often merely perfunctory. But in an atmosphere in which a man may fear for the reputation of his friend and himself if he expresses undisguised warmth or affection, it is not surprising that close friendships seldom seem to come into being. We do not refer here to the back-slapping, jolly-good-fellow type of acquaintanceships which are everywhere in evidence, but rather to the more intimate and personalized relationships that were sought and honored in times passed.

In the emotionally vacuous relationships of people today sex has been used more and more as a substitute for friendship or love. It is an extreme and somewhat bizarre paradox that in the homoerotophobic atmosphere of our culture many males seem more able to enter into sexual relationships with other males than they seem able to enter into significant friendships with other males, just as they often seem to substitute sex for love or friendship in their relationships with females.

It seems from the data we have that homoerotophobia does not do very much to preclude the possibility of overt homosexual contacts, for there is an enormous amount of homoerotophobia in our culture but no small amount of overt homosexuality. Homoerotophobia does a great deal more to distort social relationships than it does to depress the incidence of overt homosexuality. There is really more fear of being considered a "homosexual" or a "queer" by oneself and others, than there is fear of sexual relationships per se between like-sexed partners. Consider, for example, the willingness of a great many young men (and, for that matter, older men) to enter into furtive sexual relationships with other men—with or without the alibi of having received money for the bestowal of this favor; the same people might suffer an enormous loss in their sense of personal worth if they were ridiculed for some innocent gesture of affection between themselves and a friend. A great many youths of today ironically do not in the least mind being considered hustlers or part-time male prostitutes so long as no one considers them a "faggot." Many of these youths will go to bed with another man and indulge in the most eccentric sexual behavior without a qualm, but would be very disturbed by the social consequences that might ensue if they had a close, intimate friendship that did not involve overt sexual acts. But this is only one of many paradoxes that arise within a homoerotophobic environment. We must consider a few of the others.

The great need of American males—especially in youth—to be tough and aggressive, to seem to go about with a perpetual chip on the shoulder, and to become involved in brawls, street fighting, and other forms of antisocial behavior is partly a function of homoerotophobia. This behavior is affected in the interest of conformity with a stereotype of the "he-man" by those who suffer from an almost desperate fear that they might be considered as a "she-man." Sometimes it is only under the calming and liberating influence of alcohol that these males are able to afford some demonstration of affection for one another. The barroom, when it is not a site of mayhem, may be a site of effusive protestations of friendship and camaraderie accompanied by intimate gestures of affection. Little significance is ascribed to this behavior because of the bibulous circumstances.

If relationships between peers are often disturbed by subtle tensions that may be related to homoerotophobia, the effects of homoerotophobia upon fathers and sons are particularly unfortunate. These relationships are so often lacking in tangible affection as to lend credence to the idea that many males adopt a compulsive pattern of overt homosexuality in later life in an effort to compensate for the emotional indifference they felt on the part of their fathers. The American father, whose role in the home has now been reduced to little more than that of one of his children, is often prevented from entering into meaningful interaction with his sons by inhibitions that suggest fear of homosexual emotions. Often a father may fail to take an active part in the rearing of his children when they are tiny because he is convinced that it is feminine to be emotionally concerned with little children. He may express more affection for his daughters because "little girls are cute," but he may feel that to express an equal amount of affection for his sons is "sissified."

Most of the more intimate expressions of affection upon which small children thrive—those which, for example, involve direct bodily contact— emanate from the mother. She also often seems to display the greatest interest in the children. A great deal of the affection accorded a male child in our culture—perhaps most of it—comes from the mother who, often in compensation for the seeming emotional indifference of the father, may exaggerate the more intimate expressions of love to an extent where the little boy actually experiences his mother's attentions as a form of seduction.

The belief, common in America, that a "real man" lacks the more common emotions—that he knows neither fear, nor tenderness, nor sorrow, nor desire, that he knows no real emotions except those that appear in the most hostile and aggressive context—that, in other words, he is not truly human—encourages behavior on the part of older males that furthers a schism between father and son and propels the little boy toward an intense and binding relationship with his mother in search of the warmth of a truly human and close experience.

This distorted picture of what a "real man" is makes it difficult if not impossible for many fathers to participate emotionally, on a free and open basis, in the rearing of their male children. Often all that is left to them is the role of a harsh disciplinarian. But in recent times even the role of the disciplinarian—insofar as discipline plays any part in the rearing of children today—is left to the mother, and the father has become almost a complete nonentity in the home. Thus, undue emphasis is placed upon the importance of the mother, and motherhood has become fetishized to a ridiculous extent.

It is patent that all children require the love, affection, and serious interest of both a mother *and* a father. A boy in particular must feel that he is accepted and loved by his father, since it is his father to whom he looks for the kind of guidance that can only be provided by another more experienced male. Beyond a certain stage in the development of a male child the love and guidance of his father is more important to his development than the love and guidance of his mother. He must be able to identify with his father and to use him as a model of manhood, virtue, courage, industry, and other important values. Without a close relationship with their fathers most boys cannot develop a sense of inner security and personal worth. If he cannot reach his father emotionally and if his father cannot reach him emotionally, a boy will cling to his relationship with his mother beyond the stage in his development when a close, intimate relationship with his mother is desirable. Lacking an adequate father, he will attempt to find in his relationship with his mother that which only his father can give him: the sense of security as a masculine being. In other cases a boy may attempt to find what he needs by way of masculine guidance outside the home with some other male. In certain instances the guidance of an older male outside the home may be sufficient to carry a boy through to manhood. But this is merely fortuitous. Most often boys who have been rejected by their fathers seek for masculine guidance in the wrong places—usually in gangs in which the leader is not wiser, but simply more dominant or aggressive.

Most of us are aware of the ill effects when boys seek guidance, affection, and the sense of participating in manly exploits in the activities of the type of street gangs that now thrive in most of the cities of our nation. Many explanations have been offered for the existence of these gangs, and for the evils to which they so often give rise. Some of these explanations appear to be apposite. But it is seldom recognized that the existence of these gangs is also related to the failure of the American father to play any significant part in the development of his son's character. Gangs and fraternal organizations among adolescent males are common throughout the world and may be found even in the most primitive societies. But usually they are controlled by older males—the "fathers" of the community—who seek to direct the interests and activities of youth toward the values of the community. The gangs we find today in America have no such direction, and the results certainly do not reflect the values of the community—unless, ironically, certain of the less verbalized values of the community do actually find expression in the brutal activities of these gangs.

When a father plays an insignificant emotional role in the life of his son or when the father's role is entirely hostile and unsympathetic, the relationship between mother and son must bear the entire burden of the child's need for love, affection, and parental guidance. Thus the growing boy's image of his mother, and hence of all women, becomes distorted. The exaggerated role his mother has played in his development affects his future relationships with both males and females. Such a boy comes to believe that not merely a great many desirable and longed-for attributes reside in femininity, but virtually *all* desirable and longed-for attributes reside in femininity. Since he himself is a male, however, he is apt to feel rather inadequate and inferior. This feeling may make some boys attempt, as it were, to resign from their sex. Males of this sort may often be identified among the "swishes" and "drag queens" of the "gay" world as well as among certain highly effeminate males who are completely unresponsive homosexually. But this reaction may not be encountered very often. Males do not readily surrender their masculinity. More often than not under these conditions they may attempt to compensate for their feeling of inferiority as males by exaggerating the importance of masculinity while at the same time adopting a defensive attitude of contempt toward femininity. This reaction is, by no means, confined to so-called homosexuals. It may be found all too commonly among American males ratable at any point on the heterosexual-homosexual scale.

The ideal of masculinity that develops under these conditions is one in which male chauvinism, arrogance, crudeness of feeling, and even brutality become emphasized. Left with the distorted notion that only women are capable of the more tender and human emotions, this type of male seeks to express himself through the more aggressive and hostile emotions. His stereotype may be found among the hoodlums, delinquents, and bums that form so large a part of the male population of our cities, but this type of male may also be commonly found among other elements within the population as well.

Hence an exaggerated impression of the importance of the mother may produce, on the one hand, a defensive contempt for femininity and a defensive adulation of masculinity. But on the other hand, we may observe an opposite effect simultaneously. Women may become idols to be worshipped rather than beloved companions and equals, and, since no true warmth was to be found in the father-son relationship, neither is it expected by this male that warmth will be found in masculine relationships among peers. Such a male is cut off from the possibility of close, meaningful relationships with either sex and condemned to an essentially hollow and lonely life, although he may pursue numerous "affairs" with women and be "the life of the party" among his masculine acquaintances. A male of this sort has failed to develop any realistic concept either of masculinity or femininity. He tends to fetishize both masculinity and femininity and this in turn may be a further reason for him to develop an inordinately homoerotophobic position.

Such a male does not make a satisfactory father or a satisfactory husband. He tends to reject his role as a father—as his own father did before him—and act as if fathers are very unimportant. With his wife he will tend to resume his earlier role with his mother—that of an adoring but emotionally insecure son. But it is not likely that his wife will find a very deep sense of fulfillment with such a son-husband. Lacking a rich emotional life with her husband, such a wife will be tempted to turn to her children—especially her sons—for the kind of relationship which she should have with her husband. The pattern then repeats itself! The husband, because of his homoerotophobia and because of his jealousy, tends to become detached and/or hostile in his relationship with his sons. The son must play the husband to the mother in order to fulfill her needs, and must cleave to her in order to fulfill his own emotional needs, and everything is at the same point where it was in the previous generation.

This interplay between mother, father, and child creates an emotional environment that more often than not is extremely harmful to the child, and one effect of it may be to produce a compulsive and pathological type of homosexuality in the growing boy.

In a psychoanalytic study of homosexuality, Bieber and his colleagues have described emotional conditions not unlike those described above in the histories of homosexual psychiatric patients.[8] These authors found a "detached-hostile father" and "a close-intimate-binding mother" in the background of these patients more often than in the background of non-homosexual patients. This is not surprising. The father's own fear of homosexuality or, more properly, his fear of not being masculine often forces him to become unnaturally detached from his son. The same fears interfere with his relationship with his wife. Such a father may come to actually hate his son because of the relationship that subsequently develops between mother and son. The jealousy of these homoerotophobic fathers, who are really searching for a mother in their wife, resembles the kind of jealousy often found between siblings. Certainly many factors bring about these conditions within the family, but one among them that has not been given sufficient emphasis either by Bieber or by other authors is the homoerotophobia of the father. It is highly ironic that the father's own homoerotophobia may contribute to conditions that may favor a pathological type of homosexuality in his son.

The blame for this obviously distorted situation in the family has often been placed upon the supposed aggressiveness of American females and the unwillingness of modern women to assume the more passive-dependent role of the female in the past. Whatever validity may possibly reside in this observation must be tempered by the realization that the image of the male which is fostered in American life—that of an emotionally incomplete human being—makes him an inadequate father. Moreover, it makes him an inadequate husband in any context save that of an aggressive bread-winner.

In this latter role American males have excelled, as the economic and material prosperity of the country so amply demonstrates. But the spiritual wealth of contemporary American life—the maintenance of meaningful interpersonal relationships, the attainment of an adequate and secure sense of individual worth independent of material possessions, and the apprecia-tion of and joy in the nuance and variety of mental and emotional life—leaves a great deal of latitude for further development.

A male who has been so preoccupied with defending and preserving his concept of his own masculinity has hardly had either the opportunity or the courage to discover those links within his own personality between him-self and his wife. Without these links there can be no real communication between himself and the woman whom he wants to love but cannot. Under these conditions there can be no deep psychological union. For such a male the woman he "loves" becomes an altar upon which he celebrates the glory of his masculinity, a mere thing to be acted upon. He can know nothing of what will arouse, excite, delight, and satisfy her.

For any man—or woman—to become complete, and thus to become capable of sexual communication with a partner of the opposite sex, he must possess in some measure, through cultivation or intuition, certain of the qualities of the partner. He must be capable of empathizing with his mate.

No man who is anxiously preoccupied with his idea of maculinity is capable of such empathy. Moreover, the characteristics that he will tend to emphasize in himself as masculine may be more repellent than seductive to a female. While she may be seeking tenderness and consideration for her own feelings, her lover may be trying to impress her with his virility, manli-ness, and strength. Of course strength does not preclude the possibility of tenderness, and perhaps only the really strong can be really tender. But the kind of strength emphasized in a homoerotophobic atmosphere is not the kind of strength that leads to tenderness, and one may doubt whether it is real strength at all.

While some of the conflicts described in the earlier paragraphs are some-what special and do not relate directly to all males, a good many American males—as reflected in the high incidence of frigidity among American females—are inadequate lovers, in part because of the excessive burden of homoerotophobia that is thrust upon them during their development. The chief complaint that women make about their husbands or lovers is that they are insensitive, self-centered, and rough. These are among the most prominent traits that American males associate with masculinity, and their opposites—sensitivity, consideration, and tenderness—are thought by many of these males to be feminine characteristics. In adopting this somewhat distorted pose of masculinity the American male creates a barrier between himself and women that has damaging effects upon both his sexual and social relationships with women. Since he, no less than any other male, wants the love and approval of women, he is apt to try to win these by bestowing rich gifts upon his women and "spoiling" them. But as women themselves so often remark, he would have a great deal more success if, instead, he were simply more considerate and understanding.

It is interesting and important to note that the American woman has found it easier to empathize with males than the American male has found it to empathize with females. This may help to explain why she seems to understand her men better than her men seem to understand her. But it should be remembered that the American female is not confronted by homoerotophobia to anything near the same extent as the male.

Without empathy there is no chance for communication; and without communication there is no chance for satisfying sexual or social relationships to develop.

An additional paradox is that the homoerotophobic male, because he cannot empathize well with females and thus cannot know what will please them, often functions better as a homosexual partner than as a heterosexual partner. He may understand far better how to please another man sexually than how to please a woman. Because he senses that he functions better in such a role and thus achieves greater satisfaction for himself and for his partner, he may tend to repeat homosexual contacts, and with the passing of time he may become strongly conditioned to homosexual stimuli. We have already noted that homoerotophobia has more effect upon one's attitudes than upon one's actions. Many actively homosexual males are highly homoerotophobic and indeed, as we have just noted, their homoerotophobia may in a roundabout way encourage the development of homosexual preferences. This is, of course, an exceptionally ironic turn of events and helps to explain how it is that excessively homoerotophobic cultures tend to give rise to the development of exclusive homosexuality more often than less homoerotophobic cultures.

According to our necessarily limited observation of males who are exclusively homosexual throughout the greater part of their adult life, a substantial number of them, far from presenting a picture of effeminacy, are aggressively masculine (according to the stereotype of masculinity). They are also excessively homoerotophobic in the sense that the amount of guilt and remorse they feel regarding their homosexual activities and the unreal meanings they ascribe to them exceed anything found among most other males. Not a few of these individuals may be harassed by neurotic conflicts, and frequently some of them become involved in sexual activities of a frankly sadistic and/or masochistic variety.

Severely homoerotophobic cultures may tend to foster exclusive homosexuality, but it is certain that they tend to foster the type of homosexual individual who, whether exclusively homosexual or not, is more homoerotophobic than an exclusively heterosexual male. The so-called homosexuals of our culture tend to be more intolerant of themselves and of others like themselves than those whom they regard—not without some element of truth—as their oppressors. They are often their own worst enemies, and the so-called gay world is filled with calumny, pettiness, meanness, and self-mockery. What these people need in order to advance their cause as human beings is fewer victims and more martyrs. But most seem to prefer the role of the victim to that of the martyr, and not infrequently it is they themselves who create victims.

In all of the many paradoxes described throughout this chapter we may see the futility of attempting to be permissive about one aspect of sexual life while at the same time being severely prohibitionistic about some other aspect of sexual life. We encounter a great many more liberal opinions today on the subject of premarital heterosexual contacts, diverse sexual techniques in marriage, and even extramarital contacts and masturbation. But few of those who regard themselves as liberals in these matters carry their liberality to a point where it includes approval for any type of homosexual contact. Psychiatrists, clinical psychologists, marriage counselors, social workers, and even some religious leaders have pointed to the ill effects of erotophobia and have in general urged a more permissive attitude toward sex. But most of these same people have failed to see, or if they have seen, have failed to make clear that homoerotophobia is nothing but one particular aspect of erotophobia, and that homoerotophobia is one of the major symptoms of any sex-negative culture. As long as there is erotophobia there will be homoerotophobia.

If we wish to overcome the ill effect of erotophobia on heterosexual life, we will have to be prepared to go much further than we have even begun to go in recognizing the fundamental legitimacy of the sexual drive, and we will not be able categorically to exclude homosexual phenomena from recognition. Fear of homosexual feelings inevitably distorts heterosexual relationships in one way or another. We will never be able to cope with the mental hygiene problem nor the moral problem that sex in our society creates by being terribly open-minded about one aspect of sexual life while at the same time regarding some other aspect of sexual life as "taboo." When we can accept the fact that sexual feelings never degrade either the subject or the object, that they are never dangerous in themselves, and that only hate and never love need be feared, we will have become truly civilized and will no longer have to suffer the tyranny of a particular phase of barbarism.

No manifestation of the sexual drive is in itself either immoral, criminal, or pathological. But, on the other hand, any manifestation of the sexual drive may be any of these things. What is important is not whether a given type of sexual behavior is heterosexual, homosexual, or autoerotic, but what purpose it is put to, what it means to the persons involved, and its connection with the entire life pattern of the individual concerned. There are coital heterosexual acts that, viewed from any objective standpoint, are immoral in their effect, pathological in their meaning for the individual, and even criminal; there are certain homosexual relations that are none of these things. The mere modality of a person's sexual behavior will in itself tell us nothing about the moral or psychological status of the individual. It would be better if those who advise the public on sex, instead of stating these matters categorically in terms of sexual modalities, would inform the public as to what a good, satisfying, and wholesome sexual relationship consists of. In so doing they might bring about an affirmative approach to sex in which fulfillment rather than guilt is emphasized.

We must continue our discussion of homosexuality within Judaeo-Christian culture with a brief account of it in certain other subcultures before returning to the American scene.

Most European males, especially those in the southern part of the continent, tend to be less homoerotophobic than American males, and their concept of what constitutes masculinity is rather different from the American concept in a number of superficial details and in some important details. It should be remembered that the southern Europeans are the direct descendents of the peoples among whom homosexual love was not only tolerated but even placed on an exalted moral plane. Christianity was never as successful in inculcating homoerotophobic attitudes in the centers of civilization as in the barbarian North. To the present time there are closer ties with pagan antiquity in the south of Europe than in the north of Europe, and when, in addition, it is remembered that the south escaped the puritanizing influence of the Protestant Reformation (with its regression to Old Testament prohibitionism) some of these differences may be better understood.

The southern European male is likely to display certain mannerisms and habits that most American males regard as effeminate. For example, the concept of what is an acceptable amount of emotionality for a male is more liberal, and males are not expected necessarily to express less emotionality than females. Declarations and gestures of affection between males are varied and are often in evidence. Male friends may freely embrace, kiss, and affectionately fondle one another without implication of perversion or effeminacy. Kissing and embracing is expected between father and son, and the father and son who avoided such expressions of affection would be considered unnatural. Open demonstrations of affection on the part of an older male for a younger male are never considered to be in bad taste.

Modern mode of dress tends clearly to define the masculine figure. Perfumes and hair pomades are acceptable, and the southern European male may seem to be vain about his appearance. Southern European languages and speech are, from the viewpoint of foreigners, feminine in the lilt of their rhythm, their rich use of vowels, and their softness of timbre; the males no less than the females tend to exploit these features for their dramatic, rhetorical, and aesthetic effects. Though the gesticulation, gait, postures, and bodily coordination of the male are distinctly different from those of the female, these may appear more graceful than those of American males. The regularity of physical features, especially in the younger southern European male, along with his generous crop of hair and his large dark eyes, may suggest beauty rather than handsomeness to some observers, although such distinctions are highly subjective. It is useful to point to certain differences in the attitudes and behavior of European males, but the American reader should not form the impression that these males lack many of the characteristics which we in our subculture regard as masculine. They enjoy active sports, and take a distinct pride in their masculinity; like males everywhere, they respond vigorously to the physical and mental charms of women. In behaving in the manner described above these males are acting in complete conformity with the standards of masculinity current in their culture.

The continental concept of masculinity is by no means altogether incompatible with certain homosexual activities, at least for the so-called active partner; and such activities are apt to form a part of the sexual experience of a great many males up to and including early manhood. It would be difficult to escape the conclusion that most southern European males regard homosexual activities as supplementary to the relatively rare premarital heterosexual relationships that are available apart from contacts with prostitutes. In Portugal, Spain, Italy, and Greece, as across the waters in North Africa, most adolescent boys and young men accept and even seek homosexual contacts with little feeling of shame or guilt. Most often they attempt to confine their activities to the role resembling that of the male with the female, but in a situation in which need dominates they may accept the principle that "turnabout is fair play." Sometimes the role is determined by age or by social dominance. There may be a good deal of seduction of younger boys by older youths.

Romantic attachments between males during youth are not uncommon in this area, and these are seldom regarded as perverse, but are more characteristically viewed in a light not far different from that in which they were regarded by the pagan ancestors of these peoples. No one would care to have his homosexual activities announced publicly, but public exposure would incur embarrassment rather than deep-seated guilt.

The rather widespread and free practice of homosexuality among Mediterranean males seldom leads to a pattern of exclusive homosexuality either in youth or later in life. Indeed, these people have little comprehension of what is meant by "homosexuality" as a fixed pattern of behavior, and those among them that appear to be ratable as 6 or even 5 in later life seem to form a smaller group than elsewhere in Judaeo-Christendom. Some measure of homosexual experience is taken for granted as an inevitable part of the sexual and emotional development of males, and homosexual episodes up until the time of marriage occasion little anxiety in the individual or the community.

However, the male who actively seeks homosexual relationships after marriage is likely to meet with disapproval if his activities become known to the community, especially if he should choose to play the so-called passive role in anal intercourse. Expressions of disapproval, however, are seldom more than verbal and almost never involve punitive legal action, since there is no reference in the law to consensual homosexual acts that take place in privacy. Older, married males who regularly participate in homosexual contacts, like males who never marry, are regarded as peculiar but not grossly abnormal. Extremely effeminate males—the "fairies" and "faggots" of our society—are subject to good-natured ridicule, but seldom to serious abuse. Sometimes the younger of those males are treated by more vigorous males as girls, and they may be sought after as passive partners in anal intercourse. The number of these highly effeminate males in the large cities in the south of Europe, however, seems small by comparison with their number elsewhere in Judaeo-Christendom.

The essentially nonpunitive attitude toward homosexuality among younger, unmarried men in the Mediterranean region enables us to distinguish the Mediterranean attitude from that of transalpine Europe. With few exceptions, homoerotophobia increases as one crosses the Alps and proceeds northward. The more exclusively Protestant areas appear to suffer most from this phobia, and it reaches its European zenith in England. Even in England, however, public and private anxiety over homosexuality cannot be compared in intensity with the anxiety that this type of sexual behavior arouses in the United States.

As homoerotophobia increases there is generally an increase in the use of legal sanctions to suppress it; these may be reinforced by a strongly negative sentiment on the part of the public against homosexuality. The use of legal sanctions in the attempt to suppress homosexual behavior has, however, lost ground in modern times, so that among the prominent European nations only England and Germany still have laws that punish consensual homosexual relations in private, and in England Parliament may well have abolished this law by the time this book is published.

Economic factors, combined with the peculiar work psychology of the region, encourage the suppression of prostitution—homosexual or hetero-sexual—in countries like Switzerland, Holland, Denmark, and Sweden; efforts to curb free homosexual relations among adults in these countries are confined to instances in which prostitution is involved. Nevertheless, homosexual prostitution continues to exist rather widely in all of these countries, as it does in England and in the United States.

Homosexual activities, even on the part of the active partner in anal intercourse, are more strongly associated with loss of masculine status in northern Europe than in southern Europe, although it should not be imag-ined that this loss of status brings about the same degree of conflict as in the United States. Northern European males do not feel as hard pressed to maintain their masculinity as American males, and the items of behavior that are associated with loss of masculinity or with homosexuality are far fewer than in North America. In almost all of Europe, the cultivation of refinement in manners and speech is looked upon as an enviable product of education and breeding rather than as effeminacy. Coarse or aggressive public brawling is not only frowned upon but is also punished severely by the law. Refinement of taste in the arts or interest in intellectual questions in no way suggest effeminacy; nor would homosexual inclinations be imputed to the possessor of these attributes.

Habits of dress among males are rather conservative in Europe, but de-parture from the conventions would suggest bad taste or bohemianism rather than effeminacy in most cases short of outright transvestism. Certain bars, public houses, night clubs, and the like are frequented by males inter-ested in homosexual contacts throughout northern Europe, and the cus-tomers for the most part remain unmolested by the police. In several prominent northern cities there are homosexual social organizations that maintain clubhouses and sponsor social and intellectual activities. These are entirely legal and receive the full cooperation of the police.

One hears more about the exclusive homosexual and sees more persons who presumably may be rated as 5 or 6 in northern Europe than in south-ern Europe. Attitudes toward homosexuality are much more self-conscious and more definitive, and polemics on the topic are much more frequently encountered. This sort of self-consciousness and intellectualization on the theme seems to be more in evidence in the areas where Calvinism and Lutheranism have prevailed. Homosexual partnerships tend to endure longer in northern Europe than in southern Europe or America, if one may judge from hearsay and from the number of middle-aged and older homo-sexual couples who live together. Youth is not emphasized to quite the same extent, and older males do not seem to be confronted by loneliness and frustration as often, perhaps, as in America. Homosexual periodicals, often containing rather erotic illustrations and photographs, may be found on the public newsstands of the north, though never in the south.

Throughout all of Judaeo-Christendom, even in the more permissive subcultures, homosexuality is accepted or at least tolerated only so long as it is confined to specifically defined areas and widespread public attention is not focused upon it. The fundamental rejection of homosexuality on the part of Judaeo-Christian culture as a whole is revealed most clearly when, as a result of publicity through the public media of communication, a "scandal" is created, or any time that a particular subculture becomes fearful that it may be acquiring a reputation for homosexuality. At such times, although perhaps only at such times, even the most "liberal" countries pursue a policy of harassment, usually augmented by police action. It is then that personal reputations are damaged, abuses temporarily abound, and social tragedies may occur.

No quarter of Judaeo-Christendom, including Scandinavia, Holland, or Belgium, where certain so-called protective laws in the interest of homosexual citizens exist, is entirely secure for the individual who may wish to pursue a homosexual way of life. There is always some threat of social or professional inconvenience that may increase to the point of near or of actual disaster. In most countries these incidents may be relatively few, and may occur only seldom; but they are potential everywhere within Judaeo-Christendom. Even in countries that have no laws against consenting homosexual acts per se, devious legal means may be used at certain times to molest, penalize, or deport certain individuals whose homosexual activities have become scandalous or obnoxious to the community or to some public official. Instances of this have been recorded in Switzerland, France, Italy, and Greece, for example—all of which may be reckoned as very tolerant countries so far as the treatment of individuals with homosexual interests is concerned.

Sometimes the scandals that lead to persecution begin as the result of some shocking or illegal act involving homosexuality. Thus the distribution of pornography, the seduction of a child, orgiastic activities, the discovery of an organized ring of homosexual prostitution, or the occurrence of some form of brutality may bring about a public reaction in which a number of innocent persons are penalized along with the guilty. In other cases journalistic scandalmongering may be sufficient to lead to abuses. All things considered, however, these waves of hysteria are rare in Europe as compared with America, where hysteria on the subject of homosexuality and "sexual deviation" may be described as chronic.

During the earliest phase of our culture, homosexuality was condemned and suppressed as a form of idolatry and therefore as one of the most heinous of sins. By the Middle Ages homosexual behavior was also reckoned as a crime and the secular authorities of Europe, in cooperation with the Church, condemned the homosexual offender to the most brutal punishments. Nevertheless, by the time of the Renaissance, homosexuality again thrived quite openly and was embraced by some of the most prominent spirits of the age. The period of Enlightenment during the eighteenth century brought forth a number of important civil and legal reforms that facilitated the abolition of the medieval laws against sodomy in most of the leading countries of Europe during the early part of the nineteenth century. But legal reform did not mean that this mode of sexual expression was acceptable to the conscience of Judaeo-Christian man. Efforts to suppress homosexuality in modern times have consisted mainly in the use of therapeutic techniques, and it is primarily as a disease rather than as a sin or a crime that homosexuality is condemned and suppressed today. The effects upon the individual who has become involved in homosexuality are not far different from what they were in the past, however, and homosexuality continues to be the occasion for a great deal of suffering within our culture. At the end of a little book entitled *The White Paper* even Jean Cocteau, who lived in the more tolerant atmosphere of Parisian society all his life, felt the need to write the following lines:

A social vice makes a vice of my outspokenness. I haven't any more to say, and so I'll go. In France, this vice doesn't lead to the penitentiary, thanks to the longevity of the Code Napoléon and the morals of some magistrate. But I'm not willing just to be tolerated. That wounds my love of love and of liberty.

Within very recent times, as a result of the efforts of prominent sexologists and other scientists, there has been some recognition of the fact that the sexual drive may be manifested in diverse forms, and that these need not necessarily be regarded *ipso facto* as either sinful, criminal, or pathological. It has been more widely recognized by scientists that the capacity to respond to stimuli originating in an individual of the same sex is potential in all human beings, and manifest in a large number of human beings; with the wider recognition of this fact has come a tendency on the part of many scientists to reinterpret the meaning of homosexual behavior. Any effort in this direction, however, meets with impassioned and often fierce resistance on the part of those who have strongly identified themselves with the age-old sexual beliefs and mores of our culture. To suggest that homosexual behavior of any kind, no matter what part it may play in the life and personality of the individual, is not sinful or criminal or that it is anything less than "sick, sick, sick," is to bring upon oneself the concerted disapproval and ire of all of those who look upon themselves as the personal and perhaps divinely inspired guardians of righteousness.

Nevertheless, in spite of the most persistent efforts to maintain the sexual status quo in every detail, contemporary men and women have begun to question the infallibility of the dogmas upon which this status quo rests. No longer is every man certain, as he was perhaps a hundred years ago, that our traditional sexual beliefs and standards are perfect in every particular. With the growing skepticism characteristic of modern life has come an uncertainty as to whether our society is absolutely right in condemning all· of those who deviate in their sexual behavior from the verbalized ideals and pretended behavior of the group. Some have questioned whether the harassment and in some cases the outright and brutal persecution of homosexually inclined individuals tally with certain other ethical ideals such as justice, freedom, tolerance, and the dignity of the individual.

Armed with the feeling that they are asking for nothing more than their just demands, a few individuals in the more civilized and urbane quarters of Judaeo-Christendom have joined together in very recent times to protect themselves against the onslaughts of what often appears to be a callous and relentless moral bigotry. Perhaps nothing in our times is more indicative of the fundamental social changes that are taking place quietly, persistently and, for the most part unnoticed, than the emergence of what some have called "the homophile movement." This so-called movement is weak, very poorly organized, largely ineffectual, very unpopular even among those who might be expected to rally around it, and downright humorous in some of its aspects. But what is amazing is not that it accomplishes so little but that it exists at all. The existence of such a movement would have been inconceivable only fifty years ago. What its future may be few can say; but its existence indicates quite clearly a growing refusal on the part of many to be punished and humiliated for what they regard as their finest emotions.

Many so-called homosexuals are totally unaware of the significance of their position in our society, and their fondest efforts are devoted to denying to themselves and to everyone else that their social position is at all different from anyone else's. Such may sometimes be the case. It should be realized at once that homosexuality as "a way of life" is something that is almost peculiar to our own culture as a result of the unusual pressures which Judaeo-Christian culture puts upon the individual who embraces homosexual practices; even within our own culture only a very few of those millions who become involved in homosexuality make of it "a way of life." For the vast majority of those with a history of homosexuality, homosexual experiences constitute only a *part* of their sexual pattern and do not cause them to feel distinct in any way from the rest of society.

But most unfortunately, experience with homosexuality, whatever its extent, may cause a considerable number of people to feel isolated from the main current of society, and they may come to develop an attitude toward themselves that makes it quite impossible to identify with other people around them whom they regard as "heterosexuals" or "nonhomosexuals."

In other words, our attitudes toward homosexuality foster a "homosexual minority" that is in many ways similar to most other minorities. The so-called homosexual, for example, who has lost his job because of some scandal, who has been denied his veteran's benefits because of a reputation for homosexuality, or has been discriminated against in some other way, will tend to gravitate toward others like himself among whom he may find understanding and sympathy. Should such an individual wish to pursue homosexual relationships in the form of friendships and sexual alliances, he may soon find that whether or not he wishes to become part of a minority he is, in fact, part of a minority. If the same individual lived in a different culture in which homosexual episodes occasion little interest on the part of other people, he might simultaneously pursue heterosexual interests and perhaps, with the passing of time, might find that involvement in work, family life, and other activities had diverted him from his former interest in homosexual relations. Such a thing is possible even within our own society, and a majority of those who have had relatively little homosexual experience find that this is exactly what happens.

But for many, and especially for those who have an extensive amount of homosexual experience, it is almost impossible within our society not to be pressured in one way or another into a minority status, and with this status, in a great many cases, comes the assumption of a "homosexual way of life."

This way of life, as we have emphasized, is more or less peculiar to our own Judaeo-Christian culture, and it is perhaps useful in a chapter such as this to devote some space to a discussion of it. The reader, however, should not imagine that it is possible within a few paragraphs to convey a very complete picture of the "homosexual way of life." Entire chapters, and, indeed, volumes have been devoted to describing and explaining this complicated sociological and psychological pattern.

The homosexual way of life is not wholly dependent upon the mere existence of homosexual experiences in the individual's history, however few or many these may be; many individuals with a great deal of homosexual experience never become involved at all in a homosexual way of life and others do not accept it as a permanent adjustment. The homosexual way of life is dependent, rather, upon the way in which the individual reacts to his experiences with homosexuality and upon the unique sociologic pressures that face many such individuals within our society. It is essentially the social dynamics of our society that give rise to the homosexual way of life.

We must begin with the recognition that the homosexual way of life is an adjustment (or, many would say, a maladjustment) that certain individuals make to themselves and to the society around them as a result of the image they have come to accept of themselves as a "homosexual." Whatever pathology may be associated with homosexuality lies within this particular adjustment rather than in the fact of having desired and of having experienced homosexual contacts per se.

In order to accept the particular adjustment that may be called the homosexual way of life, it is first absolutely essential that the individual regard himself as a "homosexual." We should not be misled by the fact that many people who may vociferously deny to the world around them that they are "homosexual," or even that they have any particular interest in homosexuality, have nevertheless adopted an attitude toward themselves as "homosexuals." We shall later discuss briefly the individual who has adopted this attitude toward himself without simultaneously adopting the label, and—more importantly—without identifying positively with the homosexual group.

We have previously questioned the habit of making a substantive of the word "homosexual" to refer to individuals with a history of homosexual responsiveness. It has been pointed out that homosexual experiences, be they few or many, do not make a "homosexual"; nor does a preference for any particular mode of homosexual activity such as a preference for the so-called passive role in anal intercourse. Nor, in spite of a great deal of psychiatric impressionism, has it been established scientifically that the tendency to respond homosexually is regularly related to any particular item of character or personality, or any particular combination of such items. Within the group that responds homosexually may be found all types of personality, all levels of intelligence, every type of emotional adjustment and maladjustment, and every conceivable type of character from the most praiseworthy to the most reprehensible. Mere experience with homosexual contacts alone can neither make nor define a "homosexual," since if experience be used as a criterion we must acknowledge that such experience may vary almost without limit with regard to both quantity and quality. The effort to define the "homosexual" on the basis of the number of homosexual experiences in the history of the individual, or even on the basis of the individual's emotional satisfaction with such experiences, leads to an arbitrary and rather meaningless stand which will not earn unanimous approval.

Although there is in reality no such thing as a "homosexual," and, therefore, we should not refer to the "homosexual" when speaking scientifically, there has, within our society, developed a stereotype of the "homosexual," along with a great many myths and superstitions about homosexuality. This stereotype and these myths and superstitions are relevant to our discussion of the homosexual way of life and the individual's acceptance of himself as a "homosexual."

Myths about the "homosexual" and about homosexuality vary considerably and contradict each other in many particulars, so that if we were to attempt to give a complete account of all of these myths and impressions it would be necessary to write a separate volume. The myths from psychiatric, legal, and other learned literature alone would fill a great many chapters in such a volume. Most of them, however, revolve around certain basic ideas and reflect the entire evolution of the Judaeo-Christian attitude toward this subject. The sin-crime-disease triad is at the basis of most of these myths. Added to this triad is the Judaeo-Christian conviction that male homosexuality is associated with effeminacy, cowardliness, and weakness— in such contrast with the attitude toward homosexuality found among the pagans of antiquity and many so-called primitive peoples.

Thus the "homosexual" in our society is pictured as a perverted, dissolute, unscrupulous, and emotionally warped individual who is unworthy of trust and confidence. This mythological creature is also supposed to possess all of the less admirable attributes ascribed most often to the female in our society: emotional instability, physical cowardice, irresolution, social ostentation, vanity, and gossipmongering. It is of interest that in characterizing the "homosexual" as feminine, our society chooses to assign only the reprehensible traits associated with femininity, and none of the noble and admirable traits such as patience, devotion, self-sacrifice, loving gentleness, and the like. The "faggot" is not likened to a woman per se; he is likened to a mean, petty, and contemptible woman.

When all is said and done, there is no reason why, if the homosexual male is to be characterized as feminine, he should not be so characterized in such a way as to include the admirable traits associated with the female personality along with the less admirable traits. That he is not so characterized suggests a fundamental contempt on the part of our society not only for the "homosexual" but also for females. No doubt this contempt has something to do with the viewing of both females and "homosexuals" as "receptors" in the sexual act.

Cory and LeRoy draw our attention to this in the following paragraphs.

> How is it possible for society to look with such contempt upon the receptor and not on the insertor in a male homosexual act? It seems to us to be a reflection of the contempt that society has for all sexual receptors. Thus, being penetrated is viewed as being attacked, being vulnerable, hence passive, feminine, and inferior.
>
> The woman in Western culture is assigned the role of the vulnerable sex, the weaker sex, the dominated sex. Hence, it is reasoned that men who are also penetrated must be less than manly, thereby assuming feminine characteristics in a mind corrupted by thinking in terms of stereotypes.[15]

In addition to all of the attributes discussed above, the "homosexual" is credited with a number of other attributes that seem to originate in the medieval belief that sodomy, as it was called, is associated with heresy, witchcraft, and black magic. The details of this association of ideas will be discussed in a later chapter. It is sufficient to say here that the confusion led to many erroneous conclusions about homosexuality.

Many stories circulate about "homosexual freemasonry." "Homosexuals" are supposed to be organized into a secret society on an international level through which they exert unspecified but powerful influence "behind the scenes." They are supposed to be received by "others of their kind" wherever they may go throughout the world, and there has been much talk about a "homosexual conspiracy," supposedly at work in many professions such as fashion design, interior decorating, advertising, the arts, and the theater. It is the object of this conspiracy to homosexualize, as it were, the entire world, chiefly by bringing contempt upon women and by circulating the ridiculous notion that homosexuality is a superior form of love. This "homosexual freemasonry" is reminiscent of the "international Jewry" that is supposed to be "working away at the roots of our Christian heritage," and, in general, the psychology of anti-Semitism is identical to the psychology of antihomosexuality. Behind both may be found the same paranoia.

In keeping with the medieval view, homosexual practices and the effects of such practices upon the partners have been characterized as "perverse" (with all of the anxiety that word conjures up) and have become confused with sadistic and masochistic orgies and rituals. All "perversions" were lumped together in the medieval mind, and have never since become completely disentangled in popular thinking.

In this connection, the author recalls the comment of a probation officer whose job it was to consult with the "morals cases" in an effort to set them right. In speaking of "homosexuals" he informed the author that it is common practice for them to prey upon little boys. He said that one of their delights is to suck the genitals of tiny victims until they draw blood. When specific case histories were inquired after, he said that none were available at the time, but that he had heard that such practices are common among "deviates." It seemed most incongruous that anyone whose job it is to consult with others in behalf of their social adjustment should be a victim of such fantasies. But the vampire fantasy is only one among many other fantasies about "homosexuals" and "deviates" that even some people in authority harbor.

Confusion between homosexuality, sadism, and paedophilia is very common, and it is automatically assumed by many that the "homosexual" is regularly a molester of children and a sadist as well. While there are, of course, homosexual paedophiles and homosexual sadists and masochists, sadomasochism and paedophilia are no more regularly associated with homosexuality than with heterosexuality, and the vast majority of "homosexuals," like the vast majority of "heterosexuals," are emotionally repelled by sadomasochism and paedophilia.

This brief account of the attitudes and beliefs that are current in our society with regard to "homosexuals," and homosexuality, is far from complete, but it is perhaps sufficient to convey something of the atmosphere that greets the youth who has become mentally or physically involved with homosexuality. The earliest impression he has of his involvement is that it is evil, forbidden, and, above all, dangerous. All kinds of frightening implications are associated with this subject in the mind of the neophyte. Most of them are flagrantly ridiculous and are based on superstition rather than on reality. But not all such fears are groundless. The homosexual neophyte may soon learn from harsh experience how really dangerous it is in most cases to become homosexually involved when he is singled out for contempt and ridicule by others of his own age, and later when, if it is known that he is homosexually inclined, he meets with varied and repeated penalties at the hands of society. Once a boy has had anything more than the most fleeting experience with homosexuality, he must make some kind of an adjustment to the emotional conflict that this entails in our society. Adjustments vary; while it is the primary purpose of this chapter to discuss the adjustment involved when one adopts a homosexual way of life, it is useful to make a few comments upon certain other types of adjustment that commonly occur.

The conflict is not the same in character or intensity for all youths who are exposed to homosexual experiences, nor does the conflict arise within identical circumstances. Some youths have experienced a homosexual contact in which they can maintain the feeling of being entirely masculine. Often their role has been that of what Cory and LeRoy call the insertor, and they are able to reconcile their homosexual experiences with a picture of themselves as being entirely heterosexual as well, and thus beyond reproach. They may continue to have homosexual contacts throughout life, repeatedly or only infrequently, always assuming the "masculine role," and always regarding themselves as a "heterosexual." Others may have had the role of the receptor forced upon them and may have experienced no pleasure in that role. These persons may simply avoid homosexual contacts altogether, or they may seek the role of the insertor and follow a pattern like the one described above.

There are some, of course, who participate as either receptor or insertor or as both with a minimum amount of conflict because it may happen that within their group they maintain the respect of their peers on the basis of some particular accomplishments. There is a sizable number of gifted athletes, for example, who participate in homosexual contacts and experience little conflict in connection with these contacts because they are accepted by their peers. These males seldom enter into a homosexual way of life, and they seldom regard themselves as "homosexuals." Indeed, all of the adjustments to homosexuality that do not lead the individual to adopt a homosexual way of life involve some technique that enables the individual to accept himself as a "heterosexual" and not as a "homosexual." We need not enumerate the various mental mechanisms that make this possible, but since we know that far more men engage in homosexual activities than ever adopt a homosexual way of life, these techniques must be manifold and they must provide a successful adjustment to conflict over homosexuality for the average male who becomes involved.

Not all males with homosexual experience succeed, however, in maintaining a heterosexual view of themselves. Many things may conspire to bring about a situation in which the individual accepts both the label and the way of life of a "homosexual." Consider, for example, the impressionable youth who has become involved in homosexuality, and who has been exposed to the various myths and attitudes described earlier. If, for reasons that we need not elaborate here, he becomes strongly conditioned to respond to homosexual stimuli, and if he cannot renounce the pleasures that he finds in homosexuality and cannot entirely replace these with heterosexual satisfactions, he may begin to accept the stereotype. The ridicule of his fellows may leave a deep imprint upon his mind. It may not be long before he comes to think to himself, "I am one of those things . . . I am a homosexual." At the point at which one has made such an identification, the only possibility left open for a social life is that one find others like oneself with whom to associate.

The author remembers a story told him by a patient which exemplifies how such an experience can come about, and the effects it can have in determining the future of an individual. When the patient was around ten years old he made the acquaintance of a boy of thirteen who was the hero of the school. The hero's name was Philip and the patient, John, was overjoyed in the realization that he had gained the attention of so splendid a fellow. Since John was younger than Philip and far less prepossessing, he was willing to make any sacrifice in order to maintain his friendship with Philip. On their walks home from school he carried Philip's books, and he always gave a welcome ear to the boastful stories of the older boy. Philip assured John that he would have a place in the gang even though he was only ten, and that he would have the great honor of being Philip's personal servant as well.

It was not long before Philip had introduced John to the mysteries of masturbation, which Philip understood and performed with great skill, so it seemed. Indeed John, as the honored servant, was given the privilege of masturbating Philip in the secrecy of a wooded glade. The patient described his feelings for Philip at the time as those of complete love and admiration. In describing them he used the word "lyrical." Shortly afterward, when John was waiting outside the school to carry Philip's books, it occurred to him that he would never be able to tell the older boy about these lyrical feelings. While he was still lost in this saddening thought, Philip passed by but did not pause to greet his devoted admirer. The younger boy ran after his hero in the expectation of joining him. But Philip merely turned and said, "Go on. I'm not walking with you anymore. You're a queer. I don't pal around with queers."

From that instant on, the patient declared that he felt a separation between himself and other boys that changed his entire approach to life. Being a "queer" explained to him how he felt about Philip, and it explained to him also why he had not been accepted into the gang.

For a long time, of course, he felt that he was the only "queer" on earth. But later, during adolescence, when he met a boy with tastes like those he had developed in his mysterious rituals with Philip, he felt for the first time as if he had found complete acceptance. The long period of isolation was at an end. He and his new-found friend had many secret thoughts and experiences to share with one another. It was as if they lived in a world apart from which all others who were different were excluded, just as they themselves had been excluded from the outer world.

This small world of the two youths was expanded when John discovered the "gay life" of the city near his suburban home. He told his friend about it, and it was not long before the two boys were attending what seemed to be to them the glamorous parties of their sophisticated friends in town. In the atmosphere of the "gay life" John was able to find acceptance not only of his sexual tastes; he also found more acceptance of his aesthetic and his intellectual tastes. Among the youths of his own age at school or in his neighborhood, John could find little interest in the things that seemed important, glamorous, and exciting to him. To these boys John seemed like a "square," but they seemed like boorish oafs to John. There was little common ground upon which they could meet.

In the city, however, among his "gay" friends, John found a whole new world of intellectual, sexual, and aesthetic excitement. He soon became involved in a poignant love affair, and was shocked and offended when an older friend expressed skepticism about its permanence. But at least the man did not express contempt for his love. Indeed, this older friend attempted to advise and to guide the confused youth. Soon John began to look to this far more experienced man as a guide and mentor. He was the first older male who seemed to have any understanding of him, and to John understanding meant love. The two remained friends for many years, and at the time when John entered therapy he was very concerned about his friend's health, which had deteriorated through the years.

It does not require great psychological insight or wisdom to understand how the homosexual way of life fulfilled certain of John's needs. His primary conditioning to homosexuality was followed rapidly by an experience which, it is true, might have prevented another boy from pursuing homosexual activities. But a number of other circumstances, which will not be elaborated upon here, served to reinforce this conditioning, and he had learned rather traumatically that if he were to enjoy acceptance of his most "lyrical" feelings it would have to be with others who felt the same about those feelings. He always spoke of the friends in his circle as "my kind of people."

We are all in the habit of looking upon the sordid and tragic side of the homosexual way of life; and there can be little doubt that there is much that is sordid and tragic about it. But on the other hand, this adjustment cannot be condemned entirely nor absolutely for all people. Things are never so simple and never so black or white. Before emphasis is given to the seamy side of the homosexual way of life, some recognition also must be given to its value as an adjustment—the only possible adjustment for certain types of personality.

The "gay life" is not altogether or only superficial, pretentious, fantastic, and unreal. There are some aspects of it that do fulfill legitimate human needs, such as the need for companionship, understanding, and acceptance. Moreover, all human beings must find a milieu in which they can share their interests with others. It is not possible to share homosexual interests with others in ordinary society, and unless the individual with strongly developed homosexual interests wishes to remain a "lone wolf" he will gravitate toward the "gay" world. The "gay" world is easily satirized, and it is not difficult to find numerous things to ridicule in it. But every type of social clique is to some extent ridiculous and few deserve to escape the satirist's pen entirely. There are undoubtedly aspects of the "gay" life that must even be considered downright vicious. But again, viciousness is by no means confined to homosexual cliques.

It is necessary to maintain some objectivity in appraising the homosexual way of life. Most therapists, including this author, tend to criticize "gay" society and to regard the homosexual way of life as a definitely inferior emotional adjustment, without stopping to consider the alternatives presented to some people. Not even according to the most optimistic accounts can we expect to reverse the homosexual trends of every single individual who consults us as therapists, and there are many more who do not seek such a reversal even where it may be possible. For those who cannot and those who will not abandon their homosexual interests there must be recourse to some social life with others like themselves, and it is entirely understandable that these people will tend—like all minorities—to create a little world of their own. All such little worlds tend to be restricting, and involvement in the psychology typical of any minority has distinctly deleterious effects. But it also has distinct advantages; it is the advantages they provide that tend to keep these minorities intact. Wherever people come together because they are persecuted for some attribute they share in common—whether this attribute be religious, social, sexual, or political in character—group psychology will be in evidence. There can be little serious doubt that the "homosexual" *feels* persecuted, and *is* persecuted, and that consequently he will feel a strong bond in common with others who meet with his same experiences in the larger context of society as a whole.

Other types of experience may drive certain people into a homosexual way of life. Many people, for example, participate in homosexual activities on what they regard as a casual basis, only to find that our society can never regard such activities casually once they become known. The reputation for homosexuality, even in an individual ratable only as 1, 2, or 3 may be sufficient to propel that individual into the homosexual way of life. The rigid social attitudes that prevail regarding this subject constantly foster circumstances in which many people who originally may have no reason to choose between homosexuality and heterosexuality are virtually forced to do so.

Let us consider the example of an individual who in psychiatric jargon might be described as bisexual.

The story of one such person was brought to the attention of this author some years ago when a patient suffering from marked anxiety and depression came to his office. While in the Army he had been surprised during homosexual embrace with another soldier in the shower room. His discoverer reported him. He was first hospitalized and finally court-martialed. The dishonorable discharge resulting from his trial constituted an enormous obstacle during search for employment in his trade after separation from the Army. Indeed, he was completely unsuccessful in his efforts to find work in the area for which he had been trained. Moreover, word of the nature of his misdemeanor in the Army got back to some of his friends at home, and he returned to find himself the talk of the community in which he was raised.

Bitter and isolated, this young man found the only acceptance that he had known for some months in a small homosexual circle in his town. In listening to his background, and in taking his sexual history, the author felt quite convinced that this man, were it not for the circumstances described, would certainly never have become exclusively homosexual. Nor would he have adopted the homosexual way of life. Indeed, homosexuality seemed originally destined to play but a small part in his life. He had a strong interest in women and, while susceptible to the seductive behavior of men, seemed to be oriented primarily in a heterosexual direction.

By the time he entered therapy, however, some years after his unfortunate experiences, most of his friends were in the "gay" life, and he was living as the lover of another man. He had taken up work in which he was acceptable as a "homosexual" and, in a way of speaking, had become adjusted to the homosexual way of life. The adjustment was in reality only apparent in the case of this man, as his depression and anxiety revealed. Though he did not pursue them, his heterosexual interests had persisted. He explained that a few years earlier he had dated a girl regularly and had become very fond of her. When she became suspicious and resentful of some of his friends, and insisted upon knowing if he too were a "pansy," he reacted with anger and broke the relationship with her. He felt that this girl, who was far from being unsophisticated, should accept his friends who, he assured her, had been very kind to him when many others had not been. Since he was not actively homosexual at the time, and had no intention of betraying her in favor of another man, he could not understand why she would not accept him; for her to accept him, he felt, she must accept some of his closest homosexual friends. It was difficult for him to see why she could not be satisfied with his love for her, which he insisted was genuine, and he rejected the idea that in order to prove his love he must abandon friendships he cherished. After he broke up with his girl he felt quite disillusioned about the "straight world" once again, and it seemed natural for him to turn for solace where he had found it before. After some months he became attached to the man with whom he was living when he entered therapy. By the time he entered therapy this man had accepted the idea that he was a "homosexual," and he was determined to maintain a homosexual way of life without further complications.

As a result of his efforts to overcome his problems through therapy he conquered his anxiety and depression and decided to make a bid once again for an adjustment to the straight world. It is worth remarking that his friend was very helpful in bringing about a solution. He was convinced that the patient was "really straight" and that he would only find permanent happiness with a woman. Later the patient met another young lady with whom he fell in love. They were married and for some time now have lived together happily. But this man was lucky to have had the understanding and, one must add, the love of his friend and of his wife, for without both he would never have effected the changes in his life that came about during therapy. His wife is aware of her husband's homosexual trends and does not feel threatened by them so that he feels little need to act upon these tendencies. The former roommate remains a friend of this couple and, as the patient laughingly said, will probably be the godfather to their first baby.

It is often surprising to what extent acceptance of the stereotype may change an individual. Consider, for example, the "screaming faggot." It is usually supposed that very effeminate men are "born that way," or that they always acquire effeminate characteristics very early in life and so are forced into the "gay world." This may usually be the case, but is not always so. It is possible to recall a number of instances in which young men who have originally presented a typical picture of masculinity have later acquired all of the characteristics of the "screaming faggot" through direct imitation. One example comes to mind of a tough little "hustler" whose business activities forced him eventually to adopt the homosexual way of life. At the point at which he became convinced that he was a "homosexual" he took on all of the mannerisms of the stereotype and became the campiest "queen" on the avenue. No doubt, he himself was convinced that he had always been "gay," and that when he previously acted like a "butch" it was then that he was putting on airs. That is doubtful, however.

Acceptance of the idea that one is a "homosexual" does not always or even usually involve effeminate affectations, though it almost always involves a considerable loss of self-esteem. It is not possible to think of oneself as a "homosexual," with what this means in our society, and at the same time maintain a genuine sense of self-respect. It is virtually impossible to divorce the idea of being a "homosexual" from all the superstitions and distorted thinking upon which such a concept is based; no one would categorize and pigeonhole himself in such a way if he were not thoroughly indoctrinated into the type of thinking that gives rise to the stereotype in the first place. It is necessary to be clear on this point. Acceptance of one's homosexual propensities, whether these be ratable as 1 or as 6, is altogether desirable; but this is not the same as acceptance of one's self as a "homosexual." Indeed, it is hard to find anyone who regards himself as a "homosexual" who really accepts his homosexuality! Acceptance of the stereotype represents a type of adjustment rather than an appreciation of reality. In reality no one is a "homosexual" any more than anyone is a "heterosexual"—or any other reification of sexual life. Belief to the contrary only leads to homosexual chauvinism or heterosexual chauvinism. It is better and more accurate to regard oneself as a *human being* first and last, and to accept the fact that one is in the possession of various unrealized and unexplored potentialities.

Some people regard themselves as "homosexuals" in a secret and grudging way, only, from that point, to despise and to fear anyone else whom they also regard as a "homosexual." These are often very dangerous cranks who are on the verge of or in the full swim of paranoia. It is doubtful that anyone who does not have at least the secret fear that he himself is a "homosexual" would ever become highly emotional or hostile on the subject, or regard it with anything more than interested curiosity. The "closet queen" or so-called latent homosexual becomes a menace not only to himself but eventually to the entire community. He is behind most drives to "rid the community of perversion," by which effort he hopes to relieve his own unassuaged homosexual guilts and fears. Usually he succeeds only in disturbing the peace, setting aside justice, interfering with the privacy and the rights of fellow citizens, and bringing about the persecution of a defenseless group.

No picture of the "gay" life would be complete without some mention of the "fairy" or "faggot," or "queen," as we are wont to call the ultra-effeminate homosexual male. It is these individuals who have come to personify the "real homosexual" to the masses, and the masses tend to think that all "real homosexuals" are "fairies."

"Faggots," "queens," and "fairies" seem to be people who, when they say to themselves, "I am a homosexual," accept the fullest definition given this term in our society. Their impersonation of a female is usually either wholly satirical or wholly sentimental. Most go through life imitating Mae West, while a smaller number spend their days enacting the role of Elsie Dinsmore. Whether Mae West or Elsie Dinsmore, most of these eccentrics have little sexual appeal for heterosexually inclined men, who would rather have "a real woman," or for homosexually inclined men, who would rather have "a real man." It is difficult to know for whom they have any sexual appeal, although as transvestites some have succeeded in earning their living by charging unsuspecting customers a fee for intimacies that were not sufficiently intimate to reveal their lack of a vagina. When they do not take themselves seriously, the sharp-tongued humor of the "queen" may be very amusing, although when they are in a serious mood few people find them very amusing. Most other "homosexuals" consider these highly effeminate males an abomination and are excessively intolerant of them.

The "gay" scene in America includes yet another type worthy of comment. These are the "hustlers," or male prostitutes, who may be found in every large city in America and abroad. Some "queens" and "faggots" hustle for a living, but their clientele is necessarily limited in numbers because most homosexual clients prefer masculine lovers. This role is filled by young men, usually between the ages of seventeen and twenty-five, many of whom have taken to hustling as a full-time occupation. "Hustlers" do not ordinarily regard themselves as "homosexuals" but on the contrary are rather defensive about their heterosexuality and masculinity, since these are part and parcel of their stock in trade.

The life of a "hustler" and the milieu in which he works have been very candidly and rather poignantly described by John Rechy in his novel *City of Night*. The "hustler" who, like his client, is a criminal in America by virtue of existing laws, is not usually a vicious person. He may become involved in petty crimes and may occasionally "clip" (rob) his "score" (client), but ordinarily he accepts certain rules and regulations in the conduct of his commercial activities. A significant number of unemployed youths—dropouts from school, and other young men who in our progressively automated culture cannot find work—hustle in order to make a few dollars. Some boys who are employed in other work also hustle on the side to supplement their income, often in order to earn enough money to date girls. But the professional, full-time "hustler" tends to become involved in a way of life largely unknown to the part-time "hustler" who is just out of school.

The life described in Rechy's book—that in which the hustler, the "faggot," the "score," and the masculine homosexual intermingle in an atmosphere of bar life and park cruising—is but one aspect of the "gay" world, or the homosexual way of life, and should not be taken to represent the whole either in America or abroad. There are many people who are involved in a homosexual way of life who never contact "hustlers," who never frequent the bars or cruise the parks and public lavatories, and who, along with the rest of society, tend to look upon this scene as a part of the demimonde—which indeed it is. Nor is the scene described by Rechy faithfully duplicated abroad, although "hustlers" or "business-boys," as they are called, may be found in almost all European cities. Rechy's vivid account of hustling is largely an account of a special aspect of American life. The European "hustler" quite naturally works in a different milieu, in which attitudes toward homosexuality and even toward prostitution differ considerably from those encountered in America.

It is very interesting to note that most of these "hustlers" and "business-boys" seem very anxious to afford their clients satisfaction, and in their effort to do so they often have to participate in highly eccentric sexual activities that have little meaning for them personally. Many of those who patronize "hustlers," like those who patronize female prostitutes, tend to have what we call perverted desires that are often so eccentric that they cannot be fulfilled in an ordinary relationship. The tolerance—perhaps the indifference—of these "business-boys" and the equanimity with which they accept some of the most bizarre sexual demands are worthy of comment. Hidden in this willingness to please is something that perhaps not only characterizes an aspect of the personality of the "hustler," but also an aspect of the sexual potential of any human being.

Among the males who hustle, as among all males in the homosexual population, may be found individuals representing each rating from 1 through 6. But, according to the opinion of Wardell B. Pomeroy, communicated verbally to this author, most of those who become "hustlers" over any long period of time are ratable as 2. Some of these youths become so conditioned to homosexual stimuli that they spend the greater balance of their adult lives as 4s, 5s, or 6s. The latter, however, seem to be in the minority, and it is not at all unusual for a boy who has hustled over a period of several years to become involved at a later date in an exclusively heterosexual way of life.

To imagine that the world of male prostitution provides a complete picture of homosexuality or of the homosexual way of life is about as accurate as to imagine that the world of female prostitution gives a complete picture of heterosexuality or the heterosexual way of life. In either case, however, it must be admitted that certain aspects of human nature— or the human attitude toward sex—are revealed in a rather undisguised form. We may learn not a little about sex in our culture by paying some attention to prostitution.

Certain persons deny with chagrin the existence of a homosexual minority as a sociologic entity, because they arbitrarily insist that it is only possible to be born into a minority by virtue of race, religion, or ethnic origin. But such distinctions do not hold. The homosexual minority has all the vainglorious pride, all the contempt for itself, all of the chauvinism, and all the sense of alienation coupled with the desire for conformity that are characteristic of any other persecuted minority. Like other minorities, it is anxious to call attention to its great men in a rather futile effort to gain acceptance. It mocks while at the same time imitating slavishly the standards of the majority, and would consider itself honored in the extreme if it could receive accolades from the Daughters of the American Revolution or the Knights of Columbus. It has its own in-group jargon, its own in-group myths and gossip, and its own in-group characteristics of dress, manners, and speech. Like most minorities, it tends to isolate itself in ghettos, to frequent certain places of amusement and recreation, and to publish its own magazines and printed materials. It may even be said that there is a homosexual folklore.

Were it not for the extreme suppression of this group its status as a sociological minority would become all the more evident. It lacks entirely the political interest, organization, and force that certain recent writers anxiously impute to it; but that is to be expected of a minority that is so completely harassed and degraded. It cannot begin to act in its own defense and is at a stage in which its members can only function as individuals in the pursuit of self-interest. There is of course no homosexual minority outside of Judaeo-Christendom for the simple reason that there are no "homosexuals" outside of Judaeo-Christendom; there are none simply because outside of Judaeo-Christendom homosexuality seldom if ever becomes fetishized into a way of life.

As one example of the existence of a homosexual minority, which, like most minorities, has emulated and unsuccessfully adopted the standards and values of the majority, consider the attitudes our "homosexuals" adopt toward love. In almost every detail they ape and in the end caricature heterosexual values and usages. "Homosexuals" are condemned by "heterosexuals," and condemn themselves for not more regularly maintaining monogamous marriages of a sort designed for child rearing, which are only truly meaningful in the context of domesticity. We hear also of "homosexuals" bemoaning the lack of offspring and pleading for the right to adopt children. Many homosexual couples have even sought to have their unions recognized by official religious ritual.

The concept of romantic love aspired to in the affairs of most "homosexuals" is identical to that which developed during the Middle Ages and which has been the standard for heterosexual courtship ever since. This is not surprising, however, when one recalls the probable origin of romantic love in the homosexual fantasies of the troubadours.

Whether the individual with strongly developed homosexual propensities becomes a conscious member of the minority and adopts a homosexual way of life, or whether he remains totally aloof from the psychology involved in the homosexual way of life, the "homosexual" in Judaeo-Christian culture is faced with certain social realities that will make of his sexual orientation a "well of loneliness." With the exception of those few neurotic exhibitionists who accept fully the stereotype and become "faggots," those who develop pervasive homosexual interests must don a mask of hypocrisy that they are destined to wear for the remainder of their lives.

It is said that all men wear a mask, and that all men play a role in the drama that is life. This may be. Social harmony requires that everyone assume some role in life that more often than not does violence to his innermost identity. Only the rare exception who is willing to face the criticism with which he is bound to meet will reject the mask and insist upon maintaining his independence as a unique individual. Having done so he will be considered an eccentric—"a character"—and his efforts to remain apart from the "herd" will meet with considerable resistance.

But any comparison between the ordinary state of affairs described above and that in which the "homosexual" finds himself is spurious. The homosexual male must learn to be two wholly distinct people; the one whom he feels himself really to be, and the one whom he presents to the outside world. The divergence between the two is necessarily great. The disguise that he dons must completely hide his deepest longings and most heartfelt aspirations. Never must it be known abroad how he loves or whom he loves. It will never be granted to him to know the joy that comes in announcing to the world one's love and seeing others' joy in it. Whatever love he knows must remain hidden—often even from the person to whom it is addressed.

But this is only one aspect of the drama. The disguise that he assumes must not only obscure the innermost man; it must as completely as possible confute the innermost man. The outside world is a constant threat. Should he drop the mask for one moment, he may find himself disgraced, held up to scorn as a pariah, or even thrown into prison as a criminal. For him there is no security in society, no possibility of ever participating in it as himself.

Society is not there, as it is for other men, to protect him. Instead, it is one of the greatest threats to his security.

Many times the realization of this makes the "homosexual" a bitter and cynical critic of the world. He may become a pessimist and a misanthrope. At other times the unique position in which he finds himself—essentially that of an onlooker—may enable him to take a more objective view and to become a penetrating observer and critic of society. Not a little of the most telling social criticism has come from people who have been forced to look upon the world around them with the eyes of an uncompromising realist. A great deal of the humor that is common among "homosexuals"—for oddly enough these people, like members of certain other harassed minorities, may be gifted with a strong sense of humor that makes survival easier—sets into relief the many paradoxes of social life. In this context we may recall the clever and penetrating observations of Oscar Wilde and certain other gifted writers of a homosexual bent.

But the suffering that comes from a lifetime of wearing a mask of deception does not always encourage a sense of humor. More often it encourages a poignant feeling of melancholy that sometimes verges upon outright despair. This may find artistic expression in the work of gifted writers, poets, or musicians. The music of Tchaikovsky, for example, seems to express a sense of melancholy that no doubt was related to the composer's struggles with himself and his environment.

For the average person, however, a sense of alienation from the world does not give rise to artistic, critical, or scientific expression. The stress and strain imposed by so unnatural a position is often too much for the average person, and the wonder of it is that so many manage to cope with reality as well as they do under this pressure for an entire lifetime. At every turn there is potential disaster. Exposure may bring about utter ruin; social survival consists in adopting a position of, as it were, rational paranoia. Sometimes, of course, this paranoia becomes something less than rational, and the individual is plunged into a state of chronic anxiety, doubt, and suspicion.

Let us recognize unequivocally that the fear of imminent social disaster which is so apparent among many homosexually inclined individuals is not, as some psychiatrists have asserted, merely a reaction to *intrapsychic* conflicts. The threat with which these people are daily faced is a very real one, and for them to ignore it would be more psychotic on their part than for them to remain aware of it. Nor is the feeling that so many have that they are persecuted merely a paranoid delusion; for everywhere and at all times these people, if it becomes known that they are homosexual, are subject to treatment that no honest person could regard as less than persecutory. The fact that society requires that their life be conducted on the basis of complete deception is sufficient persecution to warrant a feeling of resentment. Some have argued that this feeling of resentment is unjustified because these people would have no need of deception were it not for their choice of an unacceptable orientation to sex. But the idea that this or any other sexual orientation is simply a matter of *choice* cannot be validated by any serious study of psychosexual development. Even if this orientation were entirely a matter of choice, all philosophers would not agree that such a choice warrants the bigotry and sadism of many who oppose it.

The struggle in which these people are bound to become involved is almost always a silent and anonymous one. The outside world may know nothing of it. Some have lived and died without their dearest friends, relatives, or lifetime associates ever having known of the burden they bore. During that lifetime the friends, relatives, and associates had come to know only the outer man, the man with the mask. The inner man, the real man, remained unknown and encapsulated within the disguise, for a great many so-called homosexuals never reveal themselves to anyone, even those who share the same inclinations.

Indeed, a good many of these people go through life without ever meeting anyone else whom they even recognize as having the same feelings as themselves. The isolation of some is incredible: They live an entire lifetime in the belief that they are the only persons in the world with homosexual urges. Although this was much more common in former days, when less was known and said about the subject and when many more people lived in small, intimate communities that gave rise to uncompromising conformity, it is surprising to find how many people still believe that homosexual feelings are entirely unique. Donald Webster Cory has received over 2,000 letters in response to his book *The Homosexual in America* and in response to his various talks and lectures on the subject. Among these are many letters in which people have expressed relief and even astonishment in the realization that others like themselves exist. It may be difficult for the sophisticated dweller in a large urban community to realize how it is possible for anyone to go through an entire lifetime without ever gaining knowledge of the existence of so-called homosexuals.

Even the so-called homosexual who lives in a large city, circulates freely within homosexual circles, and participates fully in a homosexual way of life must spend the greater part of his time wearing the mask. Seldom can he reveal his homosexual identity to those with whom he works, and he must maintain a pose whenever he is in public, which of course is a great deal of the time.

When, therefore, he is among other "gay" people or in a tolerant atmosphere, he may tend to emphasize rather than to mask his homosexuality. At parties, at "gay" bars, or in the privacy of his home with friends, he may appear rather extroverted and even a bit exhibitionistic in contrast with the rather subdued and remote person he may be at work or in public. But the picture he presents in "gay" life may not necessarily reflect the true nature of the inner man any more than the picture he presents in a heterosexual environment. It is the special tragedy of this individual that almost nowhere can he truly be himself. Often in "gay" society this person is so busy "letting his hair down" that he has no opportunity to reflect upon the real nature of his deepest feelings. When many people who are ordinarily subdued and distant come together in permissive surroundings for the purpose of relaxing and "being themselves," the ensuing atmosphere is usually one of forced hilarity in which no one really reveals his true identity. This is often the atmosphere of "gay society," and there can be little doubt that this is why the word "gay" has become associated with homosexuality. In reality it is quite obvious that there is very little that is very gay about homosexuality or those who are homosexual in our society.

The burden of personal anonymity is even heavier for those people who reject the homosexual way of life while still maintaining an interest in homosexuality. They represent, of course, a majority. Many things conspire to keep the ordinary person with strong homosexual tendencies within the strict boundaries of heterosexual society. To begin with, although homosexual feelings may play a substantial and even predominant part in the erotic life of a large number of people, they may by no means necessarily exclude heterosexual trends. Even if we confine our attention to those males in whom homosexual trends predominate, we will find that relatively few of them remain unaware of or unaffected by heterosexual trends. And it is equally true that those males in whom heterosexual trends predominate do not necessarily remain unaware of or unaffected by homosexual trends. Taken together these two groups represent the vast majority of all males in whom homosexual responsiveness is manifest. Yet few books on the subject of homosexuality (or heterosexuality) pay much attention to this fact, and homosexuality is discussed mainly in these books in terms of the 4 per cent of males who remain 6s throughout life. A comprehensive treatment of this subject, however, must include all males ratable from 1 through 6.

If we narrow our discussion, for the moment, to males ratable from 2 through 4 we will find within this group a large number of individuals who respond emphatically to homosexual stimuli and who either know nothing about the homosexual way of life or do not choose to enter into it. They may be prevented from taking any part in homosexual society by ignorance, fear, guilt, or indifference to the values of homosexual society. Their experiences with homosexuality may be extremely furtive, though not necessarily extremely rare, and it may not even occur to them that an interest in homosexual contacts implies participation in a homosexual way of life.

Nevertheless, many if not most of these males may meet with problems that are very similar to those of males who have abandoned heterosexuality altogether. These males are equally if not more directly confronted by the need for secrecy in connection with their homosexual interests, and refusal to participate in a homosexual way of life hardly exempts them from the many dangers that society puts in the way of any person who becomes involved in homosexual contacts. Often these men are husbands and fathers. Usually their wives remain unaware of their homosexual interests, and almost always their children remain unaware of these interests. Most of their friends and relatives know nothing of their homosexuality, and the sexual experiences they have with other men do not usually lead to extended relationships of a nonsexual nature. It is possible for them to have one or two homosexual friends or to enter into an extended affair with another man, and occasionally they may do so, but this does not imply acceptance of a homosexual way of life.

Some do, of course, become a part of the homosexual subculture and, in spite of marriage and an extensive heterosexual pattern, some of them maintain connections with homosexual society. Even more than the others we have discussed earlier, they are forced to lead a "double life." Since they maintain active connections with heterosexual society, they often have more to lose if their homosexuality is exposed. Exposure may involve their wife and their children as well as themselves, and the resulting scandal and tragedy are even greater than in the case of the single male whose entire personal life may be centered in homosexual relationships. The pressures under which this individual lives are far greater than most people would be willing to accept, and far greater than most people would be capable of enduring. It is precisely because it is so difficult to endure the pressures of a "double life" that so many people cannot maintain a bisexual orientation and feel forced to choose between exclusive heterosexuality or exclusive homosexuality.

Were it not for social influences, many more males than already do would doubtlessly participate in both heterosexual and homosexual relationships as we find them doing in other cultures. It is as if our society is willing to tolerate a large number of exclusively homosexual males—if current attitudes and practices can be called at all tolerant—in order to prevent the occurrence of an even larger number of actively bisexual males. This is a solution to "the problem of homosexuality" that apparently has not been considered suitable or even rational by most other cultures.

A "good adjustment" under circumstances like those described in the preceding paragraphs would seem impossible. Yet many of these people—indeed, most—manage to assume the ordinary duties of life, and not a few, as we may see if we inquire into the number of prominent men in whom homosexual tendencies have been marked, have actually succeeded in making a substantial contribution to the world around them. Many, as we have also seen, have assumed all the responsibilities of heterosexual life and are loving husbands and devoted fathers. It is perhaps sentimental to observe that the successful assumption of the burden of secrecy and self-denial that society places on the homosexual and the bisexual male may amount to little less than an heroic achievement in many cases. How many of these people have gone through life unrecognized, unaccepted for what they are, and unappreciated? Many more, no doubt, than is ever realized.

Does a civilized and free society really have the right to require such sacrifices from any human being?

The reader may have formed some impression of that peculiar and often morbid symptom of our sex-negative society known as the homosexual way of life. It is but one such symptom, although among the most tragic. We could enter into a more detailed account of the homosexual way of life and enlarge upon the fruitless search for permanent love that is usually defeated by a restless refuge in the satisfaction of lust made possible by the various techniques of "cruising." We might compile a list of "gay" jargon or discuss the make-believe atmosphere that permeates the social relationships of "homosexuals"—the pretentious claims to glamour, the petty rivalries, the frequent bouts of jealousy, envy, and remorse. But all this has been pictured in many novels and submitted to analysis in more ambitious texts. It is obviously a disappointing and makeshift adjustment, but it does give the individual who has been turned away from the main-stream of social life something that he could not find elsewhere; it offers him, if not true understanding and genuine sympathy, at least an escape from utter isolation and loneliness. In the "gay" life the lonely youth may find many others—a great many others—like himself. And how true it is that misery loves company! In the "gay" world he will find refutation of perhaps the first and most horrible thought he had to face when he de-clared himself a "homosexual"—the thought that he was the only person of his kind on earth.

Though our society heaps upon these people its unmitigated contempt and puts every possible barrier in the way of their happiness, the contempt of the "homosexual" for himself and the barriers he creates between him-self and his own happiness can hardly be equaled by anything imposed upon him from without. In most cases he is utterly convinced of his own depravity and the depravity of all other "homosexuals." He secretly be-lieves that his degraded role in society is no more than the circumstances warrant. *He is on the side of oppression.*

Those who have worked in the homophile movement constantly point to the absolute refusal on the part of most "homosexuals" to participate in any concerted effort to improve their lot. Even the most affluent and secure among them cannot usually be expected to cooperate. This refusal to cooperate is rationalized by endless alibis: they fear exposure; they cannot risk their jobs, their reputation, or their social position; they must consider the welfare of their family; they have neither the time nor the money to participate in this movement. Yet these same people repeatedly risk their jobs and their reputations, as well as the reputation of their families, and spend their time and their money in pursuits that are almost calculated from the start to bring disaster.

All that we have described about the "homosexual" in our society—his way of life, his self-condemnation, and his refusal to "take arms against a sea of troubles"—all this is a function of deep-seated guilt and remorse inspired by a tradition of homoerotophobia and sex-negativism that is over nineteen centuries old. Little wonder that these individuals, who have learned their lesson at an age when they were hardly capable of reason, find it quite impossible to discard beliefs and attitudes that are constantly reinforced throughout life.

No account of homosexuality within Judaeo-Christian culture—and most particularly, within American culture—would be complete without some mention of the hostility and violence with which the condemned may meet. At many junctures this hostility approaches psychotic proportions, and the violence that arises out of it becomes unequivocally criminal. For the time being, we may disregard the less extreme manifestations of hostility toward homosexuality with which one may meet in our society—such as open ridicule, legal harassment, official bigotry, and other more or less socialized and restrained expressions of hatred—but some mention should be made of the more naked forms of sadistic persecution with which the homosexual male so often meets. In a society that is peculiarly addicted to prejudice and cruelty the "homosexual" may be singled out as a particularly vulnerable victim. There are few, if any, who will come to his defense even when he becomes a target of lawless persecution; his lot, for the main part, is even more degraded than that of any member of the most harassed racial or religious minority. Defense consists mainly in maintaining a successful disguise—which, of course, may be done more readily than in the case of the Negro, or even the Jew. But, once exposed or even suspected, the "homosexual" may become prey to the most unconscionable cruelty at the hands of oppressors who regard their sadism as righteousness. Physical violence and various forms of bodily assault upon these people are common in our society and often result in murder. This violence frequently receives tacit approval, even at the official level, by the type of person who maintains the attitude that "the only good queer is a dead queer." Indeed, "queer-baiting" has become a rather popular sport in some circles. The following instance—one among many—exemplifies the usual pattern:

One spring evening in April, 1961, a young man stood waiting for a trolley near his home in San Francisco. His name was William P. Hall. He was a teacher by profession. It may be imagined that the twenty-seven-year-old man was in good spirits as he stood alone waiting for the streetcar that was to take him to a dinner engagement with a friend. He might have been surprised to see a car carrying four young men come to a precipitous halt beside him. Three of the young stalwarts descended from the car and approached him directly. Since nothing about the teacher is reported to have been particularly distinctive, let alone eccentric, he must have been taken aback when one of the approaching gang called out bluntly to him, "Are you a queer?"

However startled he may have been by this psychopathic question, the teacher's reply was more educative than anger-provoking.

"What if I asked you that question?"

Those were among the very last words spoken by William Hall. The three young hoodlums stormed the defenseless man and proceeded to beat him into a state of unconsciousness. Apparently their fists could not inflict sufficient injury upon the victim to gratify their lustful hatred, for the police later reported that investigation revealed that Hall had been struck in the head by some weapon resembling a blackjack. Their debt to the community having been paid through the attack on this man who they assumed to be a "queer," the boys removed from Hall's unconscious body a wallet containing $2.85 and left their victim lying senseless.

Early the following morning the young school teacher was found lying near the tracks by the motorman of the oncoming vehicle. He thought he saw Hall feebly waving his arms, but later he wasn't sure whether Hall had ever moved. The horrified motorman could not stop the trolley in time. Its heavy weight passed over the limp body, grinding it to death beneath relentless steel wheels. Useless attempts were made for over an hour to hoist the weight of the trolley from the mangled body, but the young teacher died before he was freed.

He met his death in this brutal fashion because a group of young toughs had presumed to diagnose him as a "homosexual"—a "sex deviate," the officials called it in their report—a "queer." The diagnosis was fatal for Hall, as the young vigilantes were out to cleanse the community of such filth. After having attacked and disabled the teacher, they continued their prowl of the city in search of other "queers"; but finding no more people to assault and murder that night, they went home to their respective beds—alone, of course.

In reporting the details of this atrocity, the *News Call Bulletin* thought it proper and meaningful to add that, "The officers made clear Hall certainly was not in that unfortunate category"—that of a "sex deviate." *Mattachine Review,* commenting upon this somewhat curious addition, said, "It is not important what 'unfortunate' category Mr. Hall may or may not have been in. Psychologists have yet to determine what constitutes a 'sex deviate' although many law enforcement and newspaper people are able to use the term glibly. Apparently they mean 'homosexual.' "

The need felt on the part of the police and press to clarify that William Hall was not a "sex deviate" is one of those subtle things people are prone to overlook without sufficient appraisal of its implicit meaning. This statement would appear to imply that the murder of Hall was all the more tragic and, perhaps, all the more criminal because the victim was *not* a "homosexual." Had Hall in fact been homosexual, would it be correct to interpret the action of these youths as in any way less criminal?

A great many people, it would appear, might answer this question in the affirmative. The young murderers certainly believed that their action was innocuous, if not virtuous. About this case Inspector Robert McLellan commented to the press, "They said they considered Hall's death justifiable homicide." He added, "They seem to regard the beating-up of whomever they consider sex deviates as a civic duty."

It is painful to observe how cruelty, intolerance, and, one must add, greed are rationalized by the most noble motives. But how is it that these youths had come to regard their predatory activities as a civic duty?

This is no idle question when one stops to consider that this "civic duty" led to thuggery, robbery, and murder. The number of youths led to such criminality under the guise of decency is far from negligible. These young men admitted that the beating they gave Hall was not the first they had ever administered to a person whom they deemed to be in the "unfortunate category." There had been many other such nights for this advanced guard of the puritan terror. When they left their friends that fateful evening they felt quite free to announce their intention of seeking prospective victims without the slightest fear of losing face. They said they knew of at least fifty other youths within the brief confines of their own neighborhood who participated in similar attacks upon "queers." Hadley Roff of the *News Call Bulletin* reported that it had been affirmed by the young vigilantes that they "keep watch on establishments patronized by homosexuals, then track down the patrons as potential victims for attack." The crusade of these youthful enemies of sexual deviation, like all such crusades, is an inspired one. They are armed and made brave by the most intoxicating of all human delusions: the feeling of self-righteousness.

The young, we know, are highly impressionable and become very easily conditioned by the unverbalized attitudes that impinge upon them from the environment. It is not without meaning that these youths, like so many others, have gained the impression that assault and battery and even murder are justifiable if the object of one's hostility is homosexual. We need not look far in order to discover the source of this impression. In a society that condones legal oppression of the sexual nonconformist, and in which almost all morality has become equated with sexual morality, it is not surprising that the young should come to believe that any other form of brutality is equally justified in the suppression and extermination of "the deviate." The ruthless attitude of these youths merely reflects the ruthless attitude of our entire society in these matters. That these boys felt no compunction about robbing the unconscious victim of their brutality, and that they felt no compunction about leaving their helpless victim to his fate is merely an analogue to similar treatment accorded the "homosexual" daily in our environment.

The activities of youth are highly instructive because they always reflect in a crude, readily ascertainable, and direct way the fundamental values of the society in which they live.

A youth goes out to hunt down a "queer" and, having found one and attacked him, then robs him of a couple of bucks. How different is this from the activities of a police force that, with the aid of cunning techniques, often entraps the "deviate" and then turns him over to a lawyer who makes a not unhandsome fee "defending" the culprit in a case of "sodomy" or "solicitation"? In one case the "queer" is a victim of concussion of the brain. In the other case the "sex deviate" is a victim of paralyzing social and psychological pressure.

There is profit for all in "queer hunting." Each takes his share, and each feels the nobler for having done so.

Our previous glimpse of homosexuality in Greece is a very different one from the sordid and depressing picture of homosexuality within our own culture. The Greeks recognized the legitimacy of the sexual drive and therefore afforded scope to its various manifestations—including, of course, homosexuality. Being a wise people, they did more than merely tolerate homosexuality; they found various ways and means to bring it into the service of civilized aims. Their ways, of course, could never be ours, for each society must find its own solutions. But our society has found no solution whatsoever to "the problem of homosexuality." We fail not only to turn homosexuality to any social good; we fail even to tolerate it. Consequently, homosexuality in our culture is a constant source of vice, crime, and disease and at very best must be considered a handicap for the individual. Because it is all of these negative things most of the time, we tend to increase the unenlightened, oppressive measures to which we have always turned. But this merely perpetuates a vicious circle. We condemn it as a vice, punish it as a crime, and treat it as a disease, but we do nothing to prevent it from becoming any of these three things. Our approach is wholly negative and the results of our approach are therefore wholly negative. Our attitudes toward homosexuality are not moral, ethical, or hygienic. We have failed to cope with the homosexual tendencies of men or to offer any possibility of bringing these tendencies into the service of the individual or the group. Of late it has become the fashion to regard homosexuality as a disease and to seek a solution to "the problem" through medical techniques. But this is merely a new version of the old negativism and must as surely fail as all of our other "solutions."

If we could stop condemning, punishing, and therapizing for just a bit, it might be possible for us to turn our attention to some means of putting this ubiquitous propensity to some constructive use instead of making it a source of personal and social tragedy. This is the real challenge with which the problem of homosexuality confronts our culture.

X

Homosexuality and the Law

Sexual phenomena, we have already seen in Chapter I, have always inspired a feeling of awe in the mass mind. Hence they are constantly invested with supernatural significance of one kind or another. We have seen this tendency at work in the puberty rites of certain so-called primitive peoples, in the institution of shamanism, and in the rituals of many religious and mystical cults. Homosexual practices have been repeatedly ascribed to gods and heroes and have been used by priests and holy men as a channel through which spiritual benefits may be conferred upon the devout.

In the West since the promulgation of Judaeo-Christian theology, however, attitudes toward homosexuality have evolved curiously. The earlier sex-positive orientation of antiquity has degenerated into an emphatically sex-negative orientation of which homoerotophobia is a conspicuous component. Homosexual love, far from being regarded as a practice of the gods to be imitated by pious mortals, is regarded in the West as a grave sin—indeed, a gross perversion—to be shunned by godly men. It is as a result of this evolution that homosexuality has become an object of official censure and severe legislation in the Western world.

It can hardly be doubted that the various peoples who later became unified in the Jewish religion, like other peoples among them, originally embraced homosexual practices not only as a part of everyday living, but also as a form of religious devotion. Prichard and other authorities point to the fact that mouth-genital and homosexual activities played a part in the religious rituals of the ancient Hebrews, and homosexual as well as heterosexual prostitution thrived in the very precincts of the temples.

The acceptance of homosexuality, however, was not destined to endure among the Hebrews as long as it did among the other peoples of antiquity. For reasons that remain obscure, this bisexual orientation was rejected by the Hebrews around 700 B.C after the return from the Babylonian Exile. Under the suasion of a supernationalistic fervor, Jewish life became infused with a feeling of separateness; "foreign" customs and usages were held in contempt. Idolatry became a cardinal sin among the Jews, and almost any practice that was associated with the religious life of non-Jews was reckoned as a form of idolatry. Male homosexual practices were severely interdicted; in the earliest stages it was as a form of idolatry rather than as a sexual crime that these activities were condemned by Jewish religious leaders. In Talmudic writings homosexuality is associated with "the way of the Canaanite," the way of the Chaldean—the way of the "heathen." Whoever participated in such "abominations" was to be put to death.

Although it was as idolatry that homosexual relations were excoriated first and foremost, the idea that such relations are "unnatural" began to obsess the Jews somewhat later. This idea almost certainly developed after the exclusion of homosexuality from Jewish life, and it is not difficult to detect that "unnatural" is almost certainly equated with "foreign," "exotic," or "unfamiliar." It is quite common for all people to insist that their own familiar ways are natural, while unfamiliar foreign customs are almost always regarded as unnatural. With the passing of time, idolatrous, heathen sex acts seemed not only unnatural; they began to appear monstrous, distorted, and perverted.

Homosexual activities are briefly mentioned—always with a negative connotation—in the Old Testament. But the awesome account of the fiery destruction of Sodom and Gomorrah loomed in the imagination of the ancient Hebrews as a constant reminder of the dangers of homosexuality—"sodomy" as it later came to be called. It was believed quite literally by pious Jews that, as a result of "unnatural sin," the Canaanites had polluted their land and had brought upon their heads the terrible wrath of Jehovah.

So ancient and so much a part of Judaeo-Christian religious tradition is the homosexual interpretation of the story of the destruction of Sodom and Gomorrah, that few believers appreciate that the story may not originally have had the meaning subsequently ascribed to it. The Reverend Doctor D. S. Bailey, in a scholarly investigation entitled *Homosexuality and the Western Christian Tradition,* raises much doubt about the traditional interpretation of the Sodom and Gomorrah myth. According to Bailey, the story of the two cities of the plain has little if anything to do with homosexuality. Rather, it is concerned with the complicated issues surrounding the topic of hospitality and the treatment of strangers—themes that have always obsessed the minds of barbaric peoples such as were the Hebrews at the time this story originated.

It was probably around 700 B.C. that the homosexual interpretation first became attached to the story of the two cities. During this period of religious revolution it is likely that the Jewish priests seized upon this myth, which by that time was quite old, to dramatize the moral dangers of this heathen and idolatrous practice.

This interpretation was believed for centuries so that, even though it is probably incorrect, it has lent additional support to a strongly homoerotophobic tradition among Judaeo-Christian peoples.

Mention has already been made of the fact that of the thirty-six crimes punishable by death in the Mosaic Law, half concern sexual relations of one kind or another. Three of these eighteen refer to so-called unnatural sex relations: sexual relations between men and animals, sexual relations between women and animals, and sexual relations between one man and another. Female homosexual relations were not stigmatized as criminal (and almost never are in modern Judaeo-Christian statutes), but such relations were considered unseemly and immoral and were ridiculed.

Of the four methods of execution, stoning was considered the most severe and was specified as the penalty for the three crimes mentioned above. In the case of homosexuality both male partners were stoned to death, as was the man or woman copulating with an animal—and also the animal, despite its lack of guilt. Homicide was justified by law if practiced in the effort to resist a homosexual advance, as by certain implications and practices it is today in some quarters of Judaeo-Christendom. Even witnesses were compelled to prevent the crime by killing the participants.

Hebraic attitudes toward homosexuality and toward sex in general were passed on to the Christians and received support and elaboration from St. Paul, who was raised in the Jewish tradition. Originally a soldier, Paul was a Roman citizen as well as a Jew and embraced the stern and uncompromising attitude toward "the law" that was characteristic of both Jews and Romans.

Thus the early Church Fathers heaped unmitigated condemnation upon homosexuality. Tertullian says that sodomistic acts are banished "not only from the threshold, but from all shelter of the Church, because they are not sins, but monstrosities." The reader may recognize some similarity in tone between this pronouncement and the quotation from the Zoroastrian text presented in an earlier chapter.

In an interesting analogy, St. Basil equates homosexual acts with idolatry, witchcraft, and murder, and recommends the same punishment for sodomy as for these other offenses.

The view of sodomy as a moral offense so grave as to preclude all possibility of repentance and redemption is reflected in a decree of the Council of Elvira, which denied communion, even at the last hour, to those who had participated in paederastia. Regarding this pronouncement Westermarck notes, "In no other point of morals was the contrast between the teachings of Christianity and the habits and opinions of the world over which it spread more radical than this." [79]

The validity of Westermarck's comment is apparent when it is realized that paederastia was an accepted and even honored practice among the peoples in whose midst the early Christians dwelt. It must have been difficult for these people to have grasped the Christian attitude toward paederastia. We must surmise that such was the case, since Christian authorities were forced to adopt radical and oppressive measures in the suppression of homosexuality throughout the Empire after Christianity became the state religion of Rome.

Precisely because homosexuality enjoyed approval among the ancients and was practiced by them on a wide scale, it was associated with paganism and censured by the Church, just as the Jews had condemned sodomy among their "heathen" neighbors. No better evidence of the approval accorded homosexual love among the ancient peoples of the Mediterranean and Near East exists than the condemnation it inspired in Jews and Christians.

During the Dark Ages sodomistic practices became equated with heresy and witchcraft, and eventually with treason as well. Early in the history of the Christian State, authorities everywhere were concerned with the suppression of paederastia. This continued well into the Middle Ages and was always exacerbated during the conversion of non-Christian elements of Europe and the Near East.

The early Christian emperors of Rome regarded homosexual practices as nothing less than a threat to the survival of their Empire. The lesson of Sodom and Gomorrah was constantly in their minds, and the participant in homosexual acts assumed a kind of fiendish as well as traitorous aspect. But in spite of official attitudes, those who opposed the Christian form of worship continued to observe many of the older pagan rituals and beliefs. It was not long before many of these practices degenerated into witchcraft, wizardry, sorcery, black magic, satanism, and devil worship, or at least were so regarded by the orthodox religion of the State. It seemed essential to Christian princes to put down all surviving remnants of paganism, not only because these were disturbing to the new order, but also because these early princes sincerely believed that for them to countenance paganism in their midst would be to invite the wrath of God. In an atmosphere of fear, superstition, religious intolerance, and social transition homosexuality, as a reminder of non-Christian life, became a target of severe disapproval.

Before the advent of Christianity the Roman State made no attempt to suppress homosexuality. The earliest Roman farmers, with their stern, family-oriented morality, may have regarded homosexual practices as something less than respectable; we cannot be certain of this since we know that their predecessors and contemporaries in Italy certainly regarded homosexuality in a favorable light. But in any event, it is clear that by the time of the earliest beginnings of the Empire paederastia was approved in Rome, and even rationalized by the finest efforts of Greek philosophy. It was common for the most renowned men to take a homosexual lover in addition to their mistresses. Of Julius Caesar it was said, not without admiration, that he was the husband of all women and the wife of all men. This reputation for bisexuality never impeded his progress toward political supremacy.

A very early Roman law known as the Lex Scautinia, which forbade paederastia between a free-born youth and a slave, is evidence of an attempt to regulate rather than to suppress homosexual behavior. However, even this mild regulation, which no doubt was promulgated in the interest of the caste system rather than in the interest of morality, had long since become a dead letter in Rome by the time of its political ascendance, and no other laws touching upon homosexual practices were ever enacted by the Romans in pre-Christian times.

But after the adoption of Christianity as the religion of the State this picture was radically changed, for reasons that have already been explained. Constantine ended the policy that persecuted Christianity and eventually recognized its official status, but he made no effort to suppress homosexuality. The first such move was made by his successor, Constantius, who issued a decree in the fourth century making homosexuality a capital crime. Under the earliest Christian emperors homosexual intercourse was punished by decapitation. Christianity, which only recently had suffered persecution and bloodshed, was now perpetrating persecution and bloodshed itself in this and in other areas.

The effete Valentinian went further than his antecedents and decreed that those who were found guilty of sodomy should be burned alive in full view of the assembled populace. The methods used by Christian leaders to enforce their will were if anything even more dreadful than those used by their pagan predecessors. Almost every method of execution and torture—except crucifixion—was practiced by Christian princes from earliest times. The earlier tolerance of the Romans toward religious heterodoxy and toward the customs of the peoples they ruled dissolved when the Roman State became Christianized and was replaced by a passion for conversion to Roman ways—the new Roman religion—which has been perpetuated in only modified form through the history of Christianized Europe. The savage imposition of sexual orthodoxy was, of course, only one aspect of this process. Roman rule had meant the surrender of worldly goods alone, and the State had never made any conscious attempt to exact spiritual conformity, but instead might be described as unusually tolerant.

After the advent of Christianity, however, Roman rule meant absolute conformity to the will of the State in spiritual as well as temporal matters. The religious life of the community had become the concern not merely of a priesthood that might differ in different areas; it had become the concern of the State. This tendency was brought to such perfection that within a few centuries State and Church were virtually one, and the head of the Church, the Pope, became the temporal ruler of Christendom. Subsequent progress toward freedom has in large measure consisted in re-effecting a separation between Church and State. This separation, however, even in the case of the most recent and most democratic nations, is only imperfect, and religious precepts still form the basis of a great deal of secular law. This is quite obvious in the area of legalized sexual moralism.

The Valentinian edict was an obvious attempt to put down paederastia through terror by the use of a punishment that vividly recalled the destruction of Sodom by fire. Death by burning was not a traditional form of execution among the Romans in pre-Christian times. It came into more frequent use with the worldly progress of Christianity, so that by the Middle Ages many people were punished in this gruesome way, especially for offenses touching upon religious belief.

These efforts to instill fear of "pagan love" apparently met with only the most modest success, just as in subsequent ages. Consequently they had to be renewed and reinforced periodically, as continues to be the case in the puritan countries today. It was the superstitious and fanatic Byzantine Emperor of the Romans, Justinian—of whom it was said, "No Roman Emperor so nearly assumed the position of a temporal Pope"—who promulgated the statute in Roman law which became the model for subsequent laws against homosexual intercourse. Justinian was known as "The Great" because of his codification of Roman law. By his time the Roman Empire in the West had collapsed under the impact of barbarism, and the Dark Ages were in full swing. It was in such an atmosphere that Justinian, terrified by the occurrence of famine, earthquakes, plague, and other natural disasters and believing these to be the result of homosexual practices, issued an edict that again condemned persons to the sword for homosexual acts "lest, as a result of these impious acts, whole cities should perish together with their inhabitants"—like Sodom and Gomorrah. The penalty for what had now come to be regarded as "sodomy" was a painful death, preceded by mutilation and castration. Two bishops were among many others known to have suffered this barbaric punishment, and their dying bodies were dragged through the streets. The entire issue had built to a frenzy, and homosexual practices would soon be regarded as a major cause of national disaster.

It is instructive to take note of the atmosphere in the court of this famous Christian law-giver. Like many legislators in subsequent ages, Justinian and those around him allowed themselves much leeway in moral matters which they did not feel they could extend to the masses. Neither Justinian nor those closest to him were paragons of virtue, but it apparently did not occur to them that it might be their own moral failings that were responsible for the outbreak of natural disasters that were to be averted by punishing sexual heterodoxy among the people. Many stories have been passed on to us concerning the psychopathic pleasures of Justinian's wife, the Empress Theodora. Among these are the accounts of her numerous affairs—heterosexual, homosexual, and incestuous—and the description of her erotic excitement upon witnessing torture, a commonplace event in early (as well as late) Christian official circles. She is said to have been highly aroused erotically—to a point where she was driven to masturbation—while observing the making of eunuchs.

After Justinian's codification of the law sodomy never again received intelligent or even rational treatment in the legal sanctions of Judaeo-Christian States until certain reforms in the penal code of France were carried out some thirteen hundred years later. Not only was the Justinian statute thought useful by subsequent authorities in putting down sexual immorality and in preventing earthquakes and other natural disasters, but it also proved to have a great political utility—as has been exploited more than once in later ages. The political advantages of this very special form of legalized moralism were detected from the start. To impute homosexuality to one's enemies and to charge them with the crime of sodomy became a profitable device. Arrests were common, and as Gibbon noted, "A sentence of death and infamy was often founded on the slight and suspicious evidence of a child or a servant . . . and paederasty became the crime of those to whom no crime could be imputed." This was the earliest but by no means the least of the abuses to which sodomy laws have been put.

The punitive attitude toward homosexuality found among early Christians is remarkable. A tendency toward cruelty may be detected in the pronouncement of Tertullian and St. Basil as well as in the decree of the Council of Elvira. No humanist can fail to deplore the lengths to which the laws of Constantius, Valentinian, and Justinian went in punishing this type of behavior. The harsh treatment accorded homosexual offenders from earliest Christian times—excommunication, denial of the last rites, decapitation, and death by fire—makes the more recent treatment of slander, harassment, imprisonment, and mandatory therapy appear extremely tolerant, and almost humane by comparison. The laws against homosexual behavior that were devised at the beginning of the Christian State established a precedence not only by interdicting such behavior under any and all conditions and making it a matter for public concern, but also by punishing it to great excess. These same tendencies are reflected in all subsequent antihomosexual legislation.

By the Middle Ages sodomy had come to be the crime "peccatum illude horribile, inter Christianos non nominandum" ("that abominable sin not fit to be named among Christians"). Death by fire had become the punishment of choice in the continental countries of Europe. In France as late as the middle and later part of the eighteenth century, persons were actually burned alive for sodomy. During the Middle Ages it was common, however, for sodomy cases—like cases of witchcraft and heresy—to be tried in ecclesiastical courts. Only if the Church "relinquished the offender to the secular arm" was he burned. The Church, it appears, usually did not deliver the sodomist for burning if he had committed only a single offense, and if he renounced his heretical sexual behavior through a public act of contrition. Most Christian commentators have maintained, perhaps apologetically, that few sodomists were put to the flames, at least in the later Middle Ages. Most are said to have escaped this horrible death through the clemency of the Church. But this assertion fails to take account of the cruel punishment of persons for sodomy and other offenses under secular laws, based upon ecclesiastical tradition, at a point in history when the European monarchies assumed greater independence from the Church. It also fails to take account of the equating of sodomy with heresy and witchcraft, which most certainly were punished by burning in a lamentable number of instances. The following excerpt from Westermarck shows clearly this medieval thinking.

> During the Middle Ages heretics were accused of unnatural vice as a matter of course. Indeed, so closely was sodomy associated with heresy that the same name was applied to both. In "La Coutume de Touraine Anjou" the word *herite,* which is the ancient form of *heritique,* seems to be used in the sense of "sodomite"; and the French *bougre* (from the Latin Bulgarus, Bulgarian), as also its English synonym (bugger), was originally a name given to a sect of heretics who came from Bulgaria in the eleventh century and was afterwards applied to other heretics, but at the same time it became the regular expression for a person guilty of unnatural intercourse. In medieval laws sodomy was also repeatedly mentioned together with heresy, and the punishment was the same for both.[13]

In an age in which Church and State were virtually one, it was easy and even logical to assume that heresy is *treason* as well; for under these circumstances the overthrow of established Christian practice would be tantamount to the overthrow of established secular authority. Thus the sodomist was not only regarded as a heretic and a witch, but also as a traitor. The reasoning went something like this: "Anyone who would practice 'pagan love' is a heretic, all heretics are witches possessed by the Devil, and all heretics and witches attempt to subvert the authority of both Church and State and are therefore traitors."

This may help to explain how it is that, even in modern times, homosexuality is associated and, by implication, even equated with treason in some countries. Those, notably in Britain and America, who insist that there is some strange connection between a predisposition toward homosexuality and a predisposition toward treason, and who therefore also insist that a "homosexual" is, automatically, "a poor security risk," would never, of course, recognize the origin of this idea in medieval habits of mind. Instead, these people point to the fact that the "homosexual" in Britain and America at least—as a result of the sodomy laws prevalent in those countries—is especially liable to blackmail by agents of foreign governments. But since the obvious remedy is never applied, nor even suggested—namely, the repeal of the ridiculous and dangerous legislation that makes certain people targets for blackmail—one must assume that the tendency to associate homosexuality with treason has its origin in a less rational and more atavistic type of thinking. Concerning this, Partridge (1958) makes the following comment:

> This lumping together by an authoritarian body of all the heresies —religious, sexual, and political—the assumption that if a man is guilty of one, he must also be guilty of the others, is of particular interest when one thinks of the tendency of some Americans (and others) during the recent Communist witch hunts in the United States, to suggest that the political default of the offenders was, in some obscure way, connected with homosexual tendencies; and that a homosexual (quite apart from his liability to blackmail) is more liable to turn Communist than a heterosexual, and is, accordingly, a greater "security risk." [65]

But the influence of medieval thinking on modern attitudes toward homosexuality is not limited to the heresy-treason complex of ideas; one may also detect the equation between homosexuality and witchcraft in much that is written on the topic. Secular propaganda that tends to encourage superstitious nonsense on this subject has continued to find its way into print today. Even journalists who otherwise may be considered sophisticated and enlightened have written on this topic in a vein which can hardly be considered less than medieval.

Some examples of this sort of journalism, half amusing and half frightening, may be found in such books as Jess Stearn's *The Sixth Man* (1961), and R. E. L. Masters' *The Homosexual Revolution* (1962).

Lamenting the supposed disappearance from the American scene of the "rosy-cheeked and laughing-eyed girl," Stearn ascribes this to "a homosexual design—male and female—to demean and degrade the traditionally American concept of soft, lovely, feminine beauty." [71] Like the witches of old, the "homosexuals" are now accused of blighting the radiant health and beauty of youth. That they are supposed to do this through the agency of the iron grip they are alleged to have upon the fashion industry rather

than through the outright use of black magic is but a modern rationalization
for a medieval concept. In New England during the witch-burning days it
was also common for people to believe that pale and wan young girls were
under the spell of some sorcerers, when in fact it was far more likely that
these young creatures were suffering from anemia brought on as a result
of profuse menstruation.

Nowadays one also reads much journalistic copy about a "homosexual
freemasonry" which is supposed to be highly organized and widely effectual
in bringing in "homosexual recruits," and which apparently does almost
everthing diabolical except meet in conclave on Walpurgisnacht.

The tendency of journalists and even of those who claim more erudition
on the subject to treat the theme of homosexuality as if it were mysterious
and uncanny is not altogether a result of previous censorship and ignorance.
It is much more likely that these writers are quite honest and candid about
their own reactions when they write on this subject as if touching upon
the realm of the diabolical. Doubtless most of them, like most of their
readers, sincerely believe some of the rather imaginative things they write
about "homosexuals." They have behind them a tradition which is at least
two thousand years old and which has its roots in a common tendency
among human beings to believe that sexual phenomena are mysteriously
related to supernatural events of one kind or another.

We must resume our account of the history of antihomosexual legislation by inquiring into conditions in England, for it is English law that
has laid the groundwork for American law in this and in other areas, and
American law will occupy a great deal of our attention in what follows
later.

By the time of Richard I, it was the practice to hang a man guilty of
sodomy. With the separation of Church and State, the State took over the
field of criminal law, including of course the enforcement of sodomy laws.
Secular authorities followed the policies established in this area by ecclesiastical authorities, except that the secular authorities were still more
prone to an indiscriminate use of capital punishment in these cases. But in
England we find a great deal of inconsistency. At a given period the law
was very stringent and seems to have been enforced with vigor. At another
period the law was less stringent and less apt to be enforced. By 1533, in
the reign of Henry VIII, sodomy was made a felony "forasmuch as there
is not yet sufficient and condign punishment appointed and limited by the
due course of the laws of this realm." But this law was repealed and re-
enacted several times, apparently because of the numerous abuses to
which it lent itself. In one form a proviso was added to prevent any witness
from profiting from the conviction of an accused sodomist.

In 1562 the original statute was revived and was not altered again in
England until 1861, when a Victorian statute reduced the penality for

sodomy to mere life imprisonment. Within the next generation (1885) the penalty, in the case of consensual sexual acts between adult males in private, was reduced to two years at hard labor. This latter law was invoked against the great British author Oscar Wilde and has since become a subject for debate in England.

Parliament recently appointed a group of experts that has come to be known as the Wolfenden Committee to study the question of homosexuality and the law in England and make recommendations for reform in this area. This committee recommended that homosexual acts between consenting adults in private no longer be considered a crime in England. The British Parliament may have finalized this recommendation by the time of this book's publication, for there is a considerable public opinion in favor of it.

It is not difficult to understand why virtually every artist, scientist, religious leader, and thinker of renown in England has come out openly in favor of the repeal of this law when the malicious mischief and outright persecution it has bred from its very beginning is made known. As in America (where, of course, similar and even harsher antihomosexual legislation prevails) this law has encouraged corruption and cruelty not only among certain criminal elements, but also among certain police officials. Even when enforced without corruption, however (which, of course, is for the main part), a sorrowful record of personal tragedy follows, not only for the offender but often for many others associated with him; this tragedy is seldom if ever offset by any worthwhile gain for anybody.

Severe sanctions touching upon homosexual and other sexual practices were retained in the penal codes of all European nations up until the end of the eighteenth century. But the rationalist fervor of the eighteenth century laid the groundwork for social and political reforms that ultimately affected the laws touching upon sexual behavior. To punish sodomy with death, it was argued by rationalists, is atrocious. When unconnected with violence, fraud, or public indecency, the law ought to take no notice of sexual acts at all. The social influence of sodomy is merely indirect, and in ordinary instances it does not violate any other person's rights. It is a vice, like habitual intoxication or adultery, but no more deserving than these of official interference.

In this spirit Napoleon dropped homosexual offenses from the "Code Pénal" of France in 1810. Thus the French penal code makes no mention of homosexual acts between consenting adults in private, and they are absolutely unpunished. Like heterosexual acts, homosexual acts are treated as a crime only when they involve an outrage to *public* decency, or they result from force or violence or one of the partners is a minor or is incapable of offering valid consent (as in the case of a dependent, an imbecile, or a mental patient).

These reforms were subsequently adopted throughout all of Christendom, with the exception of the Anglo-Saxon nations (including America) and Germany, where the spirit of French rationalism had no effect in this area of law. In substance, the Napoleonic principle is followed today in France, Belgium, Holland, Denmark, Sweden, Norway, Switzerland, Italy, Spain, Greece, Mexico, and Brazil, to offer only a few examples drawn exclusively from Judaeo-Christian nations. In non-Judaeo-Christian nations that are free of Anglo-Saxon law, consensual homosexual acts are virtually never mentioned in the legal statutes.

It is curious that in the United States, where the force of French philosophy made itself felt in the political views of the Founding Fathers, no such reform was incorporated into the penal codes of the various states. As a result of Calvinist philosophy, the freedoms guaranteed the individual under American law were not extended to that area of human relationships that touches upon "morals." American law about sexual morality remains medieval in precept and practice, and all other Anglo-Saxon countries as well as Germany, Austria, and Russia retain modified versions of medieval law.

In England, as we have already seen, the recommendation of the Wolfenden Committee has given rise to a strong and persistent movement in favor of abolition of this law.

In Germany there is strong propaganda in favor of abolition also. The present German law against homosexual acts is one of the few laws of Hitler—perhaps the only one—that has survived the downfall of the Third Reich. The Hitler regime was staunchly opposed to homosexuality, and many persons accused of homosexual practices or even homosexual "tendencies" were thrown into concentration camps as "degenerates" and "subhumans." Many, of course, perished. Others were castrated and otherwise mutilated.

During and since the Second World War, many outside of Germany have claimed that the Hitlerian regime was in some strange way friendly to homosexuality, and that certain notorious war criminals were homosexual. About the homosexuality of some of these latter individuals we cannot speak with any authority; but there is no question that the policy both of Nazi Germany and of Fascist Italy regarding homosexuality was distinctly persecutory. After the purge of Roehm, who was said to have been slaughtered in bed with a young man, open and direct persecution of all known homosexual individuals was ordered by the Nazi government and "homosexuals" were among the first to be "exterminated" as "undesirables." Later "homosexuals" were shot on sight, and the accusation of homosexuality, alone, was sufficient to justify murder. In Italy persecution was more economic than physical, but nevertheless affected many people in a very real and tangible way. In Italy today the neo-fascistic party carries on constant

though futile propaganda in favor of antihomosexual legislation. No totalitarian government during contemporary times has ever been known to
tolerate homosexuality and almost all such governments have pursued an
open policy of persecution. This should not be surprising to anyone who
understands the sociopsychological dynamics of the authoritarian state.

At the end of the war an attempt was made by rational elements within
Germany to rid the country of the antihomosexual statute. But the American and British forces of occupation did not favor liberalization in this
area and these legal reforms were successfully discouraged.

No known movement exists in Russia to repeal the oppressive antihomosexual legislation that holds sway in that country. But this is not surprising
since individual liberty is not a popular issue in Russia.

Although all but a very few civilized nations today refrain from the
attempt to control consensual homosexual acts between adults in private,
the law in many jurisdictions may nevertheless make an important distinction between consensual homosexual acts and consensual heterosexual
acts: The age at which an individual may offer legal consent to homosexual relationships is often made substantially higher than the age allowed
in heterosexual relationships. A person, for example, must be twenty-one
before he may legally participate in homosexual contacts in Holland,
Sweden, and France, whereas he may participate with impunity in heterosexual contacts at a considerably earlier age. The State permits the individual to make this decision at twenty in Switzerland, eighteen in Denmark,
and seventeen in Greece; but heterosexual contacts may be legally accepted
in these countries at a considerably earlier age. It Italy alone among the
Christian countries of the West, no distinction between heterosexual and
homosexual acts is made in the law, and the same restrictions and privileges are accorded the individual in either case upon attaining the age of
sixteen.

This distinction in the law—especially where the "age of consent" is
made unreasonably high—tends to negate any good that may come from
the legal acceptance of consensual homosexual acts in private; accordingly,
there has been a good deal of criticism by leading jurists, criminologists,
and sociologists. There are instances on record in which individuals of
twenty-one or twenty-two have been liable to severe penalties for corrupt-
ing the morals of "minors" who were eighteen, nineteen, or even twenty
years old! Moreover, some unscrupulous youths have exploited these laws
in the interests of crime and blackmail by posing as twenty-one or older,
and then "putting the screws" on the older partner.

Viewed from a certain standpoint, an unreasonably high age of consent
in these cases may be even more pernicious than the complete interdiction
of all homosexual contacts. Consider the psychological effect of such conditions upon a prepotently homosexual youth of seventeen, eighteen, nine-

teen, or twenty who lives in a country where at twenty-one he may enjoy the freedom to "act upon his nature." He is aware of the activities of other older persons all about him who share his interests, but at an age when sexual urges are certain to be most imperious, he must either risk his own safety and that of his partner, or entirely renounce the kind of satisfaction he seeks. This consideration was emphasized to the author in a discussion with Jens Jersild, Assistant Commissioner of Police and Chief of Morality Police, Copenhagen, Denmark.

For the older male sexual relations with the "minor"—even if the "minor" is twenty years old—are almost always regarded as far more criminal and are more severely punished than mere "sodomy." We have seen earlier that sexual relations between younger and older males are common throughout the mammalian species and in other human cultures have often been digni-fied by an aura of piety. There would seem to be some basis in biological and psychological factors for homosexual relationships of this kind, and it is extremely doubtful that they can be successfully suppressed through legal force.

When "sodomy" laws or other laws forbidding homosexual acts are revoked and the age of consent is made unreasonably high, the freedom that has been accorded the individual with one hand has been taken away with the other. The former "homosexual" or "sodomist" may now find himself labeled as a "sex psychopath" liable to the most severe penalties under criminal law. This kind of thing may not represent real improvement or genuine progress at all, although from the viewpoint of the person who is in the habit of regarding any type of homosexual activity as "perversion" or evil, any change in the law may represent the most radical and daring reform. The progressive and the humanitarian may justifiably support the demand, familiar in almost all Anglo-Saxon countries today, that "homo-sexual acts between consenting adults in private" be stricken from the list of criminal statutes, but the true worth of such a demand will ultimately depend upon how the word "adult" will be defined in terms of sexual behavior.

The establishment of a relatively late "age of consent" once again stems from the idea that the sexual drive is, somehow, illegitimate and that youth must therefore be "protected" against sexual manifestations until the latest possible date, particularly if the manifestation of sexuality involved is one that may be considered "depraved." As long as we persist in this view of sex we will continue to emphasize all possible dangers that may become associated with the drive and we will continue to elaborate a complicated hierarchy of sexual virtue and vice. All of this is quite understandable in terms of the predominant philosophy of our culture and in terms of the sociopsychological climate of the culture. But let us put both philosophy and emotional conviction aside, if this is possible, and examine the problem reasonably and objectively. Several important issues emerge if one adheres to the contention that the age of consent to any type of sexual act, heterosexual or homosexual, should be the same.

We need not consider the merits or demerits of the different ages of consent to heterosexual relations that have been establishd in the various penal codes of Western countries; they are almost all more realistic than those established for homosexual relations. It has generally been recognized that the individual is capable of offering valid consent to a heterosexual relationship at some point soon after the arrival of puberty. The specific year differs in various jurisdictions but usually ranges from thirteen to sixteen years of age; even the most cautious jurisdictions seldom specify an age of consent higher than eighteen. There are obvious biological and psychological reasons for not making the age of consent earlier than the arrival of puberty nor later than eighteen years.

It should be quite apparent that the palpable and concrete *social* risks that adhere to an early age of consent in the case of heterosexual relationships far exceed any that could be claimed in the case of homosexual relationships. The complications that arise from an unwanted pregnancy, especially early in life, usually affect not only mother, father, and offspring, but the relatives of the young parents as well. It is not necessary to particularize here the many personal and social problems that are created when children are born to parents too young to give them proper care.

The reasons almost always offered for a very late age of consent in the case of homosexual relationships—indeed, there are no others that could claim serious attention—are that the younger person may be morally "corrupted" by such relationships, and that early homosexual experiences may cause the individual to become a "homosexual."

Precisely what is meant by moral corruption is virtually never defined by those who are in the habit of speaking in such terms, although it may be assumed that they have in mind some kind of deterioration in the capacity to form ethical judgments. There has, however, never been any scientific study reported that validates the hypothesis that those individuals who have early homosexual experiences with others of their own age or with persons older than themselves suffer more, or less, than any other group from an incapacity to form ethical judgments. One is forced, therefore, to regard the "moral corruption" theory as an unproved hypothesis. If any scientific work is ever done with this hypothesis, it may prove possible for those who argue in favor of a very late age of consent to bring some objective arguments to bear. But until or unless such proof is forthcoming, it will be difficult for rationalists to resist the impression that this idea is in no way essentially different from the idea that adolescent masturbation is a source of moral corruption or the idea that premarital heterosexual relationships lead to a depraved sense of values.

Much has been said and written about the notion that homosexual experiences during adolescence may bring about a pattern of fixed, preferential homosexual behavior. But again, there is no reliable scientific research to validate such an opinion. The behavioral sciences have never provided evidence that prepotent homosexual trends are dependent upon adolescent homosexual experiences, and clinicians are virtually unanimous in the opinion that what they call "homosexuality" originates not in the adolescent experiences of the individual, but in the earliest interpersonal experiences of the very young child in the nuclear family.

Boys who have already acquired homosexual tendencies are of course likely to seek homosexual contacts with others of their own age. Quite frequently also they seek sexual contacts with older youths and men; indeed, in many cases involving the "seduction" of a youth by an older man it is very difficult to specify which of the two is really the seducer. But it is certain that when a boy actively seeks the sexual attentions of another younger or older male the resulting experience is the *effect* of his homosexual tendencies, not the *cause* of them. It is not too much to imagine that in those cases in which a boy has actually been seduced by an older male, it is the boy's compliance that makes the seduction possible. Most youths who have not already developed homosexual tendencies probably fail to respond to seduction and either remain entirely indifferent to homosexual advances or respond with aggression and hostility.

Most of the so-called evidence for the opinion that seduction is a cause of preferential homosexuality represents a confusion between cause and effect and is based upon the histories of prepotently homosexual males who report childhood experiences with other males. In the absence of controls, however, these data mean nothing, since a corresponding number of prepotently heterosexual males may also have a history of early homosexual experiences. Many adults who read this book and who regard themselves as fully heterosexual will be able to recall homosexual experiences, some of which amounted to seduction, in their early history.

It is difficult to document the opinion that prepotent homosexual trends arise in connection even with much earlier homosexual experiences than those of adolescence. As long ago as 1935, A. J. Rosanoff, in an article entitled "A Theory of Chaotic Sexuality" (*American Journal of Psychiatry*), stressed the idea that "Seduction can only be of lasting effect if its direction corresponds with the inherent tendencies of the subject." Unfortunately, the value of this observation and its probable truth are obscured by the implication that homosexual trends are "constitutional" or somehow entirely independent of experience. L. J. Doshay (1943), after a study of 108 boys ranging between the ages of seven and sixteen, was unable in his book *The Boy Offender and His Later Career* (Green and Stratton) to bring forth any evidence that the development of homosexual tendencies was related to seduction. Gordon Westwood (1960) in his book *A Minority—Male Homosexuals in Great Britain* (Longmans, Green and Co., Ltd.) has offered an excellent review of this topic. From his own study of 127 individuals he concluded that "The histories of the contacts in this sample do not show that seduction has any appreciable effect on the development of homosexual tendencies."

Clearly the scientific evidence does not provide a very convincing argument for the opinion that a high age of consent is necessary in order to protect the young from psychological influences that might otherwise warp their psychosexual development. Young males who already have homosexual tendencies appear to be most likely to become involved with other boys and men, and others who do not have such tendencies do not seem to acquire a pervasive or enduring homosexual pattern simply on the basis of a number of isolated sexual experiences with other males. There is no good reason, then, to put a great number of people both young and old in a position where they are liable to become enmeshed in grave legal difficulties.

But beyond these considerations there are philosophical points that would seem to support the contention that the age of consent should be the same for any type of sexual contact. Either we accept the legitimacy of sexual acts or we do not. To hold forth the contention that an individual is capable of offering valid consent to a homosexual act at twenty-one but not before, and to argue that the same individual is capable of offering valid consent to a heterosexual act at fourteen, sixteen, or eighteen is somehow intellectually, emotionally, and morally dishonest—especially when it is recognized that the latter decision may be much more significant both personally and socially than the former decision. Moreover, there is something craven in the attitude of a society that is quite willing to risk the very lives of its youth in wars and military adventures, but that quite gratuitously becomes extremely protective and prudent about youth where sex may be involved. The youth of eighteen may be exposed to grave physical and moral dangers in some war-torn area, and it may not be thought necessary even to obtain his consent before exposing him to such dangers. But the same youth and his lover may be punished and disgraced should he decide willingly to enter into a sexual relationship with his comrade. It takes more persuasive arguments than have ever yet been put forth to convince a reasonable man that these paradoxes arise from any genuine morality on the part of the social order that defends them.

In the United States homoerotophobia has reached proportions unmatched elsewhere in the world today, and this is sufficient reason alone to draw our attention to the sex codes of the various states. We have already seen that when Kinsey, Pomeroy, and Martin made their famous investigation, they found that homosexual impulses play some part in the sexual history of approximately one out of every two American males. The

Kinsey team also found, however, that the attitudes toward homosexual behavior in America tend to be more prohibitive and more negative than in most other societies.

The exaggerated importance many Americans attach to male homosexual activities is reflected in several ways, but only those manifestations of homoerotophobia that can be documented in official statutes, policies, and acts are the concern of this chapter.

In all but one of the fifty states, homosexual activities between males are prohibited by law even when carried out in private between consenting adults, and most of these laws provide inordinately severe penalties. Indeed, in most instances these penalties are the most severe now imposed anywhere on earth.

> There appears to be no other major culture in the world in which public opinion and the statute law so severely penalize homosexual relationships as they do in the United States today.[54]

In the one state, Illinois, in which this type of law was recently abolished, some citizens complain that the police continue to impose restrictions upon homosexual activities by recourse to other laws that have been reinterpreted to cover the prohibition of such activities.

The present emphasis on sexual conformity in America may be felt even at the level of the federal government; a person even suspected of homosexuality is barred from any government work. It is the policy of both the Armed Forces and the Civil Service Commission to exclude any individual suspected of homosexuality from military or civilian service. Homosexual and other "deviate" practices are regarded as immoral conduct that disqualifies the inductee, appointee, or applicant for service. Several congressional committees have attacked the induction or employment of individuals who have become involved in any way with homosexual or other unconventional sex practices. In 1950, a subcommittee of the Senate warned that these persons should not be hired because those "who indulge in such degraded activity are committing not only illegal and immoral acts, but they also constitute security risks in positions of public trust."

This policy, which received great impetus from the late Senator J. R. McCarthy of Wisconsin, has continued to hold sway at the federal level of government. Procedure includes a screening process for all civil service applicants, and the appropriate department is notified of any police record involving homosexual activity. According to one check of applications, some 1,700 applications for positions were refused for these reasons between January, 1947, and August, 1950. Since April, 1950, job holders may be sent to the Public Health Service for complete psychiatric and psychological examinations on which basis the appropriate department head decides whether to request a resignation. In the April, 1955, special issue of *Bulle-*

tin of the Atomic Scientists on matters of secrecy, security, and loyalty, the "homosexual" and the "pervert" are condemned as security risks because of liability to blackmail while the adulterer or the chronic alcoholic are ignored, although it is as yet unknown who may be the greatest security risk. No security regulations explicitly prohibit excessive drinking or heterosexual "perversions."

So-called homosexuals have been considered undesirable because they are supposed to be less stable emotionally than heterosexual persons and more given to gossip and loose talk, although absolutely no conclusive scientific research demonstrates a characterologic difference between homosexual and heterosexual persons. Such assertions must be recognized as pure impressionism, indeed, outright prejudice unworthy of belief and unworthy to form the basis of a governmental policy. Many authorities have pointed out that so-called homosexuals are not more susceptible to seduction than so-called heterosexuals and in view of the Kinsey data, that there would seem to be little or no chance of keeping our government offices free from all individuals who were ever involved in homosexual activities. The present policy only tends to make the sexual nonconformist a more ready target for the unscrupulous techniques of foreign agents and domestic criminals.

If *all* government employees felt secure in the fact that the privacy of their sexual behavior was respected by those in authority and that they would receive protection from those in authority if approached with blackmail by a foreign agent, there would be no opportunity whatsoever for any foreign agent to use sexual behavior as a means for the extortion of secret information. Having adopted a prudish and unenlightened policy in these matters, the government has not only invited the criticism of all persons both inside and outside of America who insist upon justice and fair play, but also created a situation that encourages blackmail. This policy does more to endanger than to protect national security.

Some people may be under the impression that with the end of McCarthyism has come a relaxation of this policy. Such is far from the case. It has been announced in the press as recently as September, 1966, that all male applicants for jobs in the State Department are being asked, "Have you ever engaged in a homosexual act?" This direct approach is part of the new "preventive security" described by William J. Crockett, Deputy Undersecretary for Administration. He told a Senate committee, "We personally interview the applicant and it is surprising how many admissions we get to direct questions. When we ask the questions directly they tell us and we are screening quite a number of the applicant files."

In the Armed Forces an inductee risks an undesirable or blue discharge if he becomes involved in any way with homosexuality or if his superiors are left with the impression that he may have "homosexual tendencies";

such discharge bars him from benefits or compensation or pension under regulations of the Veterans Administration.

Since almost no private enterprise will hire a man who has come into difficulty with the government in this or any other context, those who have been rejected by the Armed Forces or refused government employment as a result of such a charge may find it virtually impossible to obtain employment elsewhere. If the present wave of public sentiment continues, thousands more, many of whom are highly qualified workers, may find it impossible to earn a living.

This benighted policy affects even the most highly qualified individuals. Within recent years there have been several instances in which men with superior and even extraordinary qualifications have been dropped from public service because of the imputation of homosexuality.

This policy is not limited to those who are known definitely to have been involved in homosexuality; a person friendly to or even merely associated with another person dismissed on account of homosexuality may in turn be subject to suspicion, and he too may find himself without a job. Such a person may in effect be judged "guilty by association."

There is evidence to suggest that this continuing wave of hysteria has even affected the courts, so that it is doubtful if many of those who are accused receive justice even under the harsh policies and laws that exist at present.

In addition to severe antihomosexual legislation and job discrimination at the federal and state levels of government, homoerotophobia in America may be detected in various other official and semiofficial policies and practices. The sexual nonconformist is harassed from all sides; the police, for example, do not hesitate to raid many places where the public gathers for purposes of recreation if it is believed that "homosexuals" congregate in these places. Certain bars, taverns, and even bathing beaches have been raided in this manner, and those present have been arrested on what amount to trumped-up charges. According to such reasoning the so-called homosexual does not enjoy the right of associating in public with others who share his interests, even if prohibited sexual acts are not involved. This comes dangerously close to the implication that the mere state of being homosexual, apart from indulging in overt sexual acts, is unlawful. Thus a person may actually be arrested on some charge, such as disorderly conduct, for merely appearing to be homosexual, especially if he is in the presence of a number of other people who also appear to be homosexual.

In summary, it may be justly claimed that a person of known homosexual persuasion or even a person merely suspected of homosexual inclinations is likely to suffer common abuse as well as abridgment of his human rights in the United States more often and in many more ways than a member of any other minority. Moreover, when he is abused and deprived of his rights as a citizen and as a human being, he is less likely than a member of even the most harassed religious or racial minority to obtain the support of any other individual or group. Few will come to the defense of what is regarded as a "pervert," no matter how just his cause may be and no matter how unendurable the persecution he suffers.

We have already taken note of many of the hardships imposed upon the "homosexual" in our culture. We must now proceed to a closer examination of antihomosexual legislation and its enforcement in the United States.

Homosexual acts were punished in colonial days in America under laws derived from early English enactments or from English common law. Authorities cannot agree on whether the common-law offense in America was originally a felony or a misdemeanor. In all events, this law seems to have encouraged blackmail and malicious mischief in colonial times, as throughout history. A contemporary document states that to obtain personal property from another by threat to accuse him of sodomy is "sufficient force and violence to constitute robbery."

Although such laws were abandoned in most other civilized nations, sodomy statutes have been retained in the various American states, and the penalties prescribed in these statutes are among the most severe meted out for any type of offense, comparable to the penalties exacted for manslaughter and murder. A review of present-day statutory penalties for sodomy in the United States reveals inconsistent attitudes and extreme confusion with regard to what constitutes an illegal sex act. Maximum penalties are usually excessively severe but vary greatly throughout the states.

Three states, Colorado, Georgia, and Nevada, provide a life sentence. In Georgia this is mandatory unless clemency is recommended. This penalty is equal to that provided for premeditated murder in most modern nations.

Connecticut sets thirty years imprisonment and North Carolina, sixty. In Connecticut any person who shall have copulation "against the order of nature" is liable to imprisonment for thirty years unless forced to participate in the sodomistic act, or unless under the age of fifteen. In other words, two fifteen-year-old boys indulging in homosexual play are liable to imprisonment until the age of forty-five in Connecticut if apprehended. In North Carolina these same two boys, if given the maximum penalty, would not be released from prison until they were seventy-five, and if given the minimum sentence they would not be imprisoned for less than five years. Such penalties are patently fanatical.

At least nine states have set twenty years as the maximum period of imprisonment, another eight set fifteen years, and seventeen set ten years. But so great is the inconsistency among the states that in a few states this offense may be punished by the mere imposition of a fine.

There is little logic or agreement between the states with regard to the penalties exacted for homosexual acts. Between 1950 and 1952, for example, when New York reduced homosexual acts between consenting adults in private from the status of a felony to the status of a misdemeanor, California increased the penalty from ten to twenty years' imprisonment. Later, sodomy was brought under the indeterminate sentence in California, with a range of one year to life. Thus the same individual, as a result of having participated in identical behavior, might find himself incarcerated indefinitely or even for life in one state, while in another state he might only be required to pay a fine.

These obnoxious laws and the absurd penalties attached to them can seldom be fully enforced in any modern jurisdiction. Consequently many courts have attempted to deal with sodomy cases by the use of psychiatric probation where it is legally possible to do so. The judge may often give a suspended sentence with lengthy probation on condition that the defendant seek psychiatric treatment. But however superior this method may be to outright imprisonment, it does not preclude the need for repeal of these laws.

First, it is not possible to use this method of dealing with these cases in every state. The laws in some states allow the judge no leeway in his disposition of these cases.

Second, consenting sexual behavior between adults in private should not be legally suppressed in a free society as a matter of principle.

Third, the efficacy of psychiatric treatment in these cases and under these conditions is very doubtful, to say the least. Involuntary psychiatric treatment has little chance for success. The patient is more likely to play along with what is expected of him in the effort to extricate himself from his legal dilemma, than he is to make a genuine effort to renounce his homosexual orientation. And he will usually resume his homosexual pattern upon completion of probation. Moreover, over a period of many months or even years, such treatment may constitute an insupportable burden for most offenders. Nor do psychiatrists and psychologists enjoy being in the position of treating a "captive patient," especially if they are not entirely convinced that there is any real need for such treatment.

The substitution of medical procedures in place of punitive procedures is generally more humane, although, from the patient's viewpoint, treatment under these conditions appears punitive. But however more humane this may be, it is quite another thing to imagine that consistent enforcement of these laws could solve the "problem." This point will be discussed in greater detail toward the end of the chapter.

Homosexual acts come within the purview of vagrancy laws in some states, so that often the homosexual offender may be liable to more than one charge for the same offense. California, for example, harbors some of the most oppressive sexual legislation on earth, including among its punitive grotesqueries not only the indeterminate sentence, but also castration. The individual may be charged with an offense under the law that refers to homosexual contacts, and simultaneously with vagrancy and lewdness for the same behavior.

Vagrancy laws have been traced to the "poor laws" of medieval England that attached a laborer, like a former serf, to the land where he worked. This is yet another context in which homosexual acts are often restricted and punished by laws that are distinctly medieval in character and origin.

But to all these harsh criminal statutes must be added the enormous burden of the special, so-called sex psychopath legislation now in force in at least twenty states. The Barr-Walker Act in Pennsylvania is one example of this type of legislation.

Often under civil rather than criminal law, these statutes provide for an indefinite term of "treatment" for those classified as sex psychopaths. Simple, unaggravated homosexual acts between consenting adults sometimes come within the scope of this extraordinary legislation. Even more frightful is the application in some states of these laws to persons who are merely *accused* or merely *suspected* of some sexual irregularity. On the basis of suspicion alone, without any proof or direct evidence that an offense has actually taken place, a person may be taken into custody, denied his freedom indefinitely, and put through a rigorous psychiatric investigation. If he is adjudged a "sex psychopath," he need not be released until several psychiatric authorities are able and willing to attest that he has been "cured." But "cure" may be difficult or impossible in the case of the individual who has acquired a predominantly homosexual pattern of preference, and thus he may be retained in custody indefinitely.

Extraordinary difficulties in terminology and in diagnosis exist in this area. Since even experienced psychiatrists cannot agree on the meaning and diagnosis of sexual psychopathy, one might think that the diagnosis of sexual psychopathy would, in the legalistic context at least, be rigorously confined to the habitual molester of very young children or to those who employ outright violence and coercion in connection with the satisfaction of their sexual needs. However, such is not the case. In practice, these laws have been focused upon the exhibitionist, the voyeur, and upon the ordinary homosexual male. Indeed, uncomplicated instances of male homosexuality are quite often equated with sexual psychopathology. Numerous observers have reported that homosexual males bear the brunt of the prosecutions under these extraordinary laws.

However irritating to some elements within the community exhibitionistic or voyeuristic behavior may be, or however scandalous homosexual behavior may be, it cannot be seriously argued that either constitutes a sufficient menace to warrant the violation of basic constitutional guarantees. It might be asserted that the true sexual *criminal*—the sadistic rapist, the chronic molester of children, and the sex murderer—may warrant special treatment, even if this special treatment means putting aside traditional constitutional guarantees, although many thoughtful people feel that the social risk involved in such an unprecedented procedure is too great. But that the ordinary homosexual or the ordinary exhibitionist or voyeur should be dealt with in this fashion is little less than outrageous.

If no other point is clarified here it may be at least hoped that the inherent dangers to society and injustice to the individual that arise out of erotophobia are made obvious. Under the pressure of communal sex anxiety and hysteria atrocious laws and policies are adopted that negate every principle of civilized law-making. Our American culture is particularly and peculiarly given to this kind of sex hysteria with its attendant legislative zeal. We have special reason to resist this type of emotionalism. Under its influence we have accepted laws and punitive procedures that would only seem natural within the most totalitarian environment. Some of the sexual legislation in some of the states cannot be described with any more appropriate adjective than "Hitlerian."

There exist, of course, individuals whose behavior cannot be tolerated even in the most free of societies. Behavior that violates the person or the property of another human being, fraudulent behavior, or behavior that exploits the weakness of another human being cannot be tolerated, whether or not it is connected with sexuality. But we must be very careful never to perpetrate such behavior in the very laws that are designed to restrain it. We must not, to use the metaphor of a recent American jurist, burn down the whole house in order to roast a few lambs. The laws designed to suppress and to punish sexual fraud, sexual violence, or sexual exploitation should be written and administered in such a way as never to suppress or to punish sexual behavior that is not fraudulent, not violent, and not exploitative. Indeed, it would be far better if such laws were written in such a way as to exclude entirely the *sexual* aspect and to refer only to the *criminal* aspect which is, of course, the fraud, the violence, or the exploitation. We do not require any sex laws as such; we require only laws that protect people against *crime*.

Extreme sex legislation usually arises in an atmosphere of emotional confusion in response to some recent atrocity. At such a time and in such an atmosphere it is believed that more stringent laws can prevent the recurrence of serious crimes. But if there were any truth whatsoever to this belief, criminal sexual behavior should be at an absolute minimum in the United States, for in the United States there are a greater number of stringent and even oppressive sex laws than anywhere else on earth. Yet sex crimes in the United States are by no means at a minimum in comparison with the incidence of sexual crimes in many other nations that have no such laws.

We cannot enter into a full discussion of sex crimes or "sexual psychopathy" since this book is concerned only with homosexuality. But the larger issue is deserving of a few more words since homosexual behavior per se is universally considered to be criminal in the United States, and so-called homosexuals, as we have seen, tend to bear the brunt of sex psychopath legislation.

In order to meet with the requirements of science, morals, and just law, legislation designed to cope with the problem of sexual psychopathy—whether this psychopathy is expressed in a homosexual or a heterosexual context—should meet with the following criteria: the term "sexual psychopathy" must be given a clear-cut, limited, and meaningful definition; the enforcement and administration of this legislation must admit of "due process," and no person should be deprived of any constitutional guarantee under this legislation; no attempt should be made to enforce such legislation or even to enact it until or unless adequate facilities for treatment exist.

The term "sexual psychopath" should be strictly limited to those individuals who practice violence, fraud, exploitation, or coercion in connection with sexual gratification. It should not be applied to individuals who may merely be described as neurotic, eccentric, immoral, or unconventional in their sexual behavior, or to individuals who confine their sexual activities to acts practiced in private with the consent of the partner. In essence, the sex psychopath or sexual criminal is either a heterosexual or a homosexual rapist, a sadistic heterosexual or homosexual murderer, or a heterosexual or homosexual molester of small children.

No person should be deprived of liberty nor compelled to submit to medical or psychological treatment on mere suspicion or on the mere imputation of sexual psychopathy. The person should be taken into custody only after the commission of an overt antisocial act, and he should be retained in custody only if such an act can be proved to the satisfaction of a judge and jury. It is argued that these crimes may be prevented if persons are incarcerated before the commission of a criminal act. This may be so, and the same may be said of any type of criminal behavior. But few would argue that the potential burglar, the potential forger, or even the potential murderer should be arraigned before the commission of a specific crime, or at least before an attempt at the commission of a specific crime. Prevention in these cases as in other cases must be limited to the prevention of further crimes. The mere desire to commit a crime (sexual or otherwise) does not constitute sufficient basis to justify the restriction of a person's liberty. If people could be arrested and held in custody on the basis of mere suspicion or on the basis of a mere tendency or desire to commit some offense, our entire concept of law and justice would be routed. Yet most of the so-called sex psychopath legislation that now exists in at least twenty states defies the very principle of "due process" and puts aside fundamental constitutional guarantees.

If there is to be any significance to sex psychopath legislation being different from ordinary criminal legislation in the area of sexual offenses, then this difference should consist in providing treatment rather than punishment. But it is ridiculous to institute such legislation when no adequate facilities for such treatment exist, as is now generally the case. Adequate facilities means a staff of qualified medical and psychological specialists working with a patient within the therapeutic environment of a hospital or sanatorium rather than a prison staff working with an inmate within the punitive environment of a jail or penitentiary. Many who have been taken into custody under these laws (including many who are not true sexual psychopaths) fill state hospitals and prisons, where they are held on an indeterminate sentence without receiving anything that could be accurately described as treatment. When such a person is an ordinary homosexual male who in no sense qualifies as a true sex psychopath, the injustice of the situation is all the greater. Such an individual would be better off if he were sentenced under ordinary criminal statutes since there would at least be some limitation to the term of his sentence.

The present sex psychopath laws are questionable in so many ways that authorities in many states where these laws exist are loath to invoke them. In Pennsylvania, for example, the Barr-Walker Act has only been invoked in a handful of cases during a period of a decade. Nevertheless these questionable laws remain on the books and are actually used in some states. No doubt, they will be added to the plethora of sexual legislation in many more states in the future, in the sincere but misguided belief that they constitute some sort of progress. But unless such laws substitute therapy for punishment, and unless they meet with the requirements specified above, they will represent the worst kind of regression.

The unhealthy attitudes toward sex and the emphasis upon competition and violence that exist in America seem bound to give rise to a still greater rate of sexual criminality in the future, as they have given rise to all types of criminality. As the incidence of such crime increases so, no doubt, will antisexual legislation. People are convinced—and this seems to be particularly true in America—that laws can prevent crimes.

In reality, the growing problem of sex criminality in America can only be dealt with effectively if and when attitudes change in the direction of a more permissive but at the same time a more rational approach to sexual life. In an atmosphere in which sexual desire is constantly provoked by all the media of communication, entertainment, and advertisement, but where sexual gratification is constantly impeded by laws, hypocrisy, and misplaced ideals of virtue and vice, psychopathic sexuality is bound to thrive and increase. It is the correction of this latter circumstance, not the framing of new laws that may prove to be as benighted as the old ones, that offers the greatest possibility of solving the problem of sexual psychopathy. Those who wish really to tackle the problem of sexual crime and solve it must get at its roots instead of passing laws that are almost as atrocious and antisocial as what they are supposed to suppress.

It must be pointed out that the behavior which many ordinary criminal statutes penalize—namely, anal intercourse and mouth-genital contacts— is in no way peculiar to male homosexual relationships. This behavior often occurs in heterosexual relationships and, in the case of mouth-genital contacts, in female homosexual relationships. In practice, however, hardly anyone except homosexual males is apprehended and convicted for participating in anal intercourse and mouth-genital contacts. Sodomy laws are rarely invoked in the case of male-female relationships, and never at all in the case of lesbian relationships. In a search through the several hundred sodomy opinions reported in the United States between 1696 and 1952, the Kinsey team could not find a single case sustaining the conviction of a female for homosexual activity. Although this disparity in the interpretation and enforcement of the law is based upon a number of psychological and sociological factors, these laws are enforced selectively and are made to apply almost exclusively to homosexual males.

In some states sodomistic acts are illegal whether occurring between heterosexual or homosexual couples, although they are enforced only in the case of homosexual couples. But in other states these acts are made illegal only in the case of masculine couples. The inequity reflected in the enforcement of these laws may also be reflected in the very writing of these laws in some states.

But even when penalties for sodomy are made to apply only to masculine partners, enforcement remains selective. Anal intercourse and mouth-genital contacts between males alone are so commonplace that it is impossible to regularly enforce legislation barring such contacts. Consequently the police can make arrests for sodomy, or "indecent acts" between males only in a small fraction of the total instances in which such offenses occur. The sociologist Edwin M. Schur estimates that six million male homosexual contacts take place each year in America for every one conviction. Thus the enforcement of these laws, even when the law is made to apply only to males, must be described as flagrantly capricious. This results in a feeling of resentment at having been treated unfairly rather than a feeling of remorse on the part of those who become the victims of this capricious enforcement. Those responsible for law enforcement have the habit of "cracking down" sporadically while leaving the law unenforced at other times, so that there are waves of arrests followed by relative inactivity. All of this means that those who are arrested for sodomy must bear the brunt of a law that, if it were enforced justly and consistently, would involve tens of thousands of others. But consistent enforcement is virtually impossible in the case of sodomy laws, even where sodomy is defined in such a way as to apply only to males.

This necessarily capricious enforcement gives rise to a feeling of contempt for law in general. Many learned men have pointed out that unenforceable laws that do not reflect common behavior have no place on the books of modern states. The American Law Institute has condemned such laws and has published the observation that homosexuality "is an area in which the criminal law is ineffective if not positively harmful. Capricious selection of a few cases for prosecution among millions of infractions is unfair and chiefly benefits the seekers of private vengeance . . . Furthermore, the pursuit of homosexuals involves policemen in degrading entrapment practices and diverts attention and effort that could be employed more usefully [elsewhere]."

But even more serious abuses result from legalized moralism. Blackmail, extortion, bribery, police shakedowns, entrapment, "queer-baiting," harassment, and other evils are all encouraged by the existence of these laws.

It is well known that sodomy laws encourage and protect the blackmailer and the extortionist. Some unscrupulous individuals demand money from the so-called homosexual or even rob him, secure in the knowledge that the victim cannot call upon the police for protection for fear of being accused of a crime himself. Moreover, not all of those who are responsible for the enforcement and the administration of the law are themselves above exploiting sodomy laws to their advantage. Since those who become victims of this legislation seldom are criminals in any other context and therefore they have little experience in such matters, they are easy prey to certain conscienceless lawyers and bail-bondsmen who often tax them with exorbitant and outrageous fees. Caught up in the terror of their situation and faced by the scandalous nature of the charge brought against them, the victims of these laws are usually willing to part with whatever money they have in a frantic effort to escape conviction. Some magistrates and police have been known to yield to bribery, or even to encourage it, in the handling of these cases. The arrest and trial of homosexual citizens have become little more than a racket for the enrichment of unscrupulous police officers, bail-bondsmen, lawyers, and magistrates. These laws have probably encouraged more immorality in those responsible for their enforcement and administration than they have ever prevented in those liable to their enforcement.

As we have seen in an earlier chapter, a growing number of young hoodlums in America make a practice of "queer-baiting," comfortable in the knowledge that so-called homosexuals will almost never call upon the police for protection and that they really cannot do so. These young criminals go about, often in gangs, attacking, assaulting, and often even robbing individuals whom they regard as homosexual; in most instances their criminal behavior remains unnoticed and unchecked by the authorities. Mayhem and even murder have occurred in this context, and often those who commit these crimes do so in the sincere belief that they are ridding the community of "undesirables." These youths take their cue from the laws and from the intolerant spirit that brings about and perpetuates such laws.

Not least among the abuses encouraged by these laws are abuses that arise in the very manner of their enforcement in most cases. No doubt those in authority who practice extortion or accept bribes are in the minority, but even more honest officials may become involved in a type of illegal and unscrupulous behavior in their zeal to enforce these laws. It should be remembered that solicitation to sodomy is almost everywhere reckoned in the law as equal to the commission of sodomistic acts. Hence certain police officers, usually in plain clothes, encourage certain people whom they suspect of being homosexual to solicit a homosexual act. If the person does so they arrest him on a charge of soliciting sodomy. This technique is called entrapment and is illegal, since to encourage a crime is itself a crime.

It must be pointed out that sodomy laws tend to encourage the use of entrapment on the part of the police, since the vast majority of homosexual acts take place in private—indeed, in secrecy—between consenting partners. Without the use of entrapment or some technique very close to it, enforcement of these laws is almost impossible. Except in those rare instances in which a police officer might happen through chance to witness a homosexual act, or those equally rare instances in which some feckless person might, without encouragement, solicit a homosexual act with a police officer, it is almost necessary for the police to resort to some form of entrapment in order to make an arrest for sodomy or solicitation.

Not infrequently the police have used handsome young men as decoys. These young police officers are explicitly taught the ways and means of attracting the attention and gaining the confidence of homosexual individuals. When a police officer in plain clothes plays upon the inclinations of a homosexual suspect, makes himself extremely available to solicitation or even seems to invite such solicitation, it would surely seem that he has employed a technique of entrapment and has actually encouraged a crime.

Moreover, some defendants have claimed that they were arrested "on sight" without even having proffered an invitation to sodomy. It is easy enough for an officer in plain clothes to strike up a conversation with a known "homosexual" and simply to arrest him whether or not he suggests sexual relations. Because of the extremely tenuous nature of this charge, and because direct evidence is difficult if not impossible to obtain, no one need be the wiser in those cases in which solicitation has been falsely charged. This makes it quite impossible for a defendant to prove his innocence. One wonders how often such arrests take place at the hands of overzealous members of the "morals squad."

Other highly questionable and highly distasteful techniques have been employed in the enforcement of these laws. The police often claim that they are concerned only with those homosexual offenses that take place in public, as in the case of sexual contacts that occur in parks, public lavatories, and movie theaters.

In one city, for example, all of the benches in a particular park where "homosexuals" were known to meet were wired for sound. The police spent hours each day listening to the conversations of the people sitting on these benches. Anytime the conversation became "suggestive," or if one person propositioned the other, the police moved in to make an arrest.

Trick mirrors and even closed circuit television have been installed in the public lavatories of some cities so that the police may keep an eye on the activities in these places. If anything "irregular" occurs they appear unexpectedly to make an arrest. But before they are able to witness an illegal act they often have to watch unsuspecting members of the public in the most intimate situations for hours. In one city the police photographed the libidinous doings that went on in several of the public lavatories for weeks "in order to obtain clear-cut evidence" before they made any arrests. During such vigils, moreover, the police are called upon to play the part of a "voyeur" not only with regard to the sexual behavior of those who may be committing an offense, but also with regard to those who may be merely relieving their bladders or bowels. The entire procedure constitutes an indignity to all concerned that is hardly justified by making a few arrests on charges of indecent behavior.

Trick mirrors, closed circuit television, and secret photographs all suggest a highly voyeuristic tendency on the part of those who spend their time spying, and there is something indecent and highly offensive about such techniques. They surely constitute an unwarranted and intolerable invasion of the privacy of that majority of people who use these public facilities for perfectly legitimate reasons. It also remains to be explained why, if the surreptitious sexual activities that occasionally occur in these places are truly in the nature of a "public offense," it should be necessary to use these elaborate devices in order to spot offenders. One might think that a *public* offense would be sufficiently flagrant as to preclude the need for such methods of enforcement.

The ease with which such a large number of abuses and attendant evils may occur throws the shadow of condemnation over the very substance of these laws and demonstrates very clearly the extent to which they depart from anything that can be reckoned in the public interest. Legal literature is now filled with many cases in which entrapment has been claimed as a defense, and in view of the difficulties in the way of enforcement which such laws present, it is not very paranoid to suspect that a good deal of entrapment actually does go on in connection with the enforcement of sodomy laws.

It may be easily seen that the so-called homosexual is in a vise which presses in on him from every side. On the one hand, he himself is placed in a criminal category by the current laws on sodomy and is forced, at least to some extent, to live a kind of underworld existence in which he fears the police. On the other hand, he is a ready target for the criminal exploitation of blackmail artists, hoodlums, and unscrupulous authorities and officials. There is no direction in which he can turn to find emotional security or even justice. Liberal organizations that ordinarily defend the rights of oppressed minority groups turn away from the homosexual minority, which they either do not recognize at all as a minority or regard as a part of the "criminal element." Even organizations such as the American Civil Liberties Union whose purpose it is to protect the civil rights of citizens are loath to extend themselves in behalf of a "sex offender." These organizations have done almost nothing to help rid the community of such questionable legislation as are sodomy laws and most sex psychopath laws. Even in cases where unfair or downright illegal enforcement of such laws are involved these organizations, with very few exceptions, have done very little. But it is to be expected within a cultural milieu that perpetrates such legislation in the first place that this kind of apathy and indifference to the welfare of sexual nonconformists would be the rule.

When one considers the implications of legalized sexual moralism, the inroads that this type of legislation makes into basic human rights, and the numerous abuses to which it lends itself, it must be admitted that legislation in this area is mischievous and evil in almost every possible context. It can be defended only by the most unenlightened type of argument. It remains, moreover, a very serious question whether a free society has any right at all to assume responsibility for the moral decisions of citizens in the area of sexuality—a responsibility far more appropriate to the churches and to the conscience of the individual himself.

How then has it come to pass, when even certain of the most authoritarian regimes have seen fit to accord some measure of moral autonomy to the individual with regard to his sexual life, that one of the most modern and democratic nations on earth continues to claim the right to dictate what acts and relationships shall constitute the private sex life of adult citizens?

There is no simple answer to this question, but it should never be forgotten that the United States of America is in essence a Calvinist nation, founded by religious zealots who, precisely because of their religious fanaticism, could no longer be tolerated even within the prudish Anglo-Saxon environment that gave rise to them. Rejected in their homeland, they were forced to seek a haven in the New World in which they could realize their fondest theocratic aspirations, including the imposition of their own moral beliefs through coercion wherever and whenever necessary. The Puritan was and remains a man to whom freedom has but one meaning: *his* freedom to dictate moral law, as he sees it, to everyone else. In the words of C. L. Becker and W. L. Langer in *A Survey of European Civilization,*

Calvin's was a sterner doctrine [than that of Roman Catholics or Lutherans], and its sternness was reflected in his moral teaching and legislation. He considered it the duty of the church and state to make men moral in the strictest legalistic sense. No part of his teaching had a more profound influence on the life of the Calvinist countries than this. The civilization of America to this day shows traces of the Calvinist morality brought over to these shores by the Puritan immigrants who founded the early colonies in New England.

In England both the House of Lords and the House of Commons have at last voted by an overwhelming majority to repeal all criminal penalties against homosexual acts committed in private by consenting adults. This action has been long overdue. In view of the seventeenth-century puritan zeal that still infects much of the American legislative mentality—for "sodomy" laws are but one facet of puritan legislation that still remains effective in America—it may well be asked when the various states will begin to adjust their respective penal codes to modern life and contemporary concepts of freedom and justice. Efforts along these lines have been made during recent years in a number of the states and in at least one state, Illinois, this effort has succeeded. The recent reforms in the penal code of Illinois, however, modest as they proved to be, should not necessarily be interpreted as a precedent that will be followed in the other states. It seems much more likely that, as a result of the underlying puritan mentality, this reform will be crippled and perhaps eventually even reversed. In other states where this reform has been urged there has been no success at all, nor does it seem likely that there will be any positive action in this direction within the near future.

A recent incident in Wisconsin dramatized resistance to reform. In April, 1966, an organization known as the Young Democrats put forth a recommendation to liberalize the statute on "abnormal" sexual relations—a law, incidentally, that covers not only the acts committed by so-called homosexuals but also those committed by many so-called heterosexuals. In Wisconsin proof that one has engaged in "an abnormal act of sexual gratification" may bring a penalty of five years' imprisonment. The young reformers, who had urged "the abolition of all legal restriction on sexual relations between consenting adults which do not violate the rights of others," were met with a deluge of righteous indignation on the part of their seniors. "When the Young Democrats split into 'homocrats' and Democrats it is going too far," Governor Knowles, a Republican, said. A Republican Party newsletter charged that the recommendation was "encouraging homosexuality." One of the Democratic state senators characterized the proposal—one, it should be remembered, which has already been acted upon in almost all civilized nations—in terms of "filth . . . cancer . . . disaster!" By midweek thirty-six of the Young Democrats had publicized the fact that they supported "solidarity of the family" and were opposed to "adultery, homosexuality, and prostitution." During the scurry the recommendation was strongly condemned on the grounds that sex has no place in politics. This is a rather strange and illogical assertion since those who made this criticism must certainly believe that sex has a very definite place in the penal code! It is amusing, if at the same time saddening, to find people who have no particular claim to being learned authorities in the field of morality and theology shocked, indignant, and apparently even scandalized by a proposal that in essence has gained the public support of the Archbishop of Canterbury.

It would be very optimistic, indeed, to suppose that there has been any real change in the traditional Calvinist orientation to sex and the law, or to suppose that liberal reforms are close at hand in the United States as a whole. But this pessimistic view affords no one the excuse to ignore these issues. The tendency to legislate in the area of sexual morality and private conscience must be examined and questioned by enlightened men and women who are dedicated to the preservation and extension of freedom.

There are, of course, certain forms of behavior that no society, free or unfree, can tolerate. Obviously, any behavior that limits the freedom of another human being is not merely immoral but also criminal. Whether associated with sex or not, behavior that is violent, coercive, or fraudulent, or that is injurious to the person or property of another individual, has everywhere been regarded as criminal, and every society has attempted to suppress such behavior. But certain societies attempt to suppress not only crime, but also immorality and vice.

Let us, for the moment, consider the differences among crime, immorality, and vice.

Man is capable of a great deal of behavior that, at least according to most schools of ethical philosophy, is deplorable, immoral, and vicious. Vanity, sloth, intemperance, envy, prejudice, lasciviousness, lechery, greed, bigotry, vengefulness, cruelty, and avarice are all moral evils. And often these vices may form the basis of criminal behavior. Only in the most theocratic states, however, is it assumed that any of these vices should be directly punished under the penal code. There are no laws against vanity, greed, or envy. Although certain other vices are far more deplorable, it is almost exclusively in the area of sexual morality that vice is penalized under the law. In certain jurisdictions obscenity or lewdness, even under conditions of privacy, may be specified as crimes. But it is no more defensible— and perhaps even less so—to consider obscenity a crime than greed or vengeance. It is because our Judaeo-Christian culture places emphasis upon sexual morality, and perhaps not enough emphasis upon nonsexual morality, that obscenity and lewdness rather than vengefulness and greed are so often considered crimes.

It is recognized, however, that such vices as sloth, cruelty, prejudice, bigotry, vanity, or envy cannot be controlled through legislation and that there is some leeway for interpretation as to what particular and discrete acts represent such vices. We are not so modest in our attempts to define and to control sexual immorality, but a moment's thought makes it abundantly clear that these subtle philosophical issues are no more easily defined in the case of sexual behavior than in the case of other types of behavior. Nor is sexual morality or immorality necessarily always closely linked with other forms of morality. We do well to remember the words of the late Judge Lindsey: "I know many persons who do not conform to conventions in their sexual life, but who are moral; and I know others who conform meticulously, but who remain grossly immoral."

Because of these contingencies it remains an open question in the minds of many modern men whether it is within the legitimate province of law in a free society to define vice and virtue for the individual in the area of sexual life. Some regard such attempts on the part of law as a usurpation of rights that properly adhere to moral institutions and to the conscience of the individual. Not a few people today object to efforts on the part of governments to bring the individual into line with the interpretation of sex provided in some particular theological or philosophical system. These people insist upon the right to decide for themselves, through the exercise of their own conscience and reason, what is right and what is wrong for them no less in the sexual than in the religious sphere. Indeed, not a few people consider the right to do so a very fundamental and inalienable one that cannot be separated from other fundamental rights now recognized and acknowledged in all free societies.

We cannot attempt here to expound a philosophy that would rigidly categorize homosexual or other sexual acts as either moral or immoral. To attempt to do so would lead us beyond the scope of this book. We can, however, recognize the conditions under which homosexual acts should be considered criminal and the conditions under which such acts should definitely not be considered criminal.

Insofar as a person's sexual activities involve only himself and others who share his interests; insofar as these activities are carried out in an atmosphere of reasonable privacy, apart from the public at large; insofar as these activities do not involve either force, coercion, fraud, or deception they are, to put it plainly, of concern only to those directly involved and beyond the legitimate scope of the law.

We may regard the so-called homosexual as a sinner if we are philosophically or religiously inclined to do so. We may regard him as a sick person if we are justified in doing so by scientific considerations. But to regard the ordinary homosexual as a criminal and prosecute him as such is plainly unreasonable and unjust.

Laws directed against homosexual behavior, like all laws, are promulgated and defended in the belief that they are necessary to the general welfare of society as a whole. For example, it has been argued that in the absence of specific prohibitions against it, homosexual behavior would increase to a point where the survival of the human race would be endangered. According to this view, antihomosexual legislation is necessary because without such legislation a plague of homosexual ardor would overwhelm the population, spreading from person to person until at last the very roots of our civilization would be eaten away by the effects of "unnatural lust." We may call this the "prairie fire" view of homosexuality.

It might seem that those who put forth this defense of antihomosexual legislation ascribe altogether too much attractiveness to homosexuality. This attractiveness is pictured as so compelling as to require specific and severe opposition. Yet those who argue in this fashion are, curiously, often the very people who insist that homosexual relations are unnatural and that the desire to engage in homosexual relations can only be acquired as a result of the most extraordinary and even pathological influences. One might think that if homosexuality is "unnatural" and that if it arises only within the most eccentric context it would be self-limiting. But this inconsistency of thought is not evident to those who continue to defend legislation against homosexuality by recourse to both arguments.

In reality, the acquiring of an exclusively homosexual pattern of preference has nothing to do with laws, and laws, therefore, prove to have little effect upon the incidence of exclusive homosexuality. Nor do such laws do much to lower the incidence of nonexclusive homosexuality. Neither does the absence of such legislation, on the other hand, encourage the incidence of homosexuality. In societies in which homosexual behavior is not penalized by law and in which homosexual relationships may even meet with approval, homosexuality never becomes the predominant type of sexual outlet for the community as a whole. More often than not, these permissive societies are the very societies that have the highest birth rate.

Consider, for example, Moslem and Buddhist cultures where homosexual behavior is tolerated generously and where such behavior is common. The vast majority of males remain heterosexual, or at the most bisexual, and overpopulation, not underpopulation, is a problem. The same may be said of the more tolerant nations within Judaeo-Christendom. They are sections of Europe where homosexual practices between consenting adults in private have been legal for more than a hundred years, and where such practices occasion very little concern on the part of the community. It would be very difficult to show that homosexual behavior in these communities is any more frequent than in communities which prohibit such behavior by law, or that procreation has been affected for the worse in these more permissive communities.

It is important to note also that in the more permissive societies the integrity of the family has been maintained more stringently than in most of the societies in which homosexual behavior is prohibited by law. In other words, tolerance of homosexuality does not necessarily nor, as some have argued, regularly have an adverse effect upon the integrity of family life. In Moslem and Buddhist cultures and in the more permissive Judaeo-Christian subcultures, family ties are very strong.

Similarly, the argument that abolition of sodomy laws leads to mass depravity, to crime, and to other social evils that eventually terminate in the "decline and fall" of a civilization is definitely not borne out in the case of societies in which no laws at all against homosexual behavior exist. To the contrary. It would appear that within several of the most prohibitive nations (England, Germany, the United States, and Russia) both adult and juvenile crimes are at a new height each year, whereas within a number of other more permissive countries we find lower rates of adult and juvenile crimes.

All these dire predictions of catastrophe in connection with the abolition of antihomosexual legislation suggest a psychological and emotional state on the part of those who make them identical to that of the emperors and kings in the Dark Ages who originally framed such laws. But there is this important difference: We may excuse the superstition and hysteria of the emperors and kings on historical grounds, whereas for the modern man who thinks in such terms there really is no excuse.

Although it surely cannot be argued that freedom to indulge in homosexual relationships without legal penalty supports law and order or the solidarity of the family, neither can it be argued that sodomy laws do anything at all to encourage morality, domestic harmony, or stable social relationships. These goals cannot be attained through legislation. Morality, even in the narrow sexual sense, does not depend upon law and can never be legislated; indeed, any morality that is dependent upon fear of legal consequences is in reality no morality at all.

It is precisely the recognition that sexual conduct is a matter for personal moral decision and not a matter for legal intervention that has led many churchmen throughout the world to oppose sex laws such as those that penalize homosexual behavior. It may be argued by some that homosexual relations under particular circumstances are not immoral at all, and are therefore not deserving of punishment in any case. But even among those who regard all such relations as immoral in the highest degree, it is not a foregone conclusion that the immorality of these relations should be punished by the State, or that legislation can prevent the occurrence of such relations.

Bryan Magee in his excellent little book *One in Twenty* (Stein and Day, New York, 1966) calls attention to the righteous indignation on the part of many that tends to impede abolition of antihomosexual legislation in those jurisdictions that suffer from such legislation. He remarks, "I do not think I have ever seen an argument for keeping the law in its present state that did not rest on righteous indignation." In the next paragraph he discusses this important issue in greater detail.

> I may feel righteously indignant about adulterers—I may feel righteously indignant about liars—and in each case with at least as much justification as one could feel this emotion about homosexuals. Lying and adultery break the Ten Commandments, which homosexual acts do not, and adultery is much more disruptive of social and family life, and inflicts far more damage on children. But I do not propose that they should be made crimes, still less crimes carrying a heavy penalty of imprisonment. Nor does anyone else, so far as I know. Some people say that homosexuality is anti-social in that it is not reproductive of the race—that if everyone were homosexual the human race would die out. Here again the argument is absurd. Large numbers of people are not reproductive because they choose instead to be celibate, and this includes nearly all Roman Catholic priests. No one suggests that in behaving like this they are being anti-social. A great many married couples deliberately choose not to have children. One may think this is unwise, storing up emotional problems for themselves later in life, but nobody questions that they should be free to do so. Why should there be one rule for homosexuals and another for everyone else? There is, I fear, an element of tribalism in our attitude—the demand that deviant individuals should be punished for their deviation and made to follow the social norms. This is pernicious. The law exists not to put our tribal instincts into effect but to protect us against them, and in particular to protect the individual against the instinct of the tribe as a whole. The essence of liberal democracy is a belief that the rights of the individual should be protected against the society of which he is a member.

In a society in which true crime abounds and increases with every year, the law-abiding citizen is threatened daily by the antisocial behavior of both professional and amateur criminals, juvenile gangs menace the peace and welfare of the community, and organized crime is a multi-million-dollar business, it is rather ridiculous and not a little irritating to see the police preoccupied with the harassment and apprehension of sexual nonconformists.

The tough cop who is busy chasing fairies out of the park or participating in a raid on some gay bar might be serving the interests of the community far more substantially if he spent more of his time patrolling the streets where so many muggings take place.

The clever and handsome young officer from the "morals squad" who earns his living by playing upon the human frailties of certain frustrated middle-aged men might find more constructive use for his skills in the apprehension of a dope pusher or one of the other more insidious exponents of organized crime.

The court psychiatrist whose task it is to reverse the sexual pattern of some unfortunate individual who has become entangled in the tentacles of the law might exploit his professional knowledge in the interests of a still finer purpose if he directed his therapeutic efforts to the reclamation of some lost and confused youth.

The learned jurist who spends his day in some special court designed to handle "morals cases" might better employ his time and judgment if he heard the many cases, both civil and criminal, that now clog court rosters for years before justice is administered.

But the police and others responsible for the enforcement and administration of law do not make the laws. Their only function is to complete the work of those who do make the laws. Too much of their time and effort is devoted to enforcing and administering laws that never should have been written in the first place, with the consequence that not enough of their time and effort may be given to the enforcement and administration of laws that are in the true interest of society. Thus a great deal too much injustice prevails in the courts as a result of the enforcement of unreasonable laws at the same time that far too little real justice is meted out.

Our personal lives have become ever more dominated by the growing demands of an expanding officialdom. We are increasingly required to renounce a great many of the satisfactions that may be peculiar to us as individuals. A plethora of rules, regulations, laws, and ordinances confront us in our daily lives and make even greater inroads upon our time and freedom. We are compelled to fill out endless forms, to keep detailed records, and to disclose more and more about the nature of our private lives in order to satisfy the ritualistic compulsions of a bureaucratic state. There is practically no privacy at all left us in the conduct of our business affairs. It is expected of us that we may be called upon to testify in one sort of "investigation" or another at any moment; none of us may be absolutely certain that we ourselves will not become the subject of some sort of officious inquiry. We all now have a number, and the duties demanded of us by "society" are clearly enumerated in law and dignified by the label "service."

But in this, "The Age of Conformity," in which the only sign of protest left seems to be that which is so ineptly manifested in the antisocial behavior of juveniles, it might be hoped that at least in matters of sexual preference and taste we be accorded privacy and the exercise of personal judgment without having to endure the presumptuous authority of government. There are areas of one's feeling and experience which are intensely personal—perhaps even sacred to the individual—and over which no outside force should ever be accorded authority. It is not too much to suppose that sexual feeling and experience represent one such area.

We must recognize some limit to what the social organization may require of the individual. If we arrive at the point where that holy of holies, "society," is bound by no limitations upon its control over the individual and the official apparatus of the state may govern every detail in the life of the individual, we will have also arrived at the point where life is no longer worth living. It is a serious matter to have to observe that for many people whose sexual interests and needs do not conform with the pretended behavior of the group, such a point seems dangerously close at hand.

Consequently, many are driven to bizarre and ineffective modes of protest that in no way further the cause of freedom—sexual or otherwise— and that only tend to support the rationalizations of those who would withhold such freedom from them. In the sexual area, therefore, we tend to find either abject fear and hypocrisy in which the individual spends his life attempting to convey an image of conformity, or vainglorious boldness, expressed exhibitionistically, in which the individual spends his life attempting to convey an image of revolt. In the homosexual sphere these two extremes may be seen in the "closet queen" and the "screaming faggot," respectively.

But progress will only come about as the result of the efforts of those who will no longer conform but who have learned that an effective protest can only be based upon the recognition of one's dignity as a human being. For such a person it will not be necessary to masquerade behind a hypocritical pose either of meticulous propriety or feckless abandon.

In the final analysis, it is not the restrictions upon the freedom of the individual brought about by antihomosexual legislation that make such legislation most objectionable or expose it to the most serious criticism. This legislation is most objectionable and most liable to serious criticism for the same reason that many of our other Judaeo-Christian attitudes toward homosexuality are: they arise in an atmosphere of ignorance and denial of reality. The effort to suppress homosexuality through legal statutes and the belief that it warrants suppression ignore and obfuscate the simple facts that make it abundantly clear that homosexual responsiveness, being an integral part of the mammalian sexual heritage, has always played a substantial part in the sexual life of humans during the past, that it plays a substantial part at present, and that it will continue to do so in the future. Reason therefore demands a more realistic approach to these facts than is exemplified in attempts at suppression through legal or other means.

It is important to emphasize that no substantial reforms affecting the free practice of consenting homosexual relations will take place in isolation. Reforms in this area are dependent upon a more general program of reform affecting the entire field of sex legislation, for interdictions against homosexuality are founded upon a negative, suspicious, and fearful attitude toward sex in general. Homosexual relations were not singled out for special consideration in the Code Napoléon, nor in the Illinois reform.

These relations were permitted simply because the law refrained from dictating the nature of private, consenting sexual relations of any kind. Those who favor the repeal of antihomosexual legislation must recognize this principle and must call for the repeal of all legislation that attempts to regulate and prescribe moral decisions appropriate to the individual, whether or not such decisions involve homosexual relations.

But we may put aside the ethical and humanistic objections to antihomosexual legislation in order to consider the material objections.

The number of people who become involved in the acts which are prohibited by the legislation we have been discussing is simply too great to cope with. If anything even remotely resembling full and just enforcement of these laws were ever attempted, our prisons and houses of correction would be filled to overflowing before the first 20 per cent of the offenders had been apprehended. The extent of the dilemma posed by present statutes in the United States is clearly defined by Kinsey, Pomeroy, and Martin:

> There are those who will contend that the immorality of homosexual behavior calls for its suppression no matter what the facts are concerning the incidence and frequency of such activity in the population. Some have demanded that homosexuality be completely eliminated from society by a concentrated attack upon it at every point, and the "treatment" or isolation of all individuals with any homosexual tendencies. Whether such a program is morally desirable is a matter on which a scientist is not qualified to pass judgment; but whether such a program is physically feasible is a matter for scientific determination.
>
> The evidence that we now have on the incidence and frequency of homosexual activity indicates that at least a third of the male population would have to be isolated from the rest of the community, if all those with any homosexual capacities were to be so treated. It means that at least 13% of the male population . . . would have to be institutionalized and isolated, if all persons who were predominantly homosexual were to be handled in that way. Since about 34% of the total population of the United States are adult males, this means that there are about six and a third million males in the country who would need such isolation. [These figures would be substantially higher today as a result of an increase in the population in the United States.]
>
> If all persons with any trace of homosexual history, or those who are predominantly homosexual, were eliminated from the population today, there is no reason for believing that the incidence of the homosexual in the next generation would be materially reduced. The homosexual has been a significant part of human sexual activity ever since the dawn of history, primarily because it is an expression of capacities that are basic in the human animal.[53]

XI

Sex, Sin, and Psychiatry

Perhaps as a result of the awe which the image of the physician continues to inspire in our culture, the public most often turns to the psychiatrist rather than to the behavioral scientist for an explanation of human behavior. This seems to be particularly the case so far as sexual behavior is concerned. Although the experimental psychologist, the anthropologist, the sociologist, and also the biologist might conceivably be able to tell us more that is reliable about sexual behavior than the clinician, whose observations are necessarily confined to a highly select group of disturbed individuals drawn from a single culture, it is, nevertheless, the clinician whose opinion is most often consulted in these matters. Such is the prestige of psychiatry in our culture today (especially in the Anglo-Saxon nations) that the average person automatically assumes that psychiatric pronouncements on any aspect of sexual behavior are, so to speak, "the last word."

It is not generally recognized even by legislators, jurists, law-enforcement officials or clergymen that the sexual theories that enjoy acceptance in psychiatry today are by no means unassailable and that many psychiatric precepts are directly challenged and some even clearly refuted by the more scrupulous research of scientists outside the psychiatric fold. But the research of behavioral scientists who study sexual phenomena in the full perspective provided by cross-species and cross-cultural investigations is less familiar to the average person and plays a much smaller part in the formulation of public opinion, not only because it is more difficult for the public to grasp and assess, but also because the implications of scientific research in this area tend to be far more challenging to conventional concepts than are orthodox psychiatric views on sex. It is not too much to suppose that the extraordinary prestige that psychiatry enjoys in this age of conformity may be explained to a very large extent by the complete dedication that this branch of the healing arts has to precisely the same values and, one must add, precisely the same illusions that receive support from the other moral institutions of our culture.

Those who are in the habit of regarding psychiatry as a science may be shocked and even offended by these remarks, but they should not be. There is no reason to imagine that psychiatry is more of a science than any other branch of the healing arts and, indeed, a great deal more reason to suspect that it may be even less of a science. Medicine has been called an art throughout the ages for the good and simple reason that it *is* an art: its aim is not to understand for the mere sake of understanding, but rather to produce certain effects that seem desirable both to its practitioners and their clients. Merely because physics, chemistry, and biology have in very recent times aided the medical practitioneer in finding the ways to bring about the effects he wishes to produce, no one should conclude that medicine itself is a science. Science is absolutely amoral and is based upon the urge to understand; medicine, on the other hand, is an extremely moral calling and is based upon the urge to cure. Far from being the same, the urge to understand and the urge to cure may come into conflict at many junctions. There have of course been physicians in whom scientific motives were more prominent than therapeutic motives. But, almost without exception, these men have been condemned, excoriated, and even excommunicated from the profession by other physicians. Conservatism and even reaction against change—as is also the case with religion—have always been conspicuous tendencies within the medical profession.

From the viewpoint of those whose task it is to cure, any method which is capable of bringing about the desired results is acceptable. If tomorrow it were possible to cure headache by "the laying on of hands" physicians would include this method of treatment in their textbooks. They have done so in the past. It is only because such methods prove less reliable than more modern methods that they are no longer as often used. It is only in very recent times that physicians have resisted the temptation to use any means at hand in order to cure, and to some extent the urge to understand as well as to cure is expected in the contemporary physician because experience has shown that reliable cure can only be based upon scientific insight.

The practice of physical medicine is therefore a less fortuitous proposition today than in the past, and although medical practice remains an art, it has profited greatly from developments in the physical sciences. The practice of psychological medicine, however, is a different matter. In spite of certain contributions from biology and from experimental psychology and the other behavioral sciences, psychiatric diagnosis and therapy still depend to an alarming extent upon the feelings and intuitions, opinions, and sometimes prejudices of the practitioner. It is difficult to sort out fact from fancy in psychiatry and much that passes for fact proves upon scrutiny to be mere opinion. There is as yet in psychiatry not even any lucid formulation as to what constitutes health and disease, let alone an objective formulation, and both health and disease continue to be defined by psychiatrists in extremely vague and subjective terms.

We will not be able to evaluate psychiatric attitudes toward sexual phenomena if we do not take into consideration the history of medicine and also the peculiar psychology that always becomes involved in the human attitude toward disease.

Every human culture known to science provides evidence that sin and disease are related concepts that may become so confused as to make any distinction between them sometimes almost impossible. It is felt not only that what is regarded as sinful must be pathological, but also that what is regarded as pathological must have some connection with sinfulness.

In the case of menstruation, for example, the relationship between the idea of sin and the idea of disease is quite clear. Although scientists know that menstruation is a natural aspect of feminine physiology and that it is neither pathological nor sinful, it has been regarded as both in many cultures. In our own culture the feeling is still strong that menstruation is a punishment for evil and also that it is a form of illness. Even in contemporary times some women continue to refer to their period as "the curse" at one moment and as "the sickness" at another moment. Sexual relations with a menstruating woman are forbidden in ancient Jewish law, and the menstruating woman is considered "unclean." Upon more scrupulous investigation the word "unclean" proves to have both a hygienic and a moral connotation.

In certain other cultures as well menstruation is regarded as an illness. Wherever this is the case, sexual relations with a menstruating woman are taboo and she may even be required to live apart from the community until the menstrual flow has ceased. Often it is even forbidden to speak with her. She is considered not only ill but also tainted.

Many people are still ashamed of physical illness—not to mention mental illness—and will not admit to others that they are ill for fear of condemnation. A few generations ago, when tuberculosis was more common in Europe and America the entire subject was shrouded in shame and even the name of the disease was unmentionable in polite society. For centuries plague was interpreted as punishment for evil at the same time as it was recognized as a disease. Physical deformity of any kind has always been associated with moral corruption; hunchbacks and cripples have often been feared and quite as often persecuted because their physical deformities have been interpreted as the outward manifestation of evil. Even in more recent times certain moralists have opposed efforts to wipe out syphilis and other venereal diseases on the grounds that these diseases are punishments that God visits upon sinners for their evil deeds.

Instances in which moral and hygienic concepts become confused and even mutually dependent may be multiplied many times over. Sometimes it is possible to find instances in which a given circumstance is first regarded as sinful and/or taboo and only secondarily as pathological. Sometimes the reverse is true. But in most cases there is very little distinction made between abnormality, sinfulness, illness, and evil. Sexual phenomena, as has been sufficiently emphasized, seem in particular to inspire this kind of semantic and psychological confusion, and in the realm of sex the profane and abnormal are almost synonymous.

Because sin and disease have been confused, illnesses have been treated by religious as well as by medical means throughout the greater part of human history. The urge to cure is still suspiciously associated with the urge to purify, and the history of medicine is interwoven with superstition, magic, and religion. Originally there was no difference at all between a priest and a physician; the earliest priests were all medical specialists, and the earliest physicians were all specialists in magic and the propitiation of the gods. The witch doctor or medicine man was a priest-physician who treated not only illness but also sin by methods designed to exorcise evil spirits. Even after the separation of medicine and religion into distinct professions patients were ministered to by both physicians and priests.

The confusion between sin and disease and the relationship between medicine and religion seem even more emphatic in the case of mental ailments. We shall see later how often mental illness has been confused with sin and sin with mental illness. First, however, we will concentrate on the present-day relationship between psychiatry and religion.

Not only do people take their psychiatric problems to priests; they also take their spiritual and moral problems to psychiatrists. The distressed wife who feels that she no longer loves her husband, for example, may consult either a priest or a psychiatrist or both, and she may receive substantially the same advice and guidance from both. The clergyman who feels unable to deal with the emotional problems of his parishioner may, in a growing number of instances, refer him to a psychiatrist without the least misgiving that the parishioner's religious beliefs will be upset by the psychiatrist. The psychiatrist today may often refer cases to a clergyman for auxiliary therapy without the least misgiving that the patient's emotional difficulties will be augmented by the religious instruction he receives from the clergyman. Indeed, cooperation between psychiatry and religion has proceeded to a point where clergymen are admitted for training in certain psychoanalytic and psychotherapeutic institutes, and the devout psychoanalyst or psychotherapist today may be accorded the full respect of his colleagues even if he professes belief in every dogma of the most fundamentalist religious sect. It was not always so, however.

For a brief span during the first three or four decades of this century there was some enmity between psychiatry and religion. Religionists were fearful that certain doctrines in psychiatry—particularly those relating to sex—might be heretical in nature. During this period many clergymen of all faiths were reluctant to refer their parishioners for psychiatric treatment. Some psychiatrists seemed to be critical of traditional religious attitudes; in particular those who followed the teachings of Freud emphasized the ill effects of sexual repression and traced much of this repression to traditional religious teachings. Even the belief in God was interpreted by some psychoanalysts as a fixation of certain childhood attitudes toward the father and toward authority in general. Freud himself published a number of studies expressing skepticism toward many religious beliefs.

But this breach between psychiatry and religion—brief and superficial as it was—has been closed in recent years. The age-old communality of religion and medicine is fully intact once again. Most religionists who take pride in their modernity believe that contemporary religion has learned important lessons from psychiatry and from science in general, even though no religious institution has altered a single dogma of the traditional Judaeo-Christian sex doctrine. Psychiatrists, for their part, feel considerably chastened by the conviction that they have learned important lessons from time-honored sexual dogmas—dogmas that they apparently imagine must contain some element of truth and wisdom.

The fleeting rift between psychiatry and religion fizzled out not because religion ever made any concessions to psychiatry, nor because psychiatry made any concessions to religion, but only because both came to recognize that their differences were more apparent than real. If we examine the most radical and the most carefully worked-out of the psychiatric sex theories—Freud's Theory of the Libido or of Psychosexual Development—we may see that there is nothing in them which is at all harmful to traditional Judaeo-Christian sexual beliefs. These theories are founded upon the sexual mystique of our culture and theirs are conclusions that one would arrive at through having absorbed and accepted this mystique. Only the terminology differs from what one is used to hearing—which is probably what misled religionists at first. Freudian sex theory is so beautifully constructed and provides the conventional sexual doctrine of our religious traditions with such a perfect rationalization that, were it not for Freud's theological misdemeanors, he would have at least as good a claim to sainthood for services rendered to the Church as St. Thomas Aquinas. Aquinas stabilized the philosophical basis of organized Christianity and Freud provided the sexual doctrine of organized Christianity with some rationalistic ballast. Before Freud it was necessary to speak in such crude and outlandish terms as "abominations" and "sins against nature." Now we may refer to the same phenomena as "psychosexual regression," "pregenital fixation," or, as a compromise between the two terminologies (for the word receives currency in both religious and psychiatric jargon) "perversion."

Freudian sex theory—and most other psychoanalytic sex theories as well—assume that the sexual drive is an instinct and that as such it has inherent aims and objects. Through a long and complicated process of development that is thought to follow certain preordained stages, the sexual drive—providing everything has gone according to schedule—is supposed to reach a stage at which it is devoted exclusively to procreative aims. This final stage is called by Freudians *genitality*. The nonprocreative sexual tendencies that Freudians insist always precede the development of genital sexuality are referred to as *infantile sexuality*. Infantile sexuality is said to be distinguished by its "polymorphous perverse" character.

Thus psychoanalysts picture the sex life of the child as "perverse" and the sex life of the adult "pervert" as "infantile." This is rather a strange and even bizarre way of interpreting sexual phenomena, since it implies that the child begins his sexual life with interests which are regarded in psychiatry as pathological; according to this interpretation "perversion" is more fundamental than "normal sexuality." But this is only one of several paradoxes that arise out of the effort to interpret sexual phenomena in terms of conventional morality.

In reality, as we have seen in an earlier chapter, the sex drive has no inherent aims or objects other than the release of tension. Before this drive becomes conditioned through learning the individual may respond sexually to any sufficient stimulus. Thus very young children may respond sexually in many situations that appear "perverse" in the context of our moral beliefs, simply because they have not yet learned to avoid certain stimuli that are taboo in our culture. The so-called pervert is an individual who, for various and often multitudinous reasons, has never learned to avoid certain taboo sexual stimuli. Or he may be an individual who has never learned to respond positively and exclusively to certain approved sexual stimuli. Often various conflicts during childhood are responsible for the type of sexual learning that produces what clinicians call "perversion"; but childhood conflict is, by no means, the only factor that may facilitate the learning of socially unapproved sexual tendencies.

In addition to providing a pseudo-scientific rationalization for conventional sexual prejudices, psychoanalytic sexual doctrine provides some intellectual ballast for the notion that chastity or celibacy may afford benefits. Freud believed that the "libido"—as he often called the sex drive—may be *sublimated;* that is, he believed that the sexual drive can be diverted and that its energy may be put into the service of what he called "higher" social aims. According to this theory, the energy which might otherwise be expended in so-called perverse sexual activity—and, presumably, even the energy which might otherwise be expended in so-called normal (procreative) sexual activity—may be channeled into artistic, philosophical, and scientific activities. Indeed, these very activities have been interpreted in Freudian psychology as sublimations of infantile (perverse) sexuality.

Apart from the fact, however, that a great many artists, philosophers, and scientists have been known to have been so-called perverts who expended a great deal of their energy in the pursuit of unapproved sexual activities, the idea that sexual energy may be sublimated has become doubted even by a great many orthodox psychoanalysts. Almost no one continues to imagine that so-called genital sexuality may be "sublimated" in this way, and there is a growing question among psychoanalysts today as to whether even "pre-genital" sexuality may undergo sublimation.

Kinsey could find no evidence in support of the idea that the sexual drive may be sublimated. There was nothing to indicate that those with a very low total sexual outlet were, as a group, more energetic in cultural pursuits; nor was there anything to indicate that those with a high total sexual outlet were less energetic in cultural pursuits. In conclusion of their discussion of this topic Kinsey *et al.* remarked:

> If then, from the list of low-rating males, one removes those who are physically incapacitated, natively low in sexual drive, sexually unawakened in their younger years, separated from their usual sources of sexual stimulation, or timid or upset by their sexual suppressions, there are simply no cases which remain as clear-cut examples of sublimation . . . Certain it is that among the many males who have contributed to the present sample, sublimation is so subtle, or so rare, as to constitute an academic possibility rather than a demonstrated reality. In view of the widespread and easy acceptance of the theory, and the efforts that such a large proportion of the population has made to achieve this goal, one might have expected better evidence of its existence, at least among the sexually least active 5% of the males in the population.[53]

The assumption that psychosexual development proceeds along preordained lines that, under conditions described by certain theorists as normal, lead inevitably to an exclusive interest in heterosexual coitus is at best merely speculative, and no large-scale study of the sexual behavior of children has ever provided evidence that there is any regular and universal pattern of psychosexual development. Consequently it may not be assumed that certain types of sexual behavior are peculiar to childhood. It may be remembered that heterosexual, homosexual, and autoerotic interests may be commonly found among children and adults alike, so that it is rather meaningless to speak of one kind of sexual behavior as more "mature" than another.

The reason that religion and psychiatry have found it easy to cooperate in modern times is clear: for what religion calls sin psychiatry calls disease. Of course there may be some minor disputes as to whether to treat a given type of sexual behavior by moral or by medical means and it is true that, from time to time, even today's psychiatrists and clergymen do have their spats. But these may be easily patched up when both agree that, through one means or another, the traditional sexual heresies must be suppressed. This agreement, moreover, makes for a very comfortable arrangement when various social agencies attempt, often through direct coercion, to bring the individual into conformity with the pretended customs of the group.

The conventional orientation of psychiatry in all matters related to sex was traced in considerable detail by René Guyon in his excellent book *La Légitimité des Actes Sexuels* (published in English with the title *The Ethics of Sexual Acts*). In this book Guyon observes that:

> As between nature and convention, psychiatry always sides with convention, and brands the natural as "the abnormal." Starting from this disloyalty to its own scientific premises, psychiatry soon becomes blind to all logical conclusions.[34]

Guyon's premise, which he defends admirably from a great many different standpoints, is that all sexual acts that involve mutual consent and mutual satisfaction and do not involve violence, fraud, deception, or coercion, are legitimate ethically as well as consistent with mental health. He makes no special plea in behalf of homosexuality, but—unlike a great many others who regard themselves as sex liberals—neither does he exclude homosexuality from the sphere of moral and wholesome sexuality.

Mention has already been made of the historic attitude of medicine toward masturbation, still another instance in which sinfulness has been equated with illness. Under the moralistic headings "onanism" and "self-abuse" physicians made this benign and commonplace practice responsible not only for a catalogue of quite incredible physical ills but for insanity as well, and even in the early decades of this century medical specialists were still "treating" this supposed perversion and disease by methods ranging from moral intimidation and threat of punishment to surgery. Like homosexuality today, masturbation was considered both a cause and a result of disease. Alarmed by both the unenlightened preachments of clergymen and the absurd medical opinions of doctors, parents subjected their children to treatment that today would be considered nothing less than moral and physical assault.

Approved "therapeutic" methods included blistering the thighs of children, binding their arms in splints, and even genital mutilation in the form of circumcision and clitoridectomy. Kinsey has drawn attention to use of castration by medics as a "cure" for masturbation. In the Hospital for Epileptics at Palmer, Massachusetts, twenty-four males, half of them under fourteen years of age, were castrated for persistent maturbation and epilepsy. He reports the remarks of Flood, who discussed this treatment. "Persistent masturbators . . . unpleasant for a refined woman to see . . . it seemed an absolute necessity to try something which we had not yet tried." He also remarks on Dr. Pilcher's castrations of "confirmed masturbators" at the Kansas State Training School. A subsequent authority reported that "Our castrations first started during the administration of Dr. Pilcher who conceived the idea that castration might help control excessive masturbation and pervert sexual acts." [54] In an address given by Dr. Hawks in 1950 to the Illinois Academy of Criminology, he described the effects of castration on 330 male patients at the Kansas State Training School and concluded that the castrate is "physically a better organism."

Only the effort of a few rationalists—some of whom were not physicians at all—relieved the medical and lay public from their autoerotophobic excesses and made them see that masturbation is not only virtually a universal phenomenon but also, in a vast majority of instances, a quite harmless practice. Consequently, fewer children today are subjected to abuse from their parents and from physicians if they are discovered to have an interest in masturbation. But many myths about the harmful effects of "self-abuse" continue to circulate among the less educated, and autoerotic phenomena among adults are still condemned by many physicians as symptoms of "emotional immaturity" and "psychosexual regression."

Many physicians have cooperated in the use of castration as a punitive method in dealing with "sex offenders." In ten of our states, involuntary castration is allowed in these cases, and physicians of course perform these operations. It is interesting, in this connection, to note the strong influence cultural attitudes have upon sexual practices and punishment. In Italy, for example—a country in which the law has very little to say about private sexual acts—it might be difficult to find even a veterinarian who is willing to castrate a domestic tom-cat.

"But," many will say, "surely the attitude of modern psychiatry toward sexual practices is much less moralistic and much more permissive." Such, however, is far from being the case in reality. Recent clinical publications continue to group not only all of the traditional "perversions" but almost all other sexual behavior which deviates from conventionally established norms in the pathological category. Any sexual behavior that is not exclusively coital or that is not merely the prelude to coitus, and any sexual behavior that is not confined to a monogomous marital relationship is likely to receive the stigma of pathology from orthodox psychiatry, and there is an increasing tendency to refer all those who offend against sexual convention for "treatment." In other words, sexual immorality is still directly equated with psychopathology or is made a consequence of psychopathology, and both are defined in terms of the philosophical concepts that prevail in the Judaeo-Christian religious tradition.

Thus, it may often be that the promiscuous bachelor is urged by his friends, who regard him as a "Don Juan," to see a doctor; that the wayward husband or wife is regarded as a psychiatric case in need of treatment; that the young woman who practices prostitution as a means of increasing her income is referred by a social agency to a psychiatrist because she is thought to be suffering from a pronounced malady that has warped her judgment of right and wrong; that the teenage boy who is discovered by his teacher to have a lively interest in what she regards as "obscene literature" is sent by the school authorities to a psychological clinic for study as a possible mental case; that two youths who are caught masturbating together in a dark corner of the park are arrested and placed on psychiatric probation as dangerous "sex psychopaths." All of these have been analyzed and diagnosed as psychiatric cases by clinicians in recent publications. Sexual irregularities of any kind may be seized upon as evidence of psychopathology, and the sexual nonconformist today may be considered not only a sinner but a mental case as well.

But, as we have already seen in an earlier chapter, if all of those who ever become involved in what is now euphemistically called "socially unacceptable sexual behavior" are counted, we find that we are dealing with approximately 95 per cent of the male population.[53] This means that it is necessary to assume that almost everyone is some kind of psychiatric case according to current clinical criteria of what constitutes mental health in the sexual sphere. Clinicians have warned us that the mere frequency of a given type of sexual behavior is not necessarily an indication that the behavior in question is not pathological. But even if we heed their warnings and disregard the statistics on "socially unacceptable sexual behavior" we must still be left with the impression that current clinical views on sexual pathology are more than simply extravagant; they are downright absurd—and their absurdity should be exposed to the ridicule it deserves. It is difficult to disagree with Guyon when he writes:

> We must insist on settling this point: we must decide whether, just to please our psychiatrists, we are going to look upon everybody, or very nearly everybody, as mentally deranged; whether we are going to believe that we are, one and all of us, descended from demented societies—since our ancestors undoubtedly indulged in sexual practices which modern society regards as symptomatic of dementia.[34]

In 1948, the Indiana group deplored this tendency to equate conventionally unacceptable sexual behavior with psychopathology. In a remarkable excerpt in *Sexual Behavior in the Human Male,* Kinsey, Pomeroy, and Martin focused attention upon several of the most serious faults in the clinical approach to sexual phenomena. Their discussion is so germane and so concise that, in spite of its length, it deserves full quotation in a book such as this.

The term "abnormal" is applied in medical pathology to conditions which interfere with the physical well-being of a living body. In a social sense, the term might apply to sexual activities which cause social maladjustment. Such an application, however, involves subjective determinations of what is good personal living, or good social adjustment; and these things are not as readily determined as physiologic well-being in an organic body. It is not possible to insist that any departure from the sexual mores, or any participation in socially taboo activities, always, or even usually, involves a neurosis or psychosis, for the case histories abundantly demonstrate that most individuals who engage in taboo activities make satisfactory social adjustments. There are, in actuality, few adult males who are particularly disturbed over their sexual histories. Psychiatrists, clinical psychologists, and others who deal with cases of maladjustment, sometimes come to feel that most people find difficulty in adjusting their sexual lives; but a clinic is no place to secure incidence figures. The incidence of tuberculosis in a tuberculosis sanitarium is no measure of the incidence of tuberculosis in the population as a whole; and the incidence of disturbance over sexual activities, among the persons who come to a clinic, is no measure of the frequency of similar disturbances outside of clinics. The impression that such "sexual irregularities" as "excessive" masturbation, pre-marital intercourse, responsibility for a pre-marital pregnancy, extra-marital intercourse, mouth-genital contacts, homosexual activity, or animal intercourse, always produce psychoses and abnormal personalities is based upon the fact that the persons who do go to professional sources for advice are upset by these things.

It is unwarranted to believe that particular types of sexual behavior are always expressions of psychoses or neuroses. In actuality, they are more often expressions of what is biologically basic in mammalian and anthropoid behavior, and of a deliberate disregard for social convention. Many of the socially and intellectually most significant persons in our histories, successful scientists, educators, physicians, clergymen, business men, and persons of high position in governmental affairs, have socially taboo items in their sexual histories, and among them they have accepted nearly the whole range of so-called sexual abnormalities. Among the socially most successful and personally best adjusted persons who have contributed to the present study, there are some whose rates of outlet are as high as those in any case labelled nymphomania or satyriasis in the literature, or recognized as such in the clinic.

Clinical subjects who have such unusual items in their histories often do present psychopathologies—that is why they have gone to the clinics. But the presence of particular behavior, or the existence of a high rate, is not the abnormality which needs explanation. The real clinical problem is the discovery and treatment of the personality defects, the mental difficulties, the compulsions, and the schizo-phrenic conflicts which lead particular individuals to crack up when-ever they depart from averages or socially accepted custom, while millions of other persons embrace the very same behavior, and may have as high rates of activity, without personal or social disturbance. It has been too simple a solution to discover the sexual items in a patient's history, to consider them symptoms of a neurosis, and to diagnose the disturbance as the outcome of the departure from the established mores. It is much more difficult to discover the bases of the unstable personalities that are upset by such sexual departures, and to treat the basic defects rather than to patch up the particular issues over which the disturbances occur. Clinicians would have more incentive for using such an approach if they were better acquainted with the normal frequencies of the so-called abnormal types of ac-tivity, and if, at least as far as sex is concerned, they could acquire a wider acquaintance with the sexual histories of well-adjusted individuals.

Most of the complications which are observable in sexual histories are the result of society's reactions when it obtains knowledge of an individual's behavior, or the individual's fear of how society would react if he were discovered. In various societies, under various circum-stances, and even at various social levels of the population living in a particular town, the sex mores are fundamentally different. The way in which each group reacts to a particular sort of history de-termines the "normality" or "abnormality" of the individual's be-havior—in that particular group . . . Whatever the moral interpreta-tion (as in Moore 1943), there is no scientific reason for considering particular types of sexual activity as intrinsically, in their biologic origins, normal or abnormal. Yet scientific classifications have been nearly identical with theologic classifications and with the moral pronouncements of the English common law of the fifteenth century. This, in turn, as far as sex is concerned, was based on the medieval ecclesiastic law which was only a minor variant of the tenets of ancient Greek and Roman cults, and of the Talmudic law . . . Present-day legal determinations of sexual acts which are acceptable, or "natural," and those which are "contrary to nature" are not based on data obtained from biologists, nor from nature herself. On the contrary, the ancient codes have been accepted by laymen, jurists, and scientists alike as the ultimate sources of moral evaluations, of present-day legal procedure, and of the list of subjects that may go into a textbook of abnormal psychology. In no other field of science have scientists been satisfied to accept the biologic notions of ancient jurists and theologians, or the analyses made by the mystics of two or three thousand years ago. Either the ancient philosophers were remarkably well-trained psychologists, or modern psychologists have contributed little in defining abnormal sexual behavior.

The reactions of our social organization to these various types of behavior are the things that need study and classification. The mores, whether they concern food, clothing, sex, or religious rituals, originate neither in accumulated experience nor in scientific examinations of objectively gathered data. The sociologist and anthropologist find the origins of such customs in ignorance and superstition, and in the attempt of each group to set itself apart from its neighbors. Psychologists have been too much concerned with the individuals who depart from the group custom. It would be more important to know why so many individuals conform as they do to such ancient custom, and what psychology is involved in the preservation of these customs by a society whose individual members would, in most cases, not attempt to defend all of the specific items in that custom. Too often the study of behavior has been little more than a rationalization of the mores masquerading under the guise of objective science.[53]

It is important to emphasize here several of the points made in the paragraphs quoted above.

First, the authors point out that characterizations of certain sexual activities in terms of social maladjustment, unlike definitions of physical pathology, involve subjective determinations of what is good personal living. They do not think that such determinations lie within the scope either of psychiatry or science; they are moral determinations.

Second, the authors demonstrate that clinicians have the opportunity to observe only disturbed individuals who become involved in unconventional sexual activities. From this rather one-sided experience they are prone to conclude that all persons who are involved in unconventional sexual activities of any kind must also be disturbed. But this does not follow and, to the contrary, these authors as well as a number of other competent observers point to the fact that a great many people who (by any reasonable definition of a good social and personal adjustment) are psychologically sound become involved in conventionally unapproved sexual behavior of various kinds. The psychiatrist and clinical psychologist—and even the clergyman—tends to meet only with those individuals whose sexual behavior is a cause of emotional stress.

One of the most important points made by the Indiana team is that what really requires explanation are the personality defects, the compulsions, and the conflicts which cause certain people to become psychiatrically ill when they depart from averages or socially accepted customs while millions of others become involved in exactly the same behavior without personal or social disturbance. Kinsey and his colleagues point out that clinicians would recognize this problem in its proper perspective if "they were better acquainted with the normal frequencies of the so-called abnormal types of activity," and "if, at least as far as sex is concerned, they would acquire a wider acquaintance with the sexual histories of well-adjusted individuals."

Let us particularize these points in terms of the subject of this book. Clinicians treat so-called homosexuals who are, as they always point out, undoubtedly very disturbed people. Leaving aside the fact that there may be other so-called homosexuals who are not similarly disturbed—individuals who would hardly be expected to appear at the psychiatrist's office—clinicians, to the knowledge of this author, have never yet posed the question as to why these particular individuals have become ill. Instead, it is simply assumed either that they are ill because they are homosexual, or more often that they are homosexual because they are ill. But how can we be certain of this—especially when it may be that there are certain other so-called homosexuals who are not ill?

In the experience of this author, *all* so-called homosexuals who end up in the consultation room of the clinician—whether or not they may acknowledge the fact—are deeply disturbed by their homosexuality and, even though in many cases they may claim the very opposite, have come to the clinician with the secret or avowed motive of escaping from their homosexual urges. Though it may be paradoxical, it is often precisely because these individuals are inordinately upset by their homosexuality that they have made it an exclusive form of sexual outlet. Investigation brings to light that these patients have an entirely fantastic impression of homosexuality and of themselves as "homosexuals," and that it is these very attitudes rather than the homosexuality per se that require therapy. Therapy in all these cases should, in the opinion of this author, explore as thoroughly as possible the patient's distorted attitudes toward homosexuality in particular and toward sex in general.

Most often today the conflict of these people is construed to be a sign that homosexuality per se is a disease—or that it is based upon pathology, which amounts to the same thing—and the effort is made to reverse the patient's homosexual trends and to bring his sex life into conformity with conventional norms. Sometimes—but not as often, perhaps, as is claimed— these efforts are successful; but even where they are successful they do not by any means always lead to results that everyone could agree are desirable. This author has had the opportunity to become acquainted with many persons who were treated for homosexuality with supposedly successful results. More often than not after such "successful" therapy these individuals have either resumed their homosexual activities sometime after the termination of therapy and have continued to function poorly as "homosexuals," or, in robot-like fashion and with a supercilious air akin to that often found among religious converts, they function as "heterosexuals." In neither case, however, do they usually convey the slightest impression of ease, happiness, naturalness, or contentment.

The treatment of the homosexual patient or any other patient, if it is to be worthwhile, must bring about a confrontation on the part of the individual with his attitudes toward sex and toward himself as a sexual being. All the near and sometimes outright insanity about sex that the patient has accumulated in the erotophobic atmosphere of our culture must, as is said in clinical jargon, be "worked through" if the patient is to reach a rational sex adjustment. The object of therapy should be not that the patient accept heterosexuality, homosexuality, or autoeroticism, but simply that he accept *sexuality*. Having done so, it is entirely within his own province—and indeed his own responsibility—to discover for himself what particular modalities of the sexual drive fulfill his needs as an individual. It is very likely that a patient who receives the benefits of such therapy will be alive to a number of different sexual possibilities, but those that may constitute the greater part of his sexual pattern should be a matter of complete indifference to the therapist; certainly the therapist should never exploit his authority in order to propagandize on behalf of his own particular sexual preferences.

Therapy cannot be carried out along such lines, however, as long as psychiatrists and other clinicians consider "particular types of sexual activity as intrinsically, in their biologic origins, normal or abnormal," nor so long as the clinical arts are wedded monogamously to traditional theological interpretations of sex. It is indeed the reactions of our social organization to the various types of sexual behavior that need study and classification rather than the specific types of behavior themselves at this stage in our knowledge. The mores upon which most psychotherapeutic goals today continue to be based do not, as Kinsey *et al.* have emphasized, originate either in accumulated experience nor in scientific examinations of objectively gathered data but rather in ignorance, superstition, and the attempt of each group to set itself apart from its neighbors. Clinicians and other psychologists and social scientists might presently contribute more to the advancement of our civilization if, instead of attempting to bring everyone into conformity with the mores, they would provide us with a scientific explanation of "what psychology is involved in the preservation of these customs by a society whose individual members would, in most cases, not attempt to defend all of the specific items in that custom." Such an explanation might provide not only the basis for a saner and more healthy society but for a more enlightened sexual morality as well.

It would save a great deal of time and effort if our discussion of psychiatry could be limited to current clinical attitudes toward sexual behavior alone or, even better, limited to current clinical attitudes toward homosexuality. Unfortunately, it is not possible to grasp the fundamental objections to the clinical approach to sex and to homosexuality in particular, without knowledge of certain other points which have more general applicability.

Psychiatry and, to a lesser but nonetheless significant extent, even the behavioral sciences seem to have been unduly influenced by certain attitudes that ultimately must be regarded as subjective and clearly arbitrary. Although we imagine that any inquiry that is represented as scientific must be objective and impartial, not all such inquiries are. The social sciences in general and the clinical disciplines in particular are often

oriented to certain preconceived ideas that, when scrutinized, can hardly
be called objective or impartial. To imagine that the social sciences have
attained a degree of objectivity and reliability comparable to that of the
physical sciences is to be led astray by wishful thinking. Some who work
within the social sciences—including, of course, the clinical disciplines—
take great care to avoid falling into value judgments that are based upon
the philosophical conventions prevalent in our environment. Not a few of
these workers conscientiously attempt to distinguish fact from opinion
and, in their published works, to clarify the difference between the two.
But, apart from the fact that this may often be very difficult to do, the
pressures that are usually brought to bear upon the social scientist in his
relationships with those who enjoy authority outside the sphere of science
sometimes make it seem necessary to modify or even leave entirely un-
stated certain obvious conclusions. Often the social scientist who refuses
to accept these limitations finds it difficult or even impossible to publish his
work—not necessarily because any official censorship has been imposed
upon him, but more often simply because the policy of publishers may
stand in the way of his work getting into print. At other times excellent
work may find its way into print, only to meet with a failure on the part
of others to receive it.

There is a pervasive tendency on the part of both the scientific and the
lay public to pay attention only to that which fits comfortably with prevailing opinion and prejudice. All the rest may be simply rejected with
a remarkable air of certainty or—far worse—may be simply ignored.

Now we must scrutinize the state of mind that makes this possible. It
is very largely assumed in most of the social sciences, and to an even
larger extent in psychiatry and the other clinical areas of investigation,
that what is referred to as "the interest of society" must be served at all
costs to the individual and often the group as well, and that these interests
are always best served if both morality and mental health are defined in
terms of "adjustment" to those values and practices that are vaguely
categorized as "socially acceptable." This entire approach proves to be
based upon a type of circular reasoning that is deficient not only in logic
but also objective verification.

The expression "socially acceptable" is on the lips of an ever larger
number of people who have no clear idea of what they mean by it. Whatever value this expression may at one time have had as a means of establishing communication between people it no longer has any real meaning.
To get any sense out of this cliché one must know exactly who uses it and
how. What the judge, the legislator, or the police officer has in mind when
he uses the expression "socially acceptable" may be very different from
what the sociologist, the clinician, the journalist, the moral reformer, or
the philosopher has in mind. This cliché may be used to justify or to

condemn that which only the person who uses it regards as praiseworthy or contemptible. Yet "socially acceptable" always implies a great deal more than mere individual opinion.

It may readily be said, for instance, that male homosexuality is not "socially acceptable." But what if anything is the actual value of this statement? It is true that male homosexuality does not have the open or tacit approval of any majority within our culture, so that certainly it cannot be claimed that it is "socially acceptable." As a pure description it is quite accurate to say that homosexuality is "socially unacceptable," but beyond this what does it mean? Does it mean that homosexuality cannot be accepted or that the social acceptance of homosexuality would bring disaster in its wake? What level of social acceptance does one have in mind when using this expression? Certainly 50 per cent of the male population does not verbally express acceptance of homosexuality in public, and probably only seldom even in private. But statistics reveal that approximately one out of every two males "accepts" homosexuality to the extent at least of entertaining homosexual fantasies. Does "social acceptance" imply mass activity, positive emotional involvement on the part of a majority, or institutionalized approval or does it imply some informal kind of consensus of opinion? If it implies consensus of opinion how may this be measured? British legislators, for example, have been slow to take action on the recommendation of the Wolfenden Committee because they claim that public opinion is not in favor of legal reform. But how do they know? There is evidence to indicate that the British public as a whole today may be very susceptible to legal reforms in this area, and that at least the public is not actively opposed to such reform. Those who habitually speak for the public often do so without the slightest notion of what the public feels about a given issue. It appears that the expression "socially acceptable" is usually used by individuals who simply wish to bring credit upon their own personal views or opinions.

Another very subjective and therefore usually quite dangerous word is "adjustment." Clinicians have pointed out that life itself amounts to adjustment, and from this observation many have elaborated an extremely vague but nevertheless far-reaching concept of mental health and mental disease. The ailing patient is said to have made a "poor adjustment" and the healthy individual a "good adjustment." But what, really, is a "poor adjustment" or a "good adjustment"? The answer to this question depends far too often upon personal opinion, and even the adjectives "poor" and "good" reveal that these expressions involve value judgments.

It is quite true that all living things become modified by their environ ment and that the capacity for "adjustment" is essential to survival. But when we attempt to distinguish a "good adjustment" from a "bad adjustment" in the psychological and social spheres we are on shaky ground. It is evident that some of the most creative and useful people in history have failed to make a "good adjustment" in terms of what this usually means today in clinical jargon. Some of these people have been social misfits who did everything in their power to change their environment rather than themselves. In many cases, we owe whatever progress our civilization has made to such people. Far too often—if not always—a "good adjustment" has come to mean mere social conformity. "Adjustment" in terms of what is "socially acceptable" involves two dangerous clichés, and it may be hardly expected that any thoughtful individual who has maintained a sense of personal dignity will readily submit to someone else's judgment concerning what a "good adjustment" or what "socially acceptable behavior" is. Such a person will insist upon defining these concepts for himself. Those who are not willing or able to do so may be precisely the ones who may be properly classed as psychiatric cases.

Even if psychiatry were an exact science many of its hypotheses would remain open to question, for it must be remembered that psychiatry is forced to deal with problems that, because they are fundamentally philosophical in nature, must necessarily remain somewhat subjective.

There is much talk in psychiatry about "reality," for example. Mental health is quite often defined in terms of the capacity to grasp and to test reality. But what, it must be asked (if one accepts this definition of mental health), is reality? Philosophers have been attempting to answer this question for centuries, and no one yet feels that a completely reliable answer has been found. It may be easy to argue that a schizophrenic patient who is lost in psychosis and who believes, for example, that he is the Pope has departed in his thoughts from reality. But it is quite another thing when psychiatrists tell us that certain people are ill because they do not accept the realities defined by mere convention. We may all agree that mental health consists in the capacity to grasp and to test reality. What we cannot always agree upon, however, is precisely what constitutes reality. Many people may argue that some of the conventions that clinicians insist upon are most unrealistic and that a firmer grasp of reality would lead the individual to reject many of these convictions. In the view of these people it may be the convention-ridden person rather than the nonconformist who is ill. The psychiatrist may not claim any greater authority than any other serious, reasonably intelligent person on which conventions are realistic and which are not. When it comes to these questions the clinician is as much of a layman as anyone else and no one need stand in awe of his opinions.

No critique of the scientific status of psychiatry can fail to take into account the extent to which psychiatrists and other clinicians in the field of mental health are influenced by attitudes peculiar to their social class. The clinical outlook is very typically upper-middle-class—"bourgeois" as older writers have described it—and this is nowhere more evident than in the case of matters touching upon sex. Kinsey *et al.* stressed the extent to which attitudes toward sex are related to economic and educational background. What appears "monstrous" to one class may appear entirely "normal" to another class. Homosexuality provides an excellent example of this. Although homosexuality is most frequent in our society among individuals who may be placed in a middle-class category, it is precisely this class that is most intolerant of homosexuality. But these class differences are not confined to homosexuality nor even to broader aspects of sexual life. Psychiatric judgment may be affected in many areas by the social alliances and social prejudices of the practitioner. Vance Packard, in his book *The Status Seekers* (David McKay Company, Inc., New York) has made the following observation:

> And psychiatrists, for all their erudition, have a great deal to learn about the public they are supposed to serve, according to the findings of the Yale group of sociologists and psychiatrists . . . These psychiatrists expressed annoyance and revulsion at the behavior of lower classes that they encountered during therapy. They were shocked by the sex mores of the lower classes and they were disgusted at the wives from the lower classes who accepted beatings from their husbands as a natural and reasonable part of life.

Clinicians have every good reason to examine their social biases and to question the extent to which these biases affect the performance of their professional duties. Likewise, those who habitually accept clinical pronouncements as final should pause to consider whether or not they do so simply because so often these pronouncements reflect their own prejudices.

Until orthodox psychiatry, psychoanalysis, and clinical psychology can establish more objective criteria of mental health and mental disease, and until these disciplines can achieve at least as much detachment from conventional value judgments as is ordinarily achieved in the other social and behavioral sciences—all of which leave much to be desired—it does not seem necessary for anyone to feel called upon to accept psychiatric pronouncements as final or infallibly authoritative.

Since standards of mental health and mental disease have been defined so pervasively in terms of a "good adjustment" to "society" it is very important to examine more carefully the society that requires such adjustment. This has been done in a much more profound way by a good many of our contemporary writers and artists—particularly those of the "avant garde"—than by our psychiatrists. The consensus of opinion among those who have made such an examination hardly encourages belief in the idea that health consists in the kind of adjustments often urged in so much of the clinical literature. Some of our more thoughtful writers and dramatists, both at home and abroad, have been busily probing the mentality of a culture that within a single generation produced Nazism, Fascism, and Communism and which, while preaching a doctrine of peace, love, and brotherhood, has for centuries spawned class distinction, race hatred, religious bigotry, persecution of minorities, intolerance, and perpetual war. It is not likely that these writers nor anyone who understands their work will feel a deep moral compulsion to identify with this culture. Two world wars, along with the continuation of chronic hostility and aggression between nations and the constant threat of a third and still more terrible world war, have chilled the enthusiasm of many for a culture which vaingloriously continues to represent itself as the pinnacle of civilized life.

Some may urge with a kind of desperation that it is better to look on the bright and pretty side of things and to be grateful for the progress that our western civilization has made along certain lines. But neither chicken every Sunday, air-conditioning, nor the diversion provided by television—nor even penicillin, tranquilizers, nor adventures in outer space—may still the recent memory of Auschwitz and Hiroshima nor halt the dehumanization that comes with perpetual cold war. So long as we continue—as we are doing at this very moment—to humiliate, brutalize, torment, starve, and murder people by the hundreds of thousands, there will be a poignant need for writers who can advantage us with an unprettified picture of ourselves.

Far from imagining that mental health or even common decency may be defined in terms of adjustment to the demands of such a society, one must conclude instead that mental illness is a direct outcome of any such adjustment. Nor is mental health conspicuous among us. The average man of our times dwells in a state of mind akin to lunacy, and no one is a more faithful representative of our society than the schizophrenic patient. He best exemplifies every tendency of our times. His apathy is the apathy of the man in the street raised to a higher power. His delusions are the delusions of the man in the street brought to a kind of psychotically logical conclusion. His isolation and his failure to communicate are but more emphatic instances of the loneliness and semantic ramblings of the man in the street. His absurdities are the absurdities of the man in the street made clearer. His hebephrenic posturings, his sterotyped mannerisms, and his bizarre rituals are the posturings, mannerisms, and rituals of the man in the street practiced more conscientiously. His loss of selfhood and amalgamation into a type is the loss that, to only a slighter degree, may be observed in every man. He is, in all things, a man of our times.

In the opinion of this author, it is almost impossible for any person in the current environment of our culture to attain a state of mind commensurate with mental health. Mental health within this environment is as much a luxury as physical health would be if we were all forced to live on a diet of mud and grass. Until we are able to rid ourselves of the ageless delusions upon which we base our relationships with one another, we may not expect that sanity will ever be common in our world. But the avoidance of greater insanity does not consist in conformity; it consists in protest and in the refusal, insofar as it is humanly possible, to simply drift with the current of the times.

XII

Homosexuality and Mental Health

One of the most recent reaffirmations of the orthodox medical view of homosexuality as "perversion" and pathology appeared in 1962, in a book edited by Irving Bieber entitled *Homosexuality: A Psychoanalytic Study.* This is an account of what the authors describe as a "systematic study" of homosexuality based upon the clinical impressions and interpretations of seventy-seven members of the Society of Medical Psychoanalysts. The subjects of this study were divided into two groups. One group was composed of 106 male psychiatric patients who had been assigned the diagnosis of homosexuality by their therapists. The other group—which the authors refer to as the comparison group—was composed of 100 male psychiatric patients in whom homosexual tendencies were regarded by their therapists as insignificant or nil.

Apparently the investigators were prepared from the outset to find the homosexuality of the first group aberrant. "All psychoanalytic theories," the authors point out, "assume that adult homosexuality is psychopathologic and assign differing weights to constitutional and experiential determinants. . . . All agree that experiential determinants are in the main rooted in childhood and are primarily related to the family." [8]

It is not particularly surprising that with these particular assumptions guiding them, the investigators who contributed to this study were able to find considerable evidence to support their expectations.

This investigation began in 1952 with the formation of a Research Committee composed of ten psychoanalysts. Of the ten committee members eight were psychoanalysts with a medical background and two were psychoanalysts with a background in psychology, which is probably why the authors refer to their study as an "interdisciplinary effort." Since, however, all the investigators were adherents of psychoanalytic doctrines, it is somewhat difficult to regard this study as an "interdisciplinary effort" in any meaningful sense. At any rate, this is the first solid effort on the part of psychoanalysts to submit their generalizations about homosexual patients to some kind of scientific control and to report their impressions in quantitative terms. This precedent affords hope that an even more carefully controlled study based upon a larger and more random sample of heterosexual and homosexual males may be expected in the future although unfortunately this hope is somewhat dimmed by the authors' presentation of their main conclusions as valid and final on the basis of this pioneer effort alone.

Since the validity of any scientific conclusion is directly proportional to the objectivity of the investigators and to the extent to which the sample faithfully represents the population to which the conclusions are thought to apply, it is important to estimate both factors in the case of the Bieber study. More specifically, one must ask the following two questions: to what extent may the observations of the analysts, whose judgments the authors accept, be taken as objective and accurate? To what extent may the homosexual subjects of this study be considered representative of the entire population of homosexual males within our culture, within all other cultures, and within all the infrahuman mammalian species? It is important to insist upon a satisfactory answer to both these questions and to the second of them, in particular, since the authors offer certain broad conclusions about homosexuality that they represent as highly valid and applicable not only to homosexual males in the psychiatric population of our culture but to all homosexual males everywhere.

Before proceeding, it may be suggested that if this study had been carried out along more familiar scientific lines and if it had been published for the scientific public alone, a more accurate, if also more pedantic, title for it would have been something like, "A Comparison of Heterosexual and Homosexual Male Psychiatric Patients based upon the Clinical Impressions of 77 Psychoanalysts."

A careful reading of Bieber's book reveals quite clearly that it is not actually a study of homosexuality in any broad or comprehensive sense. It is a study of homosexuality among psychiatrically disturbed patients at the upper extreme of the heterosexual-homosexual continuum who are, moreover, drawn from a particular social class within the population of a puritanistic subculture of Judaeo-Christian civilization. The book, therefore, is a report on the homosexuality of a very special and highly select group of people.

Although the authors formulate a number of very far-reaching conclusions about homosexuality on the basis of their study of this sample, they make no attempt to relate these conclusions to other scientific data available on homosexuality within our own culture, not to mention the data available on homosexuality within other cultures and within the infrahuman species. Indeed these other data, insofar as they are accorded any attention at all by the authors, are mentioned only in passing and somewhat superciliously, as if to imply that they are of little significance. It is quite true that the homosexual behavior of infrahuman mammals and the homosexual behavior of many non-Judaeo-Christian peoples, and even the homosexual behavior of many of the males in our own culture, seems only remotely related to the various emotional complexes and familial factors identified by Bieber and his colleagues in the histories of the patients in their sample. But this affords no good reason to neglect other data nor to belittle them in a book which is published with so comprehensive a title. Nor is it easy to understand how the authors feel free to generalize the conclusions based on a study of these particular patients to all other instances in which homosexual tendencies may be found in the histories of other individuals.

We do not wish to cavil about what may seem to be trifling details, but when scientific researchers make so bold as to publish certain of the conclusions about homosexuality that are included in Bieber's book, and when these conclusions are offered as final and authoritative even in cases of which the authors must have little knowledge, it is important to insist upon unequivocal supportive data. The importance of these data becomes all the more apparent when it is realized that the conclusions of this study will in all probability be accepted as wholly authoritative and final by a great many people who, though they may not be qualified to estimate the value of this research, may nevertheless be in the position to mold public opinion and even to bring about further social sanctions that directly abridge certain rights for homosexual as well as heterosexual members of our society. Unfortunately the authors do not themselves sufficiently emphasize the limitations of their study—certain of which they seem to be unaware of—nor have they specifically addressed their book only to scientifically trained readers who may be qualified to estimate its limitations for themselves.

The conclusions of these authors are based upon the answers provided to a questionnaire by the seventy-seven psychoanalysts. In its early form the questionnaire contained items concerning the relations between the parents of the patients, the relations between the mothers and the patients, the relations between the fathers and the patients, the sexual development and functioning of the patients, the social development of the patients, the relations of the patients to women, the adaptational responses of the patients, and the psychosomatic disorders of the patients.

The questionnaire was revised during the course of the research in order to clarify certain points. For example, one group of questions was revised in order "to distinguish between parental affection and psychopathologic attitudes simulating affection," and to define " 'seductive' behavior." The reader may appreciate how difficult it may be to make a clear and readily acceptable distinction between "parental affection" and "psychopathologic attitudes simulating affection," and such a distinction must in the final analysis remain somewhat arbitrary. Such questions involve abstract concepts that may be extremely difficult to phrase clearly as well as extremely difficult to answer objectively. Questions of this kind may not be compared with such questions as "How old was the patient at the beginning of therapy?" or "How many brothers and sisters did the patient have?" Assessment of the factors that were of interest to these investigators proves difficult by any method, and certainly it proves especially difficult by use of a questionnaire. The reader may gain an even clearer picture of the vagaries involved from a few sample questions: [8]

Which parent was dominant in family decisions?

Was one parent regarded as inferior by the other?

Was contempt by one parent for the other a prominent part of parental relationship?

Questions like these are very difficult to answer objectively, especially in terms of "yes" or "no," and it should not be forgotten that the respondents were compelled to base their answers to these questions not upon their own firsthand observations of the parents, but on the basis of their impressions of the patients' impressions of the parents. One need not be a professional student of semantics in order to appreciate the difficulties involved in this kind of decision.

After the responses to this questionnaire were tabulated, it was possible to compare the analyst's impressions of the homosexual group with their impressions of the non-homosexual group. It is this comparison that forms the basis for the conclusions reached by the Research Committee.

In spite of conscientious efforts on the part of the Committee to take into consideration any element of bias or of inaccuracy on the part of the psychoanalysts, no foolproof method to rule out these factors could have been used. It is not possible to evaluate the extent to which the respondents may or may not have been influenced by extraneous factors in their judgments of the homosexual group and the comparison group. There can be little doubt that psychoanalysts accumulate certain theoretical convictions during the course of their training that may well lead to what one may call "expectations" in dealing with various classes of patients. Indeed, the psychoanalytic diagnosis of homosexuality depends to some extent upon the possibility of identifying certain emotional factors in the early history of the patient, as well as certain particular psychological characteristics during adulthood. Since the respondents themselves were responsible for the diagnosis of "homosexual" or "heterosexual," it is not too much to wonder whether certain of the very impressions that contributed to the diagnoses perseverated in the answering of the questionnaire and to wonder whether the responding analysts may have been more impressed by certain items in the history of a patient whom they regarded as a "homosexual" than they might have been by the same items in the history of a patient whom they regarded as a "heterosexual." If some method could have been devised to rule out these possibilities, the conclusions of this study would have been considerably strengthened.

In a study by Hooker, a team of clinicians found it impossible to distinguish the Rorschach records of a group of homosexual subjects from those of a group of heterosexual subjects. But in Hooker's study the judges did not know beforehand which records came from the heterosexual subjects and which came from the homosexual subjects, so that there was no chance for "expectations" to play any part in their judgments. If the histories of the subjects of Bieber's study could have been evaluated by judges who did not know beforehand which subjects were "homosexuals" and which were "heterosexuals" the results, conceivably, might have been different. But such was not the case. Not only did the respondents know that they were answering questions applicable to a "homosexual" or a "heterosexual," they themselves had also made these diagnoses.

The other source of error lies in the sample studied. Both the homosexual group and the comparison group were, as we have seen, composed of mental patients sufficiently ill as to have required extended psychoanalytic therapy. The diagnoses ranged all the way from psychoneurosis and character disorder through schizophrenia. This makes it difficult to suppose that the childhood conflicts identified in either of the groups may be readily generalized to the nonpsychiatric population.

But both groups represented a highly select population in several other important ways as well. Both groups were "well to do" economically, with a third of each reporting incomes over ten thousand dollars a year. Both groups were heavily weighted with individuals from the upper educational brackets. Both groups were heavily weighted also with individuals from the same regional background—that of New York City. All of these are important considerations when it comes to generalizing the results of this study to other classes, other educational groups, and to individuals from other regions of the country, since both sexual histories and familial histories vary considerably with regard to precisely such factors.

The greatest objection to the homosexual sample, however, is that two thirds of the homosexual subjects were individuals who were exclusively homosexual, while only one third had had sexual experiences with both males and females. Thus once again we meet with a clinical study which is very heavily oriented to the upper extreme of the heterosexual-homosexual continuum where one might expect to find the most pathology both of a sexual and a nonsexual kind. These are precisely the homosexual individuals who most often find their way to the clinician and who probably tend to resemble the homosexual stereotype in our culture more than any other group. It is very difficult to know if the results of this study have any significance for those "homosexuals," "bisexuals," or whatever the psychiatrists wish to label them, who rate toward the mid-point of the continuum and below it. It is not, for example, difficult to imagine that it would be precisely in the group at the upper extreme of the continuum that one would find the individual who had "used" homosexuality as an "escape" from heterosexuality, and this is one of the conclusions that the authors reach from their study of this sample. But a study of homosexually inclined males who are not ratable as 5 and 6 might reveal very different dynamics. After all, this is represented as a study of homosexuality, not of "homosexuals" ratable as 5 and 6. Do the findings we are about to consider apply equally to those ratable as 1, 2, 3, and 4 or, at best, only to those ratable as 5 or 6? We cannot know from this study alone.

It is also important to know whether the same results would have been forthcoming from a group of males at the upper extreme who were not burdened by any clear-cut pathology of a nonsexual variety. Some may argue that there are no such males, but that assumption remains to be proved.

There would seem to be only two ways of controlling the error that may have resulted from the choice of subjects in the homosexual group in Bieber's study. Another homosexual group composed of a far larger number of psychiatric patients with lower ratings would have to be compared with the two groups already studied; and another homosexual group composed of subjects with very high ratings who are not psychiatrically disturbed by nonsexual psychopathology would have to be compared with the two groups already studied. Actually, both of these controls should be carried out in any case before the conclusions of the Bieber study can be properly evaluated.

Strictly speaking, the most we can know from the Bieber study is the difference in familial and psychological background of mentally ill males ratable as 5 and 6 and mentally ill males ratable (probably) as 0 and 1 from a particular class, educational level, and regional environment; we may know even this only insofar as we feel able to trust the objectivity of those who responded to the questionnaire. This is very different from assuming (as, unfortunately, the authors did) that we necessarily know the psychological and familial backgrounds of all homosexually inclined males and all heterosexually inclined males.

The sociological bias of this study is really quite staggering. Both the observers and the observed represent the middle-class element of our society which is conspicuously conservative regarding sexual morality and which tends to be even more conservative in its attitudes toward homosexuality. It might be argued that if the patients were not liberated from the sexual prejudices of their class, at least their therapists were. But there is a good deal to suggest that physicians, whether or not they are psychoanalysts, are far from liberated from such prejudices. It is quite obvious that what we have in this study is a report on the interfamilial relationships of middle-class America. As such, this is an interesting and informative study; but no one should imagine that it represents the interfamilial relationships common in other classes in America, not to mention those common in other cultures.

Statistical analyses of the responses to the questionnaire showed that there was a high level of agreement between the analysts regarding the presence of certain emotional factors that we will discuss later in the histories of the homosexual patients. This has been interpreted by Bieber and his colleagues as proof that these same emotional factors are always prominent in the history of every "homosexual." But such a conclusion is by no means ineluctable. The same factors might not appear in the histories of homosexual individuals who were not psychiatrically disturbed and a different group of judges with a different set of theoretical "expectations" might have identified very different emotional factors among the same subjects. The only certain conclusion that may be drawn from this high level of agreement among the respondents is that most analysts tend to emphasize these particular emotional factors in the histories of patients whom they regard as "homosexuals." From a certain point of view, this study might be as accurately described as a report on the attitudes of psychoanalysts toward homosexual patients or as a report on the emotional elements in the histories of homosexual patients. Although the factors identified in this study are commonly referred to in much of the psychoanalytical literature on homosexuality—and, from that standpoint, cannot be considered new—other clinicians who do not subscribe to psychoanalytic views have stressed different emotional factors. In any event, the reader should realize that the agreement between the analysts may not in itself be taken as proof of certain of the conclusions upon which the authors insist.

Let us now consider some of the more significant conclusions offered by the authors of this study.

When the two groups were compared it was found that emotional conflicts during childhood were common in the case of the homosexual patients and that a particular pattern in the relationships of the prehomosexual child with both his parents could be identified. The mothers of the homosexual patients were described most often as close-intimate-binding (CIB), and the fathers were described most often as hostile-detached (HD).

Parental relationships were poor and, indeed, the prehomosexual child was viewed by the authors as a victim of the emotional pathology of his parents. Most often the mother seemed to have turned to her son for the type of relationship she desired, but never had, with her husband. The father tended to view his son as a rival for the love of his wife; hence there was a hostile breech between father and son. The authors speculate that the son had been overstimulated by a "seductive" mother and that, since he was apprehensive and guilt-ridden over heterosexuality, he had turned to other males for outlet.

On the basis of these observations, the authors conclude that all homosexuality is absolutely related to certain emotional problems of childhood and that in the absence of the kind of history that was supposed common among their homosexual patients, homosexual trends cannot develop in any adult. They view the role of both mother *and* father as crucial to the development of homosexual trends in the son. At one point, for example, they state: "We have come to the conclusion that a constructive, supportive, warmly related father *precludes* the possibility of a homosexual son; he acts as a neutralizing, protective agent should the mother make seductive or close-binding attempts." [8]

The authors reaffirm the psychoanalytic view of the sexual drive as instinctual in nature, and thus possessed of certain inherent aims. According to this view, homosexuality is a kind of mishap in the course of what psychoanalysts consider normal development. This conclusion is summarized in the following quotation: "We assume that heterosexuality is the *biologic* norm and that unless interfered with all individuals are heterosexual." [8]

It may be noted that the view expressed above is simply the reaffirmation of a theoretical doctrine and that there are no specific data from the Bieber study that compel anyone to accept this doctrine. This doctrine seems to arise from a tendency on the part of many clinicians, like many others, to think in terms of one truth and, moreover, to insist that those who fail to live by its tenets are somehow pathological.

But there is no one truth either in the sexual sphere nor in any other sphere of nature and, as we have already adequately emphasized, cross-species and cross-cultural studies have clearly revealed that many types of sexual behavior that are regarded as unnatural in the context of our conventions are in reality commonplace events among most men and animals. Primate sexuality in particular is found to be so labile that it is really very difficult to establish any norm for sexual behavior that is not immediately challenged by a plethora of exceptions. Indeed, lability and variation in sexual tastes and habits are so pronounced at the primate level that a polymorphous sexuality among human beings and other primates, especially younger males, seems to be the norm rather than any single or isolated type of behavior. We cannot, therefore, accept any doctrine that postulates heterosexuality alone as a biologic norm.

In any case, biologic norms may certainly not be established on the basis of observations drawn exclusively from a single culture. These norms may only be inferred through the kind of cross-species and cross-cultural studies that have been emphasized in this book. Such studies, as we have seen, do not support Bieber and other psychoanalysts who assume that the *conventional* norm of our culture is a *biologic* norm.

There was a good deal of evidence in the Bieber study to suggest that the homosexual patients were fearful of heterosexual relationships and that this fear of heterosexuality was promoted by the disturbed parent-child relationships to which we have briefly referred. The homosexual group, for example, evidenced a frequent fear of disease or injury to the genitals which the authors found "significantly associated with fear and aversion to female genitals." Thus, in agreement with the psychoanalyst S. Rado, the authors conclude: "A homosexual adaptation is a result of 'hidden but incapacitating fears of the opposite sex.'" [8]

From the above assumption it seems to follow logically that all adult homosexuality is a disease since, as the authors so admirably phrase it, "Any adaptation which is basically an accommodation to unrealistic fear is necessarily pathologic . . ."

No one can disagree with the idea that fear of heterosexuality is morbid and that any homosexuality that represents an accommodation to such fear is motivated by morbid trends and therefore is symptomatic of emotional pathology. If the observations of the analysts were accurate, then the homosexual patients in the Bieber study all suffered from a morbid fear of heterosexuality and we must accordingly assume that their homosexuality was a manifestation of pathology.

As a matter of fact this author accepts the account given by Bieber and his colleagues and feels that these authors have in all probability tapped a type of sexual pathology that is very common in our culture. No clinician can fail to have encountered the type of homosexual male who is pictured in the Bieber study: a male ridden by fears of the opposite sex, who has a distorted view of all women based upon a morbid attachment to his mother, who has failed throughout life to get along socially with other males, who is apprehensive, neurotic, often effeminate, and very generally describable as a tragic misfit. These males are disturbed in numerous ways. They are sick not only because they are isolated from the main current of life and persecuted by society—which may happen to any so-called homosexual—but also because of very deep conflicts within themselves which have very little to do with social attitudes toward them. These males are homosexuals because of these intrapsychic conflicts: their homosexuality originated in such conflicts and is maintained by them. Often

—indeed, almost always—they rate at the upper extreme of the continuum and it is not uncommon to find stereotyped behavior among them that is based upon an identification with the social role of women. It seems entirely appropriate to regard these males as pathological cases.

But even among those who rate 5 and 6 throughout life, these same factors may not be in evidence. There are males in whom homosexual trends are prepotent and others in whom homosexual trends play a smaller part who fail to provide any evidence of serious emotional pathology and who provide no childhood history of emotional conflicts such as those reported by Bieber, his colleagues, and other clinicians. Some of these males are in no way distinguishable from exclusively heterosexual males apart, of course, from their sexual preferences.

This author wishes to go on record as one clinician among a number of others who has had the opportunity to interview and, in several cases, to become aquainted with homosexual males who met with every reasonable standard of mental health in their relationships with themselves and with others. Throughout a period of twenty years this author has come to know approximately 1,500 homosexual males, both within the clinical setting and outside of it. He has spoken at length with many such males, treated them psychotherapeutically, examined them by standard psychological techniques, seen them both at work and away from work, in the "gay" circles and in "straight" society, lectured to organized groups of them, and maintained long-term friendships with certain of them. Among these people was to be found the kind of "homosexual" described in the clinical literature, and a good many others as well that are never described in the clinical literature. Some of these "homosexuals" were among the most disturbed people that this author ever encountered during his practice. Others were model citizens whose lives were devoted to constructive and often very creative activities. Most were concerned about their reputation and many manifested traits that often may be identified among social minorities. Some were not visibly concerned and did not manifest any traits of a minority group. The most conspicuous trait among these people, taken as a group, was a tendency to be sensitive about being "different" which in not a few cases amounted to a feeling of shamefulness.

Only within the last two years, unfortunately, has this author made any attempt to record and to systematize his observations of these individuals. But it is impossible not to be left with a general impression, and the author will offer this general impression for what it may be worth:

Homosexual males—and by this we have in mind all those ratable from 1 through 6—seem as a group to be more disturbed than other people. The American male who may be included in this category seems to be more disturbed than other males particularly when he comes from a middle-class background. He is in fact the most disturbed homosexual male that this author has ever encountered during a number of years in which he has traveled widely abroad within both homosexual and hetero-sexual circles. There is no doubt whatsoever in the mind of this author that social attitudes toward homosexuality play an enormous part in determin-ing the homosexual individual's attitudes toward himself and in determining the state of his mental health. Sick, disturbed, guilt-ridden, miserable "homosexuals" may be found "a dime a dozen" in American society and in almost equal proportion in British society. They may be found any-where within Judaeo-Christian society where this author has traveled, but their number seems to increase in direct proportion to the puritanistic elements within the given society. Thus, they are fewer in such countries as France, Italy, Greece, and Spain (where, by Judaeo-Christian standards, puritanism is less pronounced), and their number is greater in such coun-tries as the United States, Great Britain, and Germany. But, as has been emphasized, their number is at an apex in the United States, so that by comparison even England or Germany seem to produce few such troubled "homosexuals."

Explanation of this difference between the American homosexual males and the homosexual males from other societies is complicated. Perhaps relations between males and females in America are such that there are more CBI mothers and HD fathers to produce more psychopathological "homosexuals," or perhaps the inordinately homoerotophobic atmosphere of the country is sufficient to explain this difference. At any rate, any reasonably perceptive observer may note the striking difference between homosexual American males and other homosexual males.

In an effort to support their contention that all homosexuality is patho-logical, the authors of the Bieber study point to other evidence that seems to indicate that their generalizations may be applied to other individuals out-side the sample that was available to them. But the evidence to which they point is usually drawn from sources very similar to their own: the observa-tions of other clinicians, the observations of officials who had apprehended certain individuals for homosexual offenses in the Army and in civilian life, and similar sources. These observations, moreover, most clearly confirmed the observations of Bieber and his colleagues in those cases where they applied to a group most like the homosexual sample of the Bieber study. But evidence that many homosexually inclined males may be "disturbed," or even clearly neurotic, does not constitute proof of the most original points made by the Bieber group. It is easy to amass a great deal of evidence to show that homosexuality and emotional conflict are often associated, but this association may be explained in a very different way from the way it is explained by Bieber *et al.* We may not assume that all homosexuality is pathological simply because it arouses anxiety in our culture. What Bieber and other clinicians need to do in order to lend greater weight to their theories is to find some way in which to apply them convincingly to the homosexuality of individuals from non-Judaeo-Christian cultures. If all homosexuality is a disease and, moreover, a disease that is based upon the specific etiological factors hypothesized in the Bieber study, it should be easy to amass evidence from other human groups and perhaps even from the infrahuman species.

Although one must accept—almost by definition—the idea that homosexuality which is an adaptation to the fear of heterosexuality is pathological, it is quite another matter to assume that it is in this context alone that homosexuality may arise. There are doubtless many homosexual males, ratable anywhere from 1 to 6, for whom homosexuality is not an escape from heterosexuality. But so convinced are Bieber and his colleagues that homosexuality can arise only in this defensive context that they go so far as to make the following assertion:

> Clinical experience has shown that aberrant behavior is always pathologically motivated. The "doing-it-for-kicks" assumption does not adequately explain aberrant sexuality. We are committed to Rado's own proposition that homosexuality is an adaptation to fear of heterosexuality, and *we extend this proposition to account for all homosexual behavior* [italics ours].[8]

It is simply impossible to explain all homosexual behavior as an adaptation to the fear of heterosexuality, and it is difficult to understand how Bieber and his colleagues can possibly overlook or simply reject out of hand the various data that refute this interpretation. But we must draw the reader's attention to the entire context in which this assertion is made.

The authors begin by assuming that all homosexuality is aberrant. They then assume (reasonably) that all aberrant behavior must be pathologically motivated. From this assumption they then go on to assume that all homosexuality must be pathologically motivated. But this reasoning is entirely circular. The authors are saying in psychiatric jargon what the poetess said when she wrote, "A rose is a rose is a rose."

All sexual preferences are learned and must be considered a product of psychological conditioning. Innumerable factors may play a part in conditioning the sexual preferences of any individual and the assumption that homosexual preferences may be learned *only* if the individual is in flight from heterosexuality is untenable.

We need not restate the statistics from our own culture that demonstrate that heterosexuality and homosexuality may coexist in the same individual. As a matter of fact, in those cases in which homosexual trends are manifest, it is the rule rather than the exception that they coexist with heterosexual trends. There is also abundant evidence of this fact from other cultures in which large segments of the male population maintain both hetero-

sexual and homosexual interests throughout life. In the words of Ford and
Beach, ". . . one cannot classify homosexual and heterosexual tendencies
as being mutually exclusive or even opposed to each other." [22] There are,
of course, certain individuals—such as those who made up the greater
part of the homosexual sample in Bieber's study—who are exclusively
homosexual; and we may speculate that in the case of many of these individuals homosexuality is an adaptation resulting from a fear of heterosexuality. But it is difficult to suppose that such is the case with homosexually inclined individuals in whom heterosexual trends are well established and well accepted.

We are compelled to assume that homosexual stimuli may, as a result of
learning, come to have an attractiveness of their own quite apart from the
individual's positive orientation (or lack of it) to heterosexual stimuli. In
other words, it cannot be automatically assumed that homosexual tendencies regularly indicate some conflict over heterosexuality. Homosexual
tendencies may be learned whether or not there is fear of heterosexuality,
and more often than not, apparently, homosexual tendencies have nothing
to do with a fear of heterosexuality.

Scientific studies of sexual behavior have failed to support the assumption that any particular form of sexual behavior in itself provides evidence of
a disease. Most outstanding authorities in the behavioral sciences accordingly do not classify all adult homosexuality as abnormal or pathological, any
more than they classify all adult heterosexuality or all adult autoeroticism as
abnormal or pathological, although it is generally recognized by scientists
that any type of sexual behavior may in the case of a particular individual
become associated with psychopathological trends and that psychopathological trends may even form the basis for any given pattern of sexual
behavior. It is appropriate, therefore, to speak of certain homosexual as
well as certain heterosexual and autoerotic patterns as pathological, but
it does not follow that all homosexual patterns, any more than all heterosexual or all autoerotic patterns, originate in conflict and express fundamental psychopathology.

Psychoanalysts assume that adult homosexuality is always pathological
and that it is determined by constitutional as well as experiential factors.
Since a great deal of psychiatry and clinical psychology today is directly
oriented to psychoanalytic concepts, and since most clinical schools of
thought tend to be influenced by psychoanalytic concepts even when not
directly oriented to psychoanalysis, it is not too much to say that psychiatry and clinical psychology in general—though with notable exceptions—
tend to classify all adult homosexuality as pathology.

We do not subscribe to the "either-or" point of view in this book. It is
only possible to imagine that adult homosexuality is always pathological
or never pathological if one is overly impressed by abstract theories and

insufficiently acquainted with a variety of data. It is possible for any trained observer who puts himself in the position to do so to meet with individuals who have a substantial history of homosexuality without any corresponding evidence of neurosis, psychosis, psychopathy, or chronic emotional distress. Some of these individuals display not only an adequate adjustment in terms of what this means for the average person in our society, but even a superior adjustment that enables them to endure an unusual amount of stress during a considerable period of time. The number of "healthy homosexuals" with whom any one person may become acquainted is necessarily limited, but the existence of even a few such individuals refutes the contention that all homosexuality is pathological and that it always is associated with serious emotional pathology.

Explanations of adult homosexuality in terms of complexes rooted in various childhood conflicts seem to have little or no applicability to infrahuman homosexuality or to homosexuality within certain homoerotophilic cultures. To imagine, for example, that a raccoon or a baboon becomes positively conditioned to homosexual stimuli as the result of a pathological relationship with a "close-binding-intimate" mother or as the result of some other complex is little less than ridiculous. And it is hardly less ridiculous to imagine that complexes play any part in the development of homosexual interests among the peoples of various cultures in which homosexuality is expected and even encouraged. To insist, for example, that every Siwanian male develops homosexual tendencies because he has had a seductive mother and a rejecting father is extravagant, to say the least.

It would seem that when most clinicians speak of homosexuality they are speaking about a very particular type of neurotic interaction rather than a type of sexual behavior. It is doubtless true that in some unknown percentage of cases within our culture this very particular type of neurotic interaction is involved. But it is not this neurotic interaction that constitutes the fact of homosexuality, and the type of neurotic interaction that clinicians identify in the histories of their homosexual patients may not necessarily be present in all or even most sexual relationships between like-sexed partners, even in our own culture.

Since, however, most clinicians have decided beforehand that all adult homosexuality is a disorder or disease rather than simply one among a number of other manifestations of mammalian sexuality, and since it is difficult to characterize infrahuman homosexuality and the homosexuality that occurs among many non-Judao-Christian peoples as pathological, the equivocal attitude of clinicians toward some of the phylogenetic and anthropological data may be understood. Nevertheless these data exist and must be reckoned with. If they cannot be convincingly explained by clinical concepts, then it is the clinical concepts rather than the phylogenetic and anthropological data that must be discarded.

If there is such a thing as a "homosexual personality" it has not proved identifiable by the same means that have been used to identify a "schizophrenic" or a "depressive" personality. In a recent study by Hooker [43] a series of standard psychological tests was administered to thirty "homosexuals" and thirty "heterosexuals" matched for age, intelligence, and educational background. In selecting these subjects an attempt was made to exclude any person with a history of psychiatric disturbance. Thus, it may be presumed, a nonpathological element of the homosexual population was tapped. When the two groups were compared, the adjustment score of the heterosexual group was no better than the adjustment score of the homosexual group. Of still greater significance, however, was the fact that the judges—who were not informed as to which records came from the homosexual group and which came from the heterosexual group—could not distinguish a homosexual record from a heterosexual record. No "homosexual personality" emerged in the profiles provided by the homosexual group. From these results Dr. Hooker concluded that "homosexuality may be a deviation in sexual pattern which is within the normal range psychologically."

In a related study, Hooker [44] found that some of the traits and attitudes that are regarded as typical of "homosexuals" are in reality characteristics that may be found regularly among other rejected minority groups. Among these she recognized "traits of victimization" (defensive attitudes in response to a hostile environment), "protective clowning," "hatred of himself and his group," and "attitudes of dependence and passivity."

There are undoubtedly a great many individuals who participate in homosexual relationships sporadically or even regularly who never identify themselves with a homosexual minority and who therefore do not take on the characteristics of a minority. Many such persons have been identified in Kinsey's statistics and yet are never recognized by themselves or by the public at large as a part of the homosexual population. Instead, this population is judged, defined, and studied in terms of those homosexual individuals who frequent certain notorious haunts, take part in an underworld existence, come into conflict with the law, abandon heterosexuality altogether, take on the mannerisms of a stereotype, and pursue a special way of life apart from the rest of society. The others who become involved to varying extents in homosexuality, but who do not alter their attitudes toward themselves nor the pattern of their existence as a result of this involvement—perhaps three-fifths of the homosexual population—remain unidentified and almost entirely unobserved by most people, including, of course, most researchers. *The standards of mental health maintained by this latter group remain unknown to science.*

The unique childhood conflicts that clinicians ascribe to all so-called homosexuals may certainly not be identified in everyone with a history of homosexuality as an adult. Nor do the childhood conflicts that clinicians have found among homosexual neurotics and psychotics appear to be necessary to the acquirement of homosexual preferences later in life. Mention has already been made of the fact that the capacity to respond to any sufficient sexual stimulus is present in all mammals, and that this capacity may, under favorable circumstances, be realized at any point during the history of the individual. Thus, many individuals with a perfectly ordinary background acquire homosexual tastes as a result of experiences they have later in life. The incidence of homosexuality is much higher in certain trades and professions that tend to isolate males from females over a long period of time, and under these circumstances homosexual tastes and habits seem to flourish without necessarily displacing heterosexual tastes and habits. Sailors, for example, as well as fishermen, soldiers, clergymen, lumbermen, and certain others are more apt to exploit their capacity for homosexual responsiveness than the ordinary laborer or businessman who is seldom placed in a situation in which homosexual stimuli are emphasized. Similarly, this capacity is far more often exploited by males who are reared in cultures in which homoerotic stimuli are positively emphasized.

These facts are often simply ignored or denied by clinicians who insist that homosexual tastes and habits can only develop in individuals with a history of childhood conflict. For example, it is asserted in the Bieber study that homosexual behavior was "relatively uncommon" in the armed forces of Great Britain and the United States. Few statisticians have been willing to accept the incidence of homosexuality officially reported for the Armed Services of the United States, for the simple reason that homosexual behavior is illegal in the United States (and Great Britain). Consequently, homosexual activities were hidden or denied by British and American servicemen, and often when these activities came to the attention of authorities they were not officially reported—not only in order to avoid scandal for the Services, but also to protect the individuals involved against reprisal. As a result of this atmosphere of fear and secrecy it is impossible to make an even reasonably accurate estimate of the incidence of homosexuality in the Armed Services. It would be most improbable to suppose, however, that it is lower than that reported by Kinsey for civilian males.

Within the atmosphere of our own particular environment, homosexual tendencies probably arise more often within a neurotic context than heterosexual tendencies, and subsequently, homosexual tendencies are much more likely to bring about personal and social conflict than heterosexual tendencies. For these reasons any strong or prepossessing homosexual inclinations must be considered a distinct handicap for any individual within our culture; for this reason alone many so-called homosexuals need the assistance of a properly trained therapist. But to assume, as is so often done, that within an entirely different environment homosexual inclinations would as often become associated with neurotic conflicts is to go beyond the known facts.

The comments of Kinsey, Pomeroy, and Martin on this complex issue are worth quoting at some length:

> In view of the data which we now have on the incidence and frequency of the homosexual, and in particular on its co-existence with the heterosexual in the lives of a considerable portion of the male population, it is difficult to maintain the view that psychosexual reactions between individuals of the same sex are rare and therefore abnormal or unnatural, or that they constitute within themselves evidence of neuroses or even psychoses.
>
> If homosexual activity persists on as large a scale as it does, in the face of the very considerable public sentiment against it and in spite of the severity of the penalties that our Anglo-American culture has placed upon it through the centuries, there seems some reason for believing that such activity would appear in the histories of a much larger portion of the population if there were no social restraints. The very general occurrence of the homosexual in ancient Greece . . . and its wide occurrence today in some cultures in which such activity is not as taboo as in our own, suggests that the capacity of an individual to respond erotically to any sort of stimulus, whether it is provided by another person of the same or of the opposite sex, is basic in the species. . . .
>
> The opinion that homosexual activity in itself provides evidence of a psychopathic personality is materially challenged by these incidence and frequency data. Of the 40% or 50% of the male population which has homosexual experience, certainly a high proportion would not be considered psychopathic personalities on the basis of anything else in their histories. It is argued that an individual who is so obtuse to social reactions as to continue his homosexual activity and make it any material portion of his life, therein evidences some social incapacity; but psychiatrists and clinicians in general might very well re-examine their justification for demanding that all persons conform to particular patterns of behavior.[53]

Many clinicians, of course, continue to overlook facts like these or to make light of them. We read a good many inept comparisons in clinical literature between the incidence of homosexuality and the incidence of certain prevalent diseases such as the common cold. These comparisons are intended to demonstrate that the high incidence of homosexuality in no way mitigates the supposed fact that it is a disease. For example, Bieber and his coworkers make the following comment:

> Kinsey *et al.* did not regard homosexuality as pathologic but rather as the expression of an inherent capacity for indiscriminate sexual response. In support of this assumption the authors referred to the high frequency of homosexual experiences in the preadolescence of American males. Thus, an assumption of normalcy is based on the argument

of frequency though, in fact, frequency as a phenomenon is not necessarily related to absence of pathology. For example, most people in New York will contract a cold during a given period of time. This expectancy will show a normal probability distribution but respiratory infections are patently pathologic conditions.[8]

Respiratory infections are "patently pathologic conditions"; but the preadolescent homosexual experiences of American males are not "patently pathologic conditions." If the high frequency of these experiences is not to be explained as Kinsey explains it—in terms of "indiscriminate sexual response"—how then can it be explained? Surely we are not asked to believe that most preadolescent boys are mentally diseased!

If instead of bringing in the comparison between homosexuality and the common cold, these authors had attempted to explain the high frequency of preadolescent homosexual experiences among males in terms of their psychiatric theories more would have been accomplished. Instead we are given a wholly impertinent comparison that leaves us none the wiser about the meaning of an important collection of data. It is this type of evasiveness and this refusal really to confront such data that places the orthodox clinical explanation of all homosexuality as a disease in the category of a dogma rather than that of a scientific theory.

Numerous data, therefore, make it clear that one is justified in speaking of a normal or nonpathological type of homosexuality which in terms of the human race as a whole is doubtless the most frequently encountered variety of homosexuality.

On the other hand, clinical studies reveal that homosexual trends—as, for that matter, heterosexual trends—may be employed in the service of neurotic and even psychotic motives. It is even more important to be aware that serious emotional conflicts during childhood may in certain cases cause a homosexual orientation. In those cases in which homosexual trends originate in such conflicts and are maintained by such conflicts—where, for example, homosexuality is used as a defense against heterosexuality, or as a substitute for heterosexuality because heterosexual relationships are feared—one may be justified in speaking of *pathological homosexuality*.

On the surface it may be difficult to distinguish normal homosexuality from pathological homosexuality, since even the so-called normal homosexual or bisexual may suffer from conflict and anxiety induced by the uncertainty of his position in our society. But cross-cultural and cross-species data may again provide us with a clue to the difference between normal and pathological homosexuality.

Homosexuality is only very rarely an exclusive type of behavior among men and animals for any long period of time and, as we have seen, homosexual trends almost always coexist with heterosexual trends when the former are present.

Homosexual trends, moreover, are seldom related to a tendency toward effeminacy or identification with the opposite sex. In most cultures where homosexuality is practiced widely it is regarded as a typically masculine predilection, and those who participate seldom display characteristics peculiar to the opposite sex. Even within our own society, where homosexuality is regarded as a form of effeminacy and "inversion," the vast majority of actively homosexual males continue to accept a masculine role in society and are indistinguishable from other males in almost every particular except one. According to the Institute of Sex Research, fully 85 per cent of all actively homosexual males resemble exclusively heterosexual males so closely that they may not be identified as "homosexuals" even by experts.

Although "masculine" behavior and "feminine" behavior are largely defined by social and conventional criteria and therefore may vary from culture to culture, there are characteristic differences in the behavior of males and females in all cultures and in all species. We must assume, therefore, that masculine behavior and feminine behavior have some basis in biology. Most males—including the great majority of actively homosexual males—identify with the behavior of other males in many particulars, and display numerous characteristics that are distinctly different from most females.

In view of these considerations we must be somewhat suspicious of the psychological status of the male who adopts a lifelong pattern of exclusive homosexuality, especially when this pattern is accompanied by an obvious identification with the social role of the female. It may surely be expected that psychopathological influences play some part in the genesis of this type of adaptation. Fears related to one's role as a male—both sexually and socially—must be paramount in these cases, and they provide us with numerous examples of the complexes that clinicians ascribe to all homosexual males.

The subtle uses to which any type of behavior may be put and the unique connotations it may have for the individuals involved make it necessary for us to abandon any one-sided view of homosexuality or heterosexuality. Not all heterosexual phenomena are "good," "healthy," or "mature"; and not all homosexual phenomena are "bad," "unhealthy," or "immature." Both disease and health may be associated with all the major modalities of the sexual drive, and the sooner this is realized the sooner we will be able to get down to some realistic research that may lead us far beyond our present state of knowledge.

Our picture of the average "homosexual" is derived mainly from lurid fictional accounts of "perversion" and from the case histories of psychiatrists to whose doors the most harassed come. In addition, we have gained a somewhat distorted impression of homosexuality from the journalistic accounts that appear ever more frequently. Most of these accounts are based upon conditions prevailing within four or five of the largest cities of the nation. To these cities flock the most discontented and often the most eccentric and disturbed individuals within the homosexual population. A picture of homosexuality that is based upon the activities of the "gay world" in Los Angeles, Chicago, New Orleans, or New York is about as representative of homosexuality at large as is one of heterosexuality that is based upon the activities of the "fast set" in these same cities.

Throughout the nation may be found virtually millions of males who are homosexual. Their lives are generally as humdrum as those of other people and indeed consist, for the most part, of exactly the same activities. Some may come into serious difficulties because of the laws which single them out as "offenders," and others may reach an emotional impasse over their socio-sexual status that terminates in some sort of crisis. But most—indeed, the great majority—manage to make an adjustment that is acceptable to those around them and to themselves. If this were not the case, the amount of crime, mental disease, and social upheaval from within the homosexual population alone would probably more than triple the present incidence from all segments of the general population. There are within the United States at present at least 2.3 million males who are exclusively homosexual and who will remain so throughout their lives. If to this hard core of "confirmed homosexuals" we add all those with a history of homosexuality as adults, or even only those with a substantial history of homosexuality as adults, this figure must be multiplied many times over.

Considering the numbers involved, homosexuality seems actually to be a rather innocuous behavior pattern. It gives rise to relatively few serious offenders, especially when it is realized that most homosexual males who are apprehended by the police have done nothing more than proffer a sexual invitation to a bystander, who in most cases has tacitly indicated his willingness to participate. Nor is the number of homosexual males who end up in the psychiatrist's office large by comparison with the exclusively heterosexual group. Most of these individuals manage to handle their problems sufficiently well to preclude the assistance of a psychiatrist. Even though they are often confronted by legalized bigotry and by an unreasonable amount of social intolerance, it is not too much to say that these individuals contribute no more than their share of delinquency and mental disease.

We live in a day and age in which the stress of life has become so intensified and in which interpersonal relationships have become fraught with so much tension that approximately one out of every ten people becomes sufficiently disturbed to require psychiatric hospitalization. In addition to these severe cases there are many more who go through life with chronic neurotic problems for which they never seek professional aid, while many others consult psychiatrists and other therapists on an out-patient basis. In such an atmosphere it can hardly be expected that any minority group such as the homosexual group, which is subjected to an extraordinary amount of chronic emotional stress, will fare any better than the rest of the population. Present social conditions place a strain upon most people, but the extraordinary position of the homosexual person in our society might be expected to make him more vulnerable to mental illness than most other people. In addition to conflicts that arise in relationship to the environment, an unknown number of these people undoubtedly suffer from intrapsychic conflicts that have little direct connection with sociological factors. Yet few statistics point to any pervasive relationship between homosexuality and serious mental disease. The vast majority of highly disturbed psychiatric patients are overtly and exclusively heterosexual, and exclusive heterosexuality does not seem to confer any greater resistance to mental disease than that conferred by exclusive homosexuality.

A few isolated studies have suggested a higher incidence of mental disease within the homosexual population, but this relationship is by no means conclusive, although precisely these results might be anticipated. Lambert (1954) found a history of attempted suicide and severe depression much more common among a group of homosexual soldiers than among their heterosexual comrades,[57] and O'Connor (1948), studying a small series of suicides and attempted suicides, identified homosexual trends in about half of the cases.[63] In an analysis of a hundred cases of male homosexuality, Curran and Parr (1957) pointed to a large proportion of the sample which was apparently not neurotic.[16] But these studies, no matter how they may be interpreted, are emphatically limited by the fact that they are almost never based upon a random sample of the entire homosexual population.

What is needed in order to get a representative profile of the homosexual population is a study based upon a large sample in which the appropriate proportion of all those ratable as 1 through 6 is included. Such a sample would represent the entire population which has any history of homosexuality. The results could then be compared with a control group comprised of an equal number of those ratable as 0. On the basis of such a study we would be able to make a better estimate of the true effects of homosexuality on the entire group concerned rather than, at most, its effects upon a subpopulation at the upper extreme of the continuum.

But, if it is felt that "real homosexuals" are only those ratable as 5 and 6, then a much larger and much more random sample of these should be studied than have ever been reported in clinical or other literature. Among these 5s and 6s should be included not only individuals who have sought psychiatric care but also those individuals who have never experienced the need for such care.

It has been suggested by some psychoanalysts that homosexuality is a defense against schizophrenia. Other clinicians have gone even further and have declared homosexuality to be a variety of schizophrenic psychosis. But such hypotheses were not substantiated even in the study of highly disturbed homosexual patients that Bieber and his coworkers reported.

A point of view which has gained some acceptance in psychoanalytic circles is that homosexuality is a defense against schizophrenia; that is to say, if the H-patients had not become homosexual they would have become schizophrenic. Our findings do not support this hypothesis. One-fourth of the homosexual cases were diagnosed as schizophrenic; thus homosexuality obviously had not defended these homosexuals against schizophrenia. Further, there were no schizophrenic sequelae among the H-patients who became exclusively heterosexual.[8]

Where homosexuality is associated with pathology it tends to be compulsive and to veer toward exclusiveness. The individual tends to use sexual outlets as a means of coping with anxiety. This type of person, like the heterosexual "Don Juan," uses sex like the alcoholic uses alcohol—as an escape from stress and tension.

Comparisons between the alcoholic and the homosexual are very common. Here, perhaps, is the place to discuss this subject.

Homosexuality has been compared with alcoholism not merely because both are considered pathological, but because it is believed that the causes of both are similar. To some extent this might be true of a particular type of homosexual adaptation, but that this is always an apt comparison may be disputed.

One is not necessarily an alcoholic because one drinks with pleasure even if one drinks regularly, and even if one drinks to excess upon isolated occasions. Alcohol may be used for the benefit of man, and if it is not used for the wrong purposes it can be a blessing to human beings. We may say the same, to some extent, of homosexuality and of other so-called variant sexual practices.

Some people, in an effort to be helpful, have suggested that "homosexuals" should form an organization similar to Alcoholics Anonymous in order to overcome their problems. But few who make this recommendation carry the analogy between alcohol and homosexuality to its logical conclusion. If they did so they might recognize that there may be an entire class of persons for whom homosexuality is like alcohol to the "social drinker." In other words, some people are no more "addicted" to homosexuality, even though it may play some part in their lives, than the average social drinker is addicted to alcohol. Only certain fundamentally sick people abuse their homosexual propensities, just as only certain fundamentally sick people abuse alcohol.

Moralists and prudes will condemn both alcohol and homosexuality unreservedly and will see in the use of either the seeds of damnation. What they fail to see, however, is that it is those who are already damned for whom such indulgences are dangerous.

Certain cases of pathological homosexuality may respond very well to intensive psychotherapy aimed at resolving the underlying conflict within the personality. At the termination of such therapy, in those cases in which it is successful, the patient may or may not continue to manifest some interest in homosexual relations; in either case homosexual relations may play a very different part in the life of the individual, and access to a rich and rewarding heterosexual life may be opened.

This author, however, like certain other psychotherapists, does not hold to the idea that homosexual problems can be successfully resolved in an atmosphere of sex-negativism. Homosexual patients must learn to resolve the guilt and conflict they feel about their sexual preferences along with conflicts over heterosexuality. Many therapists fail to recognize the importance of this and hence may feel encouraged by the patient's guilt-laden attitude toward his homosexuality. This guilt may be interpreted as a sign that the patient "really wants to get well." But it is not possible for a homosexual patient to make true progress in therapy or to really accept heterosexuality, so long as neurotic and guilt-laden attitudes toward homosexuality or any other manifestation of the sexual drive remain unresolved.

The type of person who enters therapy with a strong desire to renounce homosexuality is often more disturbed by a nonjudgmental attitude on the part of the therapist toward homosexuality than if the therapist assumes an explicit or implicit stand against homosexuality. Some patients approach therapy in the hope of finding a therapist who will support their homosexual guilts and conflicts. Others, of course, approach therapy with the hope of finding a therapist who will relieve them of these guilts and conflicts—who, in other words, will help them to maintain their homosexuality without conflicts. Quite often these latter patients expect to be able to accept their homosexuality while maintaining a phobic attitude toward heterosexuality. We do not believe that any patient—or therapist—can take a nonjudgmental attitude toward homosexuality if he fears or despises heterosexuality. Nor, for that matter, do we believe that any patient, therapist, or any other person can unequivocally accept heterosexuality if he fears or despises homosexuality.

The only task of the therapist is to help the patient to achieve an understanding of the motivations which have led to his sexual orientation; this implies a nonjudgmental attitude on the part of the therapist in which sex per se, in all of its manifestations, is regarded without blame. No therapeutic result can be achieved when therapy is used as a method of indoctrination into the mores. The purpose of therapy is to explore with the patient the psychological source of his difficulties; its purpose is not that of bringing about a new complex of compulsive sexual ideas in lieu of those the patient brings to therapy.

The therapist, of course, can be of no aid whatsoever to the patient if he himself is an overly conventional, anxious, and prudish individual who merely wishes to proselytize for a sexual adjustment that may be none too secure in himself. It is difficult to escape the impression that some therapists who appear to be overly zealous in their desire to "cure homosexuals" are precisely the wrong kind of therapists for this type of patient; this author has seen too many cases in which "homosexuals" were more harmed than helped by such well-meaning but inept clinicians. It is of the utmost importance in a book such as this to stress the need for a proper therapy in these cases. Anyone who is tormented by homosexual problems, or to express it more comprehensively, any homosexually inclined individual who for any reason feels the need of clinical aid should be certain to choose a therapist who has had experience and success with cases in which homosexuality is involved. Not every therapist who is a competent worker is able or really qualified to deal properly with such cases. Some, to offer an analogy, are no more capable of treating homosexuality than an excellent surgeon might be capable of treating an allergy. Unfortunately there are few specialists in the field of psychotherapy for these cases so that homosexual patients often may not know where to turn for treatment unless they are fortunate enough to receive good advice. Most simply go to just any psychotherapist in the hope and expectation that he will "know best." Sometimes he does, but not always.

Because all sexual tastes and preferences originate in the experiences to which the individual is exposed, usually at an early age, rather than in anything that may be deemed hereditary or constitutional, and because these tastes and preferences are maintained only by constant reinforcement and constant repetition of the stimulus-response connection, one would expect new sexual patterns to arise easily in response to any form of psychological intervention. Sexual patterns, in other words, should be readily modified in any direction as a result of psychotherapy.

But such has not proved to be the case. Although a substantial number of individual therapists have made very optimistic claims about being able to reverse homosexual trends, more carefully controlled research has not tended to support a very realistic basis for this optimism. In spite of the most intensive psychotherapeutic procedures designed to reverse the psychosexual orientation of homosexual patients, the vast majority of these patients maintain their original sexual pattern after the termination of therapy. Many of these patients may experience less conflict over their sexual preferences, and many may exercise these preferences in a less self-destructive way as a result of therapy, but only a minority of them ever completely replace their interest in homosexual relationships with an exclusive interest in heterosexual relationships. Sexual patterns seem to be more or less firmly established by early adulthood, perhaps even by adolescence, and although these patterns may be modified to some extent by later experiences in life, the original pattern seems to persist in most cases. Seldom does a complete reversal of sexual orientation take place in later life as the result of any type of experience—therapeutic or otherwise—and such modifications as do take place are usually additive in nature; that is, new sexual responses may be added to a complex of former sexual responses. Thus, a pattern of exclusive homosexuality may, as a result of therapy or some other experience, be changed to a pattern of bisexuality in the same way that it is possible for subsequent experiences to change a pattern of exclusive heterosexuality into a pattern of bisexuality. But permanent reversal of an established pattern of sexual preferences is rare, in spite of the claims of certain therapists.

Freud had the perspicacity to recognize this fact many years ago. In *The Psychogenesis of Homosexuality in a Woman* he wrote:

> The removal of genital-inversion or homosexuality is, in my experience, never an easy matter. On the contrary, I have found success possible only under special favorable circumstances and even then the success essentially consisted in being able to open to those who are restricted homosexually the way to the opposite sex which has been until then barred, thus restoring to them full sexual function . . . To undertake to convert a fully developed homosexual is not much more promising than to do the reverse, only that for good practical reasons the latter is never attempted.

Those analysts and other psychotherapists who claim to bring about a complete reversal in the psychosexual orientation of their homosexual patients insist that anyone who is skeptical of their claims must himself be "a homosexual who does not want to get well," even though numerous investigators whose motives must be considered beyond question have agreed with Freud that such reversals are neither easy nor frequent. The results of the more optimistic therapists must be taken on faith since they have never been checked by objective investigators. Nor have these results been substantiated by an adequate follow-up study carried out three to five years after therapy.

This author knows of a great number of instances in which homosexual patients were discharged from various types of therapy as "cured," only to find that their homosexual interests revived in subsequent months or years. Some said that they had simulated a disinterest in homosexuality and a corresponding interest in heterosexuality in order to please the therapist because they were weary of therapy and wished to terminate on an amicable basis, or because they were afraid of the therapist's disapproval, or (which amounts to the same thing) were ashamed to admit that they still were homosexual. Others left therapy with the sincere belief that they had lost all interest in homosexuality; only to find at a later date that their former interest was revived by subsequent experiences. Still others feigned disinterest in homosexuality and interest in heterosexuality because they were anxious to be released from a treatment which they were compelled to take by a judge as a condition of their probation. Some of these "cured" cases were, as a result of therapy, no longer able to function well in homosexual relationships, but neither could they function well in heterosexual relationships. Such results represent a kind of "therapeutic castration" in the psychological area and may only be deplored.

It is necessary to emphasize very strongly the need for a more objective and reliable estimate of these cures, and to insist upon adequate follow-up studies before any final decisions are made regarding the prognosis of homosexuality in therapy. There is a growing tendency on the part of therapists to report cures in a rather irresponsible way, and this has established a basis for a number of possible evils.

In the first place, irresponsible or premature therapeutic claims arouse false hopes in many so-called homosexuals, as well as their parents, wives, or other interested members of their families. Many such persons leave treatment with a guilty and downcast feeling of personal unworthiness if therapeutic efforts do not lead to the results that they have been encouraged to expect from all the articles that now appear on the subject. These patients may blame themselves if they are not among the few who actually obtain the results so often promised in such articles. In such cases the patient may be more disturbed after therapy than before, and an adequate adjustment to homosexuality, as well as to heterosexuality, may have become impossible. It is no more ethical to offer false or uncertain hopes of cure to a patient than to deny such a patient hope where hope is justified. Also the rather wizened reservation that virtually all therapists make when offering a hope for success in these cases—namely, that the patient must "really want to change"—places the prime responsibility for failure upon the patient. Many patients who "really want to be cured" are not changed in spite of long-term intensive therapy, and the responsibility for the failure is no more theirs than the therapist's. Yet, as was indicated above, these patients may be left with the impression that they and they alone are responsible for the failure of the therapy to bring about the changes they expected and hoped for.

Moreover, overoptimistic and unverified therapeutic claims encourage authorities to believe that "the problem of homosexuality" may be solved already by medical means. Such an expectation, even if the most optimistic claims proved to be entirely valid, is not warranted by reality; if every therapist in the nation or in the world were to devote his practice exclusively to the treatment of homosexuality, and if in every case therapy proved successful and required only a very short time, there would still not be nearly enough therapists to make any substantial change in the incidence of prepotent homosexuality. All reliable authorities are agreed, moreover, that in the succeeding generation a whole new crop of "confirmed homosexuals" would appear upon the scene. Attempts to deal with homosexuality at the social level through medical procedure may be compared to efforts to drain the English Channel with the aid of a teaspoon.

The "problem of homosexuality" cannot be solved by medical means, except in isolated cases involving a small number of individuals. This problem—insofar as we speak of it as a social problem—must be dealt with on an entirely different basis: one that will make some allowance for the fact that homosexuality is part and parcel of our mammalian heritage. With the recognition and acceptance of this fact may come a change in the mores which may resolve many of the problems now associated with homosexuality in our culture.

It is disappointing but true that we will not be able to shunt off the social problem of homosexuality by referring it to a medical solution. Anyone who understands the psychology of sexual relations does not regard any type of sexual pattern as a medical issue. We shall have to confront homosexuality in our society as we have never done if any progress is to be made; instead of regarding homosexuality as an individual problem to be solved with the aid of a priest or a doctor, we shall sooner or later have to recognize the social significance of homosexuality and come to terms with it.

To advertise the idea that homosexuality is a "curable disease" is little less than fraudulent on the basis of the most reliable statistics that we now have. The Bieber study reports a cure of 27 per cent *of the most favorable cases treated.* There are many types of cancer with a higher incidence of cure. Yet few would feel that cancer should be represented, in a broad sense, as a curable disease. The fact that people are urged to seek proper treatment because certain cases of early cancer may be curable does not warrant the more sweeping conclusion, which would be misleading, that cancerous patients need only seek medical treatment to be certain that their problems will be over.

Similarly, simply because certain cases of homosexuality which are treated early in life under especially favorable circumstances may be reversible, one is not justified in claiming that homosexuality is on any broad basis a "curable disease." The public should be informed that such reversals are sometimes possible and also that, in the absence of such reversals, many so-called homosexuals may work out a better adjustment for themselves as a result of therapy. But neither the public nor interested public officials should be led to believe that homosexuality is fundamentally a "medical problem" or that this problem can be solved at the social level by medical means.

Let us consider the therapeutic results reported in the Bieber study. These are of special interest because they are the first results to be carefully documented from a group of therapists rather than being merely the generalized claim of an individual therapist. Psychoanalysis is the most intensive and the "deepest" form of psychotherapy presently known. It is, today, the oldest and most established form of psychotherapy. While other forms of psychotherapy have been developed by individuals and by small groups, and while many of these other psychotherapies claim superiority over psychoanalysis, psychoanalysis has had more than a sixty-year history during which its practitioners have benefited from the opportunity to exchange their experiences and views and to modify the techniques of their art so as to make it more suitable to the particular type of case involved. We may therefore expect that the therapeutic results reported in the Bieber study compare favorably with any other results presently obtainable through psychotherapeutic means.

Of the 106 homosexual patients treated, 29 were reported cured (27 per cent of the sample). These results have been cited as reason for great therapeutic optimism, and it is being asserted that homosexuality can be cured if the patient really wants to be cured. On the basis of these results certain people are leaping to some very far-reaching conclusions. But let us pause long enough to estimate the actual significance of these results.

Of the 29 individuals who were cured, 18 (or 62 per cent) had 350 hours or more of private-session therapy. Another 9 had between 150 and 350 hours of therapy and in only 2 cases was it possible to bring about a cure in less than 150 hours of therapy. Of the 29 successful cases, moreover, 23 (an overwhelming majority) "consciously wanted to change." We must consider the implications of the fact that these results do not include those who could not or would not come for therapy. Nor do they include those who did come but who, for various complex reasons, were unable to withstand the demands of psychoanalytic treatment and who terminated their therapeutic sessions relatively early. These cases with a bad prognosis are not counted in the total statistics.

Thus, under the most favorable circumstances and after virtually hundreds of hours of treatment, only 27 per cent of the cases were reported cured. These are very modest results. But to imagine that even 27 per cent of all "homosexuals" could be cured by psychoanalysis is to draw an incorrect inference from these studies, for many have no desire whatsoever to change, others could not sustain the enormous expense in time and money involved in such a treatment, and still others would begin therapy only to drop out early in the treatment.

But there is another standpoint from which these statistics may be presented, and, although it may be called more pessimistic, it may be more realistic: Of the 106 patients treated under these highly favorable circumstances, 78 (73 per cent of the sample) were not cured of their homosexuality. Whether we choose to stress the fact that 27 per cent were cured or that 73 per cent were not cured depends upon a number of factors, many of which are highly subjective. But it can hardly be denied that the significance of the failures is just as great—if not greater, considering their magnitude—than the significance of the successes. These results are quite disappointing, and therapists from other schools no doubt will insist that their own methods are more effective, although it is impossible to accept any such claim in the absence of adequately documented results.

Cory and LeRoy point to the significance of the failures, and it can hardly be denied that the points they make are worth considering:

> . . . Of those who came (or were sent) to Bieber and his co-workers for study, who struggled through analysis and underwent the torment and difficulties that it entails, many of them for literally hundreds of hours, more than 70% remained homosexuals. The writers are acquainted with hundreds of young men and women, and many older ones as well, who spent thousands of hard-earned dollars and hundreds of uncomfortable hours, seeking to overcome their imperious deviant drives, but in vain. The Mattachine Society and other groups have scores of members, some of whom readily admit that they were aided to face reality by the therapeutic sessions, but who were as overwhelmingly or as exclusively homosexual after therapy as they had been before.
>
> It would seem clear that 73% of failure is a large figure, and that this is the realistic statistic that should be publicized in order to obtain better self-understanding by the homosexual and better acceptance of him by his society. To focus attention on the 27%, as if it were a surefire majority, is misleading and dangerous.[15]

A little-publicized result of this research that has many implications for the "homosexual" is that "Improvement which was not directly related to sexual problems was reported for 97 homosexuals." [8]

Many would consider that this is the most important statement that can be made about therapy so far as a majority of these patients are concerned. From this finding we may well expect that it is possible for members of the homosexual population to receive benefits from therapy, whether or not they remain a part of this population.

A further word of caution regarding the results of the Bieber study is in order. Since no follow-up study has been done on the 27 per cent who were reported as cured, it is as yet impossible to know how many of these individuals will continue to maintain an exclusively heterosexual orientation or how many may revert to an exclusively homosexual orientation with the passing of time. It would be optimistic in the extreme to suppose that all of the 27 per cent will maintain the adaptation reached at the end of therapy throughout the rest of their lives. Indeed, this raises an important issue: It is a serious question whether these results should be represented as cures at all in the absence of adequate follow-up studies. We can only rightfully consider that those who continue to maintain their heterosexual adaptation have been really "cured" of homosexuality, and we have absolutely no way of knowing at this time how many of these subjects will do so. At the end of three years, for example, perhaps only 20 per cent will still be ratable as 0; and at the end of five years perhaps only 15 per cent will still be ratable as 0; while by the end of ten years, perhaps only 10 per cent or even fewer will still qualify for a low rating. How many, then, were really cured in any complete or permanent sense? It would undoubtedly have been better to have waited until this question could be reliably answered before making any elaborate pronouncements on this issue. In the absence of follow-up studies it is not accurate to speak in terms of cure. Instead we must conclude that prolonged psychoanalytic treatment brought about a remission of the homosexuality of 27 per cent of the patients.

Whether or not all homosexuality may be accurately regarded as psychopathological, a substantial number of persons in our culture experience serious conflict over homosexuality. Psychotherapists must be prepared to minister to the needs of any of these people who seek their help, and they must be prepared to meet the patient on his own terms rather than accepting only those who are inclined to renounce their homosexual tendencies completely. Nor should those who seek greater happiness as "homosexuals" be led to the belief—so harmful to many—that because they do not wish to "get well" they are forever trapped in their own perversity.

Prevention rather than therapy is the only acceptable social solution to the homosexual problem in our culture. In discussing prevention it is necessary to make quite clear from the start what objectives seem desirable and attainable. Although homosexuality may play no part in the lives of many, nevertheless homosexuality has some phylogenetic basis and is an abiding component of human sexuality. It has played some part in the lives of a substantial number of males throughout all of human history and within virtually every kind of cultural milieu. It will doubtless continue to do so. It is not probable that sexual contacts between like-sexed partners will ever cease to be a part of the human sexual repertory or that homosexuality per se can ever be prevented. But pathological homosexuality and the many problems that may become associated with any kind of homosexuality in our culture apparently do not have any phylogenetic basis and are a source of considerable human misery. It is these health hazards that must be prevented.

If we are to prevent pathology we must obviously remove the source of it. One can only agree with Bieber *et al.* that pathological homosexuality develops as a result of conflicts in the child that are related to both father and mother, and it would certainly seem that pathological homosexuality can only develop in a boy who has been chronically exposed to the pathological heterosexuality of both his parents. Such a child turns from heterosexuality in fear and disgust, because his experiences with his parents have left him with the abiding impression that heterosexuality involves nothing but frustration, disappointment, and misery.

No woman turns toward her son for the kind of relationship she should have with her husband if she has experienced real satisfaction in marriage. No man rejects his son if he himself feels adequate as a male. At the beginning of Chapter VIII we discussed some of the homoerotophobic factors that produce hostile-detached fathers and the kind of frustrated wives who attempt to establish a close-binding-intimate relationship with their sons, and the opinion was stressed that homoerotophobia and its various psychological ramifications are important components in the psychology of the parents of pathologically homosexual patients. But there is a good deal more than homoerotophobia to be considered. In a book such as this we cannot attempt to discuss in detail the entire subject of sex within our culture. It must be sufficient to point out that pathological attitudes toward every aspect of sex are involved in the psychology of parents who nurture a son who becomes pathologically homosexual. Indeed, it seems necessary to assume that *pathological homosexuality can only develop in an atmosphere of pathological heterosexuality*. It is perhaps even more correct to say that pathological homosexuality can only develop in an *erotophobic* environment such as that engendered by the sexual mystique of our Judaeo-Christian culture.

In recognizing this last point we have found the ultimate source not only of pathological homosexuality but also of pathological heterosexuality. All the pathology associated with heterosexuality, autoerotocism, and homosexuality in our culture has a common basis in fear, ignorance, and misunderstanding. It is of no avail to fractionalize this problem and to attempt to prevent a particular type of sexual pathology while leaving intact the ideological basis that brings all sexual pathology into being. For example, efforts to isolate the specific causes of pathological homosexuality and to prevent the development of this particular pathology are doomed from the start, because pathological homosexuality in reality is but the particular expression of a much broader pathology that originates in the entire sexual mystique of our culture. The parents of homosexual patients are themselves sexually ill, as no doubt their own parents were. To expect them to abstain from the type of behavior that brings about pathological homosexuality in their sons amounts to expecting them to recognize and to overcome their own illness. But this is more than may be expected, particularly since the attitudes that foster pathology in both parents and their children are represented as virtuous and high-minded in our culture.

Prophylaxis in the sphere of sexual pathology amounts to nothing short of a complete reorientation of our social attitudes toward all sexual phenomena. Unless we are prepared to reformulate our sexio-social concepts we must expect the same pathologies in the future that we have seen in the past; for these pathologies are directly related to and wholly dependent upon the sexual mystique prevailing within our culture.

This leads us out of the sphere of medicine and science into the sphere of philosophy and ethics. But we must pursue this topic to its logical conclusion in spite of the objections that such an effort is certain to raise. We must conclude, therefore, with a discussion of sex and morality.

XIII

Sex and Morality

Since almost all sexio-social problems—not least of all those involving psychopathology—are a result of ignorance, prejudice, fear, and misunderstanding, it may be expected that they may only be solved when and if an enlightened attitude toward sexual phenomena is fostered among us. In other words, the ultimate solution to these many problems lies in a thoroughgoing and realistic *education* in all matters touching upon sexual relationships.

However, few if any young people receive such an education today. The kind of nonsense and superstition that is passed off as sex education might better be called maleducation. At best it is insipid and irrelevant and fails to inform; at worst it is a vicious propaganda that actually misinforms. We have continued to perpetuate erroneous notions and questionable opinions under the guise of fact, and to corrupt the young and innocent with unenlightened concepts of sexual ethics that were pernicious enough hundreds of years ago but that, in the context of current social conditions, must be recognized as entirely depraved. The implication that sexual urges are somehow innately sinful, the refusal to see sexual phenomena in any terms other than those of procreation, the idea that sexual virtue consists in conforming to a set of rules related to an external pattern of behavior, the acceptance of a "double standard" of morality—all this and the mythology that arises out of it must appear grossly obscene to any thoughtful person. One can only marvel that this so-called education has not done even more harm than may be already attributed to it. As a result of it the average middle-aged New Yorker of today knows less about the similarities and differences between males and females, less about the techniques of love-making, less about the physiology and psychology of sexual relations, and less about his own and other's sexual capacities than the average Samoan youth of sixty years ago—and he is a far more disturbed and unhappy person.

It seems an unavoidable conclusion that so long as sex education amounts to little more than propaganda in support of our traditional illusions it will continue to be more harmful than helpful. If any worthwhile aims are to be realized it would seem that we must either remove sex education from the sphere of moral propaganda and confine it to a mere account of material facts, or we must evolve a new morality that is consistent with material and psychological facts and which affords a more inspired concept of virtue.

In reality, we have no choice, for a sex education that is entirely amoral and that fails to take into consideration the ethical issues that are always a part of human relationships would be no education at all. In the end it would be as misleading and destructive as is the perpetuation of a false morality. We cannot ignore moral questions; we can only attempt to find better answers to these questions than the traditional ones.

The need for a new morality in the sexual sphere has been recognized in recent times by many people, although not at the official level by any of the religious institutions in our society. An ever greater number of religious thinkers have, however, questioned our traditional concepts of sexual morality, and an increasing number of articles and books pointing out the need for a new morality are published by philosophers and religious leaders. One such publication in particular is germane to the problems raised in this book: A pamphlet entitled "Towards a Quaker View of Sex," by a group of Friends, was issued in 1963 by the Literature Committee of the Friends Home Service Committee in England. Although the views expressed in "Towards a Quaker View of Sex" may not necessarily reflect the attitude of the Friends Home Service Committee or of the Religious Society of Friends, it is nevertheless significant and to their credit that the Quakers have seen fit to publish such a pamphlet.

In section IV, under the heading "A New Morality Needed," the authors of this pamphlet point out that there are elements in the Church's attitude to sexuality throughout the centuries that seem inconsistent with some of the deepest insights in the Bible, and these authors frankly emphasize some of the defaults in the traditional Judaeo-Christian attitude toward sex. It is useful to quote some of the observations offered in this unusual document:

> We have then to reject the idea that there is anything necessarily sinful about sexual activity . . . Sexual activity is essentially neither good nor evil; it is a normal biological activity which, like most other human activities, can be indulged in destructively or creatively.
> Further, if we take impulses and experiences that are potentially wholesome and in a large measure unavoidable and characterize these

as sinful, we create a great volume of unnecessary guilt and an explosive tension within the personality. When, as so often happens, the impulse breaks through the restriction, it does so with a ruthless and destructive energy that might not otherwise have been there. A distorted Christianity must bear some of the blame for the sexual disorders of society.

In trying to summarize the feelings and judgements that have come to us in the course of our several years' deliberations, we must keep this historical survey in mind. It supports us in rejecting almost completely the traditional approach of the organized Christian church to morality, with its supposition that it knows precisely what is right and what is wrong, that this distinction can be made in terms of an external pattern of behavior, and that the greatest good will come only through universal adherence to that pattern.

The authors do not fail to relate their observations to homosexuality. In discussing the meaning of the expression, "I love you," they state, "So we are concerned with the homosexuals who say to each other 'I love you' in the hopeless and bitter awareness of a hostile criminal code and hypocritical public opinion."

The moral concepts that these authors have in mind are related to the attitudes toward one another that are manifest between two people in a sexual relationship, and these moral concepts apply equally to heterosexual and homosexual relationships.

Finally we accept the definition of sin given by an Anglican broadcaster, as covering those actions that involve exploitation of the other person. This is a concept of wrongdoing that applies both to homosexual and heterosexual actions and to actions within marriage as well as outside it. It condemns as fundamentally immoral every sexual action that is not, as far as is humanly ascertainable, the result of mutual decision. It condemns seduction and even persuasion, and every instance of coitus which, by reason of disparity of age or intelligence or emotional condition, cannot be a matter of mutual responsibility.

The authors of "Towards a Quaker View of Sex" have emphasized that morality should be creative and that the God in whose name the morality we accept is defended is a Creator rather than a rule-maker. They also emphasize that positive purposes may involve the acceptance of suffering. In the light (or darkness) of a morality that adjudges sexual feelings as inherently unrighteous and inferior, emotional maturity will seem to consist almost completely of self-control, acceptance of suffering, and other negatives. Morality, however, and also emotional maturity—without which no morality is possible—consist of self-realization. If we cannot realize our own potentialities, we have little to offer in our relationships with others. Self-realization is a duty we owe to others.

It is difficult, however, to know how self-realization is possible if one accepts a philosophy that encourages conformity with a set of rules and that defines both virtue and vice in terms of an external pattern of behavior. The time has come when we must acknowledge that no given sexual act is in itself good or evil, any more than it is in itself normal or abnormal. Global interpretations of sexual phenomena, stated dogmatically and categorically, are liable to criticism not merely because they are unscientific but also because they are in the very deepest sense immoral. They inspire neither inquiry, thought, nor any other type of effort to arrive at a personal decision. Hence they do not inspire acceptance of moral responsibility. Instead they encourage blind and even senseless conformity. It is doubtful if one may regard mere conformity, based neither upon insight nor decision, as morality. In his play *Saint Joan,* Shaw puts into the mouth of the Inquisitor the following words which are pertinent in this connection:

> The blessed St. Athanasius has laid it down in his creed that those who cannot understand are damned. It is not enough to be simple. It is not enough even to be what simple people call good. The simplicity of a darkened mind is no better than the simplicity of a beast.

Sexual morality consists of more than merely not doing certain things; it consists in doing what one does do to some purpose that may be recognized, at least by one's self, as worthy. And it consists in doing what is also worthy in the estimation of one's beloved. Sexual acts between persons who feel the worthiness of their love are morally unassailable, whatever their physical nature may be; sexual acts of any kind between persons who do not feel the worthiness of their love may not properly be deemed moral, no matter how conventional they may be.

But wholesome and ethical sexual relationships are based upon something still more fundamental even than the genuine conviction that one's love is worthy: *Sexual virtue begins with the joyful acceptance of one's own sexuality and the sexuality of other people.* Those who enter into sexual relationships with the feeling that sex is morally inferior necessarily participate in immorality, even though they may elaborate complicated justifications for such relationships.

In earliest times man was unable to recognize any connection between sexual intercourse and childbirth; the nine-month interval between the two events made the connection between them obscure in the mind of primitive man. There are even today certain so-called primitive peoples in remote regions who do not recognize that coitus is related to procreation. Sexual desire, insofar as it was accorded any meaning or interpretation, was thought by primitive man to result from possession by gods, demons, or spirits. Pregnancy, on the other hand, was also thought to result from contacts between humans and supernatural beings. Women who remained barren often went to sacred groves or other designated spots, where they thought the god or spirit would enter them and make them fertile. This same primitive concept may still be recognized in many religions today; in Christianity, for example, it is believed that the Virgin Mary conceived "without sin" in a mystical relationship with the Holy Spirit.

The most primitive concept of sex and procreation, therefore, is one in which both are regarded as entirely supernatural phenomena, but unrelated. By the time man had evolved the type of social relationships that are peculiar to what some sociologists and anthropologists have called a stage of barbarism, he had recognized the connection between sex and reproduction. At first, apparently, he was quite overwhelmed by his insight, for once he recognized the connection barbaric man elaborated complex rituals and dogmas in celebration of his discovery. It is easy to understand how, under barbaric conditions of life—where mere survival of both the individual and the group was a daily struggle—sexual morality was accorded an entirely and exclusively procreative interpretation. Whatever other values may be recognized in sexual tendencies, or ascribed to them, appeared insignificant to the barbarian when compared with the procreative function of the drive.

Later, when the development of civilization made human survival easier, other values became associated with human sexual tendencies. Love, for example, was recognized as noble and moral in its own right, and sexual pleasure itself was also valued. Under the less harassed conditions that man enjoyed as a result of the development of civilization, all of his appetitive drives were cultivated, not merely for their functional values but also for their hedonistic values. By the time human relationships had reached the level we find in ancient Egypt, Mesopotamia, Greece, and Rome, man was capable of a philosophical attitude toward life in general, not least of all toward sex and love. Sexual relationships were not shorn of their religious significance, but their religious significance had changed in accordance with the changed material conditions in a civilized society. Some concept of sexual freedom was at least recognized for men during this early stage of civilization—usually, however, at the expense of woman—and sexual phenomena were no longer viewed exclusively in procreative terms. Economic and scientific developments were not in ancient times such as to make a greater sexual freedom for women possible (although this is no longer true). Women, consequently, were denied the sexual privilege that men enjoyed, as indeed they were denied many other privileges that men enjoyed (with the exception of a brief period during Roman times).

Nevertheless, civilization had brought a new attitude toward sex: for the first time in the history of mankind heterosexual and homosexual phenomena alike were viewed in rational terms instead of only the magical and superstitious terms in which primitive and barbaric man had always viewed them. The various peoples of the ancient civilizations attempted to understand sexual phenomena in naturalistic terms and to regulate sociosexual relationships in accordance with both the material and spiritual needs of the group. Philosophers appeared upon the scene and man's mind was no longer under the control only of witch doctors, wizards, and sorcerers.

If the ancient attitude of civilized men toward sex had continued to develop along with material conditions, our sexual concepts in the West today would be entirely different. But such was not the case; ancient civilization collapsed and the world was again plunged into semi-barbarism for several more centuries to come. Before it did so, however, Christianity had taken root. This might have all been to the good, except that with it came the wholesale adoption of the Hebraic sex code with all of its many prohibitions and its monomaniacal preoccupation with procreation. This sex code undoubtedly evolved during a period when the ancient Jews had not yet emerged from barbarism, and it reflects the barbarian's obsession with an exclusively procreative interpretation of sexual phenomena. Had it not been that civilization, under the impact of barbarian invasions, collapsed and regressed once again to barbarism, it is not likely that either the Jewish or the Christian religions would have continued to preserve this code. Both, indeed, were moving away from it—in practice if not in precept —at the time of the collapse of the Roman Empire. But the return to barbarism brought about conditions that favored the type of psychology that had given rise to such a code in the first place. Hence it was reinforced by material conditions—chief among which was depopulation—and was preserved over a sufficiently long period of time to become part of religious tradition.

If one examines Christ's teachings as they are reported in the New Testament he will find little if anything that supports our traditional religious attitudes toward sex. Certainly, as has been discussed earlier, our attitudes toward marriage and family life in particular cannot be supported by anything Christ had to say in the Bible; indeed, these attitudes are rather foreign and contrary to the philosophy of Christ, in which the abandonment of close family ties is urged in favor of a far broader concept of social relationships. Our traditional attitudes toward sex have nothing to do with Christ's philosophy; they are based upon the interpolations of such of his followers as St. Paul and other lesser men who accepted the Mosaic tradition of sexual virtue in which they were raised. Christianity as we know it today is widely divergent from the teachings of Christ along a number of lines, and Christian theology is a hodgepodge of Jewish and pagan concepts that have been watered down and elaborated by minds that were almost all morally inferior to Christ's. It is possible to accept all Christ's teachings without in the least adhering to the sexual morality that has become a part of the Christian religion since his death.

The sexual morality to which we pretend today represents a mental regression and fixation on the part of Western man. In it is revealed a mixture of primitive and barbaric sexual attitudes from which the human race was emerging at the dawn of civilization and from which, to a large extent, it had freed itself at the height of Greco-Roman civilization. In this morality may be recognized the primitive belief that sexual events are supernatural and the barbaric belief that the only function of sex is procreation; little of the humanistic attitude toward sex of the ancient civilized peoples may be detected in this morality. It is a morality entirely appropriate to primitive and barbaric conditions of life, but one that must appear both vulgar and offensive in the context of civilized life. It fails to provide either guidance or inspiration to modern men and women, and insofar as it arouses any emotions at all it is only the emotions of fear and guilt. For the intellect it has absolutely no significance at all. It fails to instruct along positive lines even in the areas of marriage and family life, to which it is entirely limited, and its effect upon the mind of modern man and upon his social relationships is entirely negative. It fosters a kind of marital relationship and a kind of family psychology which in modern times is inimical to progress, and it encourages a kind of promiscuous reproduction at a time when overpopulation is one of the most serious problems that man has to face. It is a source of human discomfort, social unrest, and even mental disease and creates whole classes of individuals who are outcasts and pariahs. In the theological sphere it has produced monstrous concepts such as those of original sin and virgin birth, concepts that no man of good judgment could possibly entertain without suspending reason. It has in other words called upon modern man to sacrifice his reason, his taste, his social welfare, his sense of justice, his enjoyment of life, his dignity, and his chance to progress without offering anything in return, except possibly a feeling of complacency based upon a lazy refusal to accept change.

Man's control over natural forces has come to exceed his control over himself. Whereas formerly man was entirely dependent upon natural forces for survival, modern scientific developments have brought about a situation in which the ageless order of nature is now within man's control. Nor has man's supremacy yet reached its full potential. Continued progress in physics, medicine, chemistry, biology, and psychology will bring about still further changes in man's relationship to the material world around him.

Under these radically changed conditions many of our traditional moral concepts and religious beliefs in both the sexual and the nonsexual spheres of life appear antiquated and naïve. Any person with a sense of responsibility must recognize the need for an ideological and moral revolution comparable in scope and significance to the scientific revolution that began in recent times. It is as simple as this: If we are not able to meet the challenge of modern times and evolve a morality germane to the conditions of contemporary life we may destroy ourselves. Under these conditions every attempt to impede moral progress, every attempt to resist change, every attempt to cling to answers that are no longer pertinent must be recognized as a betrayal of life. We are concerned in this chapter only with moral questions that are related to sex, but such questions constitute a large part of the moral burden of our times.

In spite of all of the objections to a morality that is both primitive and barbaric in its approach to sexual phenomena, most moralists and many sociologists continue to view sociosexual problems from the traditional point of view. Thus, they continue to judge sexual phenomena from what amounts to an exclusively procreative point of reference. Yet it must be affirmed that the primitive ethos of a tribal psychology in which human values may not be reckoned beyond the nuclear family or at most beyond one's immediate social contacts in a small, close-knit community, must appear petty and even unrighteous in a changed world in which international relationships must be a matter of concern even for the most humble. Since procreation is thought the only purpose of sex, marriage and family life have been credited with every possible advantage for society, and it is inferred, if not openly urged, that every advantage for society as a whole is dependent upon the maintenance of these institutions along ancient and traditional lines.

It may be urged, not without reason, "It is in marriage that sexual impulses have their greatest opportunity for joyful and creative expression" because marriage provides the opportunity for an open commitment of love which is respected in society. It also forms a basis for the only arrangement that our culture has evolved for the rearing of children. It may be expected, therefore, that marriage and family life as we know them will continue to be a part of the experience of most human beings in our society for a very long time to come. But it is a different matter to assume that these institutions are perfect or that they will never change. It is also a different matter to assume that these institutions are suitable for everyone or that everyone is suitable for marriage and family life. Nor may it be assumed that every marriage is necessarily moral or that every sexual alliance outside the bounds of marriage is necessarily immoral. Both morality and immorality may be found in the most unlikely places. An enlightened morality, moreover, must allow that no one and only good exists that may be recommended to each and every person. The moral welfare of the individual as well as of the group must also be provided for in any acceptable ethical system.

We have all been instructed on the virtues of marriage and family life. There is no need here to restate these. Some of the defaults of our traditional marriage and family relationships, however, may be less apparent to many people.

We must first question the assumption that marriage and our traditional family arrangement are eternal institutions, perfect and changeless. If—as

might be expected since they are human rather than divine institutions—
marriage and family relationships change with time in accordance with
historical and material forces, it should not be assumed that these
changes are necessarily evil or that they will lead to evil. There are always
people who will point to such changes deploringly and make them both the
cause and effect of unrighteousness. It is thought by many, for example,
that if marriage and family life today are considerably different from what
they were in 1900, and greatly different from what they were in 1867, "it
is a great pity." But apart from being inevitable, many of these changes
represent progress.

Consider, for instance, the wife's position in the family a century ago.
She was to a very large extent the prisoner of an institution that exploited
her. There was little place for woman in society outside the family, and
marriage or prostitution were the only careers open to her, unless she
wanted to become an old-maid schoolmarm or librarian. She was wholly
dependent in marriage upon the generosity of her husband and had to accept
a "double standard" of morality which denied her certain freedoms that
her husband could, if he wished, avail himself of. Drudgery was her lot:
"Man may work from sun to sun, but woman's work is never done." One
pregnancy was followed by another until she was physically worn out long
before her time. Widowers in those times were far more common than
widows—a circumstance that has reversed itself in modern times. Bound
by the narrow interests of family life, most women remained ignorant of
life as a whole. They represented an uneducated, backward element of the
population. With the social, political, economic, and sexual emancipation
of women it could hardly be expected that marriage and family life would
remain the same; nor is there any good reason for supposing that they
should have. The changes wrought in these institutions have for the most
part represented progress.

We hear a great deal of talk about "Christian marriage" and "the Christian family" as if they were eternals beyond the influence of mere material
circumstance. But the Christian who lives in Manhattan today would hardly
even recognize, and certainly not approve of the Christian marriage and
family relationships of 1067, in which wife and children alike were chattels
and in which the father, insofar as he spent any time with his wife and
children, acted as a petty tyrant. The Christian home and the Christian
marriage have changed many times throughout the course of history and
will continue to do so in the future. They are mortal institutions subject
to the force of material conditions, and their moral status is no greater
than that permitted by the intellectual and social conditions that prevail
at a given time and place.

It is easy to be carried away emotionally by the mere pronouncement of
the words "marriage" and "family" because both have been excessively

mystified and, even worse, romanticized and sentimentalized. All of us tend to fetishize the institutions that have left the greatest impression upon our minds during childhood and that, during childhood, appeared to be far different from what they may have been in reality. But in spite of all this—perhaps precisely because of it—we must attempt to take a more objective look at these institutions, not as divine categories that are good regardless of their effects upon human beings and the social order, but as constantly evolving human institutions that do not entirely solve all of the problems they are called upon to solve.

We generally make two very far-reaching assumptions about the human sexual drive: that this drive may be completely satisfied in the marriage relationship, and that the demands of this drive may be entirely resisted by the average young man and woman until such time as they are married.

The first of these propositions is based on the hopeful belief that the average person is monogamous by nature or that if he may not be monogamous by nature, he can be made so without harm to himself or his spouse. The second of these propositions is based on the assumption that the sexual drive may be suppressed without harm, or that it may be, as the psychiatrists say, "sublimated" and put into the service of other motives which some people have called "higher" than mere appetitive satisfaction. It is also assumed that for every man and for every woman there is waiting somewhere what has been called "the one and only person" who can be all things to him (or her) throughout the course of an entire lifetime; it is believed that one has only to search in order to find the girl (or the boy) of one's dreams. Having been prompted to this belief by social ideals, youthful passion, and adolescent exuberance, the average young person usually finds someone who seems to possess all of the qualities promised in his (or her) dreams. This entirely delightful but altogether zany state of mind is considered the *sine qua non* for wholesome sexual relationships— otherwise one would be indulging in what has been called contemptuously "sex without love."

Having been transported by love, the two young people are quite convinced—and few would disagree with them—that marriage is the next logical step. In their marriage the lovers will be called upon to satisfy each other's every need. Each must be a devoted friend, a stimulating social companion, an aggressive breadwinner (or expert homemaker), an alluring sexual partner whose charms (no matter how often enjoyed) never stale, a wise parent, and in general the source of all things joyful, estimable, and rare.

It may be reasonably supposed that all of this is far too much to ask of any human being—especially throughout the course of an entire lifetime—and that there never was nor never will be any person who can fulfill all of the spiritual and physical needs of another person. Hence, husbands and wives alike must spend a good deal of time and effort in artful deception and flattery, trying to convince one another that each measures up to what, in the heat of adolescent passion, each thought the other was five, ten, twenty, or even forty years ago; they must sustain the illusion upon which their marriage is based and upon which their sexual relationship is justified.

But the average man or woman is not in reality gifted with the extraordinary qualities that each ascribes to the other in the heat of young love; nor is he or she usually gifted with the histrionic skills that might create the illusion of such qualities. The average person is precisely what the adjective suggests: he or she is seldom remarkable or distinguished either for beauty, character, personality, intelligence, occupational skill, talent, or any other personal attribute. Most people fail to possess in sufficient degree any characteristic that could perpetually inspire the kind of admiration that one feels at the height of love. That few continue to do so may be seen not only in the high rate of divorce in modern times, but also in the faces of so many couples who are not divorced but who are obviously disillusioned by having found each other something less than was imagined during the apex of youthful passion. Many people are surfeited with one another and bored beyond telling with the monotony that may often result from the necessity of having to find satisfaction for all of one's most intimate needs in a single individual.

Strict monogamy often produces a claustrophobic feeling in people from which they attempt to escape by dissolving one marriage and taking up another. Apart from the fact that this is no escape at all, it may be extremely harmful not only to one's partner in marriage but also to one's children. Marriage is an extremely important commitment, one that should be based upon something more realistic and something more permanent and substantial than romantic love usually proves to be. It should not, in the opinion of this author, be dissolved, if children are involved, except in the most extraordinary instances.

The concept we have evolved of romantic love, upon which we base one of the most important relationships in life, is absurdly unrealistic, egocentric, childish, and antisocial. If romantic love ever persisted for more than a few months in any majority of people, it would bring the world crashing down around our heads. People who are in love hardly have a thought for anyone else. Their reason and judgment are actually incapacitated and they have little time and almost no desire to attend to the work of the world. Love is an experience that no doubt everyone should have, but it is not an emotion upon which to base any serious relationship— particularly any relationship that involves long-term and far-reaching commitments. Nevertheless, young people are encouraged to marry "for love," and it is usually expected by both partners and by the world around them that the illusion of love will be preserved in a marriage indefinitely and in the face of every obstacle. We have seen what naked hypocrisy is often necessary to maintain this illusion. When, moreover, the romantic illusion is completely shattered—as not infrequently happens—the result is not usually friendship and a good hearty laugh together, but bitterness and disappointment that lead to divorce or chronic unhappiness in a relationship that must necessarily become more and more burdensome and degrading. Nothing, perhaps, contributes more to divorce or to unhappy marriages, than the romantic expectations with which marriage is surrounded.

We would have done much better to have based marriage and the domestic relationship on the abiding needs of human nature and to have allowed some scope for the satisfaction of certain of these needs which only rarely may be permanently fulfilled in marriage. Had we done so, we would no doubt find a much greater number of happy husbands and wives and, even more important, happy fathers and mothers with happy children. We cannot here even begin to discuss in detail some of the ill effects which the conventional concept of a good marriage has upon child-rearing.

Many people are quite incapable of the kind of single-minded devotion that is implied in marriage of any kind. An even greater number of others are incapable of being the kind of parents that we know every child is entitled to. Nor should we necessarily insist that every human being must have the kind of personality that makes him or her suitable for marriage and/or parenthood. But we do insist upon this and even make it a measure of the individual's worth and a measure of what we call in the jargon of modern times his "emotional maturity." Worse still, we expect that almost everyone will marry whether or not he possesses the attributes necessary for a close, intimate, and exclusive relationship with another person. Our demands upon the individual to marry are so great that those who remain unmarried are actually penalized in a number of ways: they are often subjected to higher taxation, they may find it difficult to obtain many types of employment, and almost always they will be urged and cajoled to marry and they will earn something of an unsavory reputation if they do not. Yet far from expecting everyone to marry and urging them to do so at the risk of various penalties, we should definitely discourage many people from marriage and having children.

Certainly in a modern world which has been radically transformed materially, one cannot urge that marriage for all is desirable in the interests of procreation and perpetuation of the species. We are now suffering seriously and dangerously from what can only be called promiscuous reproduction. It would be better for all concerned if we had far fewer children and brought them up far better than we do. The time may yet come when it will be recognized that proper parenthood involves difficult skills, talents, and accomplishments that only a few can ever hope to possess. At such a time perhaps only those who are gifted with the necessary talents and only those who have taken trouble to acquire the necessary skills will be encouraged, or even allowed, to rear children. All of these developments—and they do not seem far ahead of us—must necessarily change our entire concept of connubial love, marriage, and family life. And there is no reason to doubt that when these changes occur they will represent *progress* of a kind that may lead to social conditions that are promised only in our dreams. The elimination of poverty and of overpopulation (with all their many attendant evils) are but two of the benefits that could accrue from changes in the ideological and social approach to love, marriage, and parenthood.

The traditional Judaeo-Christian family is deserving of a few words in its own right. Far from being the source of each and every good, it is one source of a great many social and moral evils. If all the homely virtues are learned in the bosom of the family—such virtues as veracity, respect for authority, respect for property, reverence, punctuality, neatness, cleanliness, thrift, piousness, and industriousness—it should not be forgotten that many of the more contemptible vices are also learned in the bosom of the family: complacency, jealousy, bigotry, narrow-mindedness, envy, selfishness, rivalry, avarice, prejudice, vanity, and greed are readily acquired in the special psychological circumstances that prevail in the family arrangement peculiar to our culture. All of these are extremely pernicious and all are especially dangerous emotions in this atomic age.

Anyone who deplores what has been called the "breakdown" of traditional family life in the more urban and industrialized quarters of the Western world need only spend an extended period of time in other quarters of Christendom (where the traditional family has remained more intact) in order to get some impression of the seamier side of this revered institution. The superficiality of the relationships between individuals who are not related by family ties is quite incredible. Alliances are narrow; friendships are brittle, perfunctory, and seldom get beyond the formality appropriate to mere acquaintanceship. It is only relatives with whom one has real and meaningful social contact. There is little feeling for society at large and hardly any sense of social responsibility, since it is only parents, offspring, siblings, and spouses who matter. The poverty of others, for example, is of no importance so long as it does not affect one's own family; if it does then it is felt that it must be solved at the level of the family rather than at the level of society as a whole. Greed, since it is justified by the needs of the family, is in evidence on all sides, as are avarice and selfish ambition. The boredom of everyday life may become quite stultifying in an atmosphere in which no one is engaged by any issues other than those which touch upon narrow family interests. Conversation revolves around the weather, the illness of one's aging parents or in the childhood maladies of

one's offspring, papa's increase in salary, young Maria's marital expectations, or among the more adventuresome, the activities of one's cousins
or aunts in the neighboring community. Petty gossip thrives, making a
good appearance with one's neighbors is almost a life's work, and envy—
never a noble emotion—is made even more contemptible by being directed
almost exclusively to the mediocre accomplishments of those in one's
restricted environment. Prejudice and bigotry arise almost as a matter of
course because interest and experience are limited and inquiry is taboo.
The same ideas are repeated among the same people without contradiction
until, like a litany, they become completely formalized. It is felt that all
the answers to all the important questions in life have been already
achieved. People think in stereotypes and in platitudes. Cant is on the
tongues of everyone. What is familiar and what is merely habitual is accepted without question because, as one says, it is "normal." Any departure
from habit or custom, on the other hand, is said to be "abnormal." Virtue
is synonymous with orthodoxy and evil with heterodoxy.

To a very large extent the social and psychological characteristics that
may be identified with a family-oriented environment are only exaggerations of social and psychological characteristics that may be found in other
areas of our culture where family ties have been weakened. No one should
imagine that the more urbanized areas of Judaeo-Christendom escape these
limitations entirely. They may be recognized everywhere, but where life
is more directly centered in family relationships such limitations become
pronounced.

History documents some of the evils that may fall upon society as a
result of the ignoble ambitions engendered by family-centered interests.
Most of European history amounts to little more than a vulgar recital of
the ruthlessness with which certain leading families of Europe placed
dynastic interests above the interests of society as a whole.

That the narrowness of viewpoint produced by a strong family-oriented
psychology almost precludes the possibility of a generous spirit has been
repeated by philosophers as a warning time and again. What we have come
to call the "family man" and the "homebody" bring to mind what is undoubtedly one of the most dreary and uninspired pictures of male and
female. It is difficult, for example, to imagine any person who is engaged
with the world at large as a family man or a homebody. It is almost an
impossibility for any man or woman who is laden with the cares and preoccupations peculiar to family life to be very deeply concerned with others.
This, it must be supposed, was the reason why Christ called upon those
who followed him to leave house and home and break all family ties. The
philosophy he preached urged a brotherhood among men that is inimical
to a psychology in which "charity begins at home." The charity of Christ
was boundless, indiscriminate, and unencumbered by any restriction, as was

the love upon which it was based. The Roman Church may differ with Christ when it urges a sanctimonious attitude toward family upon the laity; but in requiring perpetual bachelorhood of its administrators it acts in the interests of the larger unit.

Mystics, prophets, and philosophers have almost all felt the need to abandon the restrictions of family in favor of a relatedness to all others which is uncategorical. Many of the saints felt compelled to renounce family ties for similar reasons. The Buddha also left house and home when he began his mission. Indeed, it may be noted that some of the greatest moral leaders remained unmarried or abandoned marital ties, presumably in the expectation that meditation, thought, and concern with humanity as a whole might be less encumbered without the pressures and demands of family life and the narrow alliances it implies. Among them are not only Christ and the Buddha but also Plato, Aristotle, St. Paul, Thomas Aquinas, Kant, Schopenhauer, and Nietzsche.

No one would suggest that bachelorhood is a royal road to deep thought or to selfless union with humanity. But on the other hand, it may not be assumed that bachelorhood is necessarily immaturity, selfishness, or some of the other things that it has been called by those who feel that the highest goal in life for everyone is marriage and parenthood.

The intellectual and artistic vigor of the ancient Greeks and their enlightened attitude toward ethics have been thought by some to have been achieved in part because family ties were very loose in ancient Greece. We have previously mentioned that the ancient Greek male was separated from his family at an early age and that a great deal of his education took place outside of the family. The Greek male was not by our standards a very devoted husband or father, and his alliances were for the most part with the community. There can be little question that this had a great deal to do with the Greeks' development of the concept of democracy. Democracy is unworkable unless the citizen has a strong feeling for the community. Often such a feeling is adumbrated where family ties are primary.

Certain other groups have also evolved social relationships that are more community-centered than family-centered. In some cultures children have only a very vague concept of family relationship and the rearing of children is something of a communal effort. In these cultures all adult females tend to regard all children as their own, and children, for their part, tend to regard all adult females as mothers. Often in these cultures the concept of motherhood and fatherhood is very vague. These cultures tend also to be very sex-positive in comparison with our culture. The island paradises described by explorers before the missionaries arrived were often inhabited by such groups.

If some of the pettier traits of character and personality may be linked with a family-oriented psychology, it must be remembered that far worse characteristics may arise in the same context. Consider the etiology of psychoneurosis and functional psychosis. The interpersonal conflicts or, as psychoanalysts say, "complexes" which arise in the bosom of the family— from which most of us, presumably, hardly ever free ourselves—are so many that clinicians continue to identify new ones each year. Our traditional family unit is so claustrophobic that it brings mother, father, child, and siblings into conflict at almost every juncture. The emphasis upon motherhood is so exaggerated in our culture that almost no one ever seems to outgrow his Oedipus complex. There are seventy- and eighty-year-old people who still worship at the shrine of their mother and who still, deep in their minds, rehearse in their daily relationships ancient rivalries, aspirations, hatreds, and fears learned at their mother's bosom in the shelter of the home. Yet no one can doubt that one of the most important aspects of maturity—whether defined in emotional, ethical, or sociological terms— is detachment from the family ties of childhood. To achieve such detachment requires an enormous effort on the part of individuals who have been raised in the psychological atmosphere of the family as we know it. It is doubtful that many ever achieve it in any substantial measure. Most of us, even if we are fortunate enough to escape the more clear-cut forms of mental disease, suffer the ill effects of having been exposed to conflicts that are more or less inevitable in the family as we know it.

The particular forms that marriage and family relationships assume in our culture are often defended by pointing out that every culture has recognized some form of marriage and some form of family unit. But this does not mean that every form of marriage and every kind of family arrangement is equally good; it does not mean, for example, that these institutions cannot be improved in our own culture. Indeed, it does not even mean that they will continue to exist in the future in any form which we would recognize today.

It should be remembered that all human groups have shared a very similar history until recent times—a history of deprivation, struggle, and material want. This common history has given rise to very similar institutions among different groups. Human beings have had to live together in close-knit units in order to survive. In an environment in which one out of every two infants died at birth, and in which those who survived seldom had a life-span of much more than thirty or forty years, constant pregnancy was woman's lot and the siring of children the most conspicuous sign of a man's virility. Cooperation among families eventually led to tribal alliances, and later even more complex social relationships evolved. But throughout eons of history it has been marriage, parenthood, and family ties that have constituted man's primary social means of survival. Even in more recent times economic survival has meant economic cooperation within the family, and children as well as parents have had to labor for gain and share their earnings in order to maintain a comfortable standard of living.

In our times, however, the enormous increase in material abundance that has come with man's control over his physical environment has brought about social changes that favor the development of individuality. These changes are most conspicuous in the more industrialized areas of civilization. A man or woman may survive in modern times and even be quite comfortable without a spouse or family. Restaurants, commercial laundries, cooperative dwellings, and the like have made it possible for men and women alike to live a single life in relative ease. In the more industrialized quarters we often find people postponing marriage in order to establish economic security. Thus marriage today is in many cases a result of economic security rather than the foundation of it. Ever more often we find young people leaving home to take a job and live separately from the family. Most homes today no longer include aged members of the previous generation, unmarried aunts or uncles, or a large flock of children. A greater number of the aged and young alike live alone in efficiency apartments. There has been a progressive loosening of family ties and a progressively more casual note in the marriage relationship as more wives seek employment outside the home and enjoy the feeling of economic independence. Marriage in the past was the only career for most women and the only basis for security; it no longer is. Even mothers of relatively young children may work outside the home today. Grandma too has left hearth and home, and instead of being found knitting in her rocking-chair before the fire with the household cat asleep on her lap she may be found working at the bank or even off for the day on a spree at the horse-races. Large family reunions on holidays (at which mother, father, children, aunts, uncles, grandparents, and in-laws used to convene) are hardly possible in the small apartment in which so many people live today. Many an important holiday now is spent by only a few people together in a restaurant or at the cinema. Often these people are not related by family. In not a few cases friendships have been substituted for close ties with blood relatives and escape from loneliness is sought in relationships outside the family.

It might be argued that television has done much to keep people at home nowadays, where they must necessarily associate more often with relatives. But the social value of television is highly questionable. It is true that mother, father, and children may be found together for hours at a time before the television in many homes. That there is much communication going on between them, however, would hardly be claimed by anyone who has observed these sessions carefully. In the opinion of this author, television is an additional factor in modern life that in some measure contributes to the dissolution of rich familial relationships.

Material and economic changes have, then, brought about radical changes in marriage and family life. People today do not need each other—in a material sense—as much as they have needed each other in the past. Consequently they tend to look for psychological fulfillment in these ancient institutions and, because they are not as bound to these institutions by material wants, they tend to look more objectively upon them and to be more critical of them. If psychological satisfactions are not forthcoming in a marriage, a person today is much more apt than in the past to dissolve the matrimonial relationship.

In certain ways these changes have brought about improvements in marriage. Fewer marriages today may last a lifetime, but those that do tend to be held together less by necessity and more by volition. There is greater equality between husband and wife, a much wider sphere of common interest, and more freedom from domestic monotony. The wife may have more time for her husband, and he for her; they share a greater number of experiences together and a greater number of overlapping responsibilities. All of this, on the other hand, may put a heavier strain on the marriage relationship in cases where husband and wife are not well suited to one another psychologically.

We cannot expect that marriage and family life will have quite the same urgency for men and women today as in the past, or that these institutions will remain static in the face of radically changed social and economic conditions. The changes that have already taken place are probably only the beginning of further changes that will be even more far-reaching. Certainly, as was pointed out earlier, many of these changes are in the direction of a much more pronounced individuality on the part of men and women alike. Marriage may still mean "settling down" to many people, but it does not necessarily mean settling down to a stereotyped existence. The modern wife, for example, is usually a much more individualized person than her great-grandmother was. Her role also as a mother is far less routine and far less predetermined by rigid convention. The husband and father is also more relaxed in his role. Children, too, tend to have a much more informal relationship with parents. Respect for their elders has ceased to be a discipline required of children in many modern homes, and children today are likely to be heard as well as seen. Their needs and wants and opinions play a large part in the family economy, and adolescent children in particular have so much money to spend that a large part of the national economy is devoted to supplying their wants. Commercialized entertainment is largely geared to the tastes of children and adolescents. Indeed, their tastes, attitudes, and habits are often even imitated by older people in a society which has become increasingly oriented to youth. All of this may be deplored by some as near chaos, or as decadence—and perhaps, from a certain viewpoint, it is—but such opinions must necessarily be subjective.

We are not suggesting that there should be or ever will be what Huxley called a "brave new world" in which everyone is entirely dependent upon machines and everyone is devoid of human feeling and is more or less a machine himself. There will always be a need for love, a need for companionship and for sustained, intimate relationships. Indeed, among the greatest tragedies of modern life are a pervasive sense of loneliness and an inability among people to communicate with one another. To some extent this may reflect a too rapid transition in social relationships. Perhaps when society has taken on a new stability in the future, loneliness and alienation will no longer be as conspicuous. But love, marriage, and family life will surely not be in the future what they are today, any more than they are today what they were in the past. Change is inevitable and cannot be resisted. Human institutions, although always surrounded by a nimbus of supernatural significance, serve human needs, and as human needs change so do institutions.

Our sexual conventions represent an effort to preserve the institutions of marriage and family as we have known them in the past. But these institutions have changed more rapidly and more significantly than the conventions designed to serve them. To a great extent our sexual conventions have become obsolete and often they impede progress or make it far more painful than it needs to be. Our religious institutions seem to be unresponsive to these changes, and ancient conventions are defended on the grounds that they are as meaningful today as in the past. Religious institutions have failed almost entirely to inspire a new sexual morality that is in touch with human relationships as we know them today. We are offered dead conventions in place of a living morality. Apart from being a default in itself, this failure on the part of religious institutions is dangerous because it tends to turn many people away from religion altogether so that many are left without spiritual guidance of any kind.

It is not enough to say that traditional religious attitudes toward sex fail to be meaningful to most people any longer; they are not simply hollow but actually somewhat ridiculous and inspire uncomfortable laughter in the common man and outright contempt in the more educated and thoughtful. We must face the fact that our sex code is not acceptable to any educated or thoughtful person who is unwilling to make enormous concessions to convention for its own sake. Few live by this code today. Most merely pay it lip service, and then only when called upon to do so.

Bereft of a sex code that is meaningful in terms of his daily experiences, modern man must either improvise some highly personal concept of sexual morality for himself or, if he is unable or too lazy to do so, he must live in a moral vacuum. If he accepts the traditional sex code and attempts to be guided by it he is bound to feel miserably sinful and degraded because this code is so out of touch with reality that he must violate it at every turn. Hence, there is an inordinately large number of people among us who are either immoral or amoral in terms of conventional concepts. This encourages moralists to reinforce in even harsher terms the traditional morality, and they are more likely than ever to call upon other social institutions for reinforcement of this morality, when they should be occupied with the formulation of a new morality that can inspire respect and elevate rather than degrade men and women.

But if the moral dilemma of the average man is great, the moral dilemma of the individual with prepotent homosexual tendencies is virtually overwhelming, for our religious institutions offer him no solution at all to his problems. Others may expect at least some kind of solution in marriage, although strict monogamy and premarital chastity no longer appear as very real solutions to many people. But the only alternative offered the homosexual person by our religious institutions is lifelong celibacy or lifelong sinfulness.

We have dwelt at length upon some of the moral problems that affect everyone in our culture because, ultimately, all problems of sexual morality are interrelated and can neither be adequately understood nor solved in isolation. In turning to the issues raised by homosexuality, we do not imagine that this problem is essentially different from any other engendered by our social attitudes toward sex. Our attitudes toward homosexuality are merely exaggerations of attitudes we have regarding most other aspects of sexual life. Consequently one may learn a great deal about the sex problem in general by studying the sociological aspects of homosexuality.

Up to this point, we have considered some of the more objective data available on homosexuality. On the basis of most of these data, it does not appear that we are altogether justified in maintaining many of our traditional interpretations of homosexuality. It is difficult, for example, to insist that all homosexuality is a variety of sin, crime, and/or disease. But now we must be concerned with the homosexually inclined individual simply as a human being, quite apart from whether or not we choose to regard him as a sinner, a criminal, or a mental case. He is first and foremost a human being and as such—as the person of religious feeling may wish to put it— no less a child of God than any other human being. His sexual tendencies do not in the least relieve any of us of certain moral and ethical responsibilities toward him, any more than they relieve him of certain moral and ethical responsibilities toward other people. Now we must ask what some of these mutual responsibilities are.

It is not too much to say that we have arrived at a point in our interpersonal relationships with one another at which, by common consent and common feeling, all men are accorded certain rights and certain dignities so long as they accord the same rights and the same dignities to others; we have evolved a social philosophy which recognizes the individual. Thus no man may claim certain extraordinary privileges not accorded to others, nor disclaim any responsibilities that are required of others, by virtue of his membership within a particular group, class, or segment of society. The age of the superior man and the inferior man has passed, and no one imagines that the sun above shines only for a certain class or segment of society. It follows that neither race, nationality, religious affiliation, political alliance, family connections, economic status, nor—it must be added— sexual preferences establish any just claim to rights and privileges not accorded to others; nor do these confer any immunity against one's responsibility to recognize the rights and privileges of others.

All persons may be classified in a great many different categories. Thus, for example, a person may be a middle-aged, white, heterosexual male who is married, Protestant, a member of the American Legion, of the Rolling Green Country Club, and of the Democratic party. He may have an income of twenty thousand dollars a year and he may spend part of this income on his activities as a member of the Bird Watchers of America Association. He may be a lawyer, a father of ten children, a vegetarian, a hypochondriac, a well-dressed man of fashion, a member of the City Council, a diabetic, a vestryman in his church, a graduate of State University, a descendant of the First Families of Virginia, an amateur actor, golfer, and photographer, and the fourteenth grandson of one of the Norman Barons who stood by the side of William the Conqueror in the Battle of Hastings. He is sure to be a vertebrate, a mammal, a primate, and a homo sapien. None of these things, however, adds to his rights nor detracts from his responsibilities as a human being. Though he may be classified in innumerable different categories it is as an individual that he accepts or rejects moral responsibility, and it is as an individual that he must be judged. To stereotype him as a Democrat, a white man, a Methodist, or a heterosexual is to do violence not only to his dignity as an individual, it is to do violence also to his relationships with others. It is as a human being first and foremost that we must relate to each man.

Members of all social minorities suffer to some extent from being regarded not as individuals but as stereotypes of the minority in which they may be grouped. Thus far too often we regard a man as a Negro, a Catholic, a Puerto Rican, a "homosexual," or even a doctor or a laborer rather than as a human being; we often fail to recognize his qualities as an individual and instead expect from him or even ascribe to him qualities that we imagine are essential as a representative of the group in which we place him. But virtually every human being is a member of any number of different social minorities, and none is exempt from the dehumanizing experience of being treated as a stereotype rather than an individual. Anyone reading this book may make a list of the various social minorities in which he may be classified. Many also may recall the indignities suffered when they were treated as the exponent of a category—when, in other words, they were treated as an abstraction rather than a living person.

Some minorities, of course, are more imposed upon than others; but in every case the source of the trouble may be traced to a refusal on the part of others, who themselves are members of some minority, to accept the individual. It is ironic to hear a Catholic condemning a "homosexual," a "homosexual" condemning a Negro, a Negro condemning an atheist, an atheist condemning a Republican, a Republican condemning a Jew, a Jew condemning a Puerto Rican, a Puerto Rican condemning a capitalist, etc. Behind all this is a failure on the part of many to recognize that the categories in which we place people are entirely illusory even when the category may seem to be extremely objective. This was brought out very nicely by Jean Genet when he was asked by an actor to write a play about blacks. In response to the request he answered, "But what exactly is a black? First of all, what's his color?"

We have asked throughout this book, "What exactly is a 'homosexual'?" There are endless answers to this question, some of which have some pretense to being scientific, but none is satisfactory. In the end the best that we can do is to define homosexual acts; we cannot define the "homosexual." He, whoever he may be, is always an individual and as such different from all others, including others who may also participate in homosexual acts. His worth or his lack of worth can only be known when he is known as an individual. Morality consists in part of recognizing this fact.

When a little boy looks at a little girl he sees someone who appears to be very different from himself and he immediately assumes that she is inferior. When he is a man, if he has grown in mind and spirit as well as in body, he looks at a woman and sees another person quite different from himself in certain ways, but knows that she is an equal. Both emotional and moral maturity consist in being able to absorb the paradox that all people are different but equal. Without this kind of maturity one's relationships with others are necessarily inferior. It requires nothing from us to accept others who appear to be exactly like ourselves; we give of ourselves only when we truly accept those who appear to be different from us.

Immorality does not consist in being different; it consists in not allowing others to be so. Often it is not the individual whose sexual relations depart from social custom who is immoral, but rather those who would penalize him for being different. If, for example, a law-abiding citizen who respects the rights and dignities of others is made to suffer merely for departing in his sexual preferences from the conventional norm, it is not he who is the offender; in such a case he is the victim, not the culprit.

We have arrived at a concept of morality and ethics in interpersonal relationships according to which the dignity of the human condition is respected and it is recognized that the human condition involves the kind of individuation that leads to differences among men. Men have not surrendered their right to differ among themselves, and wide differences of opinion on an endless number of issues continue to exist as, no doubt, they always will. But we no longer regard such differences as good or sufficient reason to deny another human being his right to an opinion nor or his right to live life as he sees fit—providing that he accords others the same right. We no longer automatically assume that anyone is necessarily sinful, criminal, or insane simply because he is different. We have come to recognize that life can have a different meaning for different people and that this meaning can only be recognized by the individual for himself. Intolerance and bigotry, of course, continue to be a part of life during our time; but the conscience of modern man is troubled if he recognizes intolerance and bigotry within himself, for in the atmosphere of a society that strives for greater freedom for the individual intolerance and bigotry must appear as evils.

We may summarize what we have had to say thus far by simply stating that all men must respect one another's rights, that one of the most important of these rights is the right to be different, and that no man who does not accord to others the same rights that he claims for himself can represent that his actions arise out of moral or ethical motives. A morality that is less than this is, in reality, no morality at all. Oppressive and intolerant attitudes and measures rationalized by appeals to some higher morality than is implied in the preceding sentences are simply a species of immorality in disguise. The urge to espouse or even to dictate a more lofty and austere morality than may be attainable or even recognizable to ordinary men may not be justified if its exercise involves setting aside common decency. It may be hoped that the day is past when men feel justified in destroying other men's bodies in order to save their souls.

No man need accept for himself a morality that is anything less than appears proper to him. That we do not have the right to force our moral, religious, and philosophical convictions upon others does not mean that we may not ourselves live by them. But this right should not be confused with a right to demand conformity with our own views. In a free society the state is not the mere instrument of some particular moral institution, no matter how many citizens may claim membership in that institution. The state in a free society does not legislate morality beyond the point where it protects the right of the individual to be guided in his actions by his own conscience. The only morality that the legal institutions of a free society may legitimately require of the individual is that he recognize the rights and dignities of others.

In modern times we have come to accept the idea that the individual must be guided by his own conscience in matters of religious faith and theological doctrine. Most people contend quite vehemently that every man has a right to his own convictions in these matters, even if they are the convictions of a minority or of himself alone. Any attempt on the part of a social or religious institution to impose any theological dogma or orthodoxy upon others through force would be recognized as tyranny and immorality in our time. The rights and dignities of the theological heretic and even of the atheist are respected today in all quarters of civilization.

But we have failed to extend freedom of conscience to the sphere of sexual morality, even though the sexual morality that is enforced today is part and parcel of a particular religious tradition and reflects philosophical convictions that are entirely subjective and that do not admit of objective verification. The sexual heretic is as often penalized today as was the theological heretic centuries ago. We are prone to act as if decisions involving sexual morality were entirely beyond the sphere of individual conscience and that these decisions may properly be dictated by secular law. In many places, the courtesan, the "homosexual," the vendor of literature that is offensive to conventional morality, and even the adulterer and the fornicator may be arrested and imprisoned even in cases in which their activities do not involve force, violence, deception, or fraud.

This is all a result of the continuing confusion of immorality with crime in most people's minds. It may be true that all crime is immorality; but it is not true that all immorality is crime. Except in the case of sex, we recognize that in order for immorality to amount to crime it must be harmful not merely to one's self but to another person as well; furthermore, we recognize that crime must involve harm done to another person against his will. Drunkenness may be both immoral and harmful; but we do not imagine that the drunkard who offers a drink to another drunkard who accepts the drink with pleasure has committed a crime. Nor, properly speaking, does the state ever—except in certain cases involving sex—claim the right to punish immorality or vice. When, for example, a man is imprisoned for murder or theft the law does not punish him because his acts are immoral but because his acts are criminal. So it is, at least in all just law, among civilized peoples.

There will be those who will point out that in some places gambling is made a criminal offense, and even the failure to observe Sunday as the Christian sabbath. These are anachronisms comparable to some of our anachronistic sexual legislation, but there is this difference: these laws are recognized by most people to be officious and offensive and in an increasing number of instances these laws are being revoked. On the other hand, legislation in the area of sexual morality—at least in those areas where it has been a traditional part of law—is *increasing* in our time, and such legislation is represented as desirable and just rather than as offensive and unjust.

It must be asserted that a man's or woman's moral convictions—and the acts through which he or she expresses these convictions—must be dictated by his or her own conscience alone and that sexual morality is no exception to this. Any person, of course, may seek moral instruction from religious institutions or from any other source. But it does not follow that religious institutions or any other institutions may claim any right to dictate morality by the use of force. We must, however, go further even than this: Not only should the adult individual be protected by the law from any attempt at moral coercion through official means; he should also be protected from moral coercion that involves slander, public abuse, or indignities to the person. It is not enough merely to refrain from penalizing people for acts that may be considered immoral according to prevailing standards and beliefs; people must also be protected aganist any substantial harm or abuse that may arise out of an overzealous effort on the part of another person to impose his personal morality. In many countries, for example, homosexual and other types of sexual relations are not interdicted in the penal codes, but certain people may be penalized in numerous ways for having participated in unconventional sexual relations. They may be subjected to public ridicule or other gross indignities; they may be denied government employment (or employment in private industry), veterans' benefits, housing, the right to hold public office, and a great many other rights they might enjoy if only they conformed to the conventional sex code. The pattern is familiar; we have seen it repeatedly in the case of the Negro, the Jew, and many others. These abuses should be corrected and they should be recognized in the law as misdemeanors or, if sufficiently serious, even as felonies. All citizens should be guaranteed the right to exercise their moral proclivities in the sexual as well as the theological sphere. It is no more ethical to abuse a man because he is in a sexual minority than it is to abuse a man because he is in a religious or social minority. If he is harmed by such abuse, as he must be, it is a responsibility of the social order to protect him.

The sexual heretic is often denied the rights others enjoy because his preferences are considered obscene, indecent, or offensive to public taste. Offense to public taste may be avoided by making it mandatory for all people to exercise their sexual proclivities in private (though privacy must be given some reasonable definition). But what may constitute obscenity and indecency is dependent entirely upon subjective and personal criteria. No attempt should be made to judge the obscenity or indecency of any matter that does not directly involve the public at large. Literary materials, photographs, paintings, theatrical representations and the like do not usually involve the public at large. Books, pictures, and other printed materials may be confined to one's home. Theatrical representations are usually confined to the four walls of an auditorium. Anyone may refrain from entering theaters in which spectacles offensive to his taste or morals are offered. Age limits may be established for the purchase of tickets to questionable spectacles or for the purchase of questionable printed materials. In any case, one may be sure that any commercial enterprise which is really offensive to public taste will fail. We do not need judges to decide for us what may be offensive to public taste, and we most certainly do not need judges to decide for us what is proper for us to read, see, hear, or do in the privacy of our own homes.

Too often leaders take it upon themselves to decide which of our hard-won rights must be surrendered in cases that purportedly involve obscenity or indecency, and they also insist upon being the ones to define obscenity and indecency. They are not necessarily moved in their judgments in such matters by a sense of justice or a sense of what may really constitute public welfare. Often they may be moved only by a personal feeling of revulsion. But what is repulsive to one person may be delightful to another. There is no more reason to accord some official the right to decide what is or what is not obscene than there is to accord him the right to decide whether the concept of virgin birth is morally and theologically acceptable. All moral decisions should be left to the individual and certainly they should never be enforced by law. Those who respect a more rigid and conventional sexual morality are certainly free to live by it; it is not too much to ask of these people that they allow others the same freedom.

The point is often made that all morality is a mere reflection of social mores and that if we do not all live by the mores there will be no morality at all and no order. Thus many people defend a conventional morality in which they may not personally believe, and may even go so far as to urge that the mores be enforced by law. But a thoughtful man might view this matter from an entirely opposite standpoint: He might argue that all genuine morality requires both conviction and decision, and that a conventional morality that is neither felt nor believed in is no morality at all. In any case, every moral leader in the history of the world has been a rebel against just the sort of conventionalized morality that many people today defend with the most questionable pseudoscientific and sophistic arguments. Today's heresy may be tomorrow's dogma. Certainly today's dogma was yesterday's heresy.

We need not be bewildered or intimidated by those who insist that the mores must be necessarily preserved for the sake of the common good. The common good is always served when freedom is defended and when the rights of the individual are upheld. One of the most fundamental and meaningful rights of the individual is the right to determine for himself what is moral in the sexual sphere no less than in any other sphere. This right need never be abridged in any case as long as the exercise of it does not abridge some other person's right to do the same. If it is felt that man cannot, *en masse,* live without sexual mores, then it may only be hoped that we evolve a new and far more realistic set of sexual mores than those by which so many of us continue, to our detriment, to live.

We are moving toward a new epoch in human history, an epoch in which the individual is important and in which even the group need no longer slavishly live by a vague, impersonal, and anonymous morality. The seeds for such a society were planted centuries ago by the founders of our Judaeo-Christian religions. We should attempt to avoid the paradox by which those who most vehemently profess these very religions stifle the process by which this new society may develop.

It may be argued that often those who are most unconventional in their sexual activities are precisely the people who live by no morality at all. This is often the case because it is those whose sexual needs and preferences prompt them to unconventional sex acts who have been, as it were, disinherited by others who profess moral leadership. Those in whom homosexual tendencies are prepotent, for example, may find little guidance or little understanding from moral leaders. They may feel forced to separate their sexual acts from moral considerations. But certainly not all those who are homosexual lack a moral sense. Many have applied their own moral judgment to their behavior. Many more seek moral guidance from institutions that might be expected to provide such guidance, but they find no such guidance from these institutions. Almost always they meet with negation and with what amounts to an ultimatum; they are told that they must either renounce their homosexuality or live a life of celibacy. Yet they might be quite incapable of doing either.

In the atmosphere of sexual bigotry which has become so much a part of our cultural heritage, the solution to the homosexual dilemma must appear rash to many people. Still, it is unavoidable. It amounts to this: We cannot require a more lofty morality from one class of individuals than we require from another; we cannot cater to the sexual needs of one class of individuals and ignore or even attempt to suppress the sexual needs of some other class of individuals so long as these needs do not involve violence, coercion, force, or deception.

If we do not require total renunciation of heterosexual desires on the part of the average man, we cannot require total renunciation of homosexual desires and make the exercise of them a criminal offense. If we are prepared—at least in *practice*—to accept an "easy virtue" in the heterosexual sphere—as, for example, in the case of adultery and premarital heterosexual relationships—then we must be prepared to accept an "easy virtue" in the homosexual sphere. Indeed, the concrete evils that may result from adultery or premarital sexual relationships—where these lead to broken marriages, broken homes, or unwanted pregnancies—may be far greater than the more abstract evils that may be identified with homosexuality as a result of regarding it as a sin against nature. If we evolve social means for people to fulfill their heterosexual needs, we must likewise evolve social means for people to fulfill their homosexual needs. There is no good reason to close "gay bars" when "straight bars" flourish in the same neighborhood, nor any good reason to prevent like-sexed partners from dancing together in "gay" taverns or night clubs. If we refuse to stigmatize a man and punish him for his heterosexual interests we should refuse to stigmatize a man or punish him for his homosexual interests. If the "age of consent" to a heterosexual act is sixteen or eighteen, then the "age of consent" to a homosexual act should be sixteen or eighteen. If we value love and the desire to do good by another in a heterosexual context, then we must value love and the desire to do good by another in a homosexual context.

One could multiply these examples endlessly. But in the end it all comes to the same point: there should be no rules and regulations, no requirements, no morality that applies in one sphere of erotic life but not in another, and no formal means by which one man may be set apart from another, deprived of any of his human rights, or otherwise abused.

In most civilized nations today laws against consensual sex acts of any kind have gone by the boards, and public opinion would be definitely opposed to any kind of legal device designed to dictate the nature of an individual's private sex life. In many nations the so-called homosexual has been accorded the same rights as others. He may, for example, associate with others who share his inclinations at taverns, night clubs, beaches, or other places where the public gathers for recreation. In not a few cases he even enjoys the right to speak in behalf of his sexual interests and to seek greater understanding for himself—and of himself—in social and fraternal organizations, clubs, study groups, and forums. For his own part, he has seemed willing enough to accept the rights of others, and in countries in which homosexual acts are not against the law, he is to be seen no more often before the bar of justice than any other person.

But in spite of all of this, intolerance still exists in many forms, and in some societies this intolerance amounts to naked oppression. The source of such abuses lies in certain aspects of our sexual mystique that must be corrected if we are to overcome a great many evils that affect all men and women.

Our world is faced by a great many moral challenges, and homosexuality is an important one among others. The challenge with which homosexuality presents us is manifold and puts to a test many precepts that we hold dear. We have represented our culture to the rest of the world as one in which human dignity is recognized in every man; what of the human dignity of those who may have developed homosexual tendencies? We have claimed that every man is an individual and that he must search within his own conscience for an answer to what is right; what of those who have searched and have found homosexuality to be right for them? We have claimed that love is the better part of sex and that love enobles every human relationship; what of those men and women who find that they love others of their own sex? We have claimed that no man should be denied his freedom if he respects the established rights of others; what about the freedom of the homosexual person? We have claimed that charity is the noblest virtue; what charity are we prepared to accord those who may offend our own concept of propriety?

The moral problem homosexuality presents in our culture is both a personal and a social one. It may be seen that it consists mainly in the fact that our Judaeo-Christian religions have refused to acknowledge the existence of homosexuality as a part of human experience and have, instead, represented it as originating in some inhuman and evil force that might be associated with the work of the devil. In failing to acknowledge the natural basis of homosexuality, our religious institutions have also failed to provide any ethic that can regulate and control homosexual impulses or direct them toward constructive ends. Lifelong celibacy cannot be regarded as a suitable solution to the problems of individuals who may be exclusively homosexual, for lifelong celibacy is more than can be expected of most people even when they aspire toward sainthood.

Our traditional sexual morality is at best inadequate to the needs of even those who are predisposed to long-term monogamous heterosexual relationships. Even more than others, those in whom homosexual tendencies are prepotent are left without any positive morality by which to live. They must wander in a moral desert where it is only possible to realize their needs immorally or at best amorally. It is thus that homosexuality becomes a problem for the individual and for the group.

The sexual drive is neither inherently good nor inherently evil. It becomes evil only when it is made to serve an evil purpose, and good only when it is made to serve a good purpose. But the good purposes which it may serve are as manifold as the evil ones, and certainly the good ones are not confined merely to procreation. Love, said the poet, is "a many splendored thing." In societies in which this is recognized and in which adequate provision is made in the mores for the many splendored manifestations which the sexual drive may assume, this drive serves good purposes more often than evil ones. In such societies sexual phenomena seldom become legal problems and almost never become medical problems. But sex-negative cultures give rise to every type of criminal sexuality and every type of sexual pathology. These problems, however, are always secondary in nature; at the root of them may be found a moral problem.

Before scientific knowledge provided us with the insights and the facts that we now have regarding homosexuality, it was possible for our moral institutions to avoid the issues involved or to try to deal with them through negation. This will no longer do. Knowledge no longer allows this for moral men. The statistics and other facts presented in this text constitute a challenge to Christian and Hebrew religious leaders. No longer may the problem be ignored by simply condemning homosexuality as sinful and unnatural. The Christian churches and the Hebrew congregations must offer something more constructive than guilt and renunciation to the millions of men and women who become involved in homosexual feelings. The churches must minister to them. They can no longer simply turn these men and women away and ignore their presence if they prove incapable of accepting the age-old remedy of chastity and renunciation.

The problem of homosexuality is not, as we are wont to assert in an effort to deny ethical issues, fundamentally a medical problem. For all of its pretensions, medicine can neither adequately explain nor adequately cope with this problem. So many hundreds of thousands—probably millions—are seriously involved that it is quite impossible even to attempt to deal with the problem on a medical basis. Therapy should be reserved for those who truly need it and who can benefit from it. Even if therapy for all were possible and efficacious, it is not certain that homosexual inclinations should always be approached in this manner. But if homosexuality is not a medical problem, neither is it fundamentally a legal problem—except insofar as we have made it one. The problem of homosexuality is first and last a moral problem and must receive a moral solution.

We cannot pretend to have anything like a complete solution for this problem. It is necessary to clear away prejudice and oppression before any answer can be forthcoming; for any solution that would be offered in a prejudicial and oppressive atmosphere would fail to be moral. The answer certainly can never be formulated by a single individual. Only after we have acknowledged the existence of homosexuality, seen it in its proper light, and have prepared ourselves to live with it, will moralists be able to cope with the challenge. Those who are personally involved in homosexuality must also help to formulate some answer; they cannot be excluded from any inquiry that involves questions touching upon their own lives.

But if we cannot advise the moralists in this book, it might be expected that we have some advice for those who are directly involved.

No advice may be added here for those who are homosexual beyond the few observations that were addressed earlier to all people—with one exception. To the "homosexual," because of his extraordinary burden of shame and guilt as an outcast, we would say that his first moral duty toward himself and others—no matter how challenging this duty may appear—is to accept nothing less than the same rights and the same dignities accorded to other men. He may be armed to meet this challenge by the certainty and courage that are afforded by the knowledge that he himself is careful to accord the same rights and dignities to others that he claims for himself.

We may preach pious and eloquent sermons that threaten the sexual heretic with perpetual shame on earth and eternal damnation in the life to come; still he will remain among us. We may increase our sexual statutes and enforce them in a reign of terror that makes it necessary to open concentration camps in order to contain the offenders; but there will be ever new offenders. We may therapize and propagandize until we glut our clinics and hospitals with an endless stream of patients; new patients will appear with every generation. In the end a suppressive policy will be of no avail; for homosexuality, unlike sin, does not originate in man's will to be destructive but in his will to be creative; unlike crime, it does not exploit and corrupt but instead affords inspiration; unlike disease, it is not a distortion of man's natural capacities but a utilization of them. It cannot, therefore, ever be totally or finally suppressed. Wisdom consists in accepting this fact and in attempting to *instruct* rather than to *negate*. There are, as we have pointed out, sinful, criminal, and pathological varieties of homosexuality as there are sinful, criminal, and pathological varieties of heterosexuality. These should be dealt with by improved methods of religious instruction, penal correction, and therapy. But mere unconventionality in matters of sex and love should never be confused with sin, crime, or disease.

Nothing that we may do will ever preclude the development of homosexual tendencies in a large and vital segment of the male population nor the development of certain other unconventional sexual tendencies in our times, because such tendencies are rooted in capacities that are part of our biological heritage. There will always be a new generation of youths who are sexually responsive to other males and in whom passion and love alike o'erleap the bounds of present convention. In some, homosexual tendencies will be prepotent and imperious; in the sexual pattern of others they will form only a minor part; in others still they will be hardly manifest at all; and in many, homosexual tendencies will never develop. But, however we may wish it to be otherwise, *no one sexual pattern will ever become the only sexual pattern for all men.*

Must, then, tens of millions yet unborn be condemned to the misery, loneliness, and degradation which being different almost always means in our culture? If we cannot salvage those who may have been irreparably damaged by moral isolation and despair throughout a lifetime, can we not at least make certain that there will be no new victims of intolerance and ignorance in the future? Is it not the duty of all of us to give every other man and woman an equal opportunity to live life in dignity and joy?

Perhaps someday we will find righteous answers to these questions. Perhaps social developments in the future will do much to spare those who are burdened by oppression both from within and from without.

When we have come to realize that the world belongs to all of us— when, indeed, we have come to accept the brotherhood of man—we will have ascended to a higher plane of morality in which only hatred, and never love, is condemned; a morality that is clean, fearless, and affirmative and that both acknowledges and celebrates the full range of man's amative capacities. At such a time, but no sooner, we can clasp hands with the gods and prophets of the religions to which we may now only pretend.

APPENDIX

The Heterosexual-Homosexual Rating Scale

(From *Sexual Behavior in the Human Male* by Alfred C. Kinsey, Wardell B. Pomeroy, and Clyde E. Martin)

0—Individuals are rated as 0s if they make no physical contacts which result in erotic arousal or orgasm, and make no psychic responses to individuals of their own sex. Their sociosexual contacts and responses are exclusively with individuals of the opposite sex.

1—Individuals are rated as 1s if they have only incidental homosexual contacts which have involved physical response, or incidental psychic responses without physical contact. The great preponderance of their sociosexual experience and reactions is directed toward individuals of the opposite sex. Such homosexual experiences as these individuals have may occur only a single time or two, or at least infrequently in comparison to the amount of their heterosexual experience. Their homosexual experiences never involve as specific psychic reactions as they make to heterosexual stimuli. Sometimes the homosexual activities in which they engage may be inspired by curiosity or may be more or less forced upon them by other individuals, perhaps when they are asleep or when they are drunk, or under some other peculiar circumstance.

2—Individuals are rated as 2s if they have more than incidental homosexual experience, and/or if they respond rather definitely to homosexual stimuli. Their heterosexual experiences and/or reactions still surpass their homosexual experiences and/or reactions. These individuals may have only a small amount of homosexual experience or they may have a considerable amount of it, but in every case it is surpassed by the amount of heterosexual experience that they have within the same period of time. They usually recognize their quite specific arousal by homosexual stimuli, but their responses to the opposite sex are still stronger. A few of these individuals may even have all of their overt experience in the homosexual, but their psychic reactions to persons of the opposite sex indicate that they are still predominantly heterosexual. This latter situation is most often found among younger males who have not yet ventured to have actual intercourse with girls, while their orientation is definitely heterosexual. On the other hand, there are some males who should be rated as 2s because of their strong reactions to individuals of their own sex, even though they have never had overt relations with them.

3—Individuals who are rated 3s stand midway on the heterosexual-homosexual scale. They are about equally homosexual and heterosexual in their overt experience and/or their psychic reactions. In general they accept and equally enjoy both types of contacts and have no strong preferences for one or the other. Some persons are rated 3s even though they may have a larger amount of experience of one sort, because they respond psychically to partners of both sexes, and it is only a matter of circumstance that brings them into more frequent contact with one of the sexes. Such a situation is not unusual among single males, for male contacts are often more available to them than female contacts. Married males, on the other hand, find it simpler to secure a sexual outlet through intercourse with their wives, even though some of them may be as interested in males as they are in females.

4—Individuals are rated as 4s if they have more overt activity and/or psychic reactions in the homosexual, while still maintaining a fair amount of heterosexual activity and/or responding rather definitely to heterosexual stimuli.

5—Individuals are rated 5s if they are almost entirely homosexual in their overt activities and/or reactions. They do have incidental experience with the opposite sex and sometimes react psychically to individuals of the opposite sex.

6—Individuals are rated as 6s if they are exclusively homosexual, both in regard to their overt experience and in regard to their psychic reactions.

Bibliography

1. ARIETI, S. *American Handbook of Psychiatry*. Vol. I. New York: Basic Books, 1959.
2. BAILEY, D. S. *Homosexuality and the Western Christian Tradition*. New York: Longmans, Green, 1955.
3. ———. *Sexual Offenders and Social Punishment*. London: The Church Information Board, 1956.
4. BAILEY, S. *Common Sense About Sexual Ethics: A Christian View*. New York: Macmillan, n.d.
5. BEACH, F. A. *Sexual Behavior in Animals and Men*. Springfield, Ill.: The Harvey Lectures, 1947–48, 1950.
6. BERG, C., and ALLEN, C. *The Problem of Homosexuality*. New York: Citadel Press, 1958.
7. BERGLER, E. *Homosexuality: Disease or Way of Life*. New York: Hill and Wang, 1956.
8. BIEBER, IRVING (ed.). *Homosexuality: A Psychoanalytic Study*. New York: Basic Books, 1962.
9. BUCKLEY, REV. MICHAEL J. *Morality and the Homosexual*. London: Lands, 1959.
10. CARCOPINO, J. *Daily Life in Ancient Rome*. New Haven, Conn.: Yale University Press, 1940.
11. CHESSER, E., and WALKER, K. *Odd Man Out: Homosexuality in Men and Women*. London: Victor Gollancz, 1959.
12. COLE, WILLIAM G. *Sex and Love in the Bible*. New York: Association Press, 1959.
13. CORY, D. W. *Homosexuality: A Cross Cultural Approach*. New York: The Julian Press, 1956.
14. ———. *The Homosexual in America*. New York: Greenberg, 1951, 1957.
15. ———, and LE ROY, J. P. *The Homosexual and His Society*. New York: The Citadel Press, 1963.
16. CURRAN, D., and PARR, D. "Homosexuality: An Analysis of 100 Male Cases," *British Medical Journal*, I (1957).
17. DARKE, R. "Heredity as an Etiological Factor in Homosexuality," *Journal of Mental and Nervous Diseases*, CVII (1948), pp. 251–68.

18. DURANT, W. *The Life of Greece*. New York: Simon and Schuster, 1939.
19. EDWARDES, A. *The Jewel in the Lotus*. New York: The Julian Press, 1959.
20. ENGLISH, O. S., and PEARSON, G. H. J. *Emotional Problems of Living*. New York: W. W. Norton, 1945.
21. FENICHEL, O. *The Psychoanalytic Theory of Neurosis*. New York: W. W. Norton, 1945.
22. FORD, C. S., and BEACH, F. A. *Patterns of Sexual Behavior*. New York: Harper and Bros., 1951.
23. FREUD, S. *The Basic Writings of Sigmund Freud*. Translated and edited, with an introduction by Dr. A. A. Brill. New York: Modern Library, 1938.
24. ———. *Beyond the Pleasure Principle*. New York: Bantam Books, n.d.
25. ———. *Civilization and Its Discontents*. New York: W. W. Norton, 1961.
26. ———. *An Outline of Psychoanalysis*. New York: W. W. Norton, 1940, 1949.
27. ———. *Totem and Taboo*. New York: W. W. Norton, 1952.
28. ———. *Three Contributions to the Theory of Sex*. New York: Nervous and Mental Disease Publishing Co., 1920.
29. FRIEDMAN, P. in *American Handbook of Psychiatry*. Vol. I. New York: Basic Books, 1959.
30. FRUMKIN, R. M. "Early English and American Sex Customs," *The Encyclopaedia of Sexual Behavior*. Vol. I.
31. ———. "Sexual Freedom," *ibid*.
32. GEDDES, D. P. (ed.). *An Analysis of the Kinsey Reports on Sexual Behavior in the Human Male and Female*. New York: Mentor Books, 1954.
33. GIDE, A. *Corydon*. New York: Farrar, Straus, 1950.
34. GUYON, R. *The Ethics of Sexual Acts*. New York: Alfred A. Knopf, 1934, 1947, 1958.
35. HAMILTON, G. V. "A Study of Sexual Tendencies in Monkeys and Baboons," *Journal of Animal Behavior*, IV (1914).
36. HARPER, R. A., and HARPER, F. R. "Education in Sex," *The Encyclopaedia of Sexual Behavior*, op. cit.
37. HART, H. L. A. *Law, Liberty, and Morality*. Stanford, Calif.: Stanford University Press, 1963.
38. HAUSER, R. *The Homosexual Society*. London: The Bodley Head, 1962.
39. HENRY, G. W. *All the Sexes*. New York: Rinehart, 1955.
40. HERON, A. *Towards a Quaker View of Sex*. London: Friends Home Service Committee, 1963.
41. HINSIE, L. E., and CAMPBELL, ROBERT J. *Psychiatric Dictionary*, 3rd ed. New York: Oxford University Press, 1960.
42. HIRSHFELD, DR. MAGNUS. *Sexual Anomalies and Perversions*. London: Encyclopaedic Press, 1938.
43. HOOKER, E. "The Adjustment of the Male Overt Homosexual," *Journal of Projective Techniques*, XXI (1957), pp. 18–31.
44. ———. "Preliminary Analysis of Group Behavior of Homosexuals," *Journal of Psychology*, XLII (1956), pp. 217–25.
45. HYDE, H. M. *Oscar Wilde: The Aftermath*. New York: Farrar, Straus, 1963.
46. JERSILD, J. *Boy Prostitution*. Copenhagen, G.E.C.: Gad, 1956.
47. JONES, E. *The Life and Work of Sigmund Freud*. Vol. 3. New York: Basic Books, 1957.
48. KALLMAN, F. J. "Comparative Twin Study of Genetic Aspects of Male Homosexuality," *Journal of Mental and Nervous Disease*, CXV (1952), pp. 283–98.
49. ———. "Twin Sibships and the Study of Male Homosexuality," *American Journal of Human Genetics*, IV (1952), pp. 136–46.
50. KARPMAN, B. *The Sexual Offender and His Offenses*. New York: Julian Press, 1954.

51. KEMPF, E. J. "The Social and Sexual Behavior of Infrahuman Primates with Some Comparable Facts in Human Behavior," *Psychoanalytic Review*, IV (1917).
52. KIEFER, OTTO. *Sexual Life in Ancient Rome*. New York: Barnes and Noble, 1934.
53. KINSEY, A. C., POMEROY, W. B., and MARTIN, C. E. *Sexual Behavior in the Human Male*. Philadelphia, Pa.: W. B. Saunders, 1948.
54. KINSEY, A. C., POMEROY, W. B., MARTIN, C. E., and GEBHARD, P. H. *Sexual Behavior in the Human Female*. Philadelphia, Pa.: W. B. Saunders, 1953.
55. KRICH, A. M. (ed.). *The Homosexuals as Seen by Themselves and Thirty Authorities*. New York: The Citadel Press, 1954.
56. KRONHAUSEN, P. and E. *Sex Histories of American College Men*. New York: Ballantine Books, 1960.
57. LAMBERT, K. "Homosexuals," in Medical Press, 1954.
58. LANG, T. "Studies in the Genetic Determination of Homosexuality," *Journal of Mental and Nervous Diseases*, XCII (1940), pp. 55–64.
59. LICHT, HANS. *Sexual Life in Ancient Greece*. New York: Barnes and Noble, 1932.
60. LONDON, L. S. *Abnormal Sexual Behavior*. New York: The Julian Press, 1957.
61. MAIER, N. R. F., and SCHNEIRLA, T. C. *Principles of Animal Psychology*. New York: McGraw-Hill, 1935.
62. McBRIDE, A. F., and HEBB, D. O. "Behavior of the Captive Bottle-nose Dolphin, Tursiops Truncatus," *Journal of Comparative Physicological Psychology*, XLI (1948).
63. O'CONNOR, W. A. "Some Notes on Suicide," *British Journal Medical Psychology*, XXI (1948).
64. PARE, C. M. B. "Homosexuality and Chromosomal Sex," *Journal of Psychosomatic Response*, I (1956), pp. 247–51.
65. PARTRIDGE, B. *A History of Orgies*. London: Anthony Blond, 1958, 1961.
66. PAVLOV, I. P. *Lectures on Conditioned Reflexes*. New York: Liveright Publishing Corp., 1928.
67. PLUMMER, DOUGLAS. *Queer People: The Truth About Homosexuals*. London: W. H. Allen, 1963.
68. ROBERTS, A. *Forbidden Freedom*. London: Linden Press, 1960.
69. SALTER, A. *Conditioned Reflex Therapy*. New York: Creative Age Press, 1949.
70. SHELDON, W. H. *The Varieties of Temperament*. New York: Harper and Brothers, 1942.
71. STEARN, J. *The Sixth Man*. New York: Doubleday, n.d.
72. STEKEL, W. *The Homosexual Neurosis*. Brooklyn, N.Y.: Physicians and Surgeons Book Co., 1922, 1933.
73. STERBA, R. *Introduction to the Psychoanalytic Theory of the Libido*. New York: Nervous and Mental Disease Monographs, 1942, 1947.
74. STORR, A. *Sexual Deviation*. Baltimore, Md.: Penguin Books, n.d.
75. SUTHERLAND, A., and ANDERSON, P. *Eros: An Anthology of Friendship*. London: Anthony Blond, 1961.
76. TAYLOR, G. R. *Sex in History*. New York: The Vanguard Press, 1954.
77. WELLS, HARRY I. *Sigmund Freud, A Pavlovian Critique*. New York: International Publishers, 1960.
78. WEST, D. J. *Homosexuality*. London: Gerald Duckworth, 1955.
79. WESTERMARCK, E. *The Origin and Development of Moral Ideas*. London: Macmillan, 1906.
80. WESTWOOD, G. *A Minority*. London: Longmans, Green, 1960.
81. ———. *Society and the Homosexual*. New York: E. P. Dutton, 1952, 1953.

Index

Index

The Author and His Book

WAINWRIGHT CHURCHILL is a clinical psychologist whose experience in the field of mental health has been exceptionally broad. The holder of M.A. and Ed.D. degrees from Temple University, Dr. Churchill studied psychoanalysis in New York City, where for three years he received individual instruction in the technique of psychoanalytic therapy from Dr. Theodor Reik, the eminent psychoanalyst, author, and associate of Sigmund Freud.

Dr. Churchill was formerly Director of Music Therapy at the Delaware State Hospital at a time when music was first being used in the larger mental hospitals to establish emotional rapport with the more withdrawn psychotic patients. His position as Psychological Examiner at the Camden Board of Education provided him with the opportunity to become acquainted with the emotional problems of children and adolescents.

During the summer of 1955, Dr. Churchill played a leading part in founding the Psychoanalytic Studies Institute in Philadelphia and became its first Director. Also, until 1960, he was Director of the Department of Psychoanalysis of the Philadelphia Mental Health Clinic, an Affiliate of the American College of Neuropsychiatrists, and Consultant in Psychoanalytic Psychology to the Metropolitan Hospital. He is a member of the American Psychological Association.

Sexual behavior and the many problems it presents in our society have always been of particular interest to the author, and during the years when he was Director of the Psychoanalytic Studies Institute he organized a seminar devoted to the study of male homosexuality. He soon realized, however, that many of the problems raised by male homosexuality cannot be entirely elucidated in terms of psychoanalytic psychology; and it was then that he decided to make a comprehensive study drawing upon the research not only of psychoanalysts but of other students of sexology as well. The results of these efforts are contained in the present volume.

HOMOSEXUAL BEHAVIOR AMONG MALES is set in Times Roman, a type face designed by Stanley Morison in 1932 for *The Times* of London. This book was set in type by the Harry Sweetman Typesetting Corporation, South Hackensack, New Jersey; printed by Mahoney & Roese, Inc., New York City; and bound by The Book Press, Inc., Brattleboro, Vermont.

A HAWTHORN BOOK